A CHRONOLOGICAL BIOGRAPHY
OF
MAHATMA GANDHI

A CHRONOLOGICAL BIOGRAPHY OF MAHATMA GANDHI

Anil Dutta Mishra
Saroj Kumar Jha
Sohan Raj Tater

ABHIJEET PUBLICATIONS
DELHI 110094

ABHIJEET PUBLICATIONS
2/46 Tukhmeerpur Extension
Delhi-110 094
Phone: 011-22960492, 65698474
E-mail: abhijeetpublication@gmail.com

A CHRONOLOGICAL BIOGRAPHY OF MAHATMA GANDHI

First Published 2010

ISBN 978-93-80031-52-1

PRINTED IN INDIA

Published by J.K. Singh for Abhijeet Publications, Delhi-110 094, Lasertypeset by Gaurav Graphics, New Delhi and Printed at Himanshu Printers, Delhi.

Preface

Mohandas Ḳaramchand Gandhi, popularly known as Bapu, the Father of the Nation, is remembered all over the world for his love of peace, nonviolence, truth, honesty, ethics, pristine purity and compassion and his success in using these instruments to bring together the entire Indian population and helping the country attain independence from the colonial power.

Gandhi's life was an open book. He made himself brick by brick and step by step. He reached at the top where even saint rarely reaches. He combined facts with value, theory with practice, body with soul. He conducted experiments after experiments to achieve the final goal. His entire public life was based on ethics, morality, voluntary poverty, simplicity and pristine purity.

He made title of his Autobiography as "An Autobiography: My Experiments with Truth". From early childhood he was truthful. He never bowed his head. He always upheld the self-esteem and dignity of human being. He was firm in his conviction. On the basis of four core concepts—Nonviolence, Satyagraha, Swadeshi and Swaraj, he laid the freedom struggle of India and showed way to the world.

Gandhi's approach was humanity centric. He wrote and spoke on all aspects of life. After going through the *Collected Works of Mahatma Gandhi (CWMG)* word by word, we came to the conclusion that even the whole life is not enough to understand Mahatma Gandhi and his thoughts. For that, one has to be born and reborn again and again.

Even in the era of Globalization, particularly after recent

economic crises, the whole world is debating about the inspirations one can draw from Mahatma Gandhi's words and deeds which can lead us to a harmonious whole between urban and rural, materialism and spiritualism, theory and practice, localism and globalism, ethical and unethical, pain and pleasure, love and hate, secularism and communalism, development and environment and war and peace. This is the most appropriate time when one can realize that Mahatma Gandhi's views are more relevant today than ever before or when he was alive.

Gandhi was a man of principles and great convictions and always practiced what he preached. Once, when asked for a message to humanity, Gandhi said, ***"My life is my message"***. He laid a very simple life with very few wants and needs, what he believed in and said, hold true even today in the era of globalization. Gandhi becomes a global necessity for peace, prosperity, freedom, harmony and survival of the whole human race. Gandhi provides a new hope, new force and above all a new blueprint to solve the challenges of the modern world.

Mahatma Gandhi, a multifaceted genius, applied his mind to a large number of human concerns and left an indelible impact on the social, economic and political forces of the day. He left an everlasting impact on the world at large because he always spoke and understood the language of the masses and downtrodden. He made the people fearless to fight against injustice and exploitation. He was a man far ahead of his times. Voices all over the world today are re-echoing.

Many of his ideas, however, have yet to be fully imbibed. The need of the hour is that the leaders and the people of the country must follow the Gandhian principles in thought and action. The policy makers, politicians, intellectuals and scientists must remember the **Talisman of Mahatma Gandhi**:

"Whenever you are in doubt, or when the self becomes too much with you, apply the following test.

"Recall the face of the poorest and the weakest man whom you may have seen, and ask yourself, if the step you contemplate is going to be of any use to him.

"Will he gain anything by it?

"Will it restore him to a control over his own life and destiny?

"In other words, will it lead to swaraj for the hungry and spiritually starving millions?

"Then you will find your doubts and yourself melt away."

This book provides a detailed chronological biography of Mahatma Gandhi, the greatest man this motherland had given birth. It also gives a detail account of Mahatma Gandhi's life and action starting from 2nd October 1869 till his death 30th January 1948. To make it reader and user friendly, the book is divided in eights chapters.

Chapter one gives the details of his early childhood, education, marriage, going to England, activities in London and finally becoming Mohan to Barrister.

Chapter two provides the struggle of M.K. Gandhi in South Africa. Gandhi spent twenty-one years of his life in South Africa. It is in South Africa that Gandhi experimented nonviolence with firm conviction. He established two ashrams and wrote *Hind Swaraj* or *Indian Home Rule*. It is in South Africa that Gandhi made himself and prepared to fight against injustice and finally for Independence of India.

Chapter three gives a minute account of three years of Gandhi's hectic life in India just after his arrival from South Africa. Now Mohan Das Karamchand Gandhi was known as Mahatma Gandhi, not only in South Africa and India but all over the world. During this period Mahatma Gandhi on advice of his political guru (teacher), Gopal Krishna Gokhle, toured entire India to get first hand information and understand India and Indians.

Chapter four provides a detailed account of Mahatma's initiation in Freedom Struggle. During this period, Gandhi for the first time had successfully experimented Satyagraha in Champaran in India and became undisputed leader of Indian freedom movement.

By 1920 shaking of British Empire had already been started by Mahatma Gandhi. Congress became the party of masses. New thinking within and outside Congress Party had already started. The details have been recorded in Chapter five.

In 1930 Gandhi started Dandi March (Salt Satyagraha). This satyagraha was a unique mass movement in the history of freedom struggle. By launching this movement Gandhi came on centre stage of Freedom movement. Gandhi worked for social and economic upliftment of Dalits, women, depressed and downtrodden in India. All these have been placed in the Chapter six.

1942 is a turning point in India's Freedom Struggle. In this year Gandhi started 'Quit India Movement' and gave the slogan of 'Do or Die'. And finally India got Independence on 15 August 1947. Minute details of this has been placed in Chapter seven.

Chapter eight gives the account of Gandhi's last journey which no one can escape. The independent India could not keep Gandhi alive. Reasons may be many. The fact remains that world lost the leader of nonviolence on 30th January 1948. History repeated again and the result is that the world is again in search of Gandhi.

We are sure and hopeful that the work will be a worthwhile contribution to the growing literature on Gandhi.

This work is an outcome of collective endeavour of three individuals who belong to different discipline by training and education, working at three different places with one goal to understand Gandhi and place the facts for present and future generations for bringing ethical values and self-esteem in them.

This work would not have been possible in the present form without the support and help from friends and well-wishers. There are a number of persons behind the scene whose ideas, comments and suggestions have been included in the present book. We shall be failing in our duty if we do not record our appreciation to all of them.

First and foremost, we would like to express our sincere gratitude to Prof. R.P. Misra, former Vice-Chancellor, University of Allahabad, Allahabad, and Shri T.N. Chaturvedi, former M.P. and former Governor of Karnataka, who always encourages working on Gandhi. We have no words to express our heart felt regards to them.

We are equally grateful to Prof. D. Gopal of IGNOU, Prof. Bidyut Chakarborty of Delhi University, Prof, J.N. Sharma, Department of Gandhian Thought, Punjab University, Chandigarh, Prof, A.B.S.V. Ranga Rao, Department of Social Work, Prof. RP. Dwivedi, Director, Gandhi Bhawan, Kashi Vidyapeeth, Varanasi, Dr. K.S. Bharati, Prof. and Head and Director Gandhi Bhavan, Nagpur University, Nagpur, for their cooperation and help.

As always we received full support and patience of our dear family members when we were busy with the completion of this volume.

Last but not the least, we are grateful to Mr. Jitendra Singh for bringing out the book in nice form and that too within record time.

Anil Dutta Mishra

Saroj Kumar Jha

Sohan Raj Tater

Contents

	Preface	*v*
Chapter One:	Mohan to Barrister	1
Chapter Two:	The Struggle in South Africa	5
Chapter Three:	Understanding India	176
Chapter Four:	Initiation in Freedom Struggle	187
Chapter Five:	Shaking the Foundations of the Raj	227
Chapter Six:	On Centrestage of Freedom Movement	318
Chapter Seven:	Towards Freedom	444
Chapter Eight:	Attaining Freedom	517

Chapter One

Mohan to Barrister

1869

October 2	:	Mohandas Karamchand Gandhi born at Porbandar

1876

	:	Entered primary school at Rajkot.
	:	Betrothed to Kasturbai.

1881

	:	Entered Alfred High School.
	:	Married Kasturbai.

1884-85

	:	Tried meat-eating, but abandoned it to avoid deceiving elders.
	:	Father died, aged sixty-three.

1887

November	:	Gandhiji passed Matriculation examination and joined Samaldas College at Bhavnagar.

1888

April-May	:	Diffident in his studies, was recommended to

go in for law in England; secured mother's consent to this, promising to abstain from wine, woman and meat.

August 10 : Left Rajkot for Bombay where caste meeting tried to dissuade him from going abroad.

September 4 : Despite stiff resistance from caste elders to his foreign studies, sailed for England.

October 28 : Reached London.

November 6 : Joined Inner Temple.

1889

: To make up for the social disadvantage of his vegetarianism, decided to become an "English gentleman" and started learning elocution, French, dancing and Western music, but soon reconsidered his decision and stopped lessons.

September : Called on Cardinal Manning, towards end of month, to congratulate him on his role in termination of the great London Dock Strike.

: Visited Paris Exhibition (some time between May and October)

November : Was introduced to Blavatsky and Annie Besant; but declined to become a regular member of Theosophical Society.

December : Appeared for London Matriculation but failed. During the year Theosophist influence led him to read much Theosophical and other religious literature including Edwin Arnold's *The Song Celestial*, and *The Light of Asia*, *Bhagavad Gita* in original and the *Bible*. Attended church service, and listened to famous preachers like Dr. Joseph Parker.

1890

: Early this year, came to know the periodicals The Vegetarian Messenger of Manchester and The Vegetarian of London, and Vegetarian Societies there. Attended International Vegetarian meeting with Josiah Oldfield. Started living simply; continued experiments in food;

conducted for a while Vegetarian Club with Josiah Oldfield as president, Edwin Arnold as vice-president and himself as secretary.

June : Passed London Matriculation.

September 19 : Joined Vegetarian Society and became member of executive committee.

1891

January 30 : Attended funeral of Charles Bradlaugh. Not impressed by his atheism; aversion to it being strengthened on reading Besant's *How I Became a Theosophist*.

February 20 : Made maiden speech, at Vegetarian Society meeting, in defence of Dr. Allinson's claim to membership of Society despite his anti-puritanical views on birth-control, which Gandhiji did not share.

February 21 : In article in The Vegetarian described alcohol as "that enemy of mankind, that curse of civilization".

March 26 : Was enrolled an associate member of London Theosophical Society.

May 1 : Appointed Vegetarian Society's delegate to meeting of Federal Union of Vegetarian Societies.

June 10 : Called to the Bar. During legal studies, attended lectures by Dadabhai Naoroji. Advice from Frederic Pincutt emphasizing honesty and industry filled him with hope for future as lawyer.

June 11 : Enrolled in the High Court.

June 12 : Sailed for India.

July 5-9 : Reached Bombay and learned with great grief of the passing away of his mother. Met Rajchandra (Raychandbhai), jeweller, poet and ascetic whom he was later to consider greater in religious perception than Tolstoy, and one of the three notable influences in his life. Performed expiation at Nasik for infringement of caste injunction against foreign travel. Reached Rajkot and stayed with brother Lakshmidas.

July 20 : Taken back into caste, though still ostracized by a section.

November 16 : Applied for admission as advocate of the Bombay High Court.

1892

March-April : Started attending to education of children in the family *on modern lines and adopted Western mode of diet and dress.*

May 14 : Allowed to practise in Kathiawar Agency Courts by Gazette notification.Finding practice in Rajkot difficult, proceeded to Bombay to gain experience. Made experiments in diet with friend. Abandoned first brief out of nervousness and preferred drafting memorials. Driven to seek work as teacher, but refused as not being a graduate.

: Winding up establishment in Bombay, after six months, rejoined brother at Rajkot. Working with him drawing up petitions and memorials, started making Rs. 300 a month.

Chapter Two

The Struggle in South Africa

1893

April	: Sailed for Durban, readily grasping opportunity of legal work in South Africa offered by Dada Abdulla & Co., leaving wife and child in Rajkot and intending to return in year's time.
May	: Towards close of month reached Port Natal, where he was struck by disrespect shown to Indians.
May-June	: On second or third day of arrival visited Durban Court; when asked to remove turban he preferred to leave premises. Wrote to the Press about incident; was called "unwelcome visitor", but secured considerable publicity.
	: Seven or eight days later proceeded to Pretoria on client's work. During journey by train and coach had bitter experience of colour prejudice. Resolved to fight to "root out the disease" of colour prejudice and "suffer hardships in the process". Baker, attorney and preacher, warned him of prevalence of colour prejudice and secured him lodgings in a poor woman's inn.
	: Attended Baker's prayer meetings and was introduced to Christians like Mr. Coates, a Quaker, and Misses Harris and Gabb, who became friends.

: During first week in Pretoria met Sheth Tyeb Haji Khan and addressed meeting of Indian Memon merchants on the condition of Indians in the Transvaal. Suggested and offered to help formation of association for seeking redress of grievances of Indian settlers. Stay in Pretoria gave him intimate knowledge of social, economic and political conditions of Indians in the Transvaal and the Orange Free State.

: Gandhiji had experience of regulation banning use of footpaths by Indians when he was kicked off the footpath near President Kruger's house, but refused despite pressure to sue white assailant on ground that he would never go to court for personal grievances.

August 22-September 2 : Conducted experiments in vital food. Constant contact with Mr. Coates and other Christian friends during this time prompted him to study books on Christianity and hold discussions with them but he found difficulty in accepting their interpretation of the Bible and Christianity.

1894

April : While preparing case for his client Dada Abdulla, Gandhiji realized paramount importance of facts, or truth, in legal practice. Convinced of folly of litigation, had the dispute settled by arbitration. His professional engagement over, returned to Durban.

: At farewell party saw announcement in *The Natal Mercury* of impending disfranchisement law and urged Indian merchants present to resist it. Was persuaded by them to extend his stay by a month to lead their struggle—a fateful decision.

: At this time took to serious religious study. Tolstoy's The Kingdom of God Is within You overwhelmed him.

: Corresponded with Christian friends in England. Also wrote to religious thinkers in India, like Raychandbhai whose replies to his questions on Hinduism reassured him.

May 22	:	At meeting of prominent Indian merchants set up committee to agitate against discriminatory legislation.
June 27	:	Sent telegrams to Speaker of Natal Legislative Assembly, Prime Minister Robinson and Attorney-General Escombe, requesting postponement of consideration of Franchise Law Amendment Bill till Indian petition was presented. Discussion of Bill deferred by two days.
June 28	:	Submitted to Legislative Assembly petition, signed by 500 Indians, opposing Bill and asking for Commission of Enquiry.
June 29	:	Waited in deputation on Premier; requested for week's time to present Indian case more exhaustively.
July 1	:	Attended and addressed meeting of Indians in Field Street.
July 3	:	Led deputation to Natal Governor and urged him not to sanction the Franchise Bill which received third reading in Assembly.
July 5	:	Initiated correspondence with Dadabhai Naoroji, seeking his intervention in England on behalf of South African Indians.
July 6	:	Indians presented second petition to Legislative Council, pressing for rejection of Franchise Bill.
July 7	:	Franchise Bill received third reading in Council.
July 10	:	Gandhiji petitioned Governor, requesting postponement of dispatch of the Bill to Imperial Government for Royal assent, pending Indian petition to the latter.
July 17	:	Submitted to Natal Governor lengthy mass petition signed by 10,000 Indians, addressed to Lord Ripon, Secretary of State for Colonies.
	:	Settled down in Natal to continue public work.
August 22	:	Established Natal Indian Congress to carry on sustained agitation against discriminatory legislation, becoming its first secretary; also Colonial-born Indians' Association.

September 3 : Allowed by Supreme Court to practise in Natal Courts, despite opposition by Natal Law Society. In Court, asked to remove turban, obeyed to conform to Court practice and to reserve his strength for "fighting bigger battles"

September 19 : Appeared in Gopi Maharaj case, probably his first in South Africa, and won. But subordinated legal career to public work.

November 26 : Indicated growing interest in Esoteric Christianity by becoming agent for selling its literature.

Before December 19: Addressed documented "Open Letter" to Natal Legislators.

December 19 : Circulated appeal among Europeans in Natal for sympathetic approach to problem of Indian settlers.

1895

April : Visited Trappist Monastery near Durban, where practice of vegetarianism from spiritual point of view greatly impressed him.

April 6 : Through Committee of British Indian Merchants petitioned High Commissioner against unsatisfactory award in Indian Arbitration case.

Before May 5 : Appealed to Natal Assembly against reindenture clauses in Indian Immigration Bill.

After May 14 : Appealed again to Lord Ripon concerning injustice of award leaving Indian trading rights at the mercy of the law-courts.

: Sought intervention of Lord Elgin, Viceroy of India, to protect Indian interests against discriminatory laws and disabilities.

June 17 : Defended and secured the release of indentured labourer Balasundaram. The case brought him into contact with indentured labour.

June 26 : Gandhiji petitioned Legislative Council against clauses affecting indentured labour in Immigration Bill.

August 11 : Addressed lengthy memorial to Chamberlain objecting to imposition of £3 licence fee on indenture-expired Indians. Requested Lord Elgin

		to intervene, or stop further emigration of Indian labour.
September 12	:	Chamberlain conveyed to Natal Government refusal of Imperial Government to sanction Franchise Bill in its existing form.
September 25-30	:	Gandhiji wrote to the Press denying that Natal Indian Congress was a secret organization or his being its paid employee, but accepting responsibility for drafting its Constitution.
October 22	:	British Indian Defence Committee and Johannesburg Indians telegraphed to Chamberlain protesting against interpretation of the term "British subjects" in Commando Treaty, exempting citizens from compulsory military service, as applying only to whites.
November 18	:	Natal Government forwarded fresh draft of Franchise Bill to Secretary of State for Colonies. Europeans organized meetings at Ladysmith, Salisbury, Bellair, etc., in support of Asiatic legislation
November 26	:	Gandhiji memorialized Chamberlain against discrimination in Commando Treaty.
December 16	:	Issued The Indian Franchise: An Appeal to Every Briton in South Africa.

1896

January 23	:	Gandhiji applied for appointment as a Gujarati interpreter in Natal Court.
January 27	:	The Times, London, referred to Gandhiji as one "whose efforts on behalf of his Indian fellow-subjects in South Africa entitle him to respect".
February 26	:	Gandhiji petitioned Governor of Zululand protesting against the Townships Regulations.
March 3	:	Natal Government Gazette released text of new draft Franchise Bill, introduced in legislature.
March 5	:	Petition regarding the Townships Regulations rejected by Government.
March 11	:	Gandhiji made representations to Chamberlain against the Townships Regulations.

April 27	:	Franchise Bill, in its modified form, disfranchising natives of other countries who did not enjoy parliamentary franchise there, presented to Natal Parliament.
	:	Natal Indians petitioned Legislative Assembly at Pietermaritzburg against the Bill.
May 6	:	Franchise Bill read second time.
May 7	:	Gandhiji cabled Chamberlain and the British Committee of Indian National Congress against the acceptance of Franchise Bill or any alterations thereto till Indian memorial in that behalf was presented.
May 13	:	Franchise Bill given third reading and passed in the Legislative Assembly.
May 26	:	Representatives of Durban Indian community authorized Gandhiji, who was due to leave for India, to "represent the grievances the Indians are labouring under in South Africa before the authorities and public men and public bodies in India"
June 2	:	Presented with address on behalf on Natal Indian Congress.
June 4	:	Given address by Durban Indians at farewell meeting in Congress Hall.
June 5	:	Gandhiji left for India.
July 4	:	Gandhiji reached Calcutta, having left Durban by ship on June 5. Left for Bombay via Allahabad.
July 5-6?	:	At Allahabad interviewed Chesney, editor of *The Pioneer.*
July 9	:	Reached Rajkot. Joined Sanitary Visitors' Committee at Rajkot on outbreak of the plague in Bombay.
August 14	:	Published *Green Pamphlet* at Rajkot.
August 17	:	Left Rajkot for Bombay.
August 19	:	Met Ranade, Badruddin Tyabji and Pherozeshah Mehta in Bombay.
September 11	:	Left Bombay for Rajkot, with ailing brother-in law whom he nursed up to his dying moments.
September 14	:	Reuter's cable from London to Durban released

misleading report about contents of Green Pamphlet.

September 16 : Europeans of Durban formed European Protection Association, incited by summary of Reuter's cable in Natal Papers.

September 26 : Gandhiji addressed public meeting, presided over by Pherozeshah Mehta, in Bombay.

September 29 : Bombay meeting protested against ill-usage of Indians in South Africa and decided to petition Secretary of State for India for redress.

October 11 : Gandhiji left Bombay for Madras via Poona.

October 12 : At Poona, met Gokhale, Tilak and Dr. Bhandarkar.

October 14 : Arrived at Madras.

October 26 : Addressed public meeting at Pachaiyappa College Hall, Madras.

October 31 : Reached Calcutta via Nagpur. Met Surendranath Banerjea and other leaders of public opinion.

November 12 : Received cable from Dada Abdulla, Durban, asking him to return to Natal as Voiksraad had recommended that Indians should be forced to reside in locations.

November 13 : Addressed letter to The Englishman on problems of Indians in South Africa.

November 14 (15?): Reached Bombay.

November 16 : Went to Poona and addressed public meeting under auspices of Sarvajanik Sabha.

November 20 : Returned to Bombay.

November 26 : Mass meeting of Durban Europeans under chairmanship of Harry Sparks condemned Asiatic immigration.

: Audience hissed at mention of Gandhiji's name. Colonial Patriotic Union set up.

November 30 : Gandhiji sent telegram to Viceroy at Calcutta, drawing attention to Transvaal Government's decision to force Indians to live in locations. Left Bombay for South Africa by *SS Courland* along with wife and two sons.

December 18 : Ships *Courland* and Naderi, carrying Indian

passengers, reached Durban.

December 19 : Natal Government published Notification declaring Bombay an infected port in view of the plague in some parts of Bombay Presidency. Ships put under five days' quarantine, which period was extended from time to time till January 11.

December 25 : Gandhiji addressed ship-mates at a Christmas Day gathering on Western civilization. Natal newspapers charged him later with "indulging in animated condemnation of Natal Whites" and "with desire to swamp Natal with Indians".

December 29 : Europeans of Durban advertised meeting on January 4, for demonstrating against Indians' landing.

: Newspapers full of "Asiatic invasion" story.

December 31 : Indian National Congress, in session at Calcutta, adopted, on motion of G. P. Pillai, delegate from the Natal Indian Congress briefed by Gandhiji, resolution protesting against disabilities of Indians in South Africa and appealing to the Government for remedial measures.

1897

January 2 : Letter in The Natal Advertiser supported steps to give Gandhiji and his friends a "fitting reception" when they landed in Durban.

January 13 : Gandhiji gave interview to *The Natal Advertiser.* Landed at 5 p.m. and was assaulted by a section of Durban mob, but escaped serious harm through intervention of Mrs. Alexander, the Police Superintendent's wife. Besieged later in Parsi Rustomji's house, was rescued by Police Superintendent Alexander.

January 14 : Natal Government reported incident to Secretary of State for Colonies and blamed Gandhiji for having landed at inopportune time under bad advice.

January 20 : Interviewed by Attorney-General, Gandhiji declined to have assailants prosecuted and gave

		written expression to his wish.
January 22	:	Wrote personal letters of thanks and sent gifts to Mr. and Mrs. Alexander for their help when attacked by mob.
January 28	:	Sent cable to Dadabhai Naoroji, Hunter and Bhownaggree reporting landing incidents.
January 29	:	Addressed to them letters in confirmation of cable, giving details.
February 2, 3, 4	:	Addressed letters to the Press appealing for aid for Indian Famine Relief Fund and issued circulars in English and some Indian languages for the purpose.
February 6	:	Appealed to Clergymen of Durban for rallying support for Indian famine relief.
March 2	:	Natal ministers informed Governor that Gandhiji's injuries were not serious and "in accordance with his wish, no proceedings were taken for breach of peace".
March 15	:	Gandhiji completed memorial to Chamberlain concerning the anti-Indian demonstration and subsequent developments.
March 26	:	Presented to Natal legislature petitions against anti-Indian Bills pending before them.
April 6	:	Wrote general letter to influential British and Indian friends with which were enclosed copies of memorial to Mr. Chamberlain. Original memorial delivered to Natal Governor for transmission to Chamberlain.
	:	Gandhiji released to the Press correspondence with Natal Government concerning the landing incidents.
April 13	:	Wrote to newspapers refuting allegation against him in connection with Indian immigration.
May 7	:	Informed Chairman of Central Famine Relief Committee, Calcutta, of collection by Natal Indians of £1,539-1- 9 for famine relief.
May 18	:	Interviewed British Agent at Pretoria and submitted written plea that British Government bear costs of Test Case in respect of interpretation

		of Law 3 of 1885.
June 9	:	Cabled Hunter regarding enactment of Quarantine, Dealers' Licences, Immigration Restriction and Uncovenanted Indians Protection Bills.
June 22	:	Spoke at opening ceremony of Indian Library on Queen Victoria's Diamond Jubilee Day.
July 2	:	Sent petition to Secretary of State for the Colonies regarding the four anti-Indian measures.
July 10	:	Addressed circular letter to public men in Britain and India regarding discriminatory laws.
September 11	:	Appeared in defence of Indians charged with being prohibited immigrants and had them discharged.
September 14	:	Indian Hospital opened in Durban, with Parsi Rustomji's munificence and Dr. Booth's supervision, in which, later, Gandhiji served two hours daily as medical assistant.
September 18	:	Gandhiji wrote to Dadabhai Naoroji, William Wedderburn and others about implications of Chamberlain's address at Colonial Premiers' Conference in London.
November 13	:	Wrote to *The Natal Mercury* and the Colonial Secretary repudiating allegations of organized attempts to contravene the Immigration Act.
November 15	:	Wrote to The Natal Mercury on same subject.
November 18	:	Addressed Colonial Secretary on same topic.
December 9	:	Attended Christian Mission meeting and conveyed the gift of tank from a Parsi donor (Rustomji).

1898

February 28	:	Wrote to the British Agent at Pretoria, informing him of the Transvaal Indians' intention to file Test Case in regard to Law 3 of 1885.
March 2	:	Appeared in the Somnath Maharaj case for a retail licence in respect of trading premises.

August 8	:	The Transvaal High Court ruled in Test Case that no distinction could be made between places of residence and business premises, and that Indians must reside as well as trade only in Locations specified by Government.
August 19	:	Cabled the Viceroy of India, communicating adverse decision of Court in Test Case.
August 22	:	Petitioned Indian National Congress, seeking its intervention in regard to implementation of the Locations policy by the Transvaal Government.
August 25	:	Forwarded copy of above petition to Secretary of State for India.
August 30	:	Cabled Bhownaggree and India about Test Case judgment, saying that Indians relied on Chamberlain's intercession.
September 14	:	Pleaded unsuccessfully in Dada Osman's case before Durban Town Council against refusal of trading licences to Indians on racial grounds.
November 3	:	Cabled Colonial Secretary protesting against visitors' and embarkation fees imposed under the Immigration Act.
November 19	:	Locations Notice published in Government Gazette.
November 28	:	Gandhiji represented to Indian National Congress about serious financial loss from enforcement of the Locations order.
November 29	:	Participated in inaugural ceremony of the International Printing Press in Durban set up at his suggestion.
December 5	:	Cabled India, suggesting that British friends take advantage of High Commissioner's visit to England and secure reversal of policy in regard to Locations.
December 23	:	Sought expert legal opinion from European counsel on points at issue in Licensing law.
December 31	:	Drew up petition to Secretary of State for Colonies regarding Dealers' Licenses Act, 1897.

1899

January 11 : Forwarded to Natal Governor Indian petition regarding licences.

January 21 : Addressed to the Press and public in India general letter, calling for urgent attention to Indian grievances regarding licences.

January 22 : Sought, by petition, Viceroy's intervention in regard to Licensing law.

March (prior to) 8: Undertook to translate pamphlet on plague precautions for Pietermaritzburg Town Council.

March 11 : Communicated with The Times of India and India about disabilities of Indian traders in Rhodesia.

March 20 : Contributed to The Times of India special article on plague panic in Natal, the first of a series by him on the position of Indians in South Africa.

April 25 : The Transvaal Government ordered Asiatics to remove to the Locations before July 1.

May 17 : Gandhiji addressed memorial to Chamberlain regarding Governments steps to enforce Law 3 of 1885.

May 18 : Wrote to Colonial Secretary, Pietermaritzburg, pleading that Bill to amend Indian Immigration law be modified in interests of indentured labour.

May 27 : Sent Wedderburn copy of memorial of May 17 addressed to Chamberlain.

July 6 : Communicated to Colonial Secretary information about cases of hardship resulting from operation of Dealers' Licenses Act.

July 15 : Called on State Secretary and appealed for magnanimity towards Indians.

July 20 : Waited in deputation on British Agent at Pretoria and acquainted him with problems of Indians arising out of law on Locations.

July (prior to) 27: Was interviewed by the *Star of Johannesburg* about Locations order.

July 31 : Demanded, in petition to Natal Governor, legislation to amend Licensing law and give Indians right of appeal to Supreme Court against arbitrary decisions of municipalities, Town Councils, etc., in regard to trading licences.

September 9 : Cabled Colonial Secretary for facilities to Indians to leave the Transvaal, in view of imminence of British-Boer hostilities.

October 14 : Addressed circular letter to influential people concerning refugees from the Transvaal, pressing for suspension of deposits and grant of facilities to enter Natal from Delagoa Bay

October 16 : Natal Indian Congress thanked Government for concessions to refugees.

October 17 : Meeting of English-speaking Indians decided to offer Indians, services to Natal Government on the outbreak of Boer War.

Gandhiji had medical check-up by Dr. Prince and was found fit for service in Ambulance work.

October 19 : Communicated Indian offer to Government, forwarding list of Volunteers headed by himself.

October 23 : Indian offer welcomed by Government who indicated their willingness to avail of it on suitable occasion.

October 27 : Wrote letter to *The Times of India* dealing with refugee situation and Indian offer to Natal Government to serve as stretcher-bearers.

November 1 : Circulated among Indians appeal for donations to Durban Women's Patriotic League Fund, collecting over £ 60 and himself contributing £ 3.3.0.

November 18 : In letter to *The Times of India,* reported at length on the difficulties created by Dealers' Licenses Act for Indian traders in Natal.

December 2 : Wired Colonial Secretary for details of Ambulance Corps, work and date of start.

December 4 : Informed Colonial Secretary of readiness to leave for front at moment's notice, regretted Government's tardiness in accepting offer and sent further names of Volunteers.

December (prior to) 11: Wrote to Bishop of Natal, requesting release of Dr. Booth for Ambulance work.

December 13 : Addressed meeting at Hon. Mr. Escombe's residence about aim of Indians in volunteering to serve as stretcher-bearers at the front.

December 14 : Left for the front with Ambulance Corps.

December 15 : Corps reached Chieveley and was ordered to field hospital. Colenso reverse.

December 17 : Corps left for Estcourt.

December 19 : Corps disbanded temporarily.

1900

January (prior to) 7: Gandhiji informed authorities of Indians' readiness for further Ambulance work.

January 7 : Indian Ambulance Corps reformed and stationed at Estcourt.

January 21 : Corps in action at Spion Kop; carried wounded to base under fire.

January 28 : Corps again disbanded about this time after three weeks' service.

March 1 : Gandhiji sent message of congratulations to General Buller on relief of Ladysmith.

March 8 : Circulated text of Congress message of condolence on W.W. Hunter's death.

March 14 : Addressed public meeting of Indians and Europeans held to felicitate British Generals on victory in Boer War.

March (post) 14: Contributed to *The Times of India* detailed account about doings of Indian Ambulance Corps.

March (prior to) 26: Released to Durban Press text of resolutions congratulating British Generals and their acknowledgment thereof.

April 11 : Issued appeal for donations to Durban Indian Hospital..

April 20, 24 : Addressed personal letters, forwarding presents to leaders and men of Ambulance Corps.

May 21 : Conveyed to Queen Victoria Indians' felicitations on her birthday.

July 13 : Circulated resolution thanking East India Association, London, for good work in the cause of South African Indians.

July 30	:	Appealed through Press for funds for relief of famine in India.
August 14	:	Informed Colonial Secretary of having forwarded to Turkish Ambassador in London Indians' address of felicitations to Sultan of Turkey on silver jubilee of his reign.
September 24	:	Wrote to Town Clerk, Durban, against enactment of bye-law prohibiting carrying of coloured passengers by Indian riksha-haulers in rikshas marked "For Europeans only".
October 8	:	Addressed communication to Dadabhai Naoroji concerning work of Indian National Congress for South African Indians and forwarded draft resolution thereon for ensuing Congress session.
December 6	:	Cabled Cape Town Indian leader to offer address to Lord Roberts.
December 14	:	Defended indentured Indian, Chellagadu, charged for absenting from work without permission.
December 21	:	Presided over Indian School annual function in Durban.
December 24	:	Presented petition to Natal Governor against Durban Town Council's bye-law concerning Indian riksha-haulers.

1901

January 23	:	Conveyed to Colonial Secretary on behalf of Natal Indians, condolence message on Queen's death.
February 2	:	Laid wreath on pedestal of Queen's statue in Durban and paid tribute to her at memorial meeting.
February 16	:	Communicated to Press information about Famine Fund and contributions received towards relief of famine in India.
March 19	:	Contacted Durban schools for distribution of souvenir portrait of Queen.
March 25	:	Wired High Commissioner, informing him of footpath restrictions and rigorous enforcement of anti-Indian laws, and recalling Imperial

		Government's assurance to modify, if not repeal, racial legislation.
March 30	:	Protested, in letter to Colonial Secretary, against singling him out for mention in General Buller's dispatches for services in Boer War.
April 16	:	Cabled British Committee and East India Association concerning denial of permits to refugee Indians to re-enter the Transvaal.
April 20	:	Addressed friends in England on Indian disabilities and anti-Indian laws still prevailing in South Africa.
	:	Natal Indians presented address to Lord Harris, ex-Governor of Bombay, during visit to Durban.
April 27	:	Gandhiji represented to friends in England difficulties of Indians in re-entering the Transvaal.
April 30	:	Expressed hope in letter to Colonial Secretary that in legislation to modify Indian Immigration Amendment Act, Government would maintain women labourers' wages at half those of men.
May 4	:	Addressed letter to Bombay Government bringing to their notice disabilities of Indian immigrants in South Africa.
May 9, 10	:	Represented to Military Governor, Johannesburg, and to High Commissioner undesirability of a new Immigration Department to deal with matters of Indian concern.
May 18	:	Urged in letter to East India Association and British Committee advisability of influential joint deputations to Sir Alfred Milner and to Chamberlain.
May 21	:	Expressed in letter to Revashankar Zaveri his sense of grief and loss over passing away of Raychandbhai.
June 1	:	Suggested in communication to British Committee that it form with East India Association a joint committee for concerted action in regard to anti-Indian laws in South Africa.
June 22	:	Wrote to Bhownaggree regarding joint action by British Committee and East India Association

		in respect of Indian grievances in South Africa.
August 13	:	Natal Indians presented address to Duke and Duchess of York and Cornwall.
August 23	:	Presided over meeting for formation of Durban Indians Progressive League; considered move inopportune.
September 11	:	Appeared for and secured discharge of Indian barber charged under Pass law.
October 15	:	Presented with farewell addresses by Natal Indian Congress and other Indian organizations on eve of his departure for India.
October 18	:	Returned costly gifts and recommended a trust thereof for beneficial objects.
	:	Sailed for India, promising to return within year, if community should need him.
October 30	:	Disembarked at Port Louis, Mauritius.
November 13, 16	:	Accorded receptions by Indian community of Mauritius.
November 19	:	Left Mauritius for India.
December 14	:	Reached Rajkot via Porbander.
December 17	:	Left Rajkot for Bombay; on way to Calcutta Congress, met Bhownaggree.
December 27	:	Moved resolution on South Africa at Congress session.

1902

January 19	:	Addressed public meeting at Albert Hall, Calcutta, on question of Indians in South Africa.
January 27	:	Addressed second meeting at Calcutta on work of Indian Ambulance Corps in Boer War.
January 28	:	Sailed for Rangoon.
January 31	:	Reached Rangoon.
February 2	:	Some time after this date, returned to Calcutta and stayed for several days with Gokhale.
February 21 or 22	:	Was seen off by Gokhale and Dr. P. C. Ray on tour of Benares, Agra, Jaipur and Palanpur en route to Rajkot, travelling third class. Spent a day at each place; in Benares, called on Annie Besant.

February 26 : Reached Rajkot. Settled down to practice, handling cases at Jamnagar, Veraval and other places in Kathiawar.

March 26 : Wrote to W.S. Caine, sending "Notes" on latest position in South Africa and urging efforts by British friends for redress of grievances of Indians.

March 30 : Forwarded "Notes" to India. Sent Bhownaggree copy of his resolution on South Africa adopted at Calcutta Congress.

March 31 : Writing to Khan and Nazar, pleaded that, if his presence was essential, he should be recalled to South Africa before he settled down in India.

April 8 : Wrote to Gokhale, congratulating him on his budget speech in Imperial Legislative Council.

April 22 : Contributed special article to *The Times of India* on Natal Bill to impose poll-tax on children of indentured Indians, indirectly compelling their return to India.

May 1 : Joined as Secretary, State Volunteer Plague Committee in Rajkot at about this time when outbreak of plague was feared.

May 20 : Wrote again to The Times of India, furnishing text of Natal Bill recently passed and awaiting Imperial sanction. Urged the paper to raise its voice against the injustice.

May 31 : Detailed, in special article in *Voice of India,* hardships of new poll-tax law and hoped Lord Curzon would intervene and Chamberlain use his influence with Colonies on the side of justice and fairplay.

June 3 : Urged his associates in Durban, in view of his own bad financial condition, to furnish him with funds for carrying on South' African work.

June 5 : Bombay Presidency Association forwarded memorial, prepared by Gandhiji, to Secretary of State for India, opposing Natal Act to amend Indian Immigration law by inclusion of poll-tax clause, and demanding suspension of State-regulated emigration to Colony.

July 10 : Left Rajkot for Bombay to set up legal practice there.

July 11 : Reached Bombay.

August 1 : Wrote to Gokhale, mentioning his having secured office space in Bombay, and offering him his services.

August 6 : Spoke of difficulty in legal profession, in letter to Devchand Parekh.

November 3 : Referred, in letter to Shukla, to having received cable from Natal recalling him and to his having pleaded inability to go because of physical weakness and children's ill-health.

November 14 : Communicated to Gokhale intention to leave for South Africa on November 20.

December 25 : Arrived in Durban before this date. Wrote to Natal Government, asking for change of date for deputation to Secretary of State for Colonies.

December 28 : Led deputation of Natal Indians to Chamberlain and presented memorial regarding grievances of Natal Indians.

December 28 or 29: Obtained, with the help of Police Superintendent Alexander, permit to enter the Transvaal for leading Pretoria Indians' deputation to Chamberlain.

1903

January 1 : Gandhiji reached Pretoria.

January 2 : Waited on Assistant Colonial Secretary but told that not being resident of the Transvaal, he could not be in deputation.

January 6 : British Indian Committee appealed to Lt.-Governor to permit Gandhiji to be member of deputation to Chamberlain.

January (prior to) 7: Memorial drawn up by Gandhiji presented by deputation led by George Godfrey. Addressed sometime later during the month petition to Viceroy regarding indentured Indians, requesting that Natal be advised to discontinue import of Indian labour if it could not grant elementary rights of British citizenship.

January 30	:	Wrote to Dadabhai Naoroji, reporting on the deputations to Chamberlain and suggesting prohibition of indentured emigration to Natal.
February 5	:	Wrote, in letter to Chhaganlal Gandhi, of the uncertainty of his stay in South Africa, which was 'no bed of roses'.
February 12	:	Interviewed Lt. Governor of the Transvaal concerning setting up of Bazaars.
February 16	:	Decided to settle down in Johannesburg, in view of public work, about this time enrolled to Bar of the Transvaal Supreme Court.
February 18	:	Communicated views on Bazaars to Colonial Secretary.
February 23	:	Forwarded to Dadabhai Naoroji comprehensive statement on Indian Question in the Transvaal and Orange River Colonies. Wrote to Gokhale that events in the Transvaal were progressing fast and he was "in the thick of the fight".
March 16	:	Despatched periodical statement to Dadabhai Naoroji on the situation in South Africa.
April 25	:	Wrote in The Vegetarian, offering tips to prospective emigrants to South Africa. Reported, in letter to Colonial Secretary, police high-handedness towards Indian merchants in Heidelberg.
April 27	:	Released to Press letter about Heidelberg incidents.
May 1	:	Forwarded to Lt.-Governor petition of William Hosken and other European residents of Johannesburg about Government Notice No. 356 of 1903, and expressed view that legislation to regulate immigration was more acceptable.
May 6	:	Mass meeting held in Johannesburg protesting against enforcement of anti-Indian laws which restricted Indians to Bazaars, etc., and calling for their repeal.
May 9	:	Gandhiji forwarded reports to Dadabhai Naoroji about Heidelberg and Johannesburg incidents, European petition about Notice No. 356 and the Johannesburg Mass Meeting.

May 10	:	Expressed, in letter to Dadabhai Naoroji, readiness to accept, with modifications, legislation on Natal lines to restrict immigration, and also principle of Bazaars if not imposed by law. Stated in letter to Gokhale that he had settled in Johannesburg "under very great difficulties". Requested him to study question of South African legislation to restrict Asiatic immigration and to direct movement against it in India.
May 16	:	Reported to Dadabhai Naoroji Transvaal Government move to enforce collection of £ 3 registration tax.
May 22	:	Led Indian deputation to Lord Milner, Governor of the Transvaal, in connection with compulsory levy of registration tax and general question of Indians in Colony.
May 24	:	Informed Dadabhai Naoroji of demands of Indian deputation to Lord Milner.
May 31	:	Urged in weekly communication to Dadabhai Naoroji need for relief to Indians from discrimination in Orange River Colony. Reported enactment of Bazaar law by Cape Colony and emphasized need to concentrate effort on repeal of existing legislation.
June 4	:	*Indian Opinion* commenced publication with Mansukhlal Nazar as editor.
June 6	:	Gandhiji cabled British Committee, hoping that compulsory repatriation of ex-indentured Indians would not receive sanction from Home Government.Opposed in periodical statement to Dadabhai Naoroji compulsory return of ex-indentured Indians and stressed that Location and Bazaar laws in Nạtal and the Cape Colony, if made permanent, would seriously damage Indian interests.
June 8	:	Submitted petition to Transvaal Governor, detailing disadvantages of Asiatic Office, Bazaar Notice, and prohibition of land-ownership in Locations, and demanding abrogation of discriminatory legislation and restoration of

freedom of life and trade.

June 10 : Petition presented to Natal Legislature demanding amendment of draft ordinance for Municipal franchise classing Indians with Natives.

June 23 : Suggested in petition to Natal Council modifications to Bill for restricting immigration.

June 30 : Wrote to Haridasbhai Vora, reporting success in professional practice, referring to exacting nature of his public work and expressing preparedness to settle down in Johannesburg for decade or so.

July 4 : Urged in letter to Gokhale the need of "a well-directed movement" throughout India to counteract agitation of interested parties in the Transvaal against relaxation of old anti-Asiatic laws.

July 18 : Informed Dadabhai Naoroji of passing of Municipal Ordinance despite Indian objection, and of Transvaal Government proposal to lay out 54 Locations for Indians.

July 25 : Informed Dadabhai Naoroji of Transvaal Legislative Council's resolution to enforce Bazaar Notice.

August 3 : Demanded in his weekly statement relaxation in respect of existing licences, referred to continued difficulties of Transvaal Indian refugees and refuted Milner's allegation of sanitary grounds for segregation policy.

August 4 : Cabled British Committee, India and *The Times of India* about refugee problem.

August 10 : Forwarded to Dadabhai Naoroji detailed clarification of cable of August 4.

August 24 : Petitioned Chamberlain to withhold Royal assent to Immigration Restriction Bill passed by Natal Assembly.

September 2 : Writing in Indian Opinion, expressed hope that no Indian would stoop to secure exemption from Bazaar Notice.

September 7	:	Remonstrated, in letter to Dadabhai Naoroji, against any acceptance in England of move for compulsory repatriation of indentured labour and payment of part wages in India.
November 9	:	Gandhiji reported to Dadabhai Naoroji that sites chosen for Bazaars were in out-of-the-way places.
November 16	:	Intimated in weekly letter to Dadabhai Naroroji that policy laid down in Milner's dispatch of May 1903 was not being carried out.
December 1	:	Wrote to Indian National Congress at Madras that seriousness of situation in Natal should be realised and early and earnest efforts made to secure relief.
December 11	:	Mass meeting of British Indians requested protection to all existing licences.
December 12	:	Gandhiji cabled Dadabhai Naoroji about Government's proposed amendment to Bazaar Notice proposing exemption for some Indians from liability to trade in Bazaars or Locations.
December 17	:	Appealed to Associated Chambers of Commerce at Pretoria seriously to consider amendment of Location law.

1904

January 18	:	Wrote to Dadabhai Naoroji on motion in Transvaal Legislative Council to restrict renewal of Indians' trading licences.
February 11	:	Wrote to Medical Officer of Health, Johannesburg, about overcrowding and insanitary condition in Indian Location and forewarned him of possibility of outbreak of epidemic.
February (prior to) 15	:	Visited Indian Location in Insanitary Area, Johannesburg.
February 15	:	Urged Medical Officer of Health, Johannesburg, to take immediate steps to improve sanitary conditions in Indian Location.
February 20	:	Wrote to Medical Officer of Health reiterating stand taken by him in letter of February 15.
March 1	:	Intimated Medical Officer of Health that plague

had broken out in Johannesburg.

March 18 : Informed the authorities that a number of Indians, "dead or dying" were being "dumped" in the Location; visited the suspected area accompanied by Dr. Godfrey, Dr. Pereira and a health inspector.

March 19 : Was seen by Town Clerk who informed him that Town Council could not assume any financial responsibility; improvised hospital and encouraged earth treatment; informed Town Clerk of steps Indian community was taking to combat plague.

March 21 : Was interviewed by a representative of *The Star* on plague problem.

April 5 : Wrote to Johannesburg Press about plague epidemic; released correspondence with Dr. Porter, Medical Officer of Health, Johannesburg.

April 14 : Wrote to *The Rand Daily Mail* on plague question.

April 18 : Forwarded to Public Health Committee detailed valuation of Indian Location at Krugersdrop.

April 20 : Wrote to India at length about plague epidemic.

May 11 : Supreme Court delivered judgment to the effect that the term "residence" occurring in Law 3 of 1885 did not include place of business.

September (prior to) 3: Memorial sent to Colonial Secretary on behalf of British Indian Association.

September 3 : Gandhiji wrote to The Star on question of British Indians in South Africa.

September 5 : Wrote to Dadabhai Naoroji that matters pertaining to Indian question had reached "a crisis."

October : Took over entire responsibility for and management of Indian Opinion. Visited Tongaat; read Ruskin's Unto This Last while travelling to Durban; decided to set up a colony on the lines indicated therein.

October 10 : Spoke on self-sacrifice at dinner given in his honour and for other leaders of Indian community in Durban.

October 15 : Spoke at function held in Durban to bid farewell to Madanjit, proprietor, *Indian Opinion*, on eve of his return to India.

November 3 : Wired Colonial Secretary, Pretoria, enquiring date of presentation of address to Lord Roberts.

November 10 : Anti-Asiatic Convention held at Pretoria demanding drastic steps to eliminate British Indians from the Colony.

November 11 : Presented address to Lord Roberts.

November 17 : Attended meeting of Transvaal British Indians held to protest against "Convention" proceedings in regard to Asiatic immigration into Transvaal.

November-December: Founded the Phoenix Settlement.

December 3 : Petition sent to Acting Lieutenant-Governor regarding compensation claims in respect of goods destroyed at instance of Rand Plague Committee.

December 9 : Gandhiji wrote to *The Star* regarding Indians' trading licences.

December 14 : Proposed at meeting of Natal Indian Congressfinancial assistance to Hoondamal in test case.

December (prior to) 24: Wrote to The Star, replying to venomous attack at Anti-Asiatic Convention.

December 24 : First number of Indian Opinion issued from Phoenix settlement

1905

January 10 : Spoke at opening ceremony of library in Durban.

January 13 : Wrote to G.K. Gokhale regarding Indian Opinion and his intention to open a school for Indian children.

February 17 : Visited Cape Town accompanied by Parsee Rustomjee; left for Johannesburg.

March 4 : Delivered first lecture on Hindu religion at Theosophical Society, Johannesburg.

March 9 : Spoke at function held in Johannesburg to bid farewell to L.W. Ritch.

March 11 : Second lecture on Hindu religion.

March 18 : Third lecture on Hindu religion.

March 25 : Fourth and final lecture on Hindu religion.

April 7 : Sent memorial to Natal Legislative Assembly regarding Bills "to amend and consolidate the law relating to the Municipal Corporations" and to regulate "use of firearms".

May : Was learning Tamil about this time.

May 6 : Made efforts to collect funds for earthquake relief in India.

June 7 : Presented address to Lord Selborne, new High Commissioner.

June (post) 9 : Visited Durban and Phoenix Settlement.

June 16 : Spoke at meeting of Natal Indian Congress at Durban.

July 1 : Gandhiji criticized Natal Bills concerning licences, private Locations and tax on unoccupied rural lands and occupied dwelling houses. British Indian Association represented to High Commissioner that municipal legislation discriminatory of Coloured persons in Orange River Colony could be vetoed by Lt.-Governor.

July 8 : Gandhiji asked, in *Indian Opinion,* for abolition of salt-tax in India.

July 13 : British Indian Association protested against clause 3 of Ordinance vesting control of Asiatic Bazaars in Town Councils.

July 14 : Gandhiji sought from Johannesburg Town Council assurance of facilities to Indians travelling in trams.

July 15 : Criticized, in *Indian Opinion,* Cape Immigration Act.

After July 17 : Wrote to *The Daily Express* challenging correspondent's low estimate of the number of Indian traders resident in Pietersburg before Boer War.

July 20 : Partition of Bengal announced.

July 22 : Gandhiji called upon South African politicians to reconsider treatment of British Indians in light of India's contribution to defence of Empire.

August 5	:	Contributed 10s. to Edwin Arnold Memorial Fund.
August 9	:	Poll-Tax Bill passed by Natal Legislative Council.
August 12	:	Gandhiji commended, in Indian Opinion, Lord Selborne's pronouncement that administrative injustice to Natives was a blot and a disgrace. Welcomed Natal legislature's rejection of Locations and Land Tax Bills, and Transvaal Supreme Court's judgment permitting transfer of religious property in the name of Coloured persons.
August 14	:	Denied, in letter to Haji Habib, that his lectures on religion were critical of any religion or intended to hurt anyone.
August 19	:	Called for united opposition to Bengal partition and supported boycott of British goods.
August 26	:	Praised British Association for Advancement of Science and hoped it would one day meet in India; commented on Curzon's term of viceroyalty.
August 30	:	British Indian Association objected to application to Indians of Municipal Location Bye-laws for Coloured persons in Orange River Colony.
September 1	:	British Indian Association objected to rule requiring Indian refugees to furnish European references.
September 2	:	Gandhiji attributed Japan's rise to Mikado's orders to armed forces concerning education and right conduct.
September 5	:	Natal Indians objected to Government's proposal to throw open Indian school to Coloured children, and to make no distinction in education of boys and girls.
September 9	:	Gandhiji condemned, in Indian Opinion, maltreatment of Chinese miners.
September 16	:	Gandhiji considered Gokhale outstanding among candidates for presidentship of Indian National Congress.
September 30	:	Criticized Transvaal's contentious Ordinances touching rights of Coloured persons.

October 7	:	Urged Indians in South Africa to make suitable provision for education.
	:	Condemning intolerance of Bhownaggree's moderate opinion, held that calm reasoning alone would get full measure of justice for India.
	:	Dada Osman's appeal for trading licence dismissed by Licensing Board, Durban.
October 9	:	Potchefstroom Indian Association presented address and statement to Lord Selborne.
October 14	:	Gandhiji led deputation to Lord Selborne at Potchefstroom. Warned South African Indians against plague outbreak.
	:	Welcomed reported move in India to abolish salt-tax.
October 24	:	Received Prof. Parmanand and acted host to him.
October 28	:	At Johannesburg reception, introduced Prof. Parmanand. Proposed that Natal Indian Congress set up licences committee.
	:	Hailed progress of swadeshi movement in Bengal.
November 1	:	Called for communal harmony in Bengal to strengthen anti-partition agitation.
November 11	:	Writing about Gokhale-Lajpat Rai delegation to England on behalf of Indian National Congress, appealed to Colonial statesmen to treat India, "an integral part of the Empire", with every consideration. Drew attention to hardships of Indian passengers on ships bound for South Africa.
November 13	:	Deputation of Asiatic National Convention, waiting on Lt.-Governor of the Transvaal, demanded board of control to consider applications for entry into Colony.
November 18	:	Gandhiji drew attention to discrimination against Japanese in British Colonies.
	:	Asked British Indian League of Cape Colony to oppose immigration law.
November 25	:	Called for revision of poll-tax rules and its discretionary application to poor Indians.

November 29 : Led British Indian deputation to Lord Selborne to protest against treatment meted out to British Indians in the Transvaal.

December2 : Criticized prison conditions at Stanger.Commended Bande Mataram as India's national anthem.

December 4 : As Secretary, British Indian Association, bade farewell to Sir Arthur Lawley, Governor-designate of Madras.

December 6 : Cape Colony Supreme Court decided Natal Indians had right of domicile in Cape Colony, on basis of long residence, even when unacompanied by families.

December 22 : British Indian Association protested to High Commissioner about bracketing of British Indians with Coloured persons in Orange River Colony draft ordinances.

After December 22: High Commissioner turned down Indian request for amending definition of "Coloured person" in legislation.

December 23 : Gandhiji commended cause of education to Indian youth, citing Gokhale. Deprecated third-party intervention in settlement of communal disputes in India.

December 30 : Reviewed position of British Indians in South Africa during 1905 and appealed to Indians to continue struggle "with reasonableness, ... with patience and yet with persistence". Deplored factious riots among Muslim community in Heidelberg. Acted as best man at wedding of Mr. Polak and Miss Douns.

1906

January 1 : £1 tax on Indians aged 18 or above enforced; Natal Early Closing Act came into force.

January 2 : Earthquake disaster in San Francisco.

January 20 : Mansukhlal Hiralal Nazar, at one time Editor, *Indian Opinion*, died.

February 3 : Hindi and Tamil columns of *Indian Opinion* discontinued.

February 9 : British Indian Association, in letter to Colonial Secretary, protested against changes in permit regulations.

February 10 : Association protested to Johannesburg Town Council against restrictions on Indians using tram-cars.

February 14 : Association took exception to prohibition of Indians' travelling by particular trains between Pretoria and Johannesburg.

February 16 : Association joined issue with Transvaal Leader on question of Indians using tram-cars in Johannesburg.

February 22 : In statement to Dadabhai Naoroji, Gandhiji stressed need for safeguarding Indian interests under responsible government in the Transvaal and Orange River Colony.

February 26 : Suggested to Dadabhai Naoroji that a deputation wait on British Ministers on behalf of South African Indians.

February 28 : Spoke at presentation of address by Natal Indian Congress to Abdul Kadir, retiring President.Zulu Rebellion broke out during this month.

March 7 : Gandhiji appeared for plaintiff in tram test case at Johannesburg.

Before March 10: Natal Indian Congress protested to Colonial Secretary against imposition of prohibitive fees for certificates and passes under Immigration Restriction Act.

March 10 : Gandhiji criticized resolution of the Congress of Associated Chambers of Commerce of South Africa regarding "continual influx of Asiatics". Waited in deputation on Assistant Colonial Secretary regarding permit grievances in the Transvaal.

March 11 : Addressed meeting at Pretoria.

March 12 : Appeared in tram test case and won.

March 16 : Bill to amend Cape Immigration Restriction Act of 1902 published in *Government Gazette*.

March 17 : Gandhiji exhorted Indians to volunteer their

		services to the Government on the occasion of the Zulu Rebellion.
March 19	:	In letter to Dadabhai Naoroji, drew attention to hardships under Peace Preservation Ordinance and Law 3 of 1885 in the Transvaal.
March 21	:	Addressed Coloured peoples' meeting at Johannesburg.
March 24	:	Commended Coloured peoples' petition to Imperial Government for franchise and other rights.
March 30	:	Dr. Abdurrahman met Lord Selborne regarding grievances of Cape Coloured people.
	:	Dada Osman appealed to Secretary of State for Colonies against refusal to him of trading licence.
Before March 31	:	Imperial Government set up Commission on Transvaal Constitution.
March 31	:	Gandhiji deprecated import of Indian labour for Transvaal mines.
Before April 7	:	British Indian deputation met Railway authorities at Johannesburg to represent Indian grievances. Gandhiji wrote to Leader, pointing out anomaly in restrictions on Indians' entry into the Transvaal.
April 12	:	Addressed letter to William Wedderburn on deteriorating condition of Indians in the Transvaal.
Before April 14	:	Durban Town Council passed resolution calling upon Licensing Officer not to issue fresh licences to hawkers. Natal Indian Congress decided to send deputation to England under Gandhiji's leadership. H.O. Ally waited on Sir Richard Solomon, Acting Lt.-Governor, concerning Malay Location.
April 23	:	At Durban meeting to consider future of *Indian Opinion*, Gandhiji reiterated its objects and appealed to Indian community to make it its own.
April 24	:	Welcomed establishment of Young Men's Mahomedan Association for promoting education; was entrusted with task of drafting

		its constitution. Addressed Natal Indian Congress meeting which then offered to form an ambulance corps.
Before April 26	:	Was interviewed by The Natal Mercury regarding proposed deputation to Imperial Government.
April 28	:	Criticized Natal Stores Employees' Association for irresponsible statement on Shops Act. Issued statement in reply to criticism at meetings of Young Men's Mahomedan Society about his speeches on Hinduism and policy of *Indian Opinion*.
Before May 5	:	Met General Manager, Natal Government Railways, regarding prohibition of Indians from travelling by certain trains between Johannesburg and Pretoria.
May 5	:	Appealed to Natal Government to consider Indian position regarding Land Clauses Bill in a statesmanlike manner .Commended idea of starting chamber of Indian merchants.
Before May 12	:	British Indian Association wrote to Lord Selborne regarding permits and visitors' passes. Gandhiji supported home rule for India "in the name of justice and for the good of humanity".
Before May 14	:	Constitution Commission held three meetings at Johannesburg.
Before May 18	:	Lord Selborne turned down British Indian Association's representation regarding permits.
May 18	:	Judgment favouring Indians' right to use trams awarded in Coovadia test case.
May 19	:	Johannesburg Municipality notified repeal of tram regulations and restoration of smallpox regulations which would serve to restrict the use of trams by Indians.
May 21	:	Gandhiji questioned, in Transvaal Leader, the ethics of Johannesburg Town Council's action.
May 22	:	Led representative deputation to Constitution Committee and presented Indians' viewpoint.
Before May 25	:	Lord Selborne refused to reconsider Indian stand on permits.

May 25	:	Gandhiji secured acquittal of minor boy charged with violating Law 3 of 1885.
Maw 26	:	Apropos of Queen Victoria's birthday celebrations, appealed to public men of South Africa to abjure race hatred and colour prejudice.
May 27	:	Wrote to brother, Lakshmidas, declaring his disinterestedness in worldly possessions.
May 29	:	Presented statement to Constitution Committee.
May 30	:	British Indian Association decided to include Haji Habib and Ally in deputation to England. Natal Government accepted Congress offer regarding ambulance corps.
June 2	:	Gandhiji pleaded for better amenities to deck-passengers. Addressed meeting of Indians in Durban to raise funds for ambulance work.
Before June 6	:	British Indian Committee, London, suggested Gandhiji alone proceed to England to present Indian case. Chairman, British Indian Association, and Polak not allowed to use tram in Johannesburg. British Indian Association decided to file test cases regarding permits if Government failed to redress Indian grievances.
June 8	:	Gandhiji informed Dadabhai Naoroji that deputation to England was deferred in view of ambulance work at the front.
June 9	:	Appealed to Indians for contributions to Soldiers' Fund.
Before June 13	:	Issued statement to The Natal Mercury on difficulties of Indians.
June 16	:	Indian Stretcher-Bearer Corps' pledge of allegiance published in *Indian Opinion*. Gandhiji was medically examined and certified fit.
June 21	:	Ambulance Corps received marching orders.
June 22	:	Gandhiji given rank of Sergeant-Major by Government. Entrained with Ambulance Corps. Wrote to Gokhale about Corps; invited him to visit South Africa on way back home.
Before June 23	:	Bhyat's right to a permit under Peace Preservation Ordinance vindicated in court.

June 23-July 18 : Gandhiji on ambulance duty at the front.

July 19 : Stretcher-Bearer Corps disbanded.

July 20 : Members of Corps feted at Stanger. Gandhiji spoke at Congress reception in Durban. Suggested that Indians be allowed to join permanent volunteer corps.

July 23 : Congress resolved to present medals to members of Corps. Gandhiji spoke at Diamond Jubilee Library meeting. British Indian Association emphasized necessity of sending deputation to England.

July 30 : Gandhiji sought Wedderburn's opinion on deputation's usefulness. Wrote to Principal Medical Officer of Natal Militia suggesting formation of permanent Ambulance Corps and exphasizing special training for it.

August 4 : Pointed out difficulties of Indian refugees seeking to re-enter the Transvaal.

: Wrote on differences between Lyttelton and Elgin constitutions. Colonial Secretary informed Legislative Council of Government's intention to introduce Bill to re-register Asiatics in the Transvaal. British Indian Association proposed immediate action.

August 6 : Gandhiji wrote to Dadabhai Naoroji about hardships of Transvaal Indians under proposed re-registration and suggested that latter interviewed Secretaries of State for India and Colonies.

August 7 : Sir Henry MacCallum, Natal Governor, thanked Gandhiji for services rendered by Stretcher-Bearer Corps.

Before August 9: In letter to *The Rand Daily Mail,* Gandhiji demanded full civil liberty for Indians.

August 11 : Analysed, in Indian Opinion, Colonial Secretary's statement on re-registration Ordinance.

August 12 : Spoke at Hamidiya Islamic Society exhorting Indians to organize a protest against Colonial Secretary's statement on Ordinance.

August 13 : In letter to Dadabhai Naoroji, pointed out need for equitable legislation by Imperial Government concerning the Transvaal. Natal Indian Congress petitioned Lord Elgin regarding Municipal Consolidation Bill.

August 18 : Favoured adoption of Hindustani in India for achieving nationhood.Reported Malay Location Committee's decision to challenge Town Council's rejection of petition.

August 21 : Cape Licences Act gazetted.

August 22 : Draft Asiatic Law Amendment Ordinance published in Transvaal Government Gazette.

August 25 : Gandhiji demanded British Indians be no longer classed with coloured people. British Indian Association in letter to Colonial Secretary protested against Ordinance.

August 28 : Gandhiji cabled India concerning re-registration under Ordinance; suggested commission of enquiry.

September 1 : Led deputation to Colonial Secretary at Pretoria.

September 4 : Ordinance introduced in Transvaal Assembly.

September 8 : Gandhiji described Government's persistence in enacting Draft Asiatic Ordinance as crime against humanity. British Indian Association cabled protest to Secretaries of State for India and Colonies and Viceroy of India against proposed Ordinance.

Before September 9: At meeting, Gandhiji interpreted "the Black Act" as first step to hound Indians out of country, and called for resistance.

September 9 : Spoke at Hamidiya Islamic Society meeting, on political situation in the Transvaal and stressed need to send deputation to England; advised people not to register, and offered himself to court imprisonment first.

September 11 : Mass Meeting of British Indians at Johannesburg demanded withdrawal of Ordinance; warned Indians would resort to resistance if Ordinance became law.

September 12 : British Indian Association sent Transvaal Lt.-Governor resolutions passed at Mass Meeting. Gandhiji wrote to The Rand Daily Mail, explaining his stand.

Before September 14: British Indian Association wrote to The Star affirming Indians' resolve not to submit to unbearable conditions.

September 14 : Indian woman, Punia, travelling by train, arrested and detained at Volksrust for being without separate permit.

September 15 : Punia tried, ordered to leave Colony and re-arrested at Germiston for defiance of order.

September 18 : High Commissioner informed British Indian Association that Ordinance had not yet received formal assent.

September 19 : Apropos of Punia case, Gandhiji wrote to Press criticizing Transvaal Government for its war on women and even infants.

September 20 : Declared his readiness to accept court of enquiry to investigate illegal influx of Indians into the Transvaal.

September 21 : Wrote to *Leader*, challenging its statement that Indians were bringing into Colony women of indifferent character as wives. *The Natal Mercury* published official explanation of Punia case. Indian meeting finally decided to send Gandhiji and Ally as a deputation to England.

: Lord Selborne informed British Indian Association that assent would not be given to Ordinance until deputation had visited England.

September 24 : Lord Selborne communicated to British Indian Association Lord Elgin's view that deputation would serve no useful purpose.

September 26 : Association enquired of Transvaal Governor if Ordinance had been accorded Royal sanction.

Before September 29: Lord Selborne wrote to British Indian Association, refusing to accept latter's point of view regarding Ordinance.

September 30 : Association wired Transvaal Governor requesting

		Imperial Government to withhold assent to Vrededorp Stands Ordinance till deputation had represented Indian viewpoint. Deputation accorded farewell on eve of departure.
October 1	:	Gandhiji and Ally entrained at Johannesburg for Cape Town, en route to England.
October 3	:	Deputation reached Cape Town and after reception by leading Indians, boarded s.s. Armadale Castle.
October 8	:	British Indian Association forwarded to Transvaal Governor text of cable to Secretary of State for Colonies requesting stay of Vrededorp Stands Ordinance pending representation. Association petitioned Lord Elgin regarding Vrededorp Stands Ordinance.
October 9	:	Transvaal Leader retracted statement of its Durban correspondent libelling Indian women.
October 10-11	:	Gandhiji wrote dispatches for *Indian Opinion;* was studying Tamil.
October 20	:	His answers to questions regarding Asiatic Ordinance and methods of resistance published in Indian Opinion.Deputation arrived in Southampton.
October 20	:	Gandhiji and H.O. Ally arrived at Southampton, England.Gandhiji interviewed by The Tribune and The Morning Leader. Met Dadabhai Naoroji.
October 21	:	Deputation reached London. Accompanied by Prof. Parmanand, Gandhiji visited J. H. Polak and stayed with him for the day. Met Pandit Shyamji Krishnavarma.
October 22	:	Gandhiji wrote to *The Times* answering charge of Asiatic influx into South Africa. Natal Indian Congress adopted resolution supporting Transvaal Indians' struggle against Asiatic Law Amendment Ordinance.
Before October 25	:	Gandhiji met Sir Muncherji Bhownaggree.
October 25	:	Interviewed by South Africa. Called on Ally at Lady Margaret Hospital.
October 25	:	Winston Churchill, Under-Secretary of State for Colonies, stated in Commons that Natal

Municipal Franchise Bill was under consideration of Secretary of State for Colonies.

October 26 : Gandhiji met Sir William Wedderburn and Dadabhai Naoroji. First anniversary of Bengal partition observed in India as day of mourning.

October 27 : Gandhiji interviewed by Reuter. Met Sir Muncherji Bhownaggree and Sir George Birdwood.

October 30 : Met Sir Muncherji Bhownaggree.

October 31 : Drafted representation to Lord Elgin, Secretary of State for Colonies. Met Sir Richard Solomon at House of Commons.

November 1 : Attended National Indian Association reception. Interviewed by South Africa.

November 3 : Attended London Indian Society and Pan-Islamic Society meetings.

November 6 : Met F. H. Brown, Sir Curzon Wyllie and Ameer Ali.

November 7 : Addressed Members of Parliament.

November 8 : Deputation called on Lord Elgin.

November 9 : Gandhiji and Ally met Sir Lepel Griffln and Lord George Hamilton.

November 10 : Gandhiji saw Bernard Holland.

November 11 : Met Mrs. W. C. Bannerjee.

November 13 : Called on Secretary, British Committee of Indian National Congress.

November 14 : In Commons, Churchill promised to make enquiries in regard to genuineness of petition by Dr. Godfrey and Pillay.

November 15 : Gandhiji met Mrs. Spencer Walton.

Before November 16: Met W.T. Stead and Miss Winterbottom.

November 16: Wrote to The Times and gave interview to South Africa regarding Godfrey-Pillay petition.

Before November 17: Met Theodore Morison, Sir Richard Solomon and Miss Smith.

November 20 : Dadabhai Naoroji felicitated by British and Indian admirers in London on election as President of Indian National Congress.

November 23	:	Deputation met John Morley, Secretary of State for India. Churchill stated in Commons that Vrededorp Stands Ordinance of 1906 was still under consideration.
November 23	:	Gandhiji and Ally met A.J. Balfour, A. Lyttelton, Sir Raymond West and Lord Reay.
November 26	:	Gandhiji opened discussion on British Indians in South Africa at East India Association meeting. Liberal M.P's. decided to ask Prime Minister, Sir Henry Campbell-Bannerman, to receive deputation regarding Asiatic Law Amendment Ordinance.
November 27	:	Gandhiji interviewed by The Daily News A deputation of M.P.'s met the Prime Minister who said "that he did not approve of the Ordinance and that he would speak to Lord Elgin..."
November 28	:	Met Winston Churchill. Questioned in Commons about the desirability of instituting limited Native franchise in new Constitution of Orange River Colony, Churchill expressed hope that Colonial parliament would show proper recognition of principle of "equal rights for all civilized men".
November 29	:	Gandhiji and Ally entertained friends and sympathizers at farewell breakfast in Hotel Cecil.
December 1	:	Left England for South Africa.
December 3	:	Churchill informed Commons that Secretary of State for Colonies was not able "without further consideration" to advise His Majesty that The Transvaal Ordinance should be brought into operation, and it would not "be further proceeded with at present".
December 6	:	Transvaal and Orange River Colony granted self government.
December 18	:	Transvaal Deputation arrived at Cape Town.
December 20	:	Left Cape Town for Johannesburg.
December 22	:	Reception to Deputation at Johannesburg.
December 23	:	Gandhiji spoke at meeting of British Indian Association; at Johannesburg, address was presented to him and Ally.

December 25 : Pretoria, Boksburg and Germiston Indians presented addresses to Gandhiji and Ally.

December 26 : Reception in Durban; Gandhiji appealed for unity and continuation of struggle. In India, Dadabhai Naoroji declared Swaraj as goal of Congress; Bande Mataram sung for first time at Congress session.

December 27 : Indian National Congress by resolution expressed "grave apprehension" that The policies of The Ordinance were "almost certain to be enforced" as soon as Transvaal became self-governing, unless Imperial Government continued to extend firm protection.

December 29 : Reception to Deputation by Indian community at Verulam.

1907

January 1 : Natal Indian Congress reception at Durban; Gandhiji pleaded for concerted action.

January 2 : Visited Phoenix. Gandhiji and Ally gave account of Deputation's work in England.

January 3 : Mahomedan Association meeting at Durban; Gandhiji appealed for unity and co-operation. Addressed meeting of Natal Indian Congress.

January 5 : Addresses presented to Gandhiji and Ally at meeting convened by Natal Indian Congress at Durban.

Before January 12: Gandhiji wrote to The Outlook reiterating that Indians wanted civil rights and not political power. Imperial Government sanctioned Vrededorp Stands Ordinance.

February 15 : Gandhiji appeared in permit case on behalf of Coovadia's minor son and secured acquittal.

February 18 : Churchill informed Commons that Natal Government had been refused leave to introduce legislation excluding Asiatics from trading licences, and that Colonial Office was in communication with that Government Regarding Act of 1897.

February 19 : Churchill announced in Parliament that

		compensation to Indians dispossessed under Vrededorp Stands Ordinance was subject of communication between Colonial Office and Transvaal Government.
March 2	:	British Indian Association protested to Registrar or Asiatics against taking of finger-impressions by police.
Before March 8	:	Gandhiji visited Volksrust.
March 10	:	Attended meeting of British Indian Association and Anti-Indian-Law Fund Committee.
March 11	:	Attended British Indian mass meeting.
March 19	:	Asiatic Registration Bill gazetted.
March 22	:	Asiatic Registration Bill passed in Transvaal parliament.
March 24	:	Gandhiji attended second meeting of British Indian Association and Anti-Indian-Law Fund Committee.
March 29	:	Transvaal Indian mass meeting protested against Asiatic Registration Act and offered voluntary registration.
April 4	:	Gandhiji called on Smuts at Pretoria and presented resolutions adopted at mass meeting of March 29.
April 8	:	Spoke at meeting of Natal Indian Congress in Durban.
April 9	:	Wrote to The Natal Advertiser correcting misstatement regarding unauthorized immigration into Colony.
April 21	:	Elected to committee for malaria relief at Springfield.
April 24	:	Meeting of Members of Parliament decided that deputations should wait on General Botha and Morley in regard to problems of Transvaal Indians.
April 29	:	Deputation led by Lord Ampthill waited on General Botha, who repudiated any intention of hurting British Indians' feelings in the Colony by The new measure.
April 30	:	Gandhiji in letter to *Indian Opinion* pledged that

		he would oppose Asiatic Registration Act and appealed to Indians to be steadfast in their stand. Deputation led by Sir Henry Cotton waited on Morley, who expressed willingness to address General Botha on modifications which it might be possible to introduce in regulations under Asiatic Registration Act.
May 4	:	Gandhiji spoke at meeting presenting address to Alexander, ex-Superintendent of Police, Durban.
May 6	:	Addressed Natal Indian Congress meeting bidding farewell to Omar Haji Amod Zaveri. At another meeting advised boycott of Permit Office
May 7	:	Interviewed by The Natal Mercury. Attended farewell dinner to O.H.A. Zaveri. Churchill informed Commons of General Botha's assurance that regulations under Asiatic Registration Act would be revised with a view to removing, as far as possible, undesirable conditions. Asiatic Registration Act received Royal assent.
May 10	:	Gandhiji returned to Johannesburg from Durban.
Before May 11	:	Met editor of *The Star.*
May 11	:	Addressed Committee of British Indian Association on existing situation.Wrote to *The Star* criticizing its suggestion that Indians opposing Registration Act be deported.
May 26	:	Addressed Chinese Association meeting on anti-Asiatic laws.
May 30	:	Wrote to *The Star* appealing to colonists not to enforce Registration Act and to accept voluntary registration by Indians.
June 1	:	Gandhiji attended meeting of British Indian Association which decided to send deputation to Prime Minister, General Botha, to urge acceptance of compromise proposal.
June 4	:	Botha declined to meet deputation.
June 6	:	Secretary of State for India, John Morley, indicated in Commons nature of proposed constitutional reforms in India.

June 8	: Transvaal Government Gazette announced Royal assent to Asiatic Registration Act.
June 14	: Second session of Transvaal Parliament commenced.
June 28	: Gandhiji, in interview to Rand Daily Mail, declared determination of Indians not to submit to Act.
June 29	: Spoke at Indian meeting in Volksrust to protest against Act.
June 30	: Addressed Indian meeting at Pretoria on implications of Act.
July 1	: Act enforced in Pretoria. First permit office opened. Indians notified to register within month. Campaign against registration started. Gandhiji addressed mass meeting; wrote to Rand Daily Mail that Indians in Pretoria would not submit to compulsory re-registration irrespective of consequences.
July 2	: Spoke at Volksrust meeting which resolved to adhere to gaol resolution.
July 3	: Immigration Restriction Bill published.
July 4	: Gandhiji wrote to The Star condemning Immigration Bill.
July 6	: Wrote to Rand Daily Mail that Indians would rather sacrifice everything than submit to Act.
July 7	: Spoke at meeting in Pretoria.
July 8	: Transvaal Registration Bill granted Return by Commons.
July 9	: British Indian Association submitted petition to Transvaal Legislative Assembly regarding Immigration Restriction Bill.
July 14	: Gandhiji addressed meeting of Hamidia Islamic Society at Johannesburg calling upon Indians not to submit to compulsory re-registration .
July 15	: Addressed meeting of Transvaal Football Association.
July 16	: Spoke at meeting of Indian merchants at Pretoria.
July 20	: Appealed for funds in aid of Transvaal struggle at meeting of Natal Indian Congress in Durban.

July 22 : British Indian Association submitted petition to Transvaal Legislative Council regarding Immigration Restriction Bill.

July 24 : Gandhiji arrived at Pretoria; called at Khamisa's shop where applications for registration were being received secretly at night.

July 25 : On question as to General Botha's assurance to Secretary of State for Colonies regarding administration of Asiatic Act, it was stated in Commons that no effort would be spared to make application and operation of Act as little irksome as possible and that finger-print system would be retained.

July 27 : British Indian Association wrote to Colonial Secretary refuting intimidation charge against Indians.

July 28 : Indian meeting held in Hamidia Islamic Society Hall, Johannesburg. Hartal observed in Transvaal.

July 30 : In India, editor of Hindustan sentenced to five years' rigorous imprisonment.

July 31 : Gandhiji met William Hosken in morning; addressed Pretoria mass meeting; took sole responsibility for advising Indians to oppose law and explained significance of passive resistance. Warned them of dangers of submission to Act. Gave interview to Rand Daily Mail.

Before August 5: Permit Office moved on to Pietersburg.

August 7 : In India, anniversary of Swadeshi movement observed; 20,000 Indians at meeting decided to continue boycott against Bengal's partition until it was withdrawn or modified.

August 8 : Gandhiji wrote to General Smuts suggesting amendments to Asiatic Act.

August 11 : Spoke at meeting of Hamidia Islamic Society.

August 14 : Appeared on behalf of Suleman Wadi charged with selling liquor to Natives.

August 15 : Wrote to General Smuts that result of compliance with Act would be worse than non-compliance for Indians.

August 17 : Released for publication correspondence with General Smuts.

August 19 : Wrote to The Star regarding proposal submitted to General Smuts.

August 21 : Spoke at meeting of Hamidia Islamic Society.

August 23 : British Indian Association addressed petition to Secretary of State for Colonies.

Before August 24 : Permit Office functioned at Potchefstroom and Klerksdorp.

Before August 31 : Permit Office visited Nylstroom and Rustenburg.

August 31 : Gandhiji and others gave send-off to H. O. Ally and family who left Transvaal as they did not wish to submit to Act.

September 4 : Natal Indian Congress cabled birthday felicitations to Dadabhai Naoroji. Gandhiji spoke on Indian struggle at meeting of Natal Indian Congress at Durban.

Before September 7: Attended birth anniversary celebrations of Lord Krishna organized by Sanatan Veda Dharma Sabha, Germiston.

September 11 : Wrote to Registrar of Asiatics regarding Indians detained at Komatipoort.

September 17 : Permit Office moved on to Boksburg.

Before September 21: Monster Petition addressed to Colonial Secretary circulated for signatures.

September 22 : Gandhiji addressed Hamidia Islamic Society meeting.

September 24 : Permit Office moved on to Germiston.

September 29 : Gandhiji spoke at meetings of Hamidia Islamic Society and Chinese Association.

October 6 : Addressing meeting of British Indian Association, said he would defend arrested pickets.

October 9 : Wrote to *Rand Daily Mail*.

October 13 : Attended meeting of Hamidia Islamic Society.

October 14 : Was met by Haloo, who regretted having applied for registration.

October 15 : Repudiated in court charge of intimidation

		against pickets and wrote to Commissioner of Police.
October 17	:	In India, anniversary of Bengal's partition observed as day of mourning.
October 18	:	Gandhiji wrote to *The Star* refuting intimidation charge.
October 20	:	Attended meetings of Hamidia Islamic Society and South Indians.
October 23	:	Addressed meetings of British Indian Association and Anti-Indian-Law Fund.
October 24	:	Wrote to *The Star* regarding Asiatic Registration Act.
October 27	:	Met Commissioner of Police, Johannesburg, regarding picketing. At meeting of Hamidia Islamic Society, reported on interview with Police Commissioner. Met Mahomed Shahboodeen who had been assaulted by Mahomedan priest.
October	:	In India, Bipin Chandra Pal sentenced to six months' imprisonment for refusing to give evidence in sedition case against Aurobindo Ghosh.
November 1	:	British Indian Association forwarded Monster Petition signed by 4,522 Indians to Colonial Secretary. Gandhiji wrote to *The Transvaal Leader* regarding registration of Indians.
November 9	:	At Caxton Hall, London, meeting of Mahomedans protested against treatment of Indians in Transvaal.
November 11	:	Gandhiji appeared in defence of Ram Sundar Pundit, first Indian arrested at Germiston. Spoke at meeting of Indians held after Pundit's release. Gave interview to *The Transvaal Leader.*
November 13	:	Addressed Hamidia Islamic Society meeting.
November 14	:	Appeared at Germiston in trial of Ram Sundar Pundit, who was sentenced to month's imprisonment. Hartal observed in Transvaal.
November 15	:	Gandhiji appeared in trial of pickets at Pretoria; wrote to Indian Opinion regarding Ram Sundar Pundit.
November 17	:	Met Ram Sundar Pundit in Johannesburg gaol; spoke at meeting of Hamidia Islamic Society.

November 18 :	In India, Lala Lajpat Rai released.
November 19 :	Gandhiji appeared in trial of Mahomed Shah and others at Germiston.
November 21 :	Sent *Ramayana* and *Gita* to Manilal Gandhi.
November 22 :	Wrote to G. K. Gokhale suggesting "Hindu-Muslim compact" to be made special feature of forthcoming session of Indian National Congress.
November 24 :	Spoke at meeting of Hamidia Islamic Society. Meeting of Konkanis held in Society hall.
November 27 :	Gandhiji spoke at meeting of Chinese Association.
November 30 :	Last date for registration; only 511 out of 13,000 Indians registered. During month struggle designated 'Satyagraha' for first time.
December 1 :	Gandhiji met Ram Sundar Pundit in gaol.
December 3 :	Received message from William Hosken that he should approach High Commissioner regarding Asiatic Law Amendment Act. Writing to High Commissioner, suggested appointment of judge to investigate charge of surreptitious entry by Indians.
December 6 :	Appeared in trial of Mahomed Essak.In India, terrorist attempt made on Lieutenant-Governor's train near Midnapur, Bengal.
Before December 7:	Gandhiji forwarded to High Commissioner petition of Punjabis, Pathans and Sikhs.
December 8 :	Addressed Hamidia Islamic Society meeting.
December 9 :	Appeared in trial of 37 Indians at Volksrust.
December 11 :	Defended Mahomed Essak, who was acquitted.
December 12 :	Wrote to Indian Opinion regarding prosecution of Indians.
December 13 :	Participated in reception to Ram Sundar Pundit who was released from gaol; later spoke at meeting.
December 15 :	Addressed meeting of Hamidia Islamic Society.
December 20	Telephoned to General Manager, C.S.A.R., about Indian employees at Standerton.
December 22 :	Spoke at meeting of Hamidia Islamic Society.

December 23 : In India, Mr. Allen, former District Magistrate, Dacca, shot at railway station between Dacca and Calcutta.

December 26 : General Smuts decided to prosecute Gandhiji and other pickets. Indian National Congress session commenced in Surat; split between Moderates and Extremists.

December 27 : Royal assent to Transvaal Immigration Act announced in Gazette. Gandhiji called on Acting Commissioner of Police, Transvaal and was informed of orders for arrest of himself and other pickets. Later, addressed mass meeting at Johannesburg. Gave interview to The Star.

December 28 : Conducted his own trial and appeared in defence of pickets; was ordered to leave Transvaal within 48 hours. Later, spoke at meeting in Government Square.

December 30 : Addressed meeting of Chinese Association at Johannesburg. Gave interview to Reuter. Addressed mass meeting at Pretoria.

December 31 : Was informed that his appearance in court was not required until further notice. European friends called on him and expressed sympathy. Gandhiji addressed mass meeting of Indians.

1908

January 1 : Transvaal Immigrants' Restriction Act1 (No. 15 of 1907) came into force. Mass meeting held at Surd Mosque, Fordsburg, to protest against TARA and Transvaal Asiatic Registration Act2 (Law 2 of 1907).

January 3 : Gandhiji appeared in Johannesburg Court to defend Nawab Khan and Sumandar Khan prosecuted under TARA.

January 4 : British Indian Association3 informed Receiver of Revenues that, if 'Indian traders not registered under TARA were refused licences, they would trade without them. Gandhiji pointed out in a letter to The Star that TARA rested on an unproved charge against Asiatics. Smuts in speech at Mayville said that Indians had been misled by their leaders and declared that no Parliament in the country could repeal TARA.

After January 4: Gandhiji attempted unsuccessfully to see General Smuts regarding his speech at Mayville.

January In interviews to *The Star* and *The Transvaal Leader* Gandhiji summed up Indian position against TARA

January 8 : Told Reuter that, if TARA was suspended, all Indians would be registered within a month

Before January 10 : Writing in *Indian Opinion,* reiterated Indians' determination to face imprisonment and deportation.Gandhiji adopted the term "satyagraha" as Gujarati equivalent for passive resistance.

January 10 : His last message to Transvaal Indians exhorting them to remain steadfast. Assured The Star that Indians would register voluntarily if element or compulsion in TARA was withdrawn. Addressed a meeting before his trial. Tried and sentenced to jail for two months. Declared, in final interview to *Rand Daily Mail,* that he had undertaken the struggle prayerfully and in all humility.

January 21 : Cartwright met Gandhiji in jail and they agreed upon voluntary registration by Indians in return for repeal of TARA. Addressed petition to Director of Prisons regarding Asiatic prisoners' dietscale.

January 27 : Public meetings held in Ahmednagar and elsewhere in India, protesting to Imperial Government against TARA.

January 28 : Blue book on Transvaal Asiatic legislation published in London. At meeting in New Reform Club, London, Sir W. Wedderburg declared that, since Imperial Government spent C3 million annually on defence of Transvaal, it had a right to demand that Transvaal Indians be treated in keeping with Imperial traditions. Sir M. M. Bhownaggree warned of an "Imperial danger" and M. A. Jinnah said all Indians were united in their protest against humiliating treatment of Transvaal Indians. Cartwright brought compromise letter drafted either by himself or General Smuts to Gandhiji in jail. After amending it, Gandhiji signed it along with Quinn and Naidoo at 12-30 p.m. At 2-30 p.m. Cartwright left for Pretoria to meet General Smuts. At 5 p.m. Cartwright rang up to say General Smuts had accepted the terms of compromise letter.

January 29 : Public meeting held at Bombay under chairmanship of His Highness the Aga Khan protested against TARA and appealed to Imperial Government to intervene and, failing that, to allow a retaliatory policy in India against South Africans.

January 30 : Acting Assistant Colonial Secretary wrote accepting compromise letter. Gandhiji escorted to Pretoria to meet General Smuts; settlement reached regarding voluntary registration and its validation. Learnt from Chamney that legalization of voluntary registration by Asiatics being proposed under TARA. Unsuccessfully sought another interview with Smuts. In interview to *Rand, Daily Mail* and *The Transvaal Leader* discussed the "compromise" and his treatment in prison. Addressed midnight meeting, a thousand strong, in precincts of Hamidia Mosque. Formally released from prison. Spoke at BIA meeting explaining settlement. In interview to Reuter suggested that Asiatics with domiciliary rights be assimilated in future South African nation; agreed with Smuts that indenture system in Natal should be stopped.

January 31 : All satyagrahis released. In Press interview Smuts said that Asiatics could trade without licences pending legalization of compromise. Said that demand for repeal of TARA was preposterous and Indians had not persisted in it.

February ? : In Cape general elections South African Party led by Merriman returned to power.

February 1	:	Gandhiji wrote to Smuts against Government's intention to legalize voluntary registration under TARA and proposed that this be done by amendment of TARA instead. In interview to Press, refuted charge of organized surreptitious entry of British Indians, on which TARA was based.
February 2	:	Declared at BIA meeting in Johannesburg that, if violence was to be used against those giving finger-prints, he should be first victim.
February 3	:	Met General Smuts who in Chamney's presence repeated promise to repeal TARA if Transvaal Asiatics registered voluntarily. G. K. Gokhale asked at meeting of Viceroy's Council if India Government were aware of "the depth and intensity of public feeling" at the "injustice and indignities" of Transvaal Indians. Replying for Government Findlay said that they sympathized with their Transvaal subjects and had reason to hope "current negotiations" would remove their "just grievances".
February 4	:	Lord Ampthill's all-attention motion in House of Lords. Lord Curzon also spoke.
February 5	:	The Times, London, blamed Colonial Office for "lack of imagination" in not having urged Imperial interests on Transvaal Government and brought about a settlement earlier. It called for an agreed Imperial attitude in self-governing Colonies in matters of race.
February 5-6[?]	:	In course of public speeches and Press interviews, Smuts promised freedom from arrest for violation of TARA and unlicensed trade. The law would not be repealed meanwhile. A measure to validate such registration would, however, be introduced in Parliament when it met next. Announced that aim of compromise was to reduce Colony's Asiatic population.
February 8	:	Explaining procedure for voluntary registrationin *Indian Opinion*, Gandhiji advised educated Indians not to exercise option in favour of affixing their signatures rather than finger-impressions

		on voluntary registration applications.
February 10	:	Voluntary registration began. Gandhiji assaulted by Mir Alam Khan and others; appealed from his sickbed at Doke's house that assailants be forgiven, and asked Asiatics to give their finger-prints voluntarily.
February 11	:	Dr. G. U. Pope died at Oxford.
February 15	:	"A Dialogue on the Compromise" published in Indian Opinion.1
February 22	:	Gandhiji wrote in Indian Opinion of February 22 and 29 explaining conditions under which he accepted compromise and clarifying Indian community's obligations; emphasized solidarity of Transvaal Hindus and Muslims. Wrote to Smuts, enclosing Draft Bill to amend TARA; suggested therein repeal of Peace Preservation Ordinance2 and TARA.
February 29	:	Number of voluntary registration applications at Johannesburg rose to 3,400.
March 5	:	Gandhiji left for Durban to dispel widespread misunderstanding of compromise among Pathans and others. Addressed public meeting under auspices of Natal Indian Congress at Durban.1 Another attempted assault on Gandhiji, evidently by Pathans.
March 6	:	Met Durban Pathans who insisted that he had betrayed community; reported that this conciliatory meeting was a failure. Left for Phoenix along with a "merry party" to "meet my family" after convalescence.
March 10	:	Sir Lepel Griffin died in London.
March 14	:	At dinner, said to be the first of its kind in South Africa, BIA gave gifts to whites who had helped in satyagraha campaign.
March 17	:	In Calcutta, Lord Minto declared that failure of crops in United Provinces had affected 50 million people. Famine conditions had developed in U.P. in September 1907.
March 18	:	Number of voluntary registrants in Johannesburg increased to 5,090.

March 21	:	T.J. Bennett, Proprietor-Editor of *The Times of India*, wrote to Lord Ampthill confirming representative character of Bombay meeting.
March 22	:	Men of all races including European merchants and officials exercised over question.
March 24	:	In Canada, Supreme Court nullified Government's deportation order on 146 Indians who had arrived by *S.S. Monteagle*; they were consequently released.
March 26	:	Lord Selborne speaking at Klerksdorp declared that "East is East: West is West" and that, because "white man's civilization is expensive", he could not compete with Indian trader. Suggested reservation of unoccupied portions of Empire for Asiatic settlement. British and Boer were equal partners in British Empire.
Before March 30	:	Dr. C. O'Grady Gubbins, Colonial secretary, announced Natal Government's intention to enact legislation to discontinue-immigration of indentured labour and to stop issue of licences to "Arab" traders after ten years.
March 30	:	Bill to amend Transvaal Gold Law published in *Government Gazette Extraordinary*.
April 6	:	H.S.L. Polak enrolled as attorney of Transvaal Supreme Court.
April 10	:	Transvaal Municipal Association passed resolutions saying that Natives and Coloured persons should be denied municipal franchise and right to own freehold land and made to live Locations and trade in Bazaars.
Before April 12	:	Meeting of Het Volk Congress urged that all Asiatics be moved into Bazaars. General Smuts hoped that Municipal (Consolid ation) Bill would solve problem of "Coloured people living among whites".
April 19	:	Natal Agricultural Union protested against proposed stoppage of Indian immigration; declared Indian labour necessary for Natal's industries.
April 21	:	Strike in Indian Telegraph Service.

April 22 : Sir Henry Campbell-Bannmerman died.

Before April 24: Lord Ampthill asked that Oriental immigration to colonies be discussed at an Imperial Conference.

Before April 25: BIA wrote to Smuts protesting against draft amendment to Transvaal Gold Law.

Before April 26: At congress of Progressive Party, Sir Percy Fitzpatrick said he had no faith in "coercive legislation" and "race differentiation". He called upon the white man "to justify himself" and to "outwork the Native".

Before April 27: Gandhiji returned to Johannesburg from Phoenix[?]

April 30 : Bomb incident at Muzaffarpur in India. Last day for satyagrahi traders who had been carrying on unlicensed trade to take out licences. These were issued up to December 31 to voluntary registrants and up to June 30 for traders who had not so registered.

May 2 : According to cablegram report, an Afghan lashkar about 20,000 strong crossed over into India; "unofficial war" began.

May 3 : A bomb "factory" discovered in offices of *Navasakti*. Aurobindo Ghosh, formerly of *Yugantar*, and 50 others arrested.

Before May 8 : Natal Bills published in Government Gazette.

Before May 9 : Inter-Colonial Conference, precursor of National Convention, met at Pretoria to discuss inter-state railway and customs matters, but only passed six resolutions, moved by General Smuts and prescribing procedure for attaining immediate union. Sessions lasted less than a week.

May 9 : Last date for voluntary registration by Asiatics; 8,700 applications received and 6,000 accepted.

May 12 : In telegram Chamney announced that all Asiatics entering Colony after May 9 should register under TARA. Gandhiji wrote to Smuts asking that this misunderstanding of compromise be clarified.

May 13 : Transvaal Municipal (Consolidation) Bill gazetted. Bill envisaged empowering Municipalities to deal with traders and denying hawkers right of appeal to law Courts regarding administrative decisions on licences.

May 14 : Gandhiji wrote to Cartwright saying his services as mediator might again be required.

Wrote to Lane saying that period of three months in compromise letter was never intended to apply to Asiatics returning to Colony or otherwise possessing right of re-entry; urged Smuts to accept voluntary registration of new arrivals and repeal Act.

Before May 15 : Deputy Labour Minister Mackenzie King, who returned to Canada on April 26 after consultations about Indian immigration with Imperial Government, announced in Dominion Parliament that there was no "necessity of enacting any legislation either in India or Canada" to solve problem.

May 15 : Lane wrote to Gandhiji saying Colonial Secretary could not depart from earlier decision.

Before May 16 : Gandhiji met Cartwright; decision to interview Smuts taken. *Natal Mercury, Times of Natal, The Star,* and the *Leader* deprecated Natal Bills.

May 16 : In interview to *The Star* Gandhiji welcomed Natal Bill to stop indentured immigration; condemned other two Bills. Following Smuts' emphatic refusal to extend voluntary registration facilities to Asiatics with domiciliary rights but entering after three-month compromise period, accused Smuts, in weekly news letter, of "foul play" but still hoped latter would repeal TẠRA.

May 17 : Essop Mia, Chairman, BIA, assaulted by a Pathan.

May 18 : Speaking at Y.M.C.A., Johannesburg, Gandhiji claimed that Coloured races were an integral part of the Empire and declared his faith in mission of British to raise subject races to equality with themselves.

May 20 : Writing in *Indian Opinion,* appealed to Pathan community to express disapproval of acts of violence by isolated Pathans. Writing in his newsletter on assault on Essop Mia, declared that, if one lacked the requisite courage for satyagraha, one might use arms in self-defence.

: In House of Lords, Lord Ampthill complained about "the inactivity of the Imperial Government [in the matter of Natal Bills] which have encouraged the Transvaal to imitate Natal ... thus attempting to restore a tyranny worse than under the Kruger regime".

May 21 : Gandhiji wrote to Smuts asking for public announcement of repeal of TARA.

May 22 : *The Transvaal Leader* reported that the Government was preparing a Bill legalizing voluntary registration and excepting such registrants from TARA. Lane replied stating General Smuts' inability to comply with above request. Registrar of Asiatics wrote to BIA pointing out that introduction of minors into Colony by Asiatics punishable under TARA.

May 23 : Chairman, BIA, replied that, since Indians had registered voluntarily in compliance with compromise, they considered TARA a dead letter and its enforcement, breach of compromise. Gandhiji shown draft of Transvaal Asiatics' Registration Validation Bill by Cartwright.

May 26 : BIA wrote to Colonial Secretary informing him of British Indians' decision to withdraw voluntary registration applications as the latter had gone back on his "compromise assurance." Gandhiji, Bawazeer, Naidoo and Quinn wrote to Chamney asking for return of their voluntary registration applications.

May 27 : Gandhiji explained situation at meeting of BIA Committee, which endorsed resumption of satyagraha.

May 29 : Telegraphed Chamney asking for return of application forms.

Before May 30 : Circular sent to BIA Town Committees instructing Indians to withdraw voluntary registration applications and informing them of resumption of satyagraha. Gandhiji repeated offer to defend satyagrahis free of charge.

May 30 : In letter to *Indian Opinion*, announced that satyagraha would be resumed. Telegram from Chamney, in reply to Gandhiji's of 29th, to say that latter's draft Bill for amending TIRA had been misplaced and asking for another copy. This was sent. Gandhiji wrote to Lane asking for permission to publish correspondence with Smuts between February 1 and 22.

Before June 1 : Draft "Ordinance" to restrict Asiatic immigration into Southern Rhodesia gazetted.

June 1 : Gandhiji informed over 'phone that Smuts had called Cabinet meeting to consider Indian issue; his reply would be sent on June 2.

Before June 2 : Met Chamney at Winchester House.

June 2 : Eminent white sympathizers met and reaffirmed support to Indian cause. Question in Imperial Parliament whether His Majesty's Government intended to intervene in view of threatened breach of compromise and revival of Indian agitation.

June 4 : Gandhiji invited to meet Smuts on June 6 to discuss new draft of validation Bill. In another letter Lane refused permission to publish correspondence with Smuts.

June 6 : Gandhiji met Smuts; discussed mode of validating voluntary registration, his draft amendment of TIRA and right of future Asiatic immigrants to voluntary registration. Smuts assented TARA was wholly bad and served no useful purpose. Emergence of disagreement about categories of Asiatics whose right of domicile was to be recognized under proposed legislation. Gandhiji asked for assurance of repeal of TARA, else he would move Supreme Court for return of applications. Wrote to Cartwright

		asking him to persuade Progressives not to obstruct repeal of TARA.
June 12	:	Sent Smuts a telegram announcing decision to move Supreme Court for return of applications on advice of eminent counsel. Smuts asked him to an interview the next day.
Before June 13	:	Gandhiji wrote in Indian Opinion against Rhodesia Bill for compulsory registration of Indians.
June 13	:	Met Smuts who promised decision within a week; move to approach Supreme Court put off by a week at meeting of BIA Committee. In a letter, the same day, covering discussions, Gandhiji pleaded that any amendment of TARA should protect rights of (1) pre-war refugees, (2) holders of £3 registration certificates and PPO permits; and (3) rights off would-be educated immigrants should not be jeopardized by compromise.
June 16	:	Repeal of TARA at instance of Imperial Government rumoured in Johannesburg Press.
June 19	:	Telegram asking Gandhiji to interview with Smuts next day.
June 20	:	Gandhiji met Smuts who asked to see him again on June 22 "to consider one or two minor points that remain".
June 22	:	Leader editorials saying TARA would be repealed. At meeting with Smuts, Gandhiji was shown draft amendment to TARA—an "excellent Bill" for voluntary registrants, past and future—which, however, excluded the three categories of persons and declared them prohibited immigrants. Gandhiji's proposal for referring educated Indians' issue to Supreme Court was turned clown. Smuts also refused right of judicial review of voluntary registrants' claims rejected by Registrar of Asiatics. On Gandhiji's refusal to agree to these conditions, Smuts announced decision to retain TARA and amend it to validate voluntary registration. In interviews and letters

		to Press, Gandhiji announced breach of compromise and his intention to move Supreme Court for return of applications for voluntary registration. BIA Committee endorsed proposed test case in Supreme Court. In Press statement explaining breakdown of negotiations, Smuts argued that compromise letter of January 29 did not mention repeal of TARA; he was, however, willing to repeal the Act provided Indians agreed to exclusion of the three categories of persons in amending bill. Since Gandhiji did not agree, voluntary registration would be validated by separate measure.
Before June 23	:	Aswat wrote to Chamney asking for return of application.
June 23	:	His petition for return of application filed in Supreme Court. Gandhiji and Essop Mia filed affidavits stating that Smuts had promised to repeal TARA.
June 24	:	Mass meeting in Johannesburg announced community's resolve to withdraw applications and reaffirmed resolution of September 11, 1906 not to submit to TARA.
	:	Sorabji Shapurji entered Transvaal to test right of educated Indians. In India, Tilak arrested on charge of sedition for his articles in Kesari, entitled "The Country's Misfortune" of May 12 and "These Remedies Are Not Lasting" of June 12.
June 25	:	Chamney filed counter-affidavit.
June 26	:	Smuts filed affidavit saying he had never promised to repeal Act. Chamney filed another affidavit to same effect.
June 29	:	Gandhiji and Aswat filed replying affidavits reaffirming earlier declaration about Smuts' promise.
Before July 2	:	In weekly news-letter, Gandhiji declared that satyagraha was no longer struggle for self-interest but for rights of others—the three categories of "prohibited immigrants". Burning of registration

	certificates—if "voluntary" applications were not returned—mentioned for first time as means of continuing satyagraha.
July 2	: Aswat's petition rejected by Supreme Court. Gandhiji wrote to Transvaal Press, releasing his correspondence with Smuts for publication.
July 4	: In letter to The Transvaal Leader, Rev. Doke argued that Indians' campaign against TARA was fully justified.
Before July 5	: Reported offer by Smuts, sent through white mediators, to concede right of entry to holders of £3 registration certificates and to provide for appeal to Courts against Chamney's decisions rejecting claims of voluntary registrants. In return, Indians were to agree to exclusion of educated Asiatics. Indians turned down offer.
July 5	: Meeting in Hamidia Mosque considered situation arising from Supreme Court's ruling and decided to burn registration certificates following Sunday.
July 6	: Chairman, BIA, wrote to Colonial Secretary urging legal rights of three categories of would-be Indian immigrants and explaining: (l) that Association could not barter away rights of those it did not represent and (2) that Indians could not forgo services of educated fellow-countrymen in future. Also stated community's resolve to burn certificates on July 12.
July 7	: Registrar of Asiatics instructed municipalities to demand thumbimpressions under TARA from Asiatic traders applying for licences. Gandhiji interpreted this to mean that Government wanted to bring voluntary registrants also under TARA.
July 8	: Gandhiji appeared in Court to defend Sorabji Shapurji.
July 9	: Chairman, BIA, wrote to Colonial Secretary (1) complaining that demand of thumb-impressions from Indian applicants for trading licences constituted breach of compromise and (2) saying that education test under TARA could be made very severe. Meanwhile Indians would put off mass meeting of July 12 for burning certificates.

July 10	:	Johannesburg Court ordered Shapurji to leave Colony within seven days.
July 11	:	Gandhiji sought elucidation of Smuts' offer from Cartwright.
July 14	:	Cartwright confirmed Smuts' offer over telephone. In letter to Cartwright, Gandhiji estimated number of holders of £3 Dutch registration certificates at 1000. Repeated willingness to refer educated Indians' issue to Supreme Court and to accept a severe education test but not one along racial lines, and announced his determination to carry on satyagraha. Denied Smuts' charge that he had accepted £2 from each Muslim voluntary registrant.
July 15	:	Report in *The Star* that settlement of Asiatic question was probable.
July 16	:	Chairman, BIA, wrote to The Star announcing decision of eminent Indians to take to unlicensed hawking as "protest and penance". Hawking without licences began Lord Milner, speaking on "Closer Union" at Royal Colonial Institute, London, suggested promotion of interdependence within Empire to increase understanding and reduce anti-racial prejudice in colonies.
July 20	:	Ebrahim Ismail and Suliman Bagas tried and sent to jail as unlicensed "hawkers".
	:	Gandhiji appeared in Court to defend Sorabji Shapurji; Shapurji sentenced to a month's hard labour under PPO, not TIRA. Indians wishing to enter Court assaulted by police. Addressing meeting outside (Court, Gandhiji asked traders to court arrest by trading without licences as protest against proposed deprivation of educated Indians' rights.Affidavits filed by Polak and others complaining of Police misbehaviour. Speaking at mass meeting, Gandhiji exhorted Indian traders not to affix thumb-impressions on their licence applications under TARA. Wrote that "burning of registers is postponed for time being but their collection need not be".

July 21 : Bawazeer, Chairman, Hamidia Islamic Society, arrested for hawking without licence.

July 22 : Gandhiji appeared in Court to defend Bawazeer and others. Ratanji Laloo's appeal dismissed in Supreme Court. In judgment, Justice Solomon said Asiatics might be admitted under TIRA education test. Four hundred out of 800 Indian hawkers reported to have taken out licences under TARA. Imperial Government announced they had instructed Lord Selborne not to assent to Rhodesian Asiatic legislation pending consideration by Secretary of State for Colonies. In India, Tilak sentenced to six years' transportation and fine of Rs. 1,000.

July 23 : Indian traders all over South Africa observed hartal as a mark of respect for Bawazeer. In Cape Town and Durban, meetings passed resolutions protesting against sentences on Transvaal satyagrahis. In Turkey, Sultan Abdul Hamid accepted restoration of parliamentary government.

July 26 : Gandhiji spoke at mass meeting, held to felicitate Imam Bawazeer and other satyagrahis on their release. More "voluntary" certificates and hawkers' licences handed over to BIA for burning.

July 27 : Harilal Gandhi arrested for hawking without licence. Gandhiji shown a copy, by Hosken, of Asiatic Voluntary Registration Bill—"a fraudulent bill" which equated voluntary registrants with those who had submitted to TARA and did not provide for the three categories of persons.

July 28 : Gandhiji appeared in Court to defend Harilal Gandhi and others. Harold Cox asked in House of Commons whether H. M. Government understood, in Shapurji's case, test of desirability to be "one of race or of education".

July 31 : In Imperial Parliament, Colonel Seely said self-governing colonies might exclude whomsoever they liked but must give those admitted full rights. Deputation, introduced by Sir Charles Bruce and including Sir Muncherjee, Harold Cox, G. K. Gokhale and Ritch, placed before Lord Crewe the grievances of Indians in Transvaal, Natal and Rhodesia.

Before August 1: Gandhiji wrote, in *Indian Opinion* that, "after great deliberation, Tilak's views on British rule" should be rejected. It would be "harmful, even useless" to use violence to "uproot British rule". Chinese Association decided to adopt Indian satyagrahis' methods. Chairman Quinn and other Chinese began hawking in Johannesburg.

Before August 8: In letter to *Indian Opinion* Gandhiji explained that "it was part of Harilal's education to go to gaol for the sake of the country". Speaking at Vereeniging, Lord Selborne declared that Imperial Government were bound to protect rights only of pre-war Transvaal Indians.

Before August 10: At meeting of Progressives at Witbank, Stent, Editor *Pretoria News,* referred to TARA as "unfair legislation" which Government could not enforce. Said Smuts would again be beaten in controversy by Gandhiji.

August 10 : Gandhiji defended Harilal Gandhi in Court. Addressing meeting after trial, declared that selling of satyagrahi traders' goods instead of sending them to jail was "legalized robbery" and that Smuts was responsible for "suicide of the Chinaman and death of young Mr. Naidoo". Learnt that Progressive Party would oppose repeal of TARA.

August 11 : *Transvaal Leader* editorial described "the harrying of the Asiatics" as "part of a deep statesmanlike plan"; "we have sought earnestly for the statesmanship; and we are a little tired." Bill to validate voluntary registration of Asiatics published in *Government Gazette*.

August 12 : In interview to *The Transvaal Leader* Gandhiji explained that proposed bill to validate voluntary

		registration violated terms of compromise. It did not repeal TARA, nor did it specifically exempt voluntary registrants from scope of Act. It required minors and fresh entrants to register under TARA. Daily Telegraph correspondent wrote, as quoted by Ritch, that "there was no doubt that the Government intended to repeal Registration Act.... In fact, the Registrar of Asiatics read him Some of the more important provisions of the Act... [as] approved of by Mr. Smuts".
August 12-13(?)	:	Dawad Mahomed, Parsee Rustomjee, Anglia, Randeria and other Durban leaders entrained for Johannesburg to test their domiciliary rights in Transvaal.
August 13	:	Petition to Transvaal Legislative Assembly reiterating that proposed Bill violated compromise.
August 14	:	Gandhiji wrote to Smuts appealing to him once more to respect compromise, accept his amendment of TIRA or to meet Indian leaders with a view to a settlement; failing that, certificates would be burnt following Sunday. Wrote to George Farrar, Leader of Opposition, detailing his objections to validation Bill.
August 16	:	Addressed mass meeting in Johannesburg which resolved to oppose TARA; registration certificates burnt.
August 18	:	Went to Pretoria at General Smuts' invitation to meeting attended by Botha and Smuts and members of Progressive Party. Government offered to alter validation Bill saying specifically that TARA would not apply to voluntary registrants and minors.
August 19	:	Gandhiji visited Sorabji Shapurji in prison.
August 20	:	Meeting held to consider modified version, proposed by Government, of validation Bill. Gandhiji wrote to Lane incorporating following demands of meeting: (1) repeal of TARA; (2) entry of educated Indians under-severe education test;

		(3) release of prisoners and reinstatement of Shapurji. The "letter of ultimatum" so called.
August 21	:	In Transvaal Legislative Assembly, Asiatics' Voluntary Registration Validation Bill withdrawn on Select Committee's recommendation. A new bill, Asiatics' Registration Amendment Bill "which contains [practically] everything we wanted", was read. Second reading of ARAB in Legislative Council and third reading in Legislative Assembly. Gandhiji said in interviews to The Transvaal Leader and The Star that new Bill fell short of the terms proposed by Asiatics, and that passive resistance, "a state of Suffering", would be resumed.
August 22	:	Third reading of ARAB in Legislative Council.
August 23	:	Mass meeting in Johannesburg in which more registration certificates were burnt. Mir Alam, Gandhiji's assailant, and other Pathans admitted their error and resolved "to fight to the end". In his speech, Gandhiji deprecated Sir Percy Fitzpatrick's hint that there might be racial conflict in Colony.
August 24	:	Chairman, BIA, wrote to Colonial Secretary asking Government once more, "on the eve of a fierce struggle", to give the relief sought by Asiatics.
August 27	:	Dawad Mahomed and other Natkal Indian leaders arrested in Anjuman Islam Hall, Pretoria.
August 28	:	Natal Indian leaders deported from Pretoria; Gandhiji along with others saw them off at railway station.
August 30	:	Addressed meeting of British Indians at Hamidia Mosque.
September 2	:	Asiatics Registration Amendment Act published in Government Gazette.
September 5	:	Gandhiji commended in *Indian Opinion* Col. Seely's statement in Parliament of July 31, that "those who have a right to be in the Colonies should be accorded equal rights with the whites and must be accepted as full-fledged citizens".

Thambi Naidoo, Nadirsha Cama and others deposed in affidavits that Transvaal authorities had definitely promised repeal of Asiatic Registration Act before Indian leaders decided to accept voluntary registration.

September 7 : At BIA meeting, Gandhiji asked for financial provision, in view of his suspension of legal practice, for defraying Association's office rent, Polak's expenses and Indian Opinion deficit. Left for Pretoria for collection of funds.

September 9 : Cabled SABIC reporting 175 Indians imprisoned to date and hoping Lord Ampthill and others would endeavour to obtain relief. In interview to The Star, stated that Indians were real outlanders, strangers in their own homes, and demanded equality before law. BIA petitioned Secretary of State for Colonies for repeal of Act 2 of 1907 and for establishing status of educated Indians. H. S. L. Polak and A. M. Andrews made affidavits affirming that authorities had promised repeal of Registration Act. BIA took over Gandhiji's financial responsibilities, his own needs being looked after by Kallenbach.

September 10 : Gandhiji spoke at Johannesburg mass meeting. Cachalia assumed BIA chairmanship.

Before September 12 : Gandhiji defended Randaree in Johannesburg Court.

September 13 : Presided over meeting to compose differences between Konkanis and Kanamias.

September 14 : Drew up petition to Secretary of State for Colonies on behalf of Transvaal Pathans and Punjabis, demanding repeal of Asiatic Act. Indian ex-soldiers petitioned Secretary of State for Colonies for repeal of Asiatic Act.

September 15 : Gandhiji, in Pretoria Court, defended Vally Bagas and others charged with trading without 'grocers' licences.

September 16 : Interviewed by Reuter, reiterated Indian demand for legal equality. Director of Prisons informed BIA that Medical Officer considered prisoners' diet perfectly healthy and could be changed only on medical grounds.

September 17 : Gandhiji wrote to *The Star* clarifying position regarding education test and charging Smuts with breach of promise to repeal Registration Act. Harilal Gandhi deported from Transvaal. BIA informed Director of Prisons that failure to effect diet reform would be interpreted as intention to starve Indian community into submission to Act.

September 18 : Sanction of Royal assent to new Asiatic Act reported; also decision of SABIC authorising Lord Ampthill to represent grievances of Transvaal Indians to Imperial Government. BIA protested against inclusion of animal fat in Indian prisoners' diet and demanded restoration of ghee.

September 19 : Gandhiji, along with Indian and Chinese leaders, met Hosken and communicated terms for settlement. Writing in *Indian Opinion,* exhorted Natal Indians to oppose Natal Government's Bill to restrict municipal authority for granting certain kinds of licences.BIA drew attention of Director of Prisons to ill-treatment of Syed Ali in Boksburg Gaol and demanded investigation. Lord Ampthill wrote to *The Times* stating that Validation Act undid compromise and subjected Indians again to indignities of Registration Act. BIA, Calcutta, cabled Secretarv of State for Colonies pleading for Imperial Government's protection to Transvaal Indians.

September 21 : BIA demanded from Colonial Secretary relief in Syed Ali's case; asked for prisoners' diet reform. Harilal Gandhi and others released from Volksrust Gaol, cases against them being withdrawn. New Asiatic Act came into force.

September 22 : Natal Supreme Court ruled immigrants' children subject to penalties under Immigrants' Restriction Act, 1907. Harilal Gandhi arrived in Johannesburg. Regulations under new Act published.

September 23 : Smuts rejected Indian terms for settlement. Director of Prisons denied ill-treatment of Syed Ali.

September 24 : BIA forwarded Syed Ali's affidavit to Director of Prisons. Colonial Secretary expressed inability to interfere with diet regulations in Transvaal gaols.

September 25 : BIA wrote to Director of Prisons demanding uniform diet scale for Indian prisoners and substitution of ghee for fat.

September 26 : Gandhiji arrived in Durban, advised Natal leaders to dissuade Indians entering Natal from giving thumbimpressions; commended Natal's part in Transvaal campaign.

September 28 : BIA demanded from Colonial Secretary information about diet scale for Indian prisoners. Polak repudiated Pretoria News charge that British Indians had not fulfilled their part of compromise.

September 30 : Gandhiji, in interview to *The Natal Mercury* at Durban, stressed that Indians did not want unrestricted immigration or trade, but objected to legislative discrimination. BIA cabled SABIC regarding Indian arrests and sentences under old Act and demanded its repeal.

October 2 : Gandhiji prepared draft memorandum for Johannesburg clergymen about ill-treatment of Indians. NIC1 wired Colonial Secretary about Immigration Officer's refusal to let Indian passengers disembark at Durban; cabled SABIC about Komatipoort arrest of Indians.

October 3 : Gandhiji urged Natal Indians to agitate for ending indenture system.

October 5 : Cabled SABIC about herding of 80 Indians in small, filthy room at Komatipoort.

October 6 : Left Durban for Transvaal.

October 7 : Arrested at Volksrust, along with fifteen other Indians, for entering Transvaal without registration certificates.

October 8 : Produced before Magistrate, refused to avail of bail; remanded for a week.

October 9 : BIA wrote to Colonial Secretary, Pretoria, demanding public inquiry into alleged ill-treatment of Indians returning from Delagoa Bay.

October 11 : Drew up, in Volksrust Gaol, petition to Resident Magistrate about deficient diet-scale.

October 12 : Batch of Indians including minors deported from Barberton to Portuguese territory. National Convention met at Durban.

October 13 : Gandhiji, in detention, sent message exhorting Indians to face gaol-going for sake of motherland.

October 14 : Defended Dawjee Amod and others before De Villiers, Assistant Resident Magistrate. Sent message to Indian youth before trial. Sentenced to two months' imprisonment with hard labour. On way to prison, sent message to Indians to keep "absolutely firm to the end". NIC meeting in Durban resolved to ask Government to withdraw educational order.

October 15 : Gandhiji reported at road-making work on Market Square. Reuter's Volksrust correspondent wrote, "Mr. Gandhi expressed himself as being the happiest man in the Transvaal".

October 16 : BIA, NIC in cable to Ritch resented Gandhiji being made to work on road-making. London meeting, presided over by Sir Muncherjee Bhownaggree and addressed, among others, by Lajpat Rai and Bipin Chandra Pal, protested against Gandhiji's imprisonment. Kasturba thanked sympathizers who congratulated her on Gandhiji's incarceration.

Before October 17 : Sir Pherozeshah Mehta cabled Lord Ampthill: "Public feeling in India was keenly hurt over maltreatment of Indians in South Africa" and invoked the British Government's intervention to save Indians suffering from such outrage and tyranny.

October 17 : Ritch forwarded to Colonial Office copies of BIA, NIC cables.

October 18 : Mass meeting held at Hamidia Mosque, Fordsburg.

October 21	:	In reply to question in House of Lords by Ampthill, Earl of Crewe stated he had wired Transvaal for facts about Gandhiji's arrest, and added that Gandhiji had been participating in "passive resistance campaign, and paid the penalty".
October 22	:	Viceroy of India conveyed to India Office Indian resentment of treatment of passive resisters in Transvaal, recommended considerateness and urged concession of Indian demand for entry of six educated Indians annually.
October 25	:	Gandhiji removed from Volksrust Gaol to Johannesburg in convict's garb to testify in Daya Lala's case; refused offer of cab, and marched on foot from Park Station to Fort, carrying prison knapsack.
October 27	:	Escorted from Johannesburg Gaol to High Court.
October 31	:	Secretary of State for Colonies cabled Transvaal Governor recommending acceptance of temporary admission of limited number of educated men into Transvaal.
November 3	:	Transvaal Government cabled Colonial Office that Gandhiji "was employed for two and a half days in agricultural show ground at Volksrust digging holes for trees and thereafter in municipal plantation and gaol gardens."
November 4	:	Gandhiji removed to Volksrust Gaol in convict's garb. Mass meeting held at Hamidia Mosque to consider Transvaal situation, addressed also by Europeans, passed resolution demanding right of free immigration for six educated Indians.
November 5	:	Transvaal Government replied to Colonial Office cable that Indian claim for entry of professional men was rejected after very careful consideration, that present law made provision for this, but Indians defied Act for agitational purposes.
November 9	:	Gandhiji, writing to A.H. West, declared satyagraha a religious fight and refused to obtain release, by paying fine, even to visit Kasturba lying gravely ill; addressed her farewell note.

November 14	:	Was made to work, with other prisoners, on municipal water-works, cleaning cemetery and tending soldiers' graves.
November 19	:	Fifty prisoners, from Barberton and Volksrust, released on appeal, on Supreme Court ruling that domiciled Indians returning to Colony must be allowed to register themselves.
November 22	:	Calcutta public meeting condemned failure of Transvaal Government to repeal Act 2 of 1907; Surendranath Banerjea expressed indignation that Gandhiji of "whom any nation would be proud, had been ignominiously handled through the streets of Johannesburg."
November 24	:	Polak pleaded in Court for release of Gandhiji and others on ground of gross miscarriage of justice. Johannesburg Chamber of Commerce passed resolution trusting Government would not be deflected by pressure of Indian community from enforcing law.
November 25	:	Sanderson Commission on immigration in Crown Colonies set up.
November 27	:	Attorney-General refused to order release of Gandhiji and others in Volksrust Gaol.
November 28	:	Muslims telegraphed protest against General Botha's statement that many Mahomedans had declined to join passive resistance movement. BIA wrote to Attorney-General, Pretoria, complaining of harsh treatment meted to Indian prisoners in Johannesburg Gaol.
November 29	:	Gandhiji's message from Volksrust Gaol, asking Indians to remain steadfast in their pledge, read out at Johannesburg mass meeting. BIA meeting asked Government to grant Indian demand, failing which struggle would continue.
November 30	:	Gokhale, in address to New Reform Club, London, referred to Indians' sufferings in South Africa as one of the causes for loss of faith in British rule. Col. Seely stated in Commons that, according to his information, Gandhiji had never performed hard labour on public streets.

December 1	:	BIA cabled SABIC. "Col. Seely is absolutely misinformed as to Gandhi's treatment. Forwarding affidavits." Volksrust Magistrate discharged Indian accused of refusing identification, accepting Polak's defence that section 9 of Registration Act and regulations relating thereto came into operation only then and could not apply to registered Indians arrested earlier. Annie Besant sent Gandhiji and colleagues, "a message of hope, of consolation, of friendship".
December 10	:	Lord Selborne conveyed to General Botha Imperial Government's view that Transvaal Government should extend considerate treatment to Indians with pre-war rights, admit limited number of educated Indians and repeal Act 2 of 1907 and Act 36 of 1908, and at a later date enact strict legislation on immigration.
December 12	:	Gandhiji released from Volksrust Gaol Interviewed at Volksrust, on way to Johannesburg, about illtreatment in prison. Spoke at Johannesburg reception.
December 13	:	HIS1 held meeting to honour Gandhiji and Imam Abdool Kadir Bawazeer.
December 14	:	Gandhiji addressed meeting of Tamil community at Johannesburg; later, entertained at dinner by Tamil Benefit Society.
December 15	:	General Botha communicated to Lord Selborne Government's inability to revise policy. Transvaal Colonial Secretary, in reply to Transvaal Governor, denied promise of repeal of Act 2 of 1907.
December 18	:	Gandhiji defended Naidoo and other Indian pickets at Johannesburg. Spoke at meeting of representative Europeans of Transvaal.
December 21	:	Ritch forwarded to Colonial Office copies of affidavits regarding Gandhiji's hard labour in prison.
December 23	:	Gandhiji presented Nelson, Volksrust Prison Office, Tolstoy's *Kingdom of God Is within You.*

December 24 : Appeal in Transvaal Asiatic Test Case dismissed in Pretoria Court for lack of jurisdiction.

December 26 : Gandhiji reached Durban; given rousing reception; left for Phoenix to meet Kasturba who was ill.

December 28 : In letter to Maganlal Gandhi, stressed need to strive for spiritual growth, which would ensure advance of religion and country.

December 30 : Harilal Gandhi and Randeria arrested at Johannesburg as prohibited immigrants and remanded till January 5. Pretoria News pleaded for conceding Indian demands, admitting the "persistency and unfailing good temper with which Mr. Gandhi and his compatriots are pursuing their campaign for what theyconsider to be their rights". Eight Madrasis, entitled to settle in Transvaal but refusedregistration, deported for entering Transvaal.Thambi Naidoo and others sentenced to fine of £50 or jail withhard labour for three months. Polak, who defended, filed appeal. Natal Government reissued earlier notice banning highereducation for Indian children above 14 years. Question raised in Commons.

Before December 31 : Five more men arrested and dealt with underAct 36 of 1908. Amod Mia and his brother fined £25, fortrading without licences, in Rustenburg.Indian National Congress, in resolution on South Africa,considered harsh, humiliating and cruel treatment of British Indians as injurious to British Empire.

1909

January 1 : Gandhiji entertained at dinner by Dada Osmàn, NIC Joint Secretary; addressed meeting.

Before January 2 : Dawad Mahomed, Parsee Rustomjee and M.C. Anglia detained under Registration Act for refusing to give thumb-impressions.

January 2 : Gandhiji, in Indian Opinion, exhorted countrymen, in New Year message, to adopt swadeshi. While narrating in Indian Opinion his experiences during second jail term, asserted that gaol-going was "the most effective means of fighting political disabilities". Pickets arrested in Pretoria under section 3 of Law 6 of 1894, concerning unlawful assemblies.

January 4 : Pretoria pickets informed that they were being tried under section 7 of new Act and were liable to deportation.

January 5 : Gandhiji, in interview to *The Natal Mercury,* stated that Indians were fighting with the "cleanest weapons possible". Harilal Gandhi and others remanded at Volksrust. Three Indians charged under section 7, at Roodepoort, for failing to produce registration certificates.

January 6 : Moulvi Ahmed Mukhtiar of Hamidia Mosque refused renewal of permit on ground that he had preached against Asiatic Registration Act; served with quit notice, left Transvaal for Cape. Dawad Mahomed and 31 others charged for failure to produce registration certificates.

January 7 : Gandhiji accused by *The Star,* of "quoting the breaches already made and legalized in the Asiatic law as an argument for repealing it altogether". Boksburg Indian dealers refused trading licences except for Stands in Location.

Before January 9 : Several Indians, including some Colonial-born, who were deported to Natal from Transvaal were dealt with under Regulations of Act 36 and nominally convicted for entry into Natal.

January 9 : Gandhiji attended meeting of Indian Chamber of Commerce at Durban made suggestions for Rules and Regulations of Chamber. Ritch protested to Colonial Office against Natal Government Notice banning admission of Indian students above 14 to higher-grade schools.

January 10 : Dr. Nanji operated on Kasturba, seriously ill for 3 months, in Durban. Gandhiji attended on her.

January 12 : Three Indians, charged with contravention of section 7 of Act 36 of 1908, ordered to register within 8 days.

January 18 : Gandhiji, on way to Johannesburg, arrested at Volkrust for failing to produce registration certificate. Deported and escorted to border, returned immediately and was rearrested. Released on his own recognizance, returned to Johannesburg. Supreme Court ruled deportation of registered citizens illegal.

January 20 : Gandhiji wrote to the Press stating that Indians had entered third and final phase of struggle.

: Johannesburg Town Council urged Government to deal firmly with Asiatic problem and enforce Registration Act.

January 21 : In interview to *The Natal Mercury,* Gandhiji observed it was difficult to say categorically if Indian merchants would be prepared to undergo sacrifice implied in placing all their assets at creditors' disposal. Johannesburg correspondent of Indian Opinion reported that 3 merchants were ready to follow Cachalia's example. Rand Daily Mail, commenting on meeting of Cachalia's creditors, observed that "the so-called passive resistance movement has degenerated into coercion", that "the Transvaal Government will not be bullied into making concessions by such methods", and added, "We do not think that many of the Asiatics will fall within Mr. Gandhi's little plan, and ruin themselves completely to further the cause of passive resistance when it assumes such a new and startling form." Called for Government check on picketing. Telegram in The Natal Mercury reported Johannesburg Chamber of Commerce's resentment against attempt of Indian merchants to force hands of Government. Extremist opinion supported move to confiscate inerchants' goods and to stop picketing of firms.

January 22 : Gandhiji attended meeting of Cachalia's European creditors and submitted accounts. Criticized Rand Daily Mail, for calling passive resistance an act of coercion. Naidoo's appeal against conviction under Asiatic Registration

Amendment Act dismissed by Supreme Court.

: The Soft Goods Section of Johannesburg Chamber of Commerce adopted resolution supporting Government in enforcement of Asiatic Registration Law. Bulawayo Town Council refused Indians new trading licences.

January 23 : *The Star* welcomed Supreme Court judgment in Naidoo appeal and doubted if more a few "deluded faddists will consent to sacrifice their businesses and damage their credit at the dictation of Messrs Gandhi and Cachalia". E.I. Aswat, other Indian merchants followed Cachalia's example.

January 25 : Gandhiji, in interview to Rand Daily Mail, stated he would not be satisfied until Asiatic traders got their rights in South Africa. Rand Daily Mail observed that "if the tactics of the passive resisters should spread to the Coloured and Native population of South Africa, anarchy would reign".

January 26 : Gandhiji addressed meeting of Tamilians. Wrote to Dr. Krause repudiating allegation regarding Cachalia's move.Creditors notified Cachalia of their intention to sequestrate his estate. Several Indian, including 14-year-old residents, served orders of deportation to Delagoa Bay.

January 27 : Gandhiji forwarded to Lord Cruzon statement of Indian position, hoping latter's intervention would result in happy termination of struggle. Cachalia and 31 others arrested under section 9 and produced before Magistrate. Knolwad Conference of Indians resolved not to take out licences or renew registration certificates.

January 28 : Indian merchants at Johannesburg decided to do without licences and to court imprisonment.

January 29 : Gandhiji informed of improvement in Kasturba's condition. Left for Durban. 18 Asiatics, arrested at Komatipoort as prohibited immigrants, stood trial at Barberton.

January 30 : Cachalia, Naidoo and others sentenced to 3

	months or £50 fine; Shelat to 2 months. Transvaal Government wrote to Secretary of State for Colonies denying that Gandhiji "performed hard labour in public streets", Indian prisoners were ill-treated or their religious susceptibilites hurt.
February 1 :	E.I. Aswat unanimously elected Acting Chairman of BIA during Cachalia's incarceration.
February 2 :	Lord Curzon informed Gandhiji of his discussion with Botha and Smuts and of their "anxiety to treat British Indians . . . in spirit of liberality as well as justice".
February 3 :	Parsee Rustomjee and others arrested for defying deportation orders.
February 4 :	Gandhiji removed Kasturba, convalescing after operation, to Phoenix.
February 5 :	Appeal of Randeria dismissed by Transvaal Supreme Court. Deportation of Harilal Gandhi, Dawad Mahomed and other leading Indians ordered.
February 9 :	Draft Act of Union published in Government Gazette. Dawad Mahomed and Cachalia agreed in Court to sequestration of their estates.
February 10 :	Harilal Gandhi and several others sentenced at Volksrust to terms ranging between 3 to 6 months. Imperial Government withheld assent to Asiatic Act of Rhodesia.
February 11 :	Parsee Rustomjee and others, arrested on reentering Transvaal after deportation, sentenced to 6 months.
Before February 15 :	National Convention put up Draft South Africa Act.
February 16 :	V. A. Chettiar sentenced to 3 months. General Botha in letter to Governor stated Government's stand in regard to demand for repeal of Act 2 of 1907, denied any promise was made for its repeal, and observed that 97 per cent. of Asiatic residents had actually registered and that passive resistance was breaking down.
February 17 :	More passive resisters awarded sentences from 3 to 6 months; others remanded; arrests reported from Pretoria, Heidelberg, Germiston, etc.

February 18	:	N. A. Cama sentenced to 3 months; several other prominent Indians deported or sentenced.
February 19	:	Six Indians arrested at Standerton for failure to identify themselves or produce registration certificates.
February 20	:	Leung Quinn arrested for failing to produce registration certificate and refusing identification.
February 22	:	Gandhiji left Phoenix for Johannesburg.
February 25	:	Arrested at Volksrust along with Polak and Vyas. Sentenced to 3 months or £50 fine for failure to produce registration certificate. Issued message to Tamils exhorting them to keep up struggle.
February 28	:	British Indian meeting at Hamidia Islamic Society, Vrededorp, congratulated Gandhiji, Cachalia, Parsee Rustomjee and others who had sought imprisonment; resolved to continue struggle.
March 2	:	Gandhiji's transfer from Volksrust to Pretoria Gaol ordered. Left by evening train.
March 3	:	Reached Pretoria Central Gaol. *Indian Opinion* correspondent from Volksrust telegraphed: "Mr. Gandhi has been taken to Pretoria for departmental reasons; I believe it is in order to completely isolate him. The rumour of an impending compromise is strongly discounted by the Executive of the BIA." Polak inaugurated meeting of imprisoned passive resisters' wives and relatives. E.I. Aswat and Leung Quinn sentenced to 3 months.
March 4	:	Gandhiji given work of polishing prison floor and doors. Secretary of Tamil Benefit Society and Chief Picket, K. K. Samy, sentenced to 3 months. Randeria released after serving 2 months' sentence.
March 5	:	Randeria re-arrested. Meeting of Cape Coloured people discussed Draft Act of Union, demanded representation in Union Parliament and political rights. E. S. Coovadia appointed Acting Chairman, BIA, in view of imprisonment of Cachalia and Aswat.

March 6	:	Whites started agitation to set up Locations at Barberton, Boksburg, Krugersdorp, etc.
March 7	:	British Indian meeting in Hamidia Islamic Society addressed among others by Coovadia, Kallenbach and Polak.
March 8	:	In statement on Gandhiji's imprisonment, Col. Seely observed : "Mr. Gandhi had been imprisoned because of his refusal to comply with the Transvaal Law, . . . that the Imperial Government was unable to prevent the Transvaal Government from enforcing the law relating to registration certificates."
March 10	:	Gandhiji taken in handcuffs to Court to appear as witness. Passive resisters congratulated Kasturba Gandhi on Gandhiji's third sentence of imprisonment for sake of selfrespect and honour of Asiatic communities. Chinese passive resisters congratulated Gandhiji and Leung Quinn on being sentenced, resolved to continue struggle for justice and self-respcet.
-	:	Deportation of passive resistance prisoners via Delagoa Ray to India commenced. BIA wrote to Transvaal Governor, protesting against deportation arrangement between Transvaal and Portuguese Governments.
March 11	:	Indian women held meeting in Johannesburg. Letter from Kasturba reported saying : "Had she wings, she would fly to the meeting." Letter to Transvaal Press signed by Kasturba and four others released. Doke, in letter to Johannesburg Press, referring to Gandhiji's being handcuffed, observed that "the great majority of our Colonists feel ashamed. . . that a man of the character and position of Mr. Gandhi should be needlessly insulted in this way."
March 12	:	*Indian Opinion* special correspondent in telegram stated : "Mr. Gandhi looks thin and unhealthy." Meeting of Nyasaland Indians condemned treatment of Indians in Transvaal and Imperial Government's weakness. Kimberley meeting of

non-whites expressed concern at inadequate provision in proposed Constitution to protect their interests.

March 13 : *Indian Opinion*, commenting on official statement that removal of Gandhiji from Volksrust to Pretoria Central Gaol was "simply a matter of administrative convenience", observed that "it has no other purpose than to completely isolate Mr. Gandhi, so that no breath of encouragement should reach his people from him." BIA requested High Commission to receive deputation concerning deportation policy.

March 14 : Natal Indian Congress meeting at Durban, declared support to Transvaal passive resistance, condemned deportation arrangements between Transvaal and Delagoa Bay authorities.

: BIA meeting at Johannesburg resolved to continue passive resistance "with unabated energy" till Government conceded demands.

March 15 : Draft of South Africa Act laid before South African Parliament; question raised in Commons. High Commissioner refused to see BIA deputation on deportation.

March 16 : Meeting of Indians in Delagoa Bay, addressed by Abdulla Hajee Adam and Polak on Transvaal situation and deportation arrangement, decided to send deputation to Portuguese Governor-General.

March 17 : Meeting of Kimberley Indians protested against unjust treatment of Indians in Transvaal. Transvaal Governor cabled Colonial Office that no Indians producing proof of registration were deported but only those Asiatics without domicile in South Africs, who were ordered to be deported by Magistrate. BIA, Port Elizabeth, cabled urging Viceroy's intervention on behalf of Transvaal Indians.

March 19 : Transvaal Supreme Court ruled Indians were not disabled from securing trading licences in mining areas.

March 22	:	Natal Municipal Association criticized Imperial Government for not sanctioning discriminatory provisions in Municipal Laws Consolidation Bill.
March 24	:	Meeting of BIA, East London condemned Transvaal Government's deportation policy.
March 25	:	Meeting of Indian women at Hamidia Society Hall, addressed by Mrs. Thambi Naidoo, Mrs. Polak and Miss Schlesin, formed Indian Women's Association. BIA, East London, protested against ill-treatment of Indians to High Commissioner, Colonial Office and Viceroy of India. Lord Crewe, replying to Lord Ampthill in Lords, defended, Transvaal deportation policy on ground that Indians not being Mozambique Indians ex hypothesi could be deported under Portuguese Law.
March 26	:	Moulvi Ahmed Khan of Surti Mosque examined in Court of Mr. Jordan. Registration at Pretoria reported at standstill. Schreiner, addressing meeting at Cape Town, considered colour bar a blot on Draft Union Constitution.Government of India, in reply to cable of March 17 from BIA, Port Elizabeth, assured continued "endeavours to obtain sympathetic treatment for British Indians in the Transvaal" but regretted inability to interfere in cases of penalty for noncompliance with law.
March 27	:	More arrests, convictions and deportations at Johannesburg, Vereeniging and Volksrust reported. 65 prisoners reported removed from Volksrust to Heidelberg to work on quarries.
March 28	:	BIA meeting protested against Lord Crewe's misleading statement in Parliament regarding Transvaal deportations via Delagoa Bay. Dildar Khan elected Acting Chairman, BIA. HIS resolved to protest against Transvaal Government's treatment of passive resisters.
March 29	:	Thambi Naidoo and others released after 3 months' imprisonment, felicitated by BIA. Over 150 Indians reported to be still in gaol. 13 passive

resisters including Shelat, set free at Barberton detained pending deportation arrangement with Portuguese. Transvaal Governor informed Secretary of State for Colonies that in deporting Indians, Portuguese authorities acted under their general immigration regulations. BIA, writing to British High Commissioner, countered Transvaal Government's claim that deportation policy did not apply to domiciled Indians, by citing deportation of a registered Indian's Transvaal Governor communicated to BIA reply from Secretary of State of Colonies to their petition of Septemebr 9, 1908, that Transvaal Government was unwilling to repeal Registration Act and Imperial Government not in a position to press repeal; and that views of two sides on yearly admission of six educated Indians differed only as regards method and machinery.

March 30 : Blue-book on Transvaal Indian question, published in London, revealed that Botha had disagreed with Lord Crewe's suggestion for repeal of Registration Act.

April 1 : Settlement of 20 shillings in £ liabilities effected at third meeting of Cachalia's creditors.

April 3 : Indian women at Germiston set up Association. Indian Opinion correspondent reported that passive resisters domiciled in Natal and ordered to be deported, would only be put across border at Volksrust. Indian meeting at Barberton protested against deportation policy, paid tribute to Gandhiji's "courage in facing hardships and insults, such as handcuffing, being taken from one gaol to another in a third-class compartment".

Before April 5 : BIA and HIS committee meetings congratulated Gandhiji and others on "having gone to gaol for the sake of religion and the welfare of their brethren" and resolved to continue struggle.

April 6 : BIA wrote to High Commissioner deploring latter's refusal to cable to Colonial Office representation regarding Indians' deportation.Four Transvaal Indians deported, 10 awaited deportation at Barberton.

April 7 : Polak addressed Johannesburg meeting at Hamidia Society Hall on condition of passive resisters in Diepkloof and Heidelberg gaols; BIA wrote to Acting Director of Prisons complaining of prisoners' ill-treatment. Natal Prime Minister in Parliament denied any agreement with Colonies for continuance of immigration of indentured Asiatic labour.

April 11 : Indian mass meeting at Johannesburg repudiated Botha's statement to Lord Crewe that many Asiatics were content with prevailing state of affairs; urged Imperial Government's intervention to terminate struggle.

April 12 : Question of Gandhiji being marched in handcuffs raised in Commons; Under Secretary of State for Colonies insisted that no special disability or indignity was imposed on Gandhiji as passive resister. 29 Chinese passive resisters, charged with refusal to give thumbimpressions and signatures, acquitted.

April 14 : Dr. Aburrahman inaugurated at Cape Town seventh annual Conference of African Political Organization. 16 Indians, old Johannesburg residents, deported to India via Delagoa Bay.

April 15 : Ritch made representations about Transvaal deportation policy to Colonial Office.

April 17 : *Indian Opinion* correspondent reported that Gandhiji "in the Pretoria Central Gaol, is slowly starving himself as a protest against the treatment of Indians, under the Gaol Regulations, as Kaffirs" and refusing personal allowance of ghee unless same was extended to all Transvaal Indian prisoners.

April 22 : Lord Crewe made lengthy statement in Lords on indentured labour and Indian immigration to Crown Colonies.

April 24 : Chinese passive resisters' organization commended refusal of Chinese to give finger-impressions.

April 26 : Polak, writing to Rand Daily Mail, refuted its observation that agitation was confined to a "handful of irreconcilables" or "bitter-enders"; denied a single India had "accepted" Registration law.

April 27 : New Regulations under Section 9 of Act 5 1894, published in *Government Gazette*, banned admission of Native, Indian or Coloured children to European schools.

April 29 : Cachalia and 18 other Indians released after serving 3 months sentence.

April 30 : Supreme Court ruled, in Mohamed Makda's Case, that no appeal lay against Asiatic Registrar for refusing registration.

May 1 : *Indian Opinion* explained that 97 per cent. Of Transvaal Asiatics who had already registered, according to Botha's statement, had actually registered "under voluntary registration through the efforts of the leaders of the passive resistance movement . . ."

May 4 : Indian satyagrahis in Transvaal gaols started receiving ghee as part of diet.

May 8 : P. K. Naidoo sentenced to 3 months for trading without licence at Vereeniging.

May 10 : Johannesburg Court ordered deportation of 92 Asiatics refused registration by Registrar.

May 15 : NIC protested to Colonial Secretary, against Regulations under Section 9 of Act 5 of 1894, being discriminatory against Indian students.

May 19 : Transvaal Supreme Court held that Government had no power under Notice of 1908 to cancel reservation of Location.

May 24 : Gandhiji released from Pretoria Central Gaol at 7.30 a.m.; said at meeting in Mahomedan Mosque Hall that he felt no pleasure at being free. In interview to Pretoria News, deploring deportation of 16-yearold boy to India, asserted that such methods would not break spirit of Indians. Given rousing reception on arrival at Park Station. Addressing meeting on Mosque

		grounds, exhorted Indians to resist unjust law. Welcoming Gandhiji's release on Empire Day, Pretoria News observed that Transvaal Government should "find better use for a man like Gandhi than persistent imprisonment with hard labour", that "the man is suffering for conscience' sake . . . his motives are of the highest and his methods beyond impeachment".
May 26	:	Gandhiji wrote to Johannesburg Press on jail experiences.
May 29	:	Explained in *Indian Opinion* meaning and implications of satyagraha; commenced series of articles on jail experiences. Transvaal British Indian Conciliation Committee set up by nonpassive resisters.
May 31	:	Indians in Madras Presidency presented memorial to British Parliament urging repeal of Act 2 of 1907 and sanction of right of entry to six educated Indians.
June 2	:	Gandhiji spoke at reception at West End Hall, and later at tea party to Aswat and Leung Quinn on their release.
June 3	:	Pretoria Town Council withdrew ban on use of Municipal wash-houses by Coloured persons.
June 6	:	Spoke at meeting of Transvaal British Indian Conciliation Committee, which decided to present memorial to Colonial Secretary.
June 7	:	Addressed Germiston Literary and Debating Society on "Ethics of Passive Resistance".
June 8	:	Colonial Secretary placed before House return showing Asiatic entry into Transvaal during 1909, in response to demand of G. C. Munnik, M.L.A. Polak left on propaganda tour of Cape Colony.
After June 8	:	Gandhiji demanded, in letter to The Transvaal Leader, that Munnik withdraw his charge of illegal Asiatic entry.
June 13	:	BIA Committee meeting decided personnel of deputations to England and India.
June 14	:	Colonial Secretary turned down NIC request for withdrawal of ban on Indian education imposed

by Government Notice No. 201 of 1909.

June 15 : Imam Abdul Kadir Bawazeer released. Thambi Naidoo, G.P. Vyas, N. A. Cama and U. M. Shelat arrested in Johannesburg. More Tamils arrested in Pretoria.

June 16 : Gandhiji defended Thambi Naidoo and others. Addressed Johannesburg Indian mass meeting convened to appoint deputations to England and India; meeting authorized A. M. Cachalia, Hajee Habib, V. A. Chettiar and Gandhiji to proceed to England, and N. A. Cama, N. G. Naidoo, E. S. Coovadia and H. S. L. Polak to India. A. M. Cachalia, V. A. Chettiar, E. S. Coovadia arrested. Cachalia and Chettiar sentenced to 3 months or fine of £50. BIA Chairman telegraphed Colonial Secretary requesting suspension of sentences of delegates.

June 17 : Gopal Naidoo and other Tamils, delegates-elect to India, arrested. Habibia Moslem Society, Cape Town, adopted resolution protesting against ill-treatment of British Indian Mahomedans in Transvaal.

June 18 : Colonial Secretary, rejecting BIA representation for suspension of sentences of delegates-elect, denied knowledge of their impending deputation abroad. Gandhiji in letter to *The Star* repudiated Colonial Secretary's claim. Madras Provincial Conference at Behrampore adopted resolution condemning unfair treatment of British Indians in South Africa.

June 19 : Gandhiji in Indian Opinion justified sending of deputations abroad; suggested meetings all over South Africa to express support for purposes of explaining movement and shortening struggle. Deputation of Transvaal British Indian Conciliation Committee waited on Smuts.

Before June 21 : In appeal to all Transvaal Indians, Gandhiji stressed gaol-going as the only "unfailing remedy". Justified, in letter to Habib Motan, appointment of Muslim to Viceroy's Council;

		stressed need for blood-brother relationship between Hindus and Muslims.
June 21	:	Gandhiji and Hajee Habib left Johannesburg for Cape Town en route to England. Sammy Nagappen, passive resister, sentenced to 10 days with hard labour.
June 23	:	In interview to Cape Times and Cape Argus; Gandhiji apprehended ruin of Asiatics under Union unless Imperial Government secured safeguards. Embarked for England.
	:	Smuts turned down petition of Transvaal British Indian Conciliation Committee. Coovadia, Sorabjee sentenced to 3 months.
June 25	:	Transvaal British Indian Conciliation Committee, in letter to Smuts, regretted his departure from assurances given to deputation. Polak left for Natal en route to India.
June 26	:	*Indian Opinion* reported appointment of Kallenbach as Honorary Secretary in BIA Committee meeting. BIA, Port Elizabeth, represented to Government of India necessity for "repeal of measures which are an insult to the whole of India, a source of continued strife and bitterness within the Empire, and a menace to Indian residents elsewhere in South Africa".
June 30	:	Nagappen discharged from Johannesburg Gaol in "dying condition".
July 2	:	Sir Curzon Wyllie assassinated by Madan Lal Dhingra in London. Dr. Lalkaka also killed.
July 3	:	London meeting of Indian students, presided over by Surendranath Banerjea, condemned Wyllie's murder. *Indian Opinion* reported circulation, for obtaining mass signatures, of three petitions addressed by Transvaal Indians to Queen, Dadabhai Naoroji and Bengal Chambers of Commerce, concerning repeal of Asiatic Act and removal of colour bar and racial taint from legislation.
July 4	:	Meeting of Indian women in Pretoria Location expressed indignation at arrest of some 70 Pretoria Indians.

July 6	:	Nagappen died.
July 7	:	Nagappen given public funeral by Indian community.
July 8	:	Official statement regarding Nagappen's death absolved Gaol authorities of responsibility.
Before July 9	:	Met members of Natal Cabinet and Coloured people's deputation on board the ship.
July 9	:	Bengal Provincial Congress Committee proposed Gandhiji's name as one of three nominees for presidentship of forthcoming session of Indian National Congress.
July 10	:	Gandhiji, along with Hajee Habib, arrived at Southampton; interviewed by Reuter. Reached London at 10.30 a.m.; interviewed by South Africa Associated Press Agency.
	:	Met Ritch and Abdul Caadir; called on Sir Muncherjee Bhownaggree. Wrote to Lord Ampthill for interview. Six Indians deported from Transvaal. BIA demanded, in letter to Director of Prisons, restoration of ghee in diet of Indian prisoners. Natal Indians addressed petition to Secretary of State for Colonies regarding grievances relating to indenture, franchise, trade etc.; demanded amendment of Draft Union Act.
July 11	:	Habibia Moslem Society mass meeting expressed sympathy with Transvaal and Natal deputations. British Indian League, Cape Town adopted resolution urging Imperial Government to give sympathetic consideration to Transvaal deputation. Mass meeting of Indians at Hamidia Mosque, Johannesburg, adopted resolutions urging Imperial Government to give sympathetic consideration to deputation's submission; demanded thorough and open investigation into Nagappen's death.
July 12	:	Gandhiji received BIA cable regarding Nagappen's death and release of Dawad Mahomed due to illness. William Hosken and 15 other prominent European ministers of religion and professional men petitioned Attorney-General, Johannesburg, for public

		inquiry into deaths of Nagappen and Gibbon, a white convict.
Before July 14	:	Gandhiji saw Ameer Ali.
July 14	:	Met H.E.A. Cotton, editor of India, Sir Richard Solomon and Lord Ampthill. Transvaal Indian women's petition to Queen forwarded.
July 16	:	Sir William Lee-Warner called on Gandhiji. 14 Indians deported to India from Transvaal.
July 18	:	Mass meeting at Pretoria urged Imperial Government to give sympathetic consideration to deputation's submissions.
July 19	:	Public inquiry into circumstances of Nagappen's death opened under Major Dixon.
July 20	:	Gandhiji wrote to Lord Crewe seeking private interview.
July 21	:	Met Ameer Ali, Sir William Lee-Warner and Theodore Morison.
July 22	:	Repudiated in letter to South Africa its allegation that Lord Ampthill and SABIC were associated with extremist movement in India. Deputation led by Dr. Abdurrahman and Schreiner, on behalf of Coloured people and Natives, waited on Lord Crewe.
July 23	:	Gandhiji wrote to Gokhale requesting help in Polak's work in India.
July 26	:	Gandhiji and Hajee Habib had private interview with Lord Morley. Referred in letter to Lord Morley to prohibition of Indians from land-holding, riding on tramcars, as grievances apart from Act 2 of 1907 and restriction on immigration of educated Indians.
July 27	:	House of Lords debated and passed second reading of Union Bill.
July 28	:	Col. Seely stated in Commons that definite representations had been made to General Botha regarding Transvaal Indians and that latter was "really anxious to find a solution of the question".
July 29	:	Gandhiji in letter to Lord Ampthill denied any connection between Transvaal passive resistance movement and "party of sedition" in India;

		suggested amendment of Immigration Law to give Immigration Officer power to admit only six Indians to Colony. Sent Lord Ampthill proofs of "Statement of Transvaal Indian Case". Attended suffragette meeting at St. James' Hall. Met Mrs. Pankhurst. Deputation led by Schreiner on behalf of Coloured people and Natives waited on Liberal-Labour Party members in Commons, urged it to move amendments to Union Bill.
July 31	:	Natal delegation arrived in London, received by Gandhiji. Polak reached Bombay.
August 2	:	Pretoria women set up Indian Women's Association.
August 3	:	In letter to *The Englishman,* Gandhiji corrected misstatements about Registration Act, indenture system, etc., stated that British Indians had been agitating for 15 years for abolition of indentured labour.
August 4	:	Repudiated categorically, in course of letter to Lord Ampthill, that Transvaal passive resistance movement was "formented" or financed from India or had anything to do with "party of violence" there. Major Dixon issued report of inquiry on Nagappen's death.
	:	William Hosken, Chairman of European Committee, initiated correspondence with Director of Prisons, supporting diet reform.
August 6	:	Gandhiji sent Lord Ampthill copies of "Statement" in-corporating changes and additions suggested by him.
August 9	:	Discussed with Lord Ampthill Smuts' suggestions. Forwarded to him amendment to Immigrants' Restriction Act authorizing Governor to limit number of immigrants of any nationality. Sent Lord Ampthill proofs of Doke's biolgraphy. Natal Indian delegation submitted petition to Lord Crewe. Harilal Gandhi and others released at Heidelberg. Sorabjee Shapurji released from Diepkloof Prison.
August 10	:	Gandhiji and Hajee Habib called on Lord Crewe. Gandhiji cabled BIA, Polak, regarding his

amendment to Immigration Act. Deputation on behalf of Coloured people and Natives led by Schreiner attended Labour Party meeting in Commons, which assured support for amending Union Bill. Lord Ampthill had talks with Smuts and Gandhiji, later forwarded to Smuts amendment to Immigration Act and urged him to agree to repeal of Act and admission of six Indians a year.

August 11 : Gandhiji sought Lord Crewe's intervention to stop impending deportation of 100 British Indians. Wrote to Lord Ampthill that proposed amendment of Immigration Act did not constitute "a sacrifice of any important principles". In letter to Lord Crewe, Lord Ampthill appealed to help settlement on basis of Gandhiji's formula conveyed to Smuts. Parsee Rustomjee sentenced to further term of 6 months. Indian mass meeting at Johannesburg welcomed Sorabjee Shapurjee, Harilal Gandhi and others; supported deputations; demanded Imperial Government's intervention and expressed dissatisfaction over Commission's findings about Nagappen's death.

August 12 : Natal Indian delegation informed by Lord Crewe that existing laws could not be repealed and conditions would improve after Union came into being.

August 13 : Natal Indian delegation addressed letter to Viceroy of India Forwarding statement of grievances.

August 16 : Gandhiji forwarded to Lord Crewe Mahomed Khan's complaint of ill-treatment in prison. In letter to Lord Ampthill, Obseved that inquiry substantially proved allegations about Nagappen's death.

August 17 : Madanlal Dhingra executed.

August 18 : NIC meeting at Durban supported deputation to England and criticized treatment of Transvaal Indians. Tolstoy's secretary, N. N. Gooseff,

		arrested by Russian Government on charge of distributing revolutionary literature.
August 19	:	Gandhiji purchased books for Phoenix Library.
August 20	:	In weekly dispatch to *Indian Opinion*, emphasized that Natal Indians would be free only through satyagraha. Lord Kitchener relinquished office of Commander-in-Chief of Indian Army.
August 21	:	Gandhiji met Schreiner. Witwatersrand Church Council adopted resolution urging some form of representation for Natives.
August 22	:	Gandhiji visited Whiteway countryside.
August 25	:	Suggested to Polak pice fund in aid of passive resistance struggle.
August 29	:	Smuts, in interview to Reuter, stated that "vast majority of Transvaal Indians are sick to death of the agitation carried on by some of their extreme representatives . . ."
August 30	:	Gandhiji wrote to Swami Shankeranand deprecating his criticism of Islam.
	:	Smuts wrote to Lord Ampthill on latter's proposal to Lord Crewe for repeal of Act 2 of 1907 and issue of permanent residence certificates to limited number of educated Indian immigrants. Lord Ampthill invited Lord Crewe to make statement in Parliament on Transvaal problem; later, called on him and discussed question of "right" of entry.
August 31	:	Lord Ampthill wrote to Gandhiji hoping he would not feel bound to continue passive resistance and suggested that Gandhiji clarify to Lord Crewe position in regard to "right".
September 1	:	Gandhiji informed Lord Ampthill that Smuts' proposal only accentuated racial insult, and that he could not recede from position as to question of "right".
September 2	:	Cabled Polak regarding Smuts' proposal, urged Bombay public meeting be held independently of Sheriff. Sought clarification from Lord Crewe of Smuts' interview to Reuter indicating settlement. In letter to Lord Ampthill, welcomed

		crusade implied in fresh arrests of Indians and Chinese in Transvaal. Lord Morley informed Natal delegation that their problem was concern of Colonial Office.
September 6	:	In communication to Colonial Office, stressed that he had "avoided all public activity, in order not to prejudice negotiations". In letter to Ameer Ali, declared his life devoted to demonstrating that Hindu-Muslim co-operation was indispensable condition to India's salvation.
September 7	:	Wrote to Khushalchand Gandhi that all Phoenix activities were religious.
September 9	:	BIA requested Director of Prisons, Johannesburg, to extend facilities to Muslim prisoners during Ramzan.
September 10	:	In letter to Colonial Office, Gandhiji repudiated Smuts' statement to Reuter that majority of Indians had submitted to Registration Act; asserted that strength of Indian opposition still remained unabated. Deprecated suffragette's resort to violence and declared that Indians should "never forsake the sword of satyagraha". BIA protested, in The Star, against Superintendent Vernon's statement in Court that Asiatics should be hunted out of country. Natal delegation's letter in The Times stressed three-fold disabilities of Natal Indians and appealed to Imperial Government to stop supply of indentured labour from India failing redress of grievances.
September 11	:	Reduction of grants for higher education of Indians by Natal Legislative Assembly reported by Times of Natal.
September 13	:	Gandhiji attended Pateli celebrations in London; proposed felicitations to prominent Parsi passive resisters.
September 14	:	Public meeting in Bombay appealed to Imperial Government to prevent continued injustice to Indians in South Africa, demanded stoppage of indentured labour for Natal.
September 15	:	Mass meeting at Johannesburg greeted Cachalia, Chettiar and Thambi Naidoo on release; Doke,

Howard and other Europeans spoke. 80 Chinese passive resisters arrested.

September 16 : Gandhiji and Hajee Habib had interview with Lord Crewe, expressed readiness to give undertaking that, if theoretical right of entry conceded, there would be no further agitation. 67 Chinese charged at Johannesburg for failure to produce registration certificates.

: BIA request for facilities to Muslim prisoners duing Ramzan turned down by Director of Prisons.

: Public meeting at Surat addressed by Polak.

September 17 : In letter to Manilal Gandhi, Gandhiji observed that "body should not be dearer than the soul", and he "would have preferred Kasturba's passing away without the [beef] soup; but would not have allowed it to be given to her without her consent".

Before September 18 : Natal delegation met Ali Imam of All-India Muslim League.

September 18 : Gandhiji represented to Lord Morley that denial of Ramzan facilities to Muslim prisoners would be an attack on their religion. Wrote to Lord Ampthill requesting him to enlist Sir George Farrar's active sympathy to avoid unfavourable reply from Smuts; in latter case, felt public activity by deputation necessary.

September 19 : Polak addressed public meeting at Ahmedabad.

September 22 : Meeting of Chinese passive resisters in Johannesburg pledged continued support to passive resistance movement, and sympathized with efforts of deputations abroad. E. S. Coovadia, Omarji Sale released from Diepkloof Prison.

September 23 : Gandhiji enquired of Colonial Office if any reply had been received from Smuts to cable Lord Crewe was to have sent regarding Gandhiji's amendment. Proposed to Polak institution of prizes for best essay on passive resistance from India. Public meeting at Kathore addressed by Polak. Bombay public meeting, addressed by Sir

		Pherozeshah Mehta, G. K. Gokhale and others, appealed to Imperial Government to stop ill-treatment of Indians.
September 24	:	Gandhiji met Rev. F. B. Meyer at lunch.
September 27	:	Polak and Gokhale spoke at public meeting in Poona.
September 28	:	Gandhiji addressed letter to The Advocate of India defending Polak.
September 29	:	Smuts denied, in minute, deportation of any Asiatic domiciled in Orange River Colony from Transvaal to India; asked that Gandhiji might furnish evidence of any such case. Polak addressed ladies' meeting in Poona presided over by Mrs. Ramabai Ranade.
September 30	:	Transvaal Government repudiated, in minute, complaints about ill-treatment of Indian prisoners and responsibility for Nagappen's death.
October 1	:	Gandhiji wrote to Tolstoy regarding passive resistance movement in Transvaal and Tolstoy's "Letter to a Hindoo". Spoke at dinner in honour of Ali Imam.
October 4	:	Colonial Office informed Gandhiji that initiative rested with Colonial Government whether to undertake fresh legislation on lines proposed by Smuts.
October 5	:	Gandhiji wrote to Lord Ampthill of his desire to undertake some public activity for educating influential quarters about Transvaal situation. Addressing meeting of Gujaratis in London, advised them to cultivate love for their own language.
October 6	:	In letter to Polak, emphasized need for India to see Transvaal struggle as part of her own movement for freedom and to help it. Discussed future programme with Lord Ampthill. SABIC held reception to Natal delegation.
October 7	:	Gandhiji attended suffragette meeting. Doke wrote to Rand Daily Mail giving details of Kaffir assault on Gandhiji in prison. Tolstoy replied to Gandhiji's letter of October 1.

October 8 : Gandhiji, in speech at Emerson Club, extolled way of suffering. Enquired of Colonial Office about exact position taken by Smuts; informed it of deputation's intention to educate public about Transvaal situation and failure of negotiations. Ordered printing of 2,000 copies of "Statement of Transvaal Indian Case". In message to Gujarati Punch, stressed his complete preoccupation with "the life and death struggle" in Transvaal. 67 Chinese, charged under Asiatic Ordinance, discharged.

October 9 : Sanderson Committee on Indian immigration, reported to have completed inquiry, held that abolition of Indian labour would seriously affect whites.

October 11 : Public meeting in Madras, presided over by Turkish Consul, addressed by Polak.

October 12 : Writing to Manilal Gandhi, Gandhiji declared "learning to live a good life is in itself education". Fund in aid of deported Indians started.

October 13 : Spoke on "East and West" at Hampstead Peace and Arbitration Society.

October 14 : In letter to Lord Ampthill, asserted that cessation of passive resistance was impossible "unless the theoretical right was granted". Wrote to Polak expressing his views on modern civilization, later elaborated in *Hind Swaraj*.

October 15 : Colonial Office informed Gandhiji that proposals referred to as possible basis of legislation in Transvaal were those made by Smuts and not by Gandhiji.

October 17 : Ali Imam, speaking at meeting of Indian Union Society, stressed need for Hidnu-Muslim unity. Thambi Naidoo and others, arrested in Johannesburg, sentenced to 3 months.

October 19 : Gandhiji wrote to Colonial Office asking for exact position. More Indians arrested and sentenced to 3 months. Sorabji Shapurji and S.B. Medh deported.

October 20 : E. I. Aswat, Acting-Chairman, BIA, sentenced

		to 3 months.
	:	Sorabji Shapurji and S. B. Medh arrested at Volksrust border on return to Transvaal.
October 24	:	Gandhiji presided over and spoke at Vijaya Dashami celebrations in London.
October 25	:	Indian Immigration Law Amendment Bill read for third time in Natal Legislative Assembly. Sorabji Shapurji and S. B. Medh sentenced to 6 months as prohibited immigrants.
October 26	:	Polak reported successful meetings all over Madras Presidency.
October 29	:	Gandhiji informed Lord Ampthill of decision to leave for South Africa and to challenge arrest on Transvaal border. Sought interview with Aylmer Maude to discuss matters relating to passive resistance; asked for advice regarding publication of Tolstoy's "Letter to a Hindoo". Received cable from Polak to visit India. Received cable from South Africa asking him to return.
After October 29	:	Sent message to Indian National Congress.
October 30	:	Spoke at meeting of Indian Union Society. Conveyed to Lord Ampthill his views on Indian nationalist movement and modern civilization.
November 1	:	Harilal Gandhi arrested at Volksrust, sentenced again to 6 months.
November 2	:	Gandhiji addressed meeting in London. Several Indians and some Englishmen enrolled as volunteers.
November 3	:	Colonial Office informed Gandhiji of Lord Crewe's inability "to hold out any hopes of obtaining recognition" of theoretical equality as to immigration or otherwise.
November 5	:	Gandhiji released "Statement of Transvaal Indian Case" along with summary to the Press.
November 6	:	Attended meeting of British sympathisers. In valedictory letter to Colonial Office, expressed hope Lord Crewe would still use his influence to secure removal of colour bar from Transvaal immigration laws.

November 7	:	Indian meeting at Tongaat decided to send delegation to India for stopping supply of indentured labour to Natal.
November 9	:	Gandhiji interviewed by Reuter. *The Times* reported failure of negotiations on Transvaal Asiatic legislation. Colonial Office minute recorded : "We cannot dispute the rightness of his [Gandhiji's] claim to equality before the law, it is a fundamental principle."
November 10	:	In interview to *The Daily Express*, Gandhiji stated that passive resistance campaign would continue "with unabated vigour". Wrote to Tolstoy acknowledging letter; sent copy of Doke's biography. Forwarded to Lord Crewe cable from Polak reporting public meeting in sympathy of Transvaal Indians.
November 1	:	Addressed letter to *Daily Telegraph* urging British Press to support Transvaal struggle. In letter to Gokhale, invited him to visit South Africa and participate in struggle.
	:	Wrote to Colonial Office asserting that complaints about Transvaal prison conditions were substantially true.
November 12	:	Released "Statement" to Indian Press. Addressed farewell meeting, convened by Rev. F. B. Meyer, attended among others by Dr. Rutherford, Sir Raymond West, Sir Frederick Lely, Sir Muncherjee Bhownaggree, Motilal Nehru and L. W. Ritch.
November 13	:	Gandhiji and Hajee Habib left for South Africa by *s. s. Kildonan Castle. Indian Opinion* reported setting-up in Bombay of an influential Indian Committee consisting of Sir Pherozeshah Mehta, G. K. Gokhale, M. A. Jinnah, J. B. Petit and others, to collect funds for Transvaal Indians deported to India.
November 13	:	Transvaal Indian Deputation (Gandhiji and Hajee Habib) left England for South Africa. Attempt on life of Lord Minto, Viceroy of India, at Ahmedabad.

November 13 to 22: Gandhiji wrote *Hind Swaraj* in Gujarati on board s.s. Kildonan Castle.

November 15 : Arrangements for Morley-Minto Reforms coming into force were published by Government of India.

November 16 : In Lords, Colonial Secretary told Lord Ampthill of strenuous efforts made by Colonial Office and South African Union delegates to find solution to problem of treatment of British Indians in Transvaal. He promised to publish a Blue-book containing record of recent negotiations.

November 18 : Gandhiji wrote in Gujarati "Preface to Tolstoy's Letter to a Hindoo".

November 19 : Wrote in English "Preface to Tolstoy's Letter to a Hindoo".

November 30 : Arrived at Cape Town with Hajee Habib. Interview to Cape Argus. Cabled Gokhale thanking Ratan J. Tata for donation of Rs. 25,000 in aid of Transvaal struggle. Romesh Chunder Dutt, Prime Minister to the Gaekwar of Baroda, passed away.

December 1 : Col. Seely admitted in Commons that even more stringent legislation than Immigration Law of Transvaal, which constituted racial barrier against British Indians' immigration, existed in Orange River Colony.

December 2 : Gandhiji arrived at Johannesburg. In interview to Reuter at Park Station, thanked Government for allowing his and Hajee Habib's re-entry into Transvaal.

December 3 : Addressed meeting of Tamil ladies in Johannesburg. In reply to The Star pleaded that "the theory of equality may be restored in our legislation as to immigration, which may be deliberately departed from in administration". Calcutta mass meeting protested against treatment of Transvaal Indians.

December 4 : Polak spoke at Calcutta on "non-political aspects of the South African struggle".

December 5 : Gandhiji spoke at Johannesburg mass meeting

to welcome the Deputation. Praised Hosken's Committee and European friends for support. Meeting resolved "to carry on the struggle by means of self-suffering . . . until legal and theoretical equality as to immigration of British Indians of culture with the other immigrants is restored". Gave account of his mission at Chinese meeting at Johannesburg. Travelled with Cachalia and Kallenbach to Diepkloof and met Rustomjee and Aswat in jail. Polak spoke at City College, Calcutta, on "the status and condition of Indian women in South Africa".

December 6 : Gandhiji wrote to Gokhale on financial and other aspects of Transvaal struggle and asked for £1,000 more.

December 10 : *Rand Daily Mail* advised Transvaal Government to accept Indian demand for theoretical equality.

December 20 : At Durban public meeting, Gandhiji described provision for appeal in regard to trading licences as "a bait".

December 21 : A.M.T. Jackson, Collector of Nasik, assassinated.

December 22 : Gandhiji entered Transvaal from Natal with Manilal Gandhi, Royeppen and others, but not arrested.

December 23 : Chairman, BIA, in letter to Colonial Secretary described the Railway Regulations gazetted on December 17, 1909 as "uncalled for, irritating and degrading".

December 24 : Gandhiji wrote to A. H. West on financial and other aspects of Phoenix scheme. Shelat released after 6 months' imprisonment.

December 25 : Gandhiji wrote congratulating Justice Ameer Ali on appointment as Privy Councillor.

On or before December 29: Wrote again to A.H. West regarding Phoenix.

December 29 : Indian National Congress at Lahore passed resolution expressing admiration for struggle in South Africa and urging prohibition of indenture.

December 31 : In letter to Under Secretary of State, Sir M. M. Bhownaggree drew attention to ill-treatment of Parsee Rustomjee in jail.

1910

January 1	:	*Indian Opinion* reduced in size for financial reasons.
January 5	:	Gandhiji attended Boksburg meeting, where certificates were handed in to be destroyed.
January 6	:	Rev. Charles Phillips and J. C. Gibson had interview with Gandhiji following their conversations with Lord Selborne, High Commissioner of Transvaal. In letter to J. C. Gibson, Gandhiji refuted charge that South African movement was engineered and controlled from India and that British Indians continually shifted their ground regarding their demands.
January 7	:	Spoke at dinner to Joseph Royeppen and others in Johannesburg.
January 13	:	Gokhale wrote to Gandhiji that disposal of the sums remitted was left to the latter's discretion.
January 20	:	Natal Legislative Assembly passed Indian Immigration (Licences) Act Amendment Bill.
January 27	:	Natal Legislative Council passed Indian Immigration (Licences) Act Amendment Bill.
February 1	:	Joseph Royeppen, David Andrew and Samuel Joseph tried at Volksrust and sentenced to three months' imprisonment with hard labour.
February 9	:	In Gandhiji's office, Mrs. Amacanoo and Mrs. Packirsamy took off their ornaments, vowing not to wear them till struggle was over.
February 14	:	Gandhiji spoke at Chinese reception at Cantonese Club, Johannesburg, in honour of Rev. J. J. Doke, on eve of latter's departure for America.
February 18	:	Spoke at banquet in Masonic Hall in honour of Rev. Doke. Chairman, BIA, in letter to General Manager, C.S.A.R., submitted draft railway regulations to replace those applicable to Asiatics.
February 20	:	Gandhiji addressed meeting of Natal Indian Congress in Durban.
February 23	:	Explained Transvaal struggle at meeting of Kathiawad Arya Mandal, Durban.

February 25 : Transvaal BIA, Johannesburg, sent telegram to Earl of Crewe on treatment of Royeppen and Rustomjee in Transvaal prisons and on diet-scale of prisoners. Indian Legislative Council at Calcutta passed Gokhale's resolution to prohibit recruitment of indentured labour for Natal.

February 26 : Gandhiji wrote in Indian Opinion supporting the resolve of Dr. Abdurahman and Cape Coloured people in view of their disfranchisement to observe day of Prince of Wales's arrival as day of mourning. Spoke at Durban Indian Society meeting in honour of passive resisters.

March 11 : Accompanied a number of passive resisters to Transvaal to violate immigration laws.

: In letter to Moulvi Ahmed Mukhtiar, explained that Phoenix debt was incurred during struggle.

March 17 : Told *The Star* representative that Indians had come to Johannesburg not to assert their personal rights, but to take part in struggle. President and Secretaries of Natal Indian. Congress forwarded petition to Colonial Secretary against Indian Immigration Law Amendment Bill.

March 23 : Bill to amend Indian Emigration Act, 1908, was moved by Robertson in Viceroy's Council, to give effect to Gokhale's resolution of February 25.

March 24 : Bombay Government Gazette notified that *Hind Swarajya; Universal Dawn,—Gujarati rendering of Ruskin's Unto This Last—; Mustafa Kamel Pasha's Speech,*—a Gujarati translation of the Egyptian patriot's speech delivered just before his death, in Cairo—; and *Defence of Socrates or The Story of a True Warrior*—all publications of International Printing Press— had been forfeited to His Majesty for reason that they "contain matter declared to be seditious".

April 4 : Letter to Leo Tolstoy with copy of Indian Home Rule for comment.

April 8/9 : Director of Transvaal Prisons replied to Chairman, BIA, denying complaint that prisoners were sent to Diepkloof Prison to associate them

		with hardened criminals, and declined to send them elsewhere and change present diet-scale.
April 12	:	Question on emigration of indentured Indians from India to Natal raised in Commons by O'Grady and Rees.
April 14	:	Fifty-nine Indians deported to India from Transvaal by the Umhloti. Gandhiji addressed letter to Attorney General regarding Karodia case and requested Government to use judicious discretion in obtaining warrants of arrest against Indians of standing.
April 25	:	Wrote to Gokhale indicating how Passive Resistance Fund was being used.
May 5	:	Madras public meeting protested against deportation of Indians without trial by Transvaal Government.
May 6	:	King Edward VII passed away.
May 8	:	Leo Tolstoy, in letter to Gandhiji, commenting upon Indian Home Rule, said question of passive resistance was of greatest importance not only for India but for all humanity.
May 10	:	Replying to letter from W.J. Wybergh, M.L.A. (Transvaal), Gandhiji defended views expressed in Indian Home Rule.
May 30	:	Wrote to H. Kallenbach expressing thanks for offer of farm near Lawley for use of passive resisters and their families for duration of Transvaal struggle.
June 1	:	Union of South Africa came into being.
June 2	:	In letter to Press, Gandhiji said advent of Union was no cause for rejoicing and described it as "a combination of hostile forces" arrayed against Asiatics.
June 10	:	Sir Charles Hardinge appointed Viceroy of India.
June 13	:	Twenty-six passive resisters, deported to India by Transvaal Government in April, returned to Durban by *s.s. President*.
June 18	:	In Durban, mass meeting of Indians supported passive resistance. Report of Committee on

Emigration from India to Crown Colonies and Protectorates published.

June 26 : Gandhiji spoke at Socialist Hall, Johannesburg, on "Modern v. Ancient Civilization".

June 29 : In Commons, O'Grady raised question of British Indians in Transvaal and suggested Gandhi-Smuts Conference to arrange compromise.

July 1 : Gandhiji cabled SABIC on rejection of deportees by Natal.

July 3 : Appealed for gifts to help settlers at Tolstoy Farm.

July 8 : BIA, Transvaal, presented address of welcome to Lord Gladstone.

July 9 : In reply to Secretary of State, Lord Gladstone communicated decision to increase daily ration of Indian prisoners serving sentences of up to 3 months.

July 21 : Natal Government Gazette published rules framed under Indian Immigration Law, 1891, requiring employers of indentured Indian immigrants to provide shelter for children of Indian women working in fields. Gandhiji paid tribute to G. A. Natesan for his work for passive resisters deported to India.

July 22 : Lord Morley (Secretary of State for India) expressed to Lord Crewe (Secretary of State for Colonies) his profound regret at refusal of Transvaal Ministers to make any concessions regarding observance of Ramzan in prison or to exempt high-caste Hindu prisoners from tasks involving what they regarded as religious defilement.

July 26 : In Lords, Lord Ampthill raised question of deportation of Indians from Transvaal.

July 28 : BIA cabled SABIC regarding deportation of Royeppen to Natal and Government's attempt to make minors prohibited immigrants.

July 30 : Gandhiji commented on Churchill's statement in Commons that he had given instructions that all persons imprisoned as passive resisters or as suffragettes should be spared unnecessary degradation.

August 3	:	Resolutions passed at London public meeting, under presidentship of Sir Muncherjee Bhownaggree, protesting against treatment of Indians domiciled in Transvaal and deportation via Mozambique.
August 5	:	Gokhale asked questions in Indian Imperial Council regarding Transvaal deportees.
August 6	:	Transmitting Lord Morley's communication of July 22 to Lord Gladstone, Secretary of State for Colonies said that anything offending religious susceptibilities of Indians must be a serious and permanent obstacle to a settlement.
August 9	:	Gandhiji sent rejoinder to Rand Daily Mail's leader "Asiatic Exaggeration" on Lord Morley's repudiation of harsh treatment of British Indian deportees during their enforced voyage from Delagoa Bay to Bombay.
August 13	:	Colonial Office wrote to Sir Muncherjee Bhownaggree and Ritch regarding London meeting of August 3.
August 15	:	Gandhiji wrote a letter to Tolstoy.
August 23	:	A.E. Chhotabhai, a Krugersdorp merchant, appealed against decision of Registrar of Asiatics refusing registration to his son on attaining majority. Public meeting held at Victoria Hall, Madras, to bid farewell to Transvaal deportees on eve of their departure for Transvaal. Sir S. Subramania presided; Mrs. Annie Besant attended.
August 25	:	Cape Town City Council passed resolution refusing en bloc applications of Indians for trading licences.
September 2	:	Ritch sent reply to Colonial Office letter of August 13 regarding registration law and deportation of Indians from Transvaal.
September 7	:	Tolstoy wrote to Gandhiji, supporting passive resistance.
September 10	:	Gandhiji commented in *Indian Opinion* on Magistrate Jordan's dismissal of Chhotabhai's appeal and its implications for minor Asiatics.

September 13	:	In Supreme Court, Justice Wessels heard in Chambers Chhotabhai's case and dismissed it with costs, observing that, if Government's decision about minors be true, it were a monstrous and cruel injustice.
September 17	:	Gandhiji left for Durban to receive Polak and passive resister deportees from India.
September 20	:	Spoke at a meeting of Colonial-born Indians. Spoke at Kathiawad Arya Mandal meeting organized to discuss question of welcoming deportees.
September 24	:	Wrote in Indian Opinion, congratulating Dr. Rubusana on his election as member of Cape Provincial Council for Tembuland.
September 26	:	Blue-book issued dealing with Asiatic legislation in Transvaal up to August 8, 1910.
September 28	:	Gandhiji met Polak, who reached Durban along with other deportees from India by *S.S. Sultan*.
October 4	:	Ritch, who came from England by *R.M.S. Saxon*, gave interview to *Cape Argus*.
October 5	:	Gandhiji and others spoke at reception by Kathiawad Arya Mandal, Durban, in honour of Polak and passive resisters.
October 7	:	Cape Provincial Division of Supreme Court heard application of President, British Indian League, Cape Town, against refusal by immigration authorities of leave to land to batch of Indians who desired to proceed to Transvaal.
October 8	:	Gandhiji wrote to Minister of Interior in connection with landing of deportees.
October 16	:	Death of Narayansamy.
After October 16	:	In letter to SABIC, Gandhiji described death of Narayansamy as "legalized murder".
October 25	:	Wrote to Registrar of Asiatics, requesting him to advise Principal Immigration Restriction Officer to receive applications for duplicate registration certificates from British Indians detained at Salisbury Island under court order.
November 6	:	After notice to Immigration Officer, reached Volksrust with Mrs. Rambhabai Sodha, her three

children and others on way from Durban to Tolstoy Farm.

November 7 : Appeared in Court for Mrs. Sodha. In telegram to Immigration Officer, said she did not seek right of permanent residence in Transvaal.

November 8 : Chairman, BIA, telegraphed Smuts on Mrs. Sodha's arrest and requested withdrawal of prosecution.

November 9 : Gandhiji spoke at Chinese function in honour of Ritch and Polak.

November 10 : BIA wired Minister of Interior for grant of temporary permit to Mrs. Sodha, adding Association was anxious to avoid importing women into struggle.

November 11 : Chhotabhai appeal dismissed by Transvaal Provincial Division of Supreme Court of South Africa. Committee of All-India Muslim League, London, sent representation to Secretary of State for Colonies regarding treatment of British Indians in overseas Dominions of the Crown.

November 12 : Minister of Interior refused grant of even temporary permit to Mrs. Sodha.

November 14 : Gandhiji addressed letter to Press in connection with Mrs. Sodha's case. Smuts moved second reading of Bill to consolidate and amend laws regarding naturalization of aliens.

Before November 18: Gandhiji addressed letter to members of Asiatic Conference regarding Chhotabhai case.

November 18 : At Caxton Hall, London, Polak presiding, Archdeacon Beresford Potter's paper on "Brotherhood within the Empire—with special reference to the British Indians in the Transvaal" was read. BIA decided not to join presentation of welcome address to Duke of Connaught. Ratan Tata sent to Gandhiji cheque for Rs. 25,000 in aid of Transvaal Indians' struggle.

After November 18: Chairman, Hamidia Islamic Society, conveyed respectful welcome to Duke of Connaught but expressed inability to take part in public celebration.

November 19 : Chairman, BIA, wrote to Director of Prisons regarding fast by Indian passive resisters in Diepkloof prison.

November 20 : Death of Leo Tolstoy.

November 22 : Chairman, BIA, wrote again to Director of Prisons regarding improper treatment of Indian passive resisters in Diepkloof prison.

December 4 : Gandhiji spoke at Socialist Hall, Johannesburg, on Tolstoy and his message.

December 9 : In letter thanked G.A. Natesan for securing donations and rendering help to deportees.

December 13 : Smuts stated Government's intention to introduce Immigration Bill for whole of South Africa which would provide suitable opportunity to review entire immigration policy.

December 14 : L.W. Ritch on return from South Africa told Reuter in interview that there appeared to be an earnest desire in South Africa to settle Indian problem.

December 15 : Gandhiji and others met deportees at Diepkloof after discharge from prison.

December 27 : Indian National Congress at Allahabad passed resolution expressing admiration for Transvaal Indians' struggle, urging Government of India to prohibit recruitment of indentured labour and protesting against South African policy as unwise, unrighteous and dangerous to Empire.

December 30 : Gandhiji appeared for defence in case against Mrs. Rambhabai Sodha under Immigrants' Restriction Act.

1911

January 3 : In Viceroy's Legislative Council at Calcutta, Indian Government announced decision to prohibit further emigration of indentured Indians to Natal. Gokhale expressed gratitude.

January 7 : Natal Indian Congress thanked Government of India and Gokhale for ending recruitment of indentured labour for South Africa.

January 9	:	With T. Naidoo, Gandhiji met prisoners released at Diepkloof.
January 11	:	Mrs. Rambhabai Sodha sentenced to fine of £10 and one month's simple imprisonment. Later released on bail on notice of appeal.
January 19	:	Passive resisters Quinn, Royeppen and others sentenced.
January 25	:	In case of Mahmud Chhotabhai, Chief Justice Lord de Villiers, in Appellate Division of Supreme Court, declared expulsion order null and void and ordered Registrar of Asiatics to issue registration certificate. He observed: ". . . the maintenance of liberty of the subject was of more importance than the prevention of undesirable immigration".
January 30	:	In banquet speech at Guildhall, London, Duke of Connaught expressed hope of early settlement of question of Indians in South Africa.
February 1	:	New regulations of South African Railways came into force.
February 14	:	Minister of Interior turned down request of Natal Indian Congress to alter Natal law and exempt Indian women from payment of £3 tax.
February 19	:	All-India Muslim League, London, wrote to Under Secretary of State for Colonies about South African Indians' grievances.
February 20	:	Chairman, BIA, wrote against new railway regulations to Acting General Manager, South African Railways.
February 24	:	Writing to Times of Natal, Polak condemned slavery in Natal.
February 25	:	Union of South Africa Government Gazette Extraordinary published text of Immigrants, Restriction Bill (1911). Indentured Indian labourers of a Stanger estate-owner offered passive resistance.
February 27	:	Stanger passive resisters sentenced and sent to prison.
February 28	:	Protector of Indian Immigrants secured release of Stangermen. Smuts told Parliament that

Asiatics belonged to an ancient race and they could not be generally treated as barbarians.

March 2 : First reading of Immigrants' Restriction Bill. In letter to P.S. to Minister of Interior, Gandhiji sought clarification whether under Section 1 of new Bill Asiatics who might pass education test could enter and remain in Transvaal without being liable to take out registration under Act 36, 1908. Wrote to R. Gregorowski, a Johannesburg lawyer, seeking opinion on interpretation of Immigrants' Restriction Bill.

March 4 : Lane in reply to Gandhiji's letter stated that Asiatics admitted as immigrants under new Immigration Bill "would not fall under registration laws and would not be restricted to provincial limits". In letter to Lane, Gandhiji requested that new Bill be so amended in Committee as to make the assurance given "absolutely clear" He also sought legal protection for wives and minor children of registered Asiatics.

March 9 : Natal Indian Congress meeting passed resolution against Immigration Bill.

March 11 : Chairman, BIA, sent telegram to Members of Parliament at Cape Town requesting that new Immigration Bill be so amended as to cover objections raised by BIA. In cable to Natesan, Gokhale and SABIC (London), Gandhiji said new Bill was satisfactory in principle because it recognized legal equality and would end passive resistance if amended to exempt educated Indians from operation of Registration Act and to protect minor children and wives.

March 12 : Mass meeting of Indians at Cape Town protested against Immigration Bill.

March 13 : Minister of Interior moved second reading of Immigration Bill in Assembly.

March 15 : Petitions of Cape, Natal and Transvaal Indians presented to Parliament.

March 16 : In letter to *Pretoria News,* Gandhiji clarified

		misunderstanding created by his interview.
March 17	:	Sent telegram to P. S. to Smuts regarding amendment of new Bill.
March 18	:	In telegram sent by Acting Chairman, Chinese Association, to Secretary to Minister of Interior, the Chinese joined hands with BIA in request for amendment of Immigrants' Restriction Bill to remove colour or racial bar, to afford protection to wives and minor children of legal residents and to provide for entry of a limited number of cultured Chinese into Union.
March 20	:	Gandhiji sent telegram and wrote to P. S. to Smuts regarding relief under new Immigration Bill. Natal Indian Congress in telegram to P.S. to Minister of Interior opposed amendment to new Bill imposing racial bar against entry into Orange Free State of Asiatics admitted into Union under education test.
March 21	:	Lane telegraphed Gandhiji that Smuts would favourably consider question of providing for women and children of persons lawfully resident, but regarded Gandhiji's attitude on Free State question as "unfair" .
March 22	:	Gandhiji telegraphed reply to P. S. to Minister of Interior on Free State question.
March 23	:	European British Indian Committee meeting at Johannesburg approved Gandhiji's latest correspondence with Minister of Interior regarding new Immigration Bill and urged Government to accept proposed solution.
March 24	:	P. S. to Smuts informed Gandhiji that there would be "no colour or racial bar of any kind whatsoever appearing in Immigration Bill or any amendment which the Government intend to move". Regarding Orange Free State, Smuts proposed leaving situation as it was under existing law of Province. In telegram to P.S. to Smuts, Gandhiji said racial bar would certainly be created if educated Asiatic immigrants were upon entering Orange Free State confronted with Asiatic registration law.

March 25	:	Left for Cape Town.
March 26	:	Durban mass meeting under auspices of Natal Indian Congress protested against new Immigration Bill.
March 27	:	Gandhiji's interview with Smuts at Cape Town.
March 29	:	Natal Indian Congress in telegram to Finance Minister protested against new Poll-tax Bill. In letter to Lane, Gandhiji said amendments to be moved regarding domicile, marriage and parental relationship by Smuts to Immigration Bill requiring evidence to be furnished to immigration officer might "open the door to favouritism, corruption and bribery".
Before March 30	:	Interview to *Cape Argus*.
March 30	:	Gandhiji Spoke at meeting of Cape Town United Hindu Association held in honour of L. W. Ritch and himself.
Before April 1	:	In Klerksdorp, European owners of Stands, as ordered by Public Prosecutor under Gold Law, served notices of eviction on Indian tenants.
April 1	:	Government of India issued notification prohibiting recruitment of indentured labour for South Africa with effect from July 1, 1911.
April 2	:	Gandhiji attended meeting of Cape British Indian Union held to demand changes in Union Immigrants' Restriction Bill so as to protect Cape rights.
April 5	:	In letter to L.W. Ritch, Gandhiji expressed feeling that UIRB would not be passed without the amendment asked for. Wrote to Maud Polak about hardship to Transvaal Indians under the Gold Law and about Klerksdorp persecution. In Natal Provincial Council, G. H. Hulett moved resolution seeking Union legislation to grant Provincial Council Control over issue of trading licences.
April 6	:	In Union Parliament, T. L. Schreiner asked for abolition of £3 tax consequent upon the stoppage of indenture. General Smuts, answering, refused to interfere and informed House that attitude

in India being discouraging very few indentured Indians might come to Natal before July 1.

April 7 : Gandhiji sent to E.F.C. Lane his alternative proposals for ending TVL struggle: either amendment of UIRB to exempt educated immigrants from operation of TVL registration law and Clauses 1 to 6 of Orange Free State Constitution, and protection of existing rights, especially of wives and minors, or dropping of UIRB and amendment of Transvaal Immigrants' Restriction Act.

April 8 : Sought confirmation from E.F.C. Lane that six educated Indians a year would be allowed to enter Union or TVL. whichever of his two proposals be adopted.

April 11 : Deputation of Durban Indian leaders met Mayor to discuss position of Indians during Coronation celebrations.

April 15 : L. W. Ritch commenced legal practice in Gandhiji's Johannesburg office.

April 17 : Joseph Royeppen, Leung Quinn and other passive resisters released.

April 19 : Smuts, in interview, told Gandhiji he would pass UIRB in current or following session; explained why "we do not want Asia to come in" and appealed for peace; asked Gandhiji to agree to the Governor General having power to make regulations regarding education test; assured him Mrs. Sodha would not be arrested should her appeal fail. In letter to Smuts, Gandhiji urged him to settle the question of the entry of six educated Indians a year so that passive resistance could be suspended.

April 20 : Communicated to E.F.C Lane unwillingness of Natal Indian Congress, British Indian Association1 and Cape Indians to cease passive resistance unless TVL problem was settled. Expressed hope that this alternative solution would still be adopted during session and asked for Smuts' decision.

April 21 : E.F.C. Lane informed Gandhiji that Government could not proceed with UIRB during the current session; Government keenly desired solution of "vexed question" and would deliberate over a settlement during the recess; mean-while Indians should stop passive resistance. Gandhiji met E.F.C. Lane. Told him passive resistance could be suspended if certain assurances were given. Lane telephoned Smuts who agreed to some assurances being given.

April 22 : Gandhiji, in letter, informed E.F.C. Lane that passive resistance could be suspended provided Smuts gave certain assurances. Smuts, in reply to above, expressed intention to introduce legislation, during following session, which would: (a) repeal Act 2 of 1907, subject to reservation of rights of minor children; (b) give legal equality for all immigrants; (c) empower registration of passive resisters who, but for their resistance, would have been entitled to it, anything under Act 36 of 1908 not withstanding. (d) empower the regularizationof issue of temporary certificates to educated passive resisters (not more that five or six) then in TVL. Smuts added that if Gandhiji gave assurance of suspension of passive resistance he would ask Governor General to favourably consider releasing passive resistance prisoners. Appeal of Rambhabai Sodha dismissed by Court.

April 24 : Gandhiji, speaking at Kimberley meeting of Indians, said they were "nearing a solution of the difficult question".

April 25 : Smuts withdrew UIRB in Union Assembly.

April 26 : Gandhiji returned tö Johannesburg.

April 27 : At meeting of Indians in Johannesburg, Gandhiji explained correspondence with Smuts regarding Provisional Settlement and advised acceptance of proposals. Meeting decided: (a) to call of passive resistance if Smuts fulfilled his pledges; (b) to send H. S.L. Polak to England in place of Gandhiji and A.M. Cachalia. *Indian Opinion*

		announced that TVL Chinese had decided to accept proposals for Provisional Settlement.
April 28	:	Gandhiji, in interview to *The Star* about Provisional settlement, announced intention to retire from public life after finalization of Settlement.
April 29	:	Gandhiji met E.F.C. Lane. Gave, in letter to E.F.C. Lane, British Indians' interpretation of the terms of the Settlement and sought Smuts' confirmation; made request for R.M. Sodha being allowed to register, for reinstatement of a government servant, who had been removed for passive resistance, for release of Chinese prisoners, etc.
May 1	:	BIA petitioned Secretary of State for Colonies regarding grievances of TVL Indians, including those arising from Law 3 of 1885, the Gold Law and Townships Act. Gandhiji addressed Vrededorp farewell meeting for Joseph Royeppen.
May 3(?)	:	Gandhiji met Smuts.
May 4	:	Wrote to E.F.C. Lane regarding categories of Indians and Chinese who might apply for voluntary registration. Wrote to A.E. Chotabhai thanking him for £300 sent for professional services in connection with his son's case and saying he intended to hand over Phoenix to trustees and would use sum for school there.
Before May 8	:	Harilal Gandhi left home without informing Gandhiji.
May 8	:	Gandhiji wrote to H.S.L. Polak giving him estimate of expenses for his visit to England and India and telling him of Smuts' favourable response to demands of passive resisters. Writing to Dr. Pranjivan Mehta, suggested that six Natal satyagrahis be educated in England at Dr. Mehta's expense; mentioned his resolve not to practise law.
May 15	:	Natal Indian Congress addressed Memorandum to Secretary of State for Colonies regarding

	proposed arbitrary education test, curtailment of existing rights in UIRB, and £3 tax on ex-indentured Indians. Harilal Gandhi returned to Tolstoy Farm from Delagoa Bay.
May 16 :	Klerksdorp Indians appealed to Minister of Interior for withdrawal of notices under Gold Law and repeal of the Law.
May 17 :	Transvaal Draft Municipal Councils Ordinance1 (Draft Local Government Ordinance) published in Government Gazette.
Before May 18 :	Harilal Gandhi left home finally for India.
May 18 :	Gandhiji wrote to Minister of Interior asking for Smuts' answer to his proposals regarding Provisional Settlement contained in his letter of April 29, 1911. In House of Commons, questions asked regarding Gold Law and Township Act and resulting hardships to TVL Indians.
May 19 :	Smuts informed Gandhiji that: (a) passive resisters with valid claims to registration, but deported under TARA or TARAA, could apply for registration by December 31, 1911; (b) Asiatics with valid claims to registration, who left South Africa owing to passive resistance, though not deported, could apply for registration provided both of above categories did not exceed 30; (c) about 180 Chinese and Indians in South Africa, refused registration under the voluntary system, could apply by December 31, 1911; (d) the seven educated Indians now in TVL named by Gandhiji would receive temporary authorization for residence pending alteration of law, when permanent documents would be issued. Smuts also expressed hope Asiatic community would regard acceptance of requests as final settlement and said that on hearing from Gandhiji passive resistance prisoners would be released. Gandhiji, in reply to above, said 180 Asiatic passive resisters included also those who could not apply under either the voluntary system or any of the Asiatic laws; construed absence of disclaimer to terms of Provisional Settlement as set forth in

		his letter of April 29 as endorsement thereof and requested telegraphic reply. Wrote to Gokhale apprising him of good results secured by passive resistance and of the hardships of Indians in TVL, Natal and the Cape.
May 20	:	Smuts in telegram to Gandhiji informed him that: (a) 180 Asiatics included also those who failed to apply in time on grounds of three years' pre-war residence in TVL; (b) existing individual rights would not be taken away but various provinces would be affected by future general and uniform legislation; (c) well-known or educated registered Asiatics need not give thumb or finger-impressions for taking out licences. Gandhiji, in reply, conveyed acceptance of the Provisional Settlement on behalf of the BIA and gave list of passive resisters to be released.
After May 20	:	Drafted statement for proposed British Indian Deputation to Smuts.
May 22	:	BIA published notice in *Indian Opinion* asking passive resisters eligible to register under the Provisional Settlement to submit their names to Honorary Secretary.
May 23	:	Gandhiji, in interview to Reuter, explained Provisional Settlement.
May 26	:	Drafted letter to Registrar of Asiatics enclosing list of Chinese entitled to register under Provisional Settlement and also names of three Mahomedans for special certificates.
May 27	:	Writing in *Indian Opinion*, expressed satisfaction at Provisional Settlement but warned that passive resistance would be resumed if Smuts did not keep his promise to repeal TARA and amend TIRA or if fresh anti-Asiatic legislation was introduced.
May 30	:	In london, H.S.L. Polak spoke on South African Indian problem at meeting of League of Honour.
May 31	:	Gandhiji wrote to G. A. Natesan expressing satisfaction with Provisional Settlement and praising Natesan's work.

June 1	:	Klerksdorp Indians informed that Minister of Interior could not make any alternations in Gold Law.
June 2	:	Gandhiji at Park Station saw off R. M. Sodha, leaving for India. Five passive resisters released under Provisional Settlement. South Africa British Indian Committee1 wrote to Colonial Office regarding operation of Gold Law and Townships Act in TVL and other hardships of Indians.
June 3	:	Gandhiji, writing in Indian in *Indian Opinion,* set forth the achievements of satyagraha to date.
June 5	:	Gandhiji and L.W. Ritch addressed gathering at Johannesburg after passive resisters' football match. BIA sent petition to TVL Administrator and Provincial Council protesting against TDMCO.
June 6	:	BIA wrote to Secretary of Interior on behalf of Klerksdrop Indians regarding operation of Gold Law.
June 9	:	Gandhiji attended banquet given to William Hosken in Johannesburg.
June 10	:	Writing in *Indian Opinion,* criticized TDMCO as being designed to crush Asiatic hawkers.
June 15	:	At Roodepoort, Tamblin, a white, charged under Gold Law for sub-letting Stand to Asiatics.
June 16	:	Gandhiji spoke at farewell to Sorabji Shapurji in Durban.
June 17	:	H.S.L. Polak wrote for SABIC to Colonial Office regarding TVL Indians' grievances, including hardships caused by Gold Law and Townships Act and £3 tax on ex-indentured Indians.
June 19	:	Natal Indian leaders informed Town Clerk, Durban, that they could not participate in official Coronation festivities because of racial discrimination shown. First meeting of Imperial Conference in London under presidentship of Secretary of State for Colonies.
June 19 (?)	:	India Office Memorandum to Imperial Conference on position of British Indians in Dominions.

June 21	:	Gandhiji, along with Natal Indian leaders, met Mayor of Durban regarding Coronation celebrations.
June 22	:	Coronation of King George V at Westminster Abbey. In Durban, Indians boycotted celebrations.
June 24	:	Gandhiji, writing in *Indian Opinion,* affirmed loyalty to the King.
June 27	:	Indian Immigration Board deputation discussed with Smuts problem of finding other labour, immigration from India having stopped. In house of Commons, Sir William Bull asked question regarding operation of TVL Gold Law and Townships Act against Indians.
June 30	:	Justice Wessels of TVL Division of Supreme Court in judgment ruled that no Indian could bring more than one wife into the country and "that must be a woman who actually was a wife."
July 1	:	Gandhiji, writing in *Indian Opinion,* praised H.S.L. Polak's work in England.
After July 1	:	Wrote to Dr. Pranjivan Mehta seeking monetary assistance to the extent of £1,000 for expanding activities at Phoenix.
July 4	:	Wrote to Dr. Murison regarding antituberculosis work in Durban.
July 5	:	BIA and Hamidia Islamic Society wrote to Secretary for Interior, asking whether Justice Wessels' judgment would affect the existing practice of permitting Mahomedans to bring in more than one wife as sanctioned by their religion.
July 8	:	Gandhiji, writing in *Indian Opinion,* discussed Justice Wessels' ruling in Bai Rasul's case that an Indian may bring in only one wife; said it was not possible to have in British Dominions laws insulting to any recognized religion.
July 11	:	At Rodepoort, Tamblin sentenced by Magistrate to £2 fine or 10 days' imprisonment under Gold Law for subletting Stands to Asiatics.
July 12	:	In House of Commons, questions asked regarding TDMCO.

July 20	Lord Ampthill and Sir M.M. Bhownaggree wrote for SABIC to Colonial Office regarding treatment of Indians in Colonies and attitude of Imperial conference; requested that General Botha be asked to receive deputation.
Before July 22	BIA and Hamidia Islamic Society informed by Smuts that Justice Wessels' ruling regarding immigration of Mahomedans' wives had been noted and Smuts would consider individual cases of hardship brought to his notice.
About July 26	SABIC wrote to Colonial Office regarding entry of Indian wives into Natal.
July 28	H.S.L. Polak spoke at Universal Races Congress in London.
July 31	Farewell address signed by Gandhiji and A. M. Cachalia presented to H. Kallenbach on his departure for Europe. Anti-Asiatic Conference at Potchefstroom decided to form an organization to protect interests of whites against Asiatics.
August 2	SABIC wrote to Colonial Office regarding entry of Indian wives into TVL.
August 3	L.W. Ritch served with notice by Krugersdorp Resident Magistrate against transferring or sub-letting Stands owned by him to Coloured persons and violating Gold Law.
August 5	Gandhiji, writing in Indian Opinion, advised Natal Indians to help Dr. Murison's campaign against tuberculosis in Durban.
August 12	Wrote to Secretary for Interior saying he would try to complete by August 21, 1911, list of passive resisters covered by Provisional Settlement. Writing in Indian Opinion on notice served on L. W. Ritch under Gold Law, called on Indian to remain firm.
August 13	Addressing BIA meeting in Johannesburg, explained that L. W. Ritch was prepared to face imprisonment to protect Indians' rights of equitable ownership in Krugersdorp.
August 14	*The Times,* London, wrote on UIRB and Provisional Settlement.

August 15	: BIA wrote to Secretary for Interior seeking his intervention in preventing prosecution of L. W. Ritch for having Coloured persons on property registered in his name at Krugersdorp.
August 18	: Amended rules for employment of women and children of indentured Indians published in Union Government Gazette.
August 19	: Gandhiji, writing in Indian Opinion, congratulated L. W. Ritch and TVL Indians on their decision to resist Government's attempts to oust Indian merchants under God Law and Townships Act.
August 21	: Forwarded to Registrar of Asiatics revised, though not yet final, list of indians covered by Provisional Settlement.
August 22	: Union Ministers' minutes to Governor General on £3 tax and TDMCO.
August 28	: Governor General forwarded to Colonial Office Union Ministers' minutes on £3 tax in Natal and TDMCO. TVL Division of Supreme Court upheld appeal by Tamblin against Roodepoort Magistrate's sentence under Gold Law.
September 3	: Gandhiji addressed meeting at Johannesburg held to celebrate Dadabhai Naoroji's birthday.
September 5	: Reuter cable announced famine in Punjab and Rajasthan.
September 6	: SABIC wrote to Colonial Office regarding harassment under Gold Law and Townships Act of Indian equitable owners of property in Krugersdorp, Klerksdorp and Roodepoort.
September 7	: H.S.L. Polak wrote to *Cape Times* regarding anti-Asiatic agitation.
September 9	: Gandhiji, writing to Maganlal Gandhi, declared that money spent by individuals in constructing houses on their share of Phoenix land could not be returned to them.
September 16	: In Durban, Natal Indian leaders formed "The Anti-£3 Tax League".
September 23	: Gandhiji, writing in *Indian Opinion*, welcomed

		decision of Germiston Indians oppose move by Town Council to prohibit their trading in Georgetown Location.
September 24	:	In letter to Dr. Pranjivan Mehta, said he was preparing himself for work in India.
September 27	:	Gandhiji, along with Tolstoy Farm's schoolboys, attended football match at Johannesburg.
September 28	:	Italy invaded Turkish territory.
September 30	:	Wrote in *Indian Opinion* regarding Natal Indian Congress inquiry whether he could preside at the forthcoming session of Indian National Congress, and his conditional willingness.
October 1	:	Indians served a month's notice by Germiston Municipality to vacate Stands in Georgetown Location. "The Germiston Indian Association" formed.
October 2	:	Gandhiji attended meeting of Muslims at Johannesburg held to condemn Italy for waging war against Turkey.
October 7	:	Wrote in letter to Harilal Gandhi of invitation to preside at the Indian National Congress.
October 9	:	BIA wrote to TVL Administrator regarding Town Council notice on Germiston Indians to vacate Georgetown Location.
October 10	:	Gandhiji wrote to Dr. Pranjivan Mehta saying it was not clear from whom the invitation to preside at the Indian National Congress had come, but he had accepted it on condition that his presence was really necessary and his freedom was not compromised. Said he would go to India the moment matters were settled in South Africa.
October 22	:	Informed Dr. Pranjivan Mehta that cable regarding presidentship of Indian National Congress was inquiry not invitation; that he had cabled that his name be not considered. Also informed him of Manila Doctor's intention to attend Congress session in India.
October 23	:	Spoke at Johannesburg function to celebrate Gujarati New Year's Day.

October 24 : Wrote to Gokhale, requesting help for Manilal Doctor in his efforts against indenture system.

October 30 : Wrote to Gokhale inviting him to visit South Africa; also explained misunderstanding over presidentship of Indian National Congress.

November 6 : A.M. Bhyat opend store in Boksburg in premises registered in name of L.W. Ritch.

November 8 : In Boksburg, mass meeting of whites protested against opening of store by A.M. Bhyat; asked Government to proceed against L.W. Ritch, under Section 131 of Gold Law.

November 11 : Gandhiji, in Indian Opinion, expressed resolve to fight tooth and nail against £3 tax; also called for funds to help the famine-stricken in India.

November 13-15: At Bloemfontein, South African Agricultural Union Annual Conference passed resolution urging Government to stop issue of trading licences and transfer of land to Asiatics.

November 14 : *Indian Opinion* announced Reuter's news that, Gandhiji having withdrawn, Pandit Bishen Narayan Dhar would be elected President of Indian National Congress. Colonial Office replied to part of H. S. L. Polak's SABIC letter of June 17, saying that Union Ministers' minute of August 22 on the £3 tax correctly represented the facts, that the legislation was passed with full consent of Imperial Government and that it supported Union Ministers' refusal to repeal its provisions.

November 15 : At Indian Women's Association Bazaar in Johannesburg, Gandhiji read out address to Mrs. Vogl.

November 18 : Gandhiji, in *Indian Opinion,* condemned as breach of faith, Natal Government's attempt to realize £3 tax from re-indentured Indians after their circular of April, 1910, granting exemption. Natal Indian Congress wrote to Minister of Justice requesting him to abide by Government circular of April, 1910, and not realize £3 tax from re-indentured Indians.

November 25 : Gandhiji, in *Indian Opinion,* called on Natal Indians to take steps for abolition of £3 tax.

December 6 : In House of Lords, Lord Lamington moved for production of correspondence between Colonial Office and Union Government regarding position of British Indians in TVL; asked for information on working of TVL Gold Law, Townships Act and TDMCO.

December 7 : Gandhiji, in letter to E.F.C. Lane, suggested that if general legislation could not be passed in the current session of Union Parliament, TIRA should be amended.

December 8 : In letter to Gokhale, renewed invitation to visit South Africa.

December 9 : Writing in *Indian Opinion,* asked Indians to contribute liberally to Famine Relief Fund.

December 20 : Spoke at Chinese rally in Johannesburg to pay homage to Alex Benson.

December 21 : Wire from E.F.C. Lane from Pretoria inviting Gandhiji to meet him and see draft of new Immigration Bill1.

December 22 : Gandhiji saw draft of UIRB (1912).

On or after December 26: H.S.L. Polak, Chintamani and Sorabji Shapurji spoke at Indian National Congress in Calcutta. Resolutions passed deploring South African Indians' disabilities, demanding retaliatory measures and urging Government to totally stop indenture system. Polak in his speech announced Gokhale's intention to visit South Africa the following year.

December 30 : Gandhiji, in *Indian Opinion,* condemned refusal of authorities to allow an Indian boy, Nathalia, entry into Natal and called for matter to be taken to higher courts.

1912

January 1 : Inaugural meeting of African Political Organization held at Johannesburg under presidentship of Dr. Abdurrahman.

January 4 : Labour Conference at Bloemfontein demanded

		abolition of indenture system.
January 4 (?)	:	Dr. Porter reported serious outbreak of smallpox in Malay Location, Johannesburg.
January 5	:	BIA complained to Secretary for Interior regarding case of an infant below one year for whom Durban immigration authorities had demanded a visitor's pass.
January 6	:	*Indian Opinion* reported famine in Bombay Presidency, Kathiawad, Ahmedabad and Kaira. Writing in *Indian Opinion,* Gandhiji appealed for funds for famine relief in India; commended H.S.L. Polak's work at Indian National Congress, and welcomed decision of Gokhale to visit South Africa as "joyful news".
Janaury 9	:	H.S.L. Polak wrote to Government of India regarding £3 tax on ex-indentured Indians.
January 12	:	Gandhiji, in letter to Gokhale, welcomed his visit to South Africa; suggested visit on way to London. L.W. Ritch received legal notice to deliver title-deed and posession of Boksburg Stands to Government in cancellation of his ownership.
January 13	:	Gandhiji, in *Indian Opinion,* warned Indians not to conceal cases of smallpox.
January 15	:	Gave interview to *Evening Chronicle* on TDMCO, small-pox, trading licences, etc.
January 16	:	Cases of plague discovered in Durban.
January 18	:	Durban Indians formed Plague Committee to help Public Health Department.
	:	Gandhiji met M. Chamney.
Before January 20	:	Indian hawkers informed that they would be refused licences to hawk in Kimberley. Supreme Court dismissed appeal of Indian minor, Mahomed Hassan, against Government's refusal to register him on ground that he was over 16 years of age when he arrived.
January 29	:	Gandhiji wrote to E.F.C. Lane saying the gazetted version of UIRB(1912) differed somewhat from the draft he had seen; discussed Sections 5, 7,

25 and 28. Abdoolla Hajee Adam, founder-president of Natal Indian Congress, died.

January 30 : First reading of UIRB(1912) in Union Assembly. Gandhiji wired Smuts regarding Sections 5, 7, 25 and 28. Received reply to above that second reading of Bill was not until February 8 and matters mentioned were being considered.

January 31 : In wire to Gandhiji, Secretary for Interior upheld Sections 5, 7, 25 and 28 of Bill.

February 1 : Gandhiji wired E.F.C. Lane expressing dissatisfaction with reply of January 31 and requesting alterations in Sections 7 and 8. Said he was refraining from public action pending reply.

February 3 : Writing in *Indian Opinion* on the Bill, said it did not quite fulfil Smuts' promise. Criticized provisions vesting power in immigration officers to determine domiciliary rights of wives and minors, taking away right of Judicial appeal and disturbing existing rights of interprovincial movement of educated persons. Wired Cape British Indian Union to pass resolutions against these provisions. In Gujarati section of *Indian Opinion,* translated and commented on important sections of the Bill.

February 4 : Meetings held in Cape and Natal to protest against Bill.

February 7 : Secretary for Interior replied to Gandhiji's wire of February 1, saying the Bill nowhere excluded appeal to law courts; system of domicile certificates all over Union was quite impossible; Section 8 of the Bill regarding sworn declaration required in OFS was being considered. Appealed to Gandhiji to persuade his compatriots to accept Bill. In reply to above, Gandhiji wired asking for amendment in Bill to secure existing legal rights regarding interprovincial immigration of educated Asiatics; said he would still postpone public action pending reply.

February 8 : Smuts replied that he hoped to give satisfactory assurances regarding above.

	:	Gandhiji wired that nothing short of assurance of retaining existing legal position would do. Reserved right to criticize Bill regarding other features not covered by Provisional Settlement.
February 9	:	Natal division of Supreme Court confirmed magistrate's decision that N. Mudaly was liable to pay £3 tax in spite of having entered on contract of service on expiry of indenture.
February 10	:	Gandhiji, writing in Indian Opinion, severely criticized UIRB(1912) for its policy of Asiatic exclusion and for interfering with vested rights. Hoped Government would sympathetically consider Indian protests.
February 11	:	At Kimberley, mass meeting of Indians held to protest against the Bill.
February 12	:	Gandhiji received H. Kallenbach at Krugersdorp on his return from Europe.
February 13	:	In TVL Supreme Court, appeal of Fatima Jussat against Barberton magistrate's refusal to allow her entry dismissed by Justice Wessels on ground that a Mahomedan could bring in only one wife.
February 15	:	Gandhiji wrote to E.F.C. Lane that he still awaited reply and that he intended to take legal opinion regarding UIRB (1912) in matter of appeal to law courts. Wrote to R. Gregorowski seeking legal opinion on certain provisions of the Bill. BIA and Hamidia Islamic Society wired Minister of Interior seeking his intervention in Fatima Jussat's case.
Before February 17	:	Petition setting forth Cape Indians' objections to UIRB(1912) submitted to the Senate and House of Assembly.
February 17	:	Gandhiji commented in *Indian Opinion* on Supreme Court judgment on N. Mudaly's appeal.
February 18	:	Sorabji Shapurji arrived from India.
February 19	:	In House of Lords, Lord Ampthill raised debate on TVL Indians.
February 21	:	Gandhiji telegraphed Registrar of Asiatics regarding visiting permits for Khoja representatives of the Aga Khan.

February 22	:	L.W. Ritch and A.M. Bhyat summoned by Supreme Court in connection with the Boksburg Stands.
February 24	:	Gandhiji wrote to E.F.C. Lane informing him of Counsel's opinion that UIRB(1912) ousted jurisdiction of law courts, except by way of mandamus and took away certain existing rights; requested that the defects might be remedied.
February 27	:	In Imperial Legislative Council, Calcutta, Gokhale asked questions regarding indentured labourers in Natal.
Februrary 29	:	BIA wired reminder to Minister of Interior regarding Fatima Jussat's case.
March 2	:	BIA informed telegraphically by Minister of Interior that Fatima Jussat's case did not warrant his intervention.
March 4	:	At All-India Muslim League session in Calcutta, resolution passed regarding South African Indians; H.S.L. Polak also spoke. In Imperial Legislative Council, Calcutta, Gokhale's resolution on total abolition of indentured labour for Colonies defeated by 11 votes.
March 5	:	BIA wrote to Secretary for Interior again seeking intervention in Fatima Jussat's case.
March 7	:	In Imperial Legislative Council, Calcutta, Gokhale asked question on removal of Indians from Vrededorp Township.
March 9	:	Gandhiji, writing in *Indian Opinion*, deplored refusal of Colonial Office to intervene in the case of Indian minor, Nathalia, who had been refused entry into Natal; also called on Indians to fight against deportation of Fatima Jussat. At Johannesburg farewell to Pragji Khandubhai Desai and Surendrarai Medh, commended their work as satyagrahis.
March 13	:	In letters to BIA and Hamidia Islamic Society Minister refused to reconsider his decision in Fatima Jussat's case.
March 16	:	Gandhiji, writing in *Indian Opinion*, commended Gokhale's efforts to get resolution on total

		abolition of indenture passed in the Imperial Legislative Council.
March 26	:	Meeting of Indian South African league held in Madras passed resolutions regarding ill-treatment of Indians in South Africa, UIRB(1912) and ending of indenture.
March ?	:	White Paper containing correspondence between Union and Imperial Governments regarding position of British Indians under Gold Law and Townships Act published in London.
April 1	:	Gandhiji, in public letter to Ratan Tata, gave account of receipts and expenditure of Passive Resistance funds.
April 2	:	At Pretoria, White League Congress pledged itself to preventing equality between whites and Coloured persons.
April 4	:	Gandhiji, writing to E.F.C. Lane, enquired whether UIRB(1912) would come up that session or be abandoned.
April 11	:	Writing to E. F. C. Lane, drew attention to remark of Acting Secretary for Interior and hoped this would not mean exclusion of educated persons from OFS.
April 15	:	The *Titanic* sank in the Atlantic.
April 19	:	H.S.L. Polak wrote to Government of India regarding rights of Indian owners of property in South Africa, specially in Boksburg, and regarding entry of Mahomedan wives into South Africa.
April 24	:	Magistrate Jordan at Johannesburg, in case of Hassin Mahomed's wife, declared that her marriage could not be considered valid and she had no right to be in TVL.
April 27	:	H.S.L. Polak wrote to Government of India regarding Germiston Location.
April 28	:	Gandhiji, A. M. Cachalia, L. W. Ritch, Sorabji Shapurji, Thambi Naidoo and others spoke at meeting held in Germiston Location.
April 29	:	In House of Commons, question asked regarding Nathalia's case.

Before May 4	:	In letter to *Sporting Star* Gandhiji opposed division of Asiatics into higher and lower classes for purposes of admission to the Wanderers Ground. Re-elcted patron of the Natal Indian Football Association.
May 11	:	Writing in *Indian Opinion,* condemned Magistrate Jordan's decision disallowing wives of polygamous marriages from entering TVL.
May 14	:	Letter from E.F.C. Lane enclosing proposed change in Section 28 of UIRB(1912) concerning sworn declaration required in OFS and informing Gandhiji of Smuts' intention to settle the question of domicile.
May 16	:	Gandhiji criticized TVL Provincial Council's decision to refuse separate school for Indians at Johannesburg. In House of Commons, question asked regarding quit notice served on Germiston Indians; Colonial Secretary expressed inability to interfere.
May 21	:	Gandhiji, replying to E.F.C. Lane, expressed satisfaction that Government were willing to settle the difficulty about declaration in OFS and about domicile rights under UIRB(1912).
May 30	:	Second reading of the Bill moved in Union Assembly.
May 31	:	Gandhiji wrote to E.F.C. Lane regarding interprovincial movement of educated Indians under the Bill.
Before June 1	:	Cape British Indian Union's petition regarding trading licences presented in House of Assembly.
June 1	:	Writing in Indian Opinion on "An Unfortunate Case", Gandhiji described the cruel treatment of an indentured Indian woman by her employer and condemned the whole indenture system.
June 6	:	Case against L.W. Ritch and A.M. Bhyat heard in Supreme Court, Pretoria.
June 7	:	Gandhiji went to Pretoria and met M. Chamney and E.F.C. Lane.
June 22	:	In Union Assembly debate on second reading of UIRB(1912) Smuts expressed Government's

		keenness to pass measure, if possible, that session.
June 24	:	Union Parliament prorogued until September 23, 1912 and Bill shelved.
June 25	:	Gandhiji telegraphed Secretary for Interior enquiring about Government's intentions regarding the Bill and future of Provisional Settlement in view of prorogation of Parliament.
June 26	:	Gandhiji wired SABIC regarding notices served on European owners of Vrededorp Stands to remove Asiatic occupants within three months. Spoke at meeting of Tamil Benefit Society on UIRB (1912).
June 27	:	Meeting of Cape British Indian Union held to discuss situation arising from shelving of the Bill.
June 28	:	Gandhiji and Kasturba left for Durban.
June 29	:	Arrived in Durban. Spoke at Durban farewell to Dawad Mahomed and other Haj pilgrims.
June 30	:	resided at prize-giving ceremony at H. L. Paul's Indian Educational Institute at Durban.
July 3	:	Gandhiji saw off Dawad Mahomed who left for Mecca. H.S.L. Polak wrote to Government of India regarding Indian education in Natal.
July 5	:	Gandhiji left Durban for Johannesburg.
Before July 6	:	In case regarding Boksburg Stands, Supreme Court decided against L.W. Ritch and A.M. Bhyat; ordered Ritch to deliver possession of Stands and ejected Bhyat.
July 6	:	Gandhiji wrote to E.F.C. Lane enquiring about Government's intentions regarding UIRB(1912) and future of Provisional Settlement.
July 7	:	Arrived in Johannesburg from Durban.
July 11	:	Met M. Chamney, Registrar of Asiatics.
Before July 13	:	Cousins appointed Acting Immigration Officer, Natal.
July 13	:	andhiji, in Indian Opinion, criticized Dr. Murison's statement that Indians were given to lying. Condemned the circular issued by the Natal Immigration Officer, Cousins, laying down

evidence required for entry of Indian wives. Advised Natal Indian Congress to fight about stoppage of issue of domicile certificates.

July 16 : Informed by Acting Secretary for Interior that Government would introduce amended measure next session; meanwhile, administration of existing legislation would continue.

July 17 : In reply to Secretary for Interior, said he understood Provisional Settlement would continue pending passage of satisfactory legislation and therefore a certain number of educated Asiatics would be admitted for the year; would submit names on confirmation. In House of Lords, Lord Ampthill gave instances of violation of spirit of Provisional Settlement; said Abraham Fischer [who had replaced Smuts as Minister of Interior] was less amicable towards Indians than Smuts.

July 19 : Acting Secretary for Interior confirmed that previous year's Provisional Settlement would continue pending passage of legislation and six educated Indians would be admitted for the year.

July 20 : Gandhiji, in *Indian Opinion,* again criticized Natal Immigration Officer, Cousins, for wanting fresh proof from those returning from India; desired Natal Indian Congress to take up matter. Advised Indians to render Dr. Murison all help and no conceal cases.

July 21 : Spoke at meeting in Johannesburg held to mourn death of Mrs. Tilak.

July 22 : Wrote to Registrar of Asiatics demanding that waiting accommodation be provided for Indians with business in his office. Wrote to Secretary for Interior requesting that R. M. Sodha be issued trading licence without being asked to produce registration certificate. Spoke at Johannesburg farewell party for V. A. Chettiar.

July 23 : Met M. Chamney.

July 25 : Gokhale cabled Gandhiji that he would sail from England for South Africa on October 5.

July 26	:	Gandhiji informed by M. Chamney that no accommodation for Indians visiting his office could be provided. Natal Indian Congress wrote to Secretary for Interior protesting against circular issued by Immigration Officer Cousins requiring proofs of marriage from immigrant Indian wives. Manila Doctor left Cape for Fiji.
July 29	:	Gandhiji wrote to Registrar of Asiatics again regarding waiting accommodation at his office.
July 30	:	Gokhale appointed member of Royal Commission on Indian Public Services.
July 31	:	A.O. Hume died.
August 1	:	Gandhiji spoke at banquet given by Johannesburg Tamil Community to V. A. Chettiar. Ratan Tata made a third donation of Rs. 25,000/-towards Passive Resistance Fund. Bombay public meeting condemned treatment of Indians in Colonies, particularly in South Africa.
August 3	:	Gandhiji, in *Indian Opinion,* advised Germiston Indians not to shift to unhealthy site chosen for new Asiatic Bazzar. Wrote to Minister of Interior regarding right of educated persons to earn livelihood; asked for decision regarding trading licence for R. M. Sodha.
August 10	:	Went to Roodepoort and Krugersdorp with A. M. Cachalia. Writing in Indian Opinion, called on Indians to unite in according fitting welcome to Gokhale on his arrival in South Africa.
August 11	:	Returned to Tolstoy Farm.
August 16	:	Registrar of Asiatics informed Gandhiji that R. M. Sodha and other specially exempted educated Asiatics could not be issued trading licences pending legislation validating their residence.
August 17	:	Writing in *Indian Opinion,* drew attention of Indians to report of a second outbreak of smallpox in Johannesburg and called for help to Dr. Porter in fighting the disease.
August 22	:	Spoke at Johannesburg Theosophical Lodge. In interview to *The Transvaal Leader* opposed compulsory segregation of Coloured races as

		measure to check smallpox.
August 25	:	Spoke at BIA meeting held to arrange welcome to Gokhale; announced Aga Khan's intention to visit South Africa and East Africa.
August 30	:	Left for Durban with Kasturba and others.
August 31	:	Arrived at Durban; proceeded Phoenix. Wrote in *Indian Opinion* on the late A.O. Hume. Commented on the case of five Indians returning to Cape Town, who were refused entry because the ship bringing them had been delayed by bad weather.
September 4	:	H.S.L. Polak and Mrs. Polak arrived in Durban from India.
September 7	:	Gandhiji, in *Indian Opinion* commended work done by H.S.L. Polak in India.
September 12	:	In Johannesburg Magistrate's court, proceedings commenced to compel whites to eject Coloured tenants from Stands at Vrededorp.
September 14	:	Phoenix Trust Deed published in *Indian Opinion*. Gandhiji, writing in *Indian Opinion* criticized illegal actions of Natal Immigration Officer, Cousins, regarding Indians seeking entry. Announced intention to discontinue advertisements in *Indian Opinion*.
	:	Left Durban for Johannesburg.
October 5	:	Gokhale left England for South Africa.
October 8	:	Montenegro declared war on Turkey.
October 9	:	Gandhiji met M. Chamney.
October 16	:	In letter to Harilal Gandhi, explained why he chose Sorabji Shapurji rather than him for study of law in England.
October 18	:	Left for Cape with H. Kallenbach and others.
October 20	:	Arrived in the Cape.
October 21	:	Met Cousins. Gokhale Reception Committee wrote to Botha to suspend £3 tax on ex-indentured Indians in view of Gokhale's approaching visit.
October 22	:	Gokhale arrived in Cape Town. Reception in City Hall; Mayor presided. General address read by

		Dr. A. H. Gool. Addresses presented by Hindu Association, Konkney Muslim League and Tamil Community. Speeches by Gandhiji, W. P. Schreiner and Dr. Abdurrahman. Speech in reply by Gokhale. Gandhiji, in interview to Cape Argus, said Gokhale would investigate the whole Indian question in South Africa.
October 23	:	Gokhale had interviews with W. P. Schreiner and Sir Fredric Smith. Also met Reception Committee; discussed grievances.
October 24	:	Interview with John X. Merriman at Civil Service Club. Left for Kimberley, accompanied by Gandhiji. Deputation of Indians at Wellington.
October 25	:	At De Aar, deputation of Indians. Met Mrs. Cronwright Schreiner (Olive Schreiner). Special train from Kimberley with 200 Indians met Gokhale's train at Modder River. Reception at Beaconsfield by Mayor and others. Reached Kimberley at 5.30 p.m. Received by Mayor and others. Reception in Town Hall, Mayor presiding. Gandhiji addressed gathering.
October 26	:	Visit to the mines. J. McLaren called to state Bloemfontein Indians' grievances. Banquet in City Hall at 8.45 p.m., with Mayor of Beaconsfield in chair; Gandhiji spoke.
October 27	:	Indian Reception at Constantia Hall. In evening, Gokhale and Gandhiji left Kimberley at 6 p.m. Presentation of addresses at Windosorton, Christiana and Bloemhof. Leading Europeans present at all these places.
October 28	:	At Klerksdorp, met by special train from Johannesburg carrying over 200 persons. Reception at Exchange Hall at 6.30 a.m., with Mayor presiding. Statement of grievances by British Indians. Reached Potchefstroom, 8.30 a.m. Reception and addresses at the Town Gardens.
	:	Reached Krugersdorp, 2.00 p.m. Received by Mayor; presentation of addresses at station. Drove to Indian Location, Burghersdorp. Reached Johannesburg, 4.00 p.m. Received by

		Mayor at station. Addresses presented by BIA (read out by Gandhiji), by Johannesburg Hindus, Hamidia Islamic Society, Tamil Benefit Society, Patidar Association, Pietersburg Indians and Cradock Indians.
October 29	:	Reception to Gokhale at Carlton Hotel by Johannesburg European Committee. Speeches by Patrick Duncan, Drummond Chaplin and William Hosken. Gokhale, in reply, explained the object of his mission to South Africa.
October 30	:	Creswell and other M.L.A.'s and Portuguese Consul called on Gokhale.
	:	The Transvaal Leader representative interviewed Gandhiji and Gokhale. Gokhale received Parsee deputation. In afternoon, Gokhale and Gandhiji attended conference at William Hosken's house.
October 31	:	Banquet at Masonic Hall by BIA, with the Mayor presiding. Speeches by Mayor Ellis, William Hosken, Patrick Duncan, J. J. Doke, L. W. Ritch, Gokhale and Gandhiji.
November 1	:	Gokhale entertained by Chinese Association. Interviewed Pathan Deputation, Essop Mia Deputation, Habib Motan Deputation, Merchant's Deputation. Reception by TVL Women's Asociation; address presented by Mrs. Vogl. Indian meeting at Drill Hall.
November 2	:	Gokhale and Gandhiji left for Tolstoy Farm.
November 3	:	Gandhiji wrote to Srinivasa Sastri regarding Gokhale's visit and his proposed departure for India.
November 5	:	Gokhale, with Gandhiji, returned to Johannesburg after two days' rest at Tolstoy Farm. Tea at Drummond Chaplin's ; met Sir Percy Fitzpatrick.
November 6	:	Visited Germiston and Boksburg Locations. Called on Ellis. Left for Natal.
November 7	:	Addresses presented at Newcastle and Dundee. Received people at Ladysmith. Arrived in Maritzburg. Reception in Town Hall; Gandhiji spoke.

November 8	:	Discussed Indians' grievances at meeting in Indian High School. Interview with Licensing Officer. Luncheon at Camden Hotel by Maritzburg Reception Committee; Gandhiji spoke. In afternoon, left by special train for Durban. Arrived in Durban. Received at station by Mayor, Chief Magistrate and others. Procession to Mr. Moosa's house. In evening, Reception at Town Hall, with Mayor presiding. Speeches by Mayor and others. Addresses presented. Gandhiji also spoke.
November 9	:	Merchants' Deputation. Distributed prizes at Childrens'; Sports at Albert Park.
November 10	:	In morning, heard grievances of £3 tax-payers at meeting at Lord's ground. In afternoon, went by special train to Isipingo, returning at 5 p.m. In evening, motored to Phoenix.
November 11	:	Left Phoenix in afternoon and returned to Durban. In evening, banquet in Drill Hall, Sir David Hunter presiding; Gandhiji also spoke.
November 12	:	Visited Sydenham College. Met Chamber of Commerce. Visited Mount Edgecombe; met indentured Indians there. Attended Reception Committee meeting held to thank Parsee Rustomjee. Left for Pretoria.
November 13	:	On the way, addresses presented at Volksrust, Standerton and Heidelburg.
	:	In evening, reached Pretoria. Received at station by Deputy Mayor, M. Chamney and others.
November 14	:	In morning, interview with Ministers—Botha, Smuts and Fischer. In evening, Reception at Town Hall; Gandhiji also spoke.
November 15	:	In morning, motored to Johannesburg to see Wyndham. Lunch with Governor General. In afternoon, left for Lawley.
November 16	:	Governor General sent to Imperial Government confidential minute regarding his talk with Gokhale.
November 17	:	Gokhale and Gandhiji met Sir Thomas Smartt at Chaplin's house. Called on Chairman,

		Hamidia Islamic Society, Chairman, Patidar Association and Mr. Phillips. Left for Lourenco Marques, 8.45 p.m.
November 18	:	Banquet at Lourenco Marques; Gandhiji also spoke. Took steamer for Beira.
November 20	:	Arrived in Beira.
November 21	:	Address presented at Beira.
November 23	:	Left Beira.
November 25	:	Arrived in Mozambique. Address in the city. In afternoon, left Mozambique.
November 26	:	On board ship, Gandhiji promised Gokhale he would not leave for India without arranging for work to be carried on in South Africa in his absence; affairs would probably be left in H.S.L. Polak's hands.
November 27	:	Arrived in Zanzibar. Visited city. Function in Victoria Gardens.
November 28	:	Address presented in city in afternoon. Gokhale, Gandhiji and H. Kallenbach sailed by s. s. president.
November 29	:	In morning, reached Tongaat. In afternoon, parted from Gokhale. Gandhiji and H. Kallenbach boarded *S.S. Trebora,* travelling deck class.
November 30	:	Gandhiji and H. Kallenbach reached Zanzibar.
December 1	:	Reached Dar-es-Salaam. Landed. Gandhiji wore Indian dress.
December 3	:	Address presented in Dar-es-Salaam.
December 6	:	Left Dar-es-Salaam.
December 7	:	Arrived in Mozambique.
December 8	:	Left Mozambique
December 13	:	Gandhiji arrived in Delagoa Bay. Detained before being permitted to land.
	:	Gokhale reached Bombay.
December 14	:	Gandhiji arrived in Johannesburg and went to Lawley. At Bombay, Gokhale addressed public meeting on position and problems of Indians in South Africa.

December 18	:	Gandhiji left for Durban.
December 21	:	Interview with Sir John Hulett in Durban.
December 22	:	The Dayal brothers, coming from India to the Transvaal along with their wives, disallowed landing at Durban by Immigration Officer, Cousins.
December 28	:	Gokhale's resolution demanding total abolition of indenture system passed at Indian National Congress at Bankipore. Writing in Indian Opinion, Gandhiji condemned terrorist's attempt at Delhi on Lord Hardinge's life.
December 30	:	Agjee and Ameappan, both having remarried, and returning from India, reached Durban. Agjee's wife disallowed to land and Ameappan's wife refused admission.

1913

January 2	:	Gandhiji left Durban.
January 3	:	Gokhale Reception Committee, Durban, wired Minister of Interior regarding cases of Agjee and Ameappan.
Before January 4	:	Gajjar, a Cape Indian, visiting Durban, declared a prohibited immigrant. H. S. L. Polak wrote to Secretary to Minister of Interior regarding harassment of the Dayal brothers by Counsins, Natal Immigration Officer; also wrote to *The Natal Mercury* regarding the Dayal brothers and Gajjar. *The Natal Mercury,* in editorial, severely condemned Cousins.
January 4	:	Gandhiji arrived in Johannesburg. Writing in *Indian Opinion,* commended Gokhale's speeches on South African Indian problem at Bombay and at Indian National Congress at Bankipore. In another article, discussed changes effected in layout and content of *Indian Opinion.* Commenced a series of articles on general knowledge about health in Gujarati section of *Indian Opinion.*
January 7	:	A.M. Cachalia wrote to Secretary to Minister of Interior regarding Dayal brothers.

January 8 : Prosecution of Dayal brothers, detained at Volksrust, ordered by Registrar of Asiatics.

Before January 11: Cousins replaced by Harry Smith as Natal Immigration Officer.

January 11 : Contribution of Rs. 2,500 by Nizam of Hyderabad to Passive Resistance funds announced in *Indian Opinion*.

Before January 18: Gandhiji and school shifted from Tolstoy Farm to Phoenix.

January 18 : *Indian Opinion* announced Gandhij's decision to go to India about the middle of the year, if expected Immigration Bill was passed in forthcoming session of Parliament. Gandhiji wrote in Indian Opinion of Government's failure to keep their promise regarding British Indians entitled to residence in TVL or Union and hinted at possibility of a conflagration in the community.

Before January 24: H.S.L. Polak met Chief Immigration Officer, Natal, regarding entry of Agjee and Ameappan's wives.

Before January 25: Split between Botha and Hertzog during Gokhale's visit to South Africa reported in *The Star.*

January 25 : Report in *The Times of Natal* regarding Government's decision to abolish £3 tax on ex-indentured Indians. Gandhiji, in Indian Opinion, welcomed above reported decision. In another article, discussed provision in proposed Financial Relations Bill granting Provincial Councils power to legislate regarding trading licences; called upon Indians to offer vigorous protest.

January 27 : BIA informed by Under-Secretary for Interior that prosecution against the Dayal brothers would be withdrawn and their registration effected.

January 31 : In Union Assemby, T. Schreiner protested against colour discrimination in Arms and Ammunition Bill.

February 1 : BIA wrote to Ministry of Interior asking that Indians coming from India and claiming rights of residence in TVL be issued visiting passes by Immigration Officers at the coast.

February 7 : In Union Assembly, Minister of Finance stated that repeal of £3 tax on Indians was still under consideration . Ministry of Interior informed BIA that all enquiries regarding Indians arriving at ports and claiming rights of entry must be made at the port of entry.

Before February 8: Minor son of M. A. Kotwal, on return to Durban after temporary absence, disallowed landing despite possession of domicile certificate as his father was not in Natal. Had to obtain Supreme Court interdict to avoid deportation. Minor son of Moulvi Abdul Vahed of Cape Town, on arrival aboard the Markgraf, detained at Durban and sent away by same ship, unprotected.

February 8 : Gandhiji, in *Indian Opinion,* criticized "tyrannical powers" vested in immigration officials.

February 11 : In House of Lords, Lord Ampthill asked question regarding outcome of Gokhale's visit to South Africa and moved for Papers. Under-Secretary for Colonies replied the visit was unofficial and he had no Papers to lay before House.

February 13 : BIA again wrote to Ministry of Interior urging that Indians returning from India be granted visiting passes at ports of entry.

February 14 : Gandhiji, in letter to Gokhale, mentioned that, owing to internal troubles in Botha cabinet, the promised legislation would again be postponed; if so, he would not be able to leave for India about the middle of the year. Said ministers were not carrying out their assurances and Immigration Acts were being administered with ever-growing severity.

Feburary 24 : Under-Secretary for Interior informed BIA that arrangements at ports for TVL Indians seeking entry could not be altered.

Feburary 28 : M. A. Goga lost appeal against Licensing Officer's refusal to transfer his trading licence to himself and son.

March 3 : In Union Parliament, Financial Relations Bill, mentioning proposed abolition of £3 tax on ex-indentured Indians, passed second reading.

March 4 : BIA wrote again to Secretary for Interior regarding removal of hardships at ports for TVL Indians already registered or eligible to register.

March 8 : Dawad Mahomed returned to South Africa after tour of Middle East and India.

March 9 : The Johannesburg Indian Literary and Debating Society formed; Gandhiji elected patron.

March 14 : In Cape Supreme Court, Justice Searle rejected Hassan Esop's appeal against deportation of his wife, Bai Miriam, on the ground that she was not Hassan Esop's lawful wife as her marriage had been contracted according to Mahomedan custom.

March 15 : Gandhiji, writing in *Indian Opinion,* explained procedure and evidence required for entry of minors and wives into TVL.

March 20 : A TVL Syrian appealed to High Court that two Stands in Wolhuter Township be registered in his name on ground that Syrians were exempt from laws applying to Indians and Coloured Persons; judgment reserved.

Before March 22: Gandhiji, commenting in *Indian Opinion* on case of Ebrahim Cassim's minor son, Hassan Mia, said that Union Government's insistence on production of birth certificates of minors seeking entry showed that it wanted to create difficulties or to stop entry of children altogether.

March 24 : Wrote to Private Secretary to Minister of Interior asking that out of six names of educated British Indians submitted by Gandhiji for entry for the past year, the two rejected by Registrar of Asiatics be restored, in keeping with terms of Provisional Settlement. Enquired whether proposed Immigration Bill embodying Provisional Settlement would be brought up during current session of Parliament.

March 26 : Tamil Benefit Society meeting held at Johannesburg to consider Justice Searle's judgment in Bai Miriam's case.

Before March 29: Master of Natal Provincial Division of Supreme

		Court, in the case of Bai Janubi, a Mahomedan widow, questioned validity of her marriage for assessing succession duty and demanded that Supreme Court ruling be obtained.
March 29	:	Gandhiji, commenting in Indian Opinion on above case, ascribed this "unexpected calamity" to new interpretation of an old law.
March 30	:	Mass meeting of Indians in Hamidia Islamic Society Hall, Johannesburg, called to consider the Searle judgment, expressed distress and requested Government to introduce remedial legislation recognizing validity of marriages solemnized according to Indian religions.
April 1	:	Financial Relations Act, No. 10 of 1913, came into operation.
April 3	:	Text of new Immigration Bill published in *Union Gazette Extraordinary.*
April 9	:	Gandhiji telegraphed Minister of Interior Bill was open to serious objections from Indian standpoint as it disturbed several existing rights. Wrote to E.F.C. Lane that Searle judgment on Indian marriages had shaken foundation of Indian society in South Africa.
After April 9	:	In wire to BIA expressed disapproval of Immigration Bill.
April 10	:	Forwarded to Minister of Interior copies of resolutions passed at mass meeting of March 30.
April 12	:	Gandhiji detailed in *Indian Opinion* new Bill's failure to fulfil terms of Provisional Settlement of 1911, reminded British Indians of lesson of "finding pleasure in pain" if Government failed to grant relief.
April 14	:	Immigration Restriction Bill read for first time in House of Assembly.
April 15	:	In telegram to Minister of Interior, Gandhiji asked for retention of Natal Immigration Act and protection to wives and minor children of educated Indians; regretted interpretation of reference to passive resistance as threat. Wrote to Secretary for Interior for amending Union

		marriage laws to legalize non-Christian marriages.
April 16	:	Governor-General Gladstone wrote to Government hoping that "ministers are considering whether some small practical concessions can be made without taking legislative action".
Before April 19	:	Kasturba Gandhi decided to join struggle and court arrest.
April 19	:	Gandhiji informed Gokhale of Kasturba's decision. Gokhale sailed for England.
April 26	:	Immigration Restriction Bill read for second time in Assembly.
April 27	:	Gandhiji arrived in Johannesburg from Phoenix, addressed Vrededorp mass meeting, which adopted resolution against Immigration Bill.
After April 27	:	Cabled Chaplin, Merriman, Smartt, Alexander, Schreiner and Ampthill reiterating objections to Immigration Bill, and revival of passive resistance if Government failed to grant relief.
Before April 28	:	At Johannesburg consulted European Committee about Immigration Bill; was interviewed by *The Star*.
April 30	:	Minister of Interior defended in Assembly legislation to control Asiatic influx.
May 3	:	Gandhiji wrote in *Indian Opinion:* "If struggle is revived, the impending third campaign will be the purest, the last and the most brilliant of all."
May 4	:	Sonja Schlesin, Secretary, TIWA, wired Minister of Interior its decision to offer satyagraha on issue of Indian marriages.
May 8	:	Gandhiji opened Hindu temple at Verulam. SSC cabled Governor-General urging that immediate enactment of legislation to remove Indians' legal disabilities was matter of Imperial importance.
May 11	:	Cape British Indian Union meeting protested against Immigration Bill and Searle judgment.
May 14	:	Gandhiji in letter to Chaplin, feared Imperial Government was not informed of full text of Bill.

May 16 : Colonial-born Indians held mass meeting in Johannesburg protesting against Bill.

May 17 : Gandhiji; writing in *Indian Opinion,* asked for total acceptance of British Indians' demands.

May 19 : In letter to Ministry of Interior, declared passive resistance a certainty if Government failed to carry out promise of relief; BIA clarified in letter its demand for lawful recognition of monogamous Indian marriages.

May 24 : Gandhiji wired Chaplin and others stating that official amendments to Bill were inadequate.

May 26 : Bill read for third time in Assembly and passed on to Senate for concurrence. Chaplin wired Gandhiji Government's acceptance of amendment as putting marriage question right.

May 27 : Gandhiji, in cable to Duncan, Schreiner and others, held amendment insufficient as it required registration of marriages, Bill ran counter to spirit of Settlement. Telegraphed Minister of Interior drawing attention to unfulfilled terms of Settlement.

May 28 : Chaplin cabled Gandhiji conveying Smuts' willingness to do all he could for Indians. Immigrants' Restriction Bill, renamed Immigration Regulation Bill, read for first time in Senate.

May 29 : Gandhiji wired Schreiner and Alexander that registration of Indian marriages was superfluous, in absence of any case of undesirable women entering South Africa. Minister of Interior denied prospect of any legislation validating Indian marriages, or having given undertaking that Indians could bring in wives of polygamous marriages. Governor-General Gladstone cabled SSC urging that latter influence Indian Government to dissuade Gandhiji from resuming passive resistance; assured he was doing his best for abolishing £3 tax.

May 30 : Gandhiji telegraphed Minister of Interior, stating that marriage certificates were not in vogue in

		India, that marriage law should be consistent with Provisional Settlement terms. Minister of Interior moved second reading of Bill in Senate.
June 2	:	Gandhiji released statement from Durban that Immigration Bill violated two principal conditions of 1911 Settlement and hoped Senate would retrieve measure. Indian women in Winberg took pledges not to carry passes.
June 5	:	Natal Immigration Law Amendment Bill regarding £3 tax introduced in Assembly.
	:	Immigration Regulation Bill passed second reading in Senate.
After June 5	:	In telegram to Minister of Interior and members of Parliament, Gandhiji urged exemption of men, in addition to women, from payment of £3 tax.
June 7	:	In letter to Gokhale indicated date of his return to India indefinite, if satyagraha was resumed. Writing in Indian Opinion, declared inevitability of passive resistance if grievances were not redressed.
June 9	:	Immigration Regulation Bill read third time in Senate.
Before June 11	:	Gandhiji issued statement from Durban that proposal to exempt women alone from £3 tax betrayed assurance of repeal given to Gokhale.
June 11	:	Immigration Regulation Bill passed.
June 12	:	Colonial-born Indian Association, Durban, adopted resolution protesting against Immigration Bill, decided to advise Indians not to pay tax.
June 13	:	Immigration Regulation Bill finally discussed in Assembly. Gandhiji criticized SSC's statement in Commons on June 11, charged Union Government with deceiving Imperial Government about Immigration Bill.
June 14	:	Called upon Indians, through Indian Opinion, to resist implementation of Immigration Act.
June 16	:	BIA telegraphed Governor-General to withhold sanction to Bill on ground that it deprived Indians of rights hitherto enjoyed.

June 18	:	Lord Ampthill, in letter to London Time , deplored passage of Immigration Bill, hoped British Parliament would have chance to discuss Bill before Royal assent.
June 19	:	William Wedderburn wrote to Gandhiji about serious condition of Gokhale's health, expressed anxiety at latter's decision to return to India for resuming public work.
June 20	:	Gandhiji, in letter to Gokhale explained implications of Bill, expressed preparedness to drop satyagraha if Fischer promised redress of grievances; and wrote of his anxiety to meet Gokhale in India, to sit at his feet and to work under and learn from him.
June 21	:	Cabled Gokhale from Durban, en route to Transvaal, expressing misgiving about success of mission to Minister of Interior.
June 22	:	Gandhiji's second brother, Karsandas Gandhi, died at Rajkot.
June 28	:	Gandhiji wrote to Ministry of Interior expressing readiness for negotiations to avoid passive resistance.
July 1	:	Obtained expert legal opinion regarding Act 22 of 1913 with reference to immigration and Indian marriages.
July 2	:	Had interview with Gorges, Secretary for Interior.
July 5	:	Orange Free State women decided to resist Pass laws.
July 10	:	Polak left for London to assist Gokhale represent South African Indians' case.
July 12	:	Gandhiji, writing to Gokhale, reported Smuts' preoccupation with other problems and working readiness for prolonged struggle; offered him Polak's services in event of settlement.
July 15	:	Regulations under Immigration Regulation Act gazetted.
Before July 17	:	Smuts wrote to Gandhiji to defer discussions till Railway strike resolved.
July 19	:	Gandhiji returned from Rand in view of Smuts' inability to hold talks because of strike situation.

July 21 : Wrote, in letter to J.B. Petit, that voluntary contributions would be accepted; acknowledged receipt of £8720.

July 26 : *Indian Opinion* reported that Gandhiji, "in accordance with Smuts' wish, refrained from taking any action because of the unexpected troubles of the Government"

July 29 : Gandhiji cabled Gokhale from Durban that industrial crisis hampered progress of negotiations about settlement. Reached Johannesburg.

July 30 : Lord Ampthill said in Lords that Immigration Regulation Bill was not in accordance with Provisional Settlement and requested Imperial Government to ask Union Government that Bill be withheld until amended.

August 1 : Immigration Regulation Act came into force.

Before August 2: 34 women in Bloemfontein jailed for not carrying passes.

August 7 : In London, Gokhale met Fischer and discussed questions of £3 tax and Indian marriages. Gandhiji wrote to Jamnadas Gandhi that Kallenbach and Manilal would go with him to India and the press would continue to function.

August 11 : J.B. Petit telegraphically remitted Gandhiji £400 as India's contribution to Passive Resistance Fund.

August 12 : SABIC represented to Under-Secretary of State for India against provisions of Financial Relations Act, 1913, as oppressive to Indian traders.

August 15 : Rev. Joseph J. Doke passed away at Umtali.

Before August 16: Motilal Nehru, President, United Provinces Congress Committee, telegraphed Viceroy that Imperial Government be urged to withhold Royal assent to Immigration Bill.

August 23 : Gandhiji wrote in Indian Opinion on Doke.

August 24 : Wrote from Johannesburg to Private Secretary to Minister of Interior that official interpretation of new Act threatened "existing and acquired rights" of Indians. Spoke at Doke memorial service in Baptist Church, Johannesburg.

August 29	:	Maganlal Gandhi served with summons for employing Sarjoo, an Indian ex-indentured labourer convicted for failure to pay arrears Of £3 tax. Polak left England for South Africa.
September 4	:	Gandhiji left Johannesburg for Phoenix. Maganlal Gandhi cautioned and discharged in Sarjoo's case.
September 10	:	Gandhiji telegraphed Private Secretary to Minister of Interior on question of polygamous marriages; considered resumption of passive resistance imperative, if amendment of law not effected.
September 11	:	Zoroastrian Anjuman, Durban, wrote to Secretary for Interior objecting to regulations under Immigration Act.
September 12	:	Cachalia informed Government of Indians' decision to resume passive resistance.
September 13	:	Gandhiji announced in Indian Opinion that the negotiations had "proved abortive".
September 15	:	Passive resistance revived; pioneer party of passive resisters, twelve men and four women, including Kasturba Gandhi, left Durban for Volksrust by train to cross border. Prominent Transvaal Indian merchants resolved to fight against Gold Law and Townships Act.
September 16	:	Parsee Rustomjee and other passive resisters charged at Volksrust as prohibited immigrants under new Act. Gandhiji wrote to Harilal Gandhi in India to return to South Africa with his wife, ready for imprisonment as passive resister. Kasturba, along with other passive resisters, arrested.
September 20	:	Advised Indians to court arrest by hawking or trading without licences or by declining to produce them when demanded.
September 21	:	Clarified Indian stand, resort to passive resistance, in *The Natal Mercury.*
September 22	:	Passive resisters deported to Natal border, but, on re-crossing border, were re-arrested and taken to Volkstust.

September 23 : Kasturba Gandhi sentenced to three months' imprisonment with hard labour, other passive resisters to one to three months.

September 24 : Gandhiji asserted, in *Indian Opinion,* that £3 tax was crux of the struggle.

September 25 : Left Durban for Johannesburg. At Maritzburg and Ladysmith, received from Indians assurances of support to struggle. At latter place, refused to leave compartment reserved for Europeans as ordered by conductor. Budrea and three other passive resisters, who accompanied Gandhiji, arrested at Volksrust.

September 27 : Gandhiji reached Johannesburg.

September 28 : Wrote to Ministry of Interior about gravity of struggle and appealed for reconsideration. BIA mass meeting at Vrededorp addressed by Gandhiji, Kallenbach and Ritch, resolved to continue struggle till Government redressed grievances.

September 29 : In interview to *The Transvaal Leader,* Gandhiji indicated that struggle would be confined to about a hundred resisters. More instances of passive resistance by crossing the Border and hawking without permits.

September 30 : Gandhiji refuted *The Transvaal Leader* report that influential Indian merchants were opposed to passive resistance. Budree and his companions deported; re-arrested on re-crossing Border, sentenced to three months' hard labour. S. B. Medh, Pragji Desai and Manilal Gandhi arrested for hawking, sentenced to seven days' labour. Johannesburg Indian merchants in letter to *The Transvaal Leader,* denied its allegation.

Before October 1: Zoroastrian Anjuman telegraphed Minister of Interior associating itself with passive resistance movement.

October 1 : Indian mass meeting held under Anjuman Islam, Durban, adopted resolutions supporting movement.

October 2 : Kallenbach and twelve women left Johannesburg for Maritzburg to court arrest.

October 3 : Anjuman Islam held meeting at Grey Street Mosque, Durban; passed resolution protesting against marriage laws. Polak arrived at Johannesburg; interviewed by *Rand Daily Mail.*

Before October 5: Parsee Rustomjee and other prisoners in Maritzburg Gaol resolved to fast until gaol authorities returned sacred thread and gave up compulsory vaccination.

October 5 : Gandhiji addressed, in Johannesburg, meeting of Patidar Association which adopted resolution supporting passive resistance; similar meetings held at Germiston and Pietermaritzburg.

October 6 : Two Mahomedan women from Durban crossed Border at Volksrust, got arrested.

October 7 : S.B. Medh, Pragji Desai and Manilal Gandhi, on completing sentences, hawked in Johannesburg; taken to court in handcuffs, they were charged with non-production of certificates and released on their own recognizances.

October 8 : Bai Fatima Mehtab, her mother, son and attendant left Durban for Volksrust to court arrest.

October 9 : Gandhiji attended Johannesburg Hindus' meeting, which pledged to support passive resistance. Medh, Pragji Desai and Manilal Gandhi sentenced to 10 days' imprisonment with hard labour.

October 10 : Seven passive resisters, on way to Charlestown, detained at Volksrust, but not arrested.

October 13 : P.K. Naidoo, Jiwan Premji and nine others went out hawking in Johannesburg to court arrest.

October 14 : Mrs. Mehtab and party sentenced at Volksrust to three months' imprisonment with hard labour. Naidoo, Bhawani Dayal and Ramnarayan charged with inciting Railway workers to create disturbance, sent to gaol.

Before October 15: Drummond Chaplin at meeting in Durban, criticised £3 tax and Government policy of appointing Immigration Officers on Appeal Board.

October 15 : Gandhiji released statement reiterating Indian demands, need for fresh legislation on question of marriages and £3 tax. Hosken, Chairman, European Committee, wrote to Minister of Interior supporting Indians' demand, offering mediation.

October 16 : Colonial-born Indians at Newcastle passed resolution approving Gandhiji's policy,

: Charges against Medh, Pragji Desai, Manilal Gandhi, Veerasamy Francis and seven others under Asiatic Act were withdrawn on instructions from Pretoria.

October 17 : Gandhiji visited Natal Coalfields near Newcastle, urged indentured Indians to strike untill Government promised repeal of £3 tax. Campaign entered new phase. 78 workers struck work, four arrested and sentenced to two weeks with hard labour. Over 3,000 indentured Indian miners decided to strike. Hindustani Association, Durban, held meeting in support of passive resistance, declared confidence in Gandhiji's leadership. Interviewed by Reuter's Agency in London, Fischer considered modus vivendi possible if Indians abandoned theoretical questions, adopted practical stand.

October 18 : Fifteen passive resisters proceeded from Newcastle to Volksrust to court arrest.

: Polak assured Newcastle Magistrate and mine managers that Indians would not use force.

October 19 : At Durban Gandhiji attended meeting of Indians which criticized his policy and passed vote of no confidence in him. Left Durban for Newcastle. Hamidia Islamic Society meeting at Vrededorp protested against Smuts' reported contemptuous reference to Muslim divorce law.

October 20 : Twenty-two Railway workers at Dannhauser struck work. About 3,000 Indians from Newcastle, Cambrian and Durban Navigation Collieries struck work.

October 21 : Gandhiji left Newcastle for Johannesburg to attend meeting of European Committee. Had private and informal interview with Lord Emmett. Eleven Indian women arrested at Newcastle, who admitted having peacefully advised miners to suspend work, sentenced to three months' hard labour under Vagrancy Act.

Before October 22: At Dannhauser meeting, over 1,000 Indians decided to strike. Committee formed in Durban with Dawad Mahomed as Chairman to collect funds and provisions for strikers.

October 22 : Gandhiji wired Gokhale from Johannesburg that strikers would resume work it Government promised to repeal £3 tax. Told Rand Daily Mail representative six collieries affected, 2,000 miners idle; reprimanded paper for attempt through biased reports to create schism among Indians. Returned to Newcastle, on tour of Hatting Spruit, Elandslaagte, in strike area. 1,500 strikers at Dannhauser decided to walk to Border, court arrest.

Before October 23: Gandhiji, from Newcastle, wired Botha that strike, in protest against £3 tax, would be ended if Government promised repeal. In telegram to Press, said that he was advising miners to court arrest, leaving mines. Manilal Gandhi and four others arrested at Volksrust for hawking.

October 23 : Gandhiji informed Press that movement of strikers leaving mines to court arrest or march to Volksrust was imminent. The Natal Mercury reported 9 coal mines closed down due to strike.

October 24 : Gandhiji wrote to Maganlal Gandhi that he proposed to lead 2,000 men into Transvaal. Six Indians accompanying him to Johannesburg deported; and, on re-entering, re-arrested and sentenced to 3 months' hard labour. Sixteen Newcastle colliery strikers sentenced to two months' hard labour.

Before October 25: Gandhiji cabled G.A. Natesan denying The Times of India report of October 21 about split among Indians concerning passive resistance.

October 25 : Addressed employers of Indian labour at Durban Chamber of Commerce, and in interview to The

Natal Mercury attributed coal mine strike to Government's failure to repeal £3 tax.

October 26 : Gandhiji addressed Indian miners at Hindu Temple, Dundee. Eight hundred more miners joined strike. Germiston Indian Association resolved on passive resistance against Municipality for erecting double fence between Asiatic Bazaar and Native Location. Ladysmith Indians supported strike, formed committee to help families of passive resisters.

October 27 : NIC held meeting, cabled Gokhale supporting movement. Six passive resisters arrested at Volksrust, four sentenced to 3 months' imprisonment. Five Colonial-born Indians including Albert Christopher and Ruben Joseph left Durban for strike area. "Army" of passive resisters informed of march commencing following day.

October 28 : Gandhiji telegraphed Minister of Interior, stressing basic issues, appealing for reconsideration of tax question upon merits. The march from Newcastle began. General Smuts denied at South African Party meeting, he had promised Gokhale repeal of £3 tax.

After October 28: NIC cabled Gokhale regarding Government's denial of promise to repeal £3 tax; Gokhale confirmed definite promise given.

October 29 : Gandhiji with Ballengeich Indian miners left Ingogo in morning for Volksrust. Informed Gokhale that he was marching with strikers to court arrest; requested assistance to get Polak settled in London. Indian strikers refused to accept Government's directive through mine-owners to resume work. NIC charged Government with bad faith in repudiating promise to repeal tax. Pragji Desai sentenced to three months on charge of trespassing on Newcastle mine property.

October 30 : Gandhiji reached Charlestown with 200 men; telegraphed Minister of Interior to enquire into forcible vaccination of women prisoners; wired1

Indian Opinion that about 5,000 Indians affected in the strike area, 4,000 were being led and supported, including 300 women and 600 children; 300 passive resisters were in gaol. 300 marchers led by Thambi Naidoo and 200 by Albert Christopher left Newcastle; some 150 Indians of Ballengeich Colliery arrested.

October 31 : Gandhiji informed Secretary of Justice that if Indians, who had surrendered themselves, were not arrested, they would march into Transvaal. About 200 men and women led by A. D. Pillay left Newcastle on march to Volksrust, another 500 by train.

November 2 : Gandhiji had, under his charge, 1,500 passive resisters stationed at Charlestown.

November 3 : Informed Reuter that he contemplated moving 1,500 men into Transvaal for courting arrest; if not arrested, would proceed to Tolstoy Farm. The Natal Advertiser reported over 2,000 Indians camping there with 500 arrived from Ladysmith.

Before November 4: Gandhiji cabled Gokhale reporting situation regarding march.

November 4 : 1,700 passive resisters started march from Newcastle.

Before November 5: Ladysmith railway men joined strike. 175 Ballengeich strikers, remanded till November 10, discharged because of Government's inability to accommodate them.

November 5 : Gandhiji telephoned General Smuts asking for assurance of repeal of £3 tax, for "march" to be stopped; Smuts refused. Gandhiji reaffirmed to *The Natal Mercury* determination to lead march. 700 Indian passive resisters left Newcastle. London Indians' meeting declared that Indians denied citizenship rights in the Colonies could not share Imperial obligations; expressed admiration for heroism of Mrs. Gandhi, others.

: At Dundee, several Indians sentenced to fine, imprisonment for refusing to work till £3 tax repealed.

Before November 6 : Gandhiji cabled Gokhale reporting strike situation; he would lead "great march" on November 6.

November 6 : Led at 6.30 a.m., "great march" consisting of 2,037 men, 127 women and 57 children, from Charlestown; addressed marchers halfway between Charlestown and Volksrust. At Volksrust border, Police Superintendent and Immigration Officer interviewed Gandhiji and Kallenbach. Marchers broke through Police cordon, crossed border. Gandhiji arrested at 8.30 p.m. at Palmford railway station; marchers continued their journey.

November 7 : Gandhiji appeared in Volksrust court; was released on £50 bail; case remanded till November 14; motored 33 miles, rejoined marchers at Paadekraal en route supplied medicines to old and infirm among passive resisters there. Telegraphed Minister of Interior for permission to continue march with other strikers, else Government should take over responsibility for looking after marchers. Indians of Umhloti Valley Sugar Company struck work.

November 8 : Gandhiji arrived at Standerton; arrested and released on recognizances of £50; case remanded till November 21. Column continued march. Interviewed by Reuter, Gandhiji felt sure government would repeal £3 tax.

November 9 : Arrested at about 3 p.m. at Teakworth near Greylingstaad on Dundee warrant, charged with inducing strike; not allowed to speak to satyagrahis, taken secretly to Balfour for the night. Marchers led by Polak proceeded to Greylingstaad.

November 10 : Gandhiji's request for remand, permission to take marchers to Tolstoy Farm rejected by magistrate, forwarded to Government. Gandhiji took pledge to take one meal a day "till a repeal of the tax was promised,". Column continued march; reached Balfour; 2,000 marchers declared prohibited immigrants, arrested and deported to Natal by special train. Polak, Kallenbach arrested at Charlestown for aiding and abetting prohibited immigrants enter Transvaal; cases remanded till November 13. Passive resisters in Maritzburg Gaol went on three-day fast.

Before November 11: Gandhiji, in a message, praising marchers' courage and sacrifice, appealed to those not courting arrest to forgo a meal a day to provide food for strikers.

November 11 : Gandhiji sentenced by Dundee Magistrate to £60 fine or to nine months' imprisonment with hard labour; preferred latter; exhorted strikers, in message, to continue strike till £3 tax was repealed. Writing to Maganlal Gandhi from Dundee Gaol, gave instructions regarding financial arrangements; was allowed fruit diet. Polak and Kallenbach remanded.

November 12 : 1,500 strikers cleared off Verulam; thousands of indentured Indians struck on plantations from Tongaat to Umgeni.

November 13 : Gandhiji removed to Volksrust Gaol where Kallenbach and Polak were lodged.

November 14 : Made statement before Volksrust Court; convicted on evidence furnished by himself, sentenced to further 3 months.

November 15 : Appeared as witness for Crown against Kallenbach, who was sentenced to 3 months. Passive resisters locked up in barracks on Mount Edgecombe denied food; NIA secured telegraphic permission to feed strikers.

November 16 : In Durban, all Indian labour on railways, sugar refineries, dock and corporation struck work; clash between strikers and police; 16 Indians injured, one succumbed.

November 17 : Gandhiji appeared as witness in case in which Polak was sentenced to 3 months.

November 18 : Gandhiji transferred to Maritzburg Gaol, Kallenbach to Krugersdorp and Polak to Boksburg. 7,000 to 8,000 reported on strike in Durban. SSI expressed to SSC grave concern at India's resentment of harsh treatment to Natal Indians, called for authoritative statement.

November 19	:	Jamnadas Gandhi, four others, crossed Transvaal border from Kimberley.
November 20	:	264 strikers from Harbour, 5 leaders sentenced to 7 days' imprisonment with hard labour. Bombay women, meeting in Servants of India Society Hall, resolved to mobilize sympathy, funds for South Africa Indians.
November 21	:	Sorabji Rustomjee, Christopher arrested. Strike in Maritzburg; Thambi Naidoo arrested.
November 24	:	In Madras, Lord Hardinge made sympathetic pronouncement regarding South Africa Indians.
November 25	:	West, acting Editor of Indian Opinion, arrested at Phoenix, charged with "harbouring indentured people". Two Indians shot dead by police on Beneva Estate.
	:	Strikers arrested at Verulam, other places, sentenced to 7 days' imprisonment.
November 26	:	West appeared before Court, remanded for a week. 94 strikers from Platt's sugar estates sentenced to 7 days' imprisonment.
November 27	:	NIC cabled Gokhale of violent official repression of passive resisters; urged intervention with Indian, Imperial Governments, also telegraphed Minister of Justice, Pretoria, for facilities to inquire into cases of police assault on Indians. Skirmish between strikers and, police at Mount Edgecombe resulted in death of 6 Indians.
November 28	:	Gokhale speaking in Delhi referred to South Africa Indians' desperate plight.
November 30	:	Mass meetings at Durban, Johannesburg, Maritzburg, Newcastle, other towns expressed loyalty to leaders, supported Gokhale's demand for impartial inquiry.
December 1	:	All-India and South Africa League deputation waited on SSI regarding South Africa Indians' grievances.
December 2	:	25 men crossed Transvaal border from Charlestown, sentenced to 3 months with hard labour. BIA Chairman forwarded to Governor-General resolutions of Indian mass meeting.

December 3	:	50 to 60 passive resisters transferred from Maritzburg Gaol to Durban Gaol on hunger strike since November 30 NIA informed. Surendranath Banerjea, A.C. Mazumdar addressed public meeting at Calcutta in support of South Africa Indians.
December 4	:	Durban Gaol superintendent, interviewed by West, denied hunger strike; Chief Magistrate enquiring into matter.
December 6	:	Schlesin, West refused permission to see hunger strikers.
December 10	:	Public meeting in Bombay passed resolutions condemning treatment of Indians in South Africa; Sir Pherozeshah Mehta spoke.
December 11	:	Government appointed Commission with Sir William Solomon as Chairman, Ewald Esselen, J. S. Wylie as members, to inquire into disturbances.
December 14	:	Gandhiji wrote from Bloemfontein Gaol to Miss West at Phoenix.
December 15	:	Public meetings at Johannesburg, Cape Town, Durban, Maritzburg, Kimberley and Potchefstroom protested against composition of Commission.
December 16	:	Lord Willingdon, Governor of Bombay, referred to South Africa question as "in its very essence a highly Imperial question".
Before December 17	:	Gokhale cabled Gandhiji that Rev. C. F. Andrews and W. W. Pearson would visit South Africa to inquire into conditions of Indians. Inquiry into Indian deaths at Hillhead barracks and on Mount Edgecombe estates on November 27 commenced at Verulam.
December 18	:	Gandhiji, Polak and Kallenbach released at Pretoria on Solomon Commission's recommendation. Gandhiji reached Johannesburg in the evening; addressed mass meeting; resolutions not to give evidence before Commission adopted; later, interviewed by The Natal Mercury Commission of inquiry started

session at Pretoria. 31 passive resisters, including five women, sentenced to 3 months for crossing Border.

December 19 : Gandhiji, Polak and Kallenbach left for Durban.

December 20 : Taken in procession to NIA office, Gandhiji announced mass meeting next day for deciding about tendering evidence to Commission. In interview to The Natal Mercury stated that Indian community would boycott Commission unless Government appointed Europeans free from anti-Asiatic bias. Transvaal women passive resisters released from Durban Gaol.

December 21 : Gandhiji appeared at Durban Indians' mass meeting dressed as indentured Indian; announced decision to eat once a day—as mark of "inward mourning" for Indians shot dead during strike. Meeting resolved not to give evidenced before Commission but to renew struggle; recommended inclusion of W. P. Schreiner and Sir James Rose-Innes in Commission, urged release of all passive resisters. Gandhiji later wrote to Minister of Interior forwarding resolutions passed at mass meeting. Received Gokhale's cable not to boycott Commission.

December 22 : Parsee Rustomjee, Chhaganlal Gandhi, Ramdas Gandhi released from Durban Gaol; Kasturba Gandhi, Kashi Gandhi, Santok Gandhi, Solomon Royeppen and others from Maritzburg Gaol. Gandhiji spoke at reception to released passive resisters; later, at Maritzburg mass meeting, exhorted Indians to give up luxuries as mark of mourning.

: Cabled Gokhale about stand in regard to reconstitution of Commission, mass enthusiasm for passive resistance.

After December 22 : Wrote to *The Natal Advertiser* about ill-treatment of passive resisters in gaol.

December 22 : Gandhiji cabled Gokhale, citing instances of anti-Asiatic attitude of Esselen and Wylie, and official repression against passive resistance prisoners.

Gokhale cabled Gandhiji to send Polak to England. Gandhiji and colleagues cabled Ampthill Indian community's resentment against Solomon Commission. In letter to The Natal Mercury, rated the cause higher than South African sympathy.

December 24 : Smuts wrote to Gandhiji declining to appoint more members on Commission.

: Gandhiji cabled Gokhale inability to withdraw struggle; conveyed to Gokhale, Ampthill, assurance of support to it by religious leaders, Press, European Committee.

December 25 : Wired Minister of Interior denying joint letter was ultimatum, and promising to safeguard interests of employers of Indian labour, sought interview.

December 26 : Appealed to Gokhale to urge Viceroy's intervention with Imperial Government for appointing additional member to Commission on behalf of Indians and planters. Gandhiji wrote to Senator Campbell thanking him for his effort to secure repeal of £3 tax. Informed Gokhale that passive resisters' oath did not set January 1 as date for revival of struggle. In another cable, advised Gokhale to hold up remittance of funds as movement was likely to be postponed.

: Indian National Congress at Karachi denounced ill-treatment of South Africa Indians; eulogized Gandhiji's heroic leadership, demanded ban on indenture system and decided to send deputation to England.

Before December 27 : Gandhiji emphasized, in interview to Reuter, Indian loyalty to Union and Imperial Governments, and anxiety to avoid resumption of passive resistance.

December 27 : Assured Gokhale, in cable ; postponement of march till Robertson's arrival in South Africa. Hoped Viceroy or SSI would not impair European sympathy. Informed Maritzburg Indian mass meeting of negotiations, but alerted it for struggle.

December 28 : Gokhale wired Viceroy Gandhiji's promise not to revive march till Robertson's arrival. Viceroy advised Gokhale Robertson leaving on January 1. Gokhale cabled Gandhiji for details of ill-treatment, objections levelled against Commission personnel.

December 29 : Gandhiji cabled Gokhale long statement. Minister of Interior replying to Gandhiji's telegram of December 25, appreciated conciliatory tone of Indian leaders, asked Gandhiji to send in writing points for discussion. Gandhiji pressed Minister of Interior to nominate two additional members on Commission; expressed readiness to advise acceptance of one-man Commission under Solomon with enlarged terms of reference; pleaded for release of prisoners, interview for settlement. Clarified to the Natal Mercury that march would not be resumed on January 1, 1914. Governor-General cabled Colonial Office regarding conciliation move.

December 30 : Gandhiji assured Gokhale that Indians would certainly wait a week or even more till Robertson had chance to look into situation. Criticising the Natal Mercury editorial, reiterated Indian community united in determination to preserve honour through passive resistance.

December 31 : Informed Gokhale of inability to send Polak to England in view of situation. Gokhale released to Press Gandhiji's statement on Solomon Commission and related matters.

1914

January 1 : Gandhiji wrote to Senator Campbell defending movement, denying passive resistance was connected with violence. Sir Benjamin Robertson left Bombay en route for South Africa.

January 2 : C. F. Andrews and W. W. Pearson arrived in Durban. Gandhiji spoke at reception. Cabled Gokhale about Andrews' arrival, effort for nominating impartial European on Commission.

January 3 : In cable to Gokhale, asked for Harilal's return to join passive resistance.

January 4 :	Addressed Indian Hawkers' Association reception in honour of Andrews and Pearson. Gave interview to Reuter.
January 5 :	Hurbatsingh 70-year-old satyagrahi serving 3 months' sentence died of pneumonia in Volksrust Gaol.
January 7 :	Gandhiji, And Andrews, left for Pretoria for interview with Smuts.
Before January 8:	Several Indians killed in police firing at Blackburn Estates.
January 8 :	Gandhiji sought interview with Smuts.
January 9 :	Gandhiji, Andrews arrived in Pretoria; in interview to Pretoria News, assured that passive resisters would not embarrass Government till railway strike was settled.
January 11 :	Benjamin Robertson arrived in Durban.
January 12 :	Mrs. Sheikh Mehtab and her mother, Hanifa Bibi, released from Maritzburg Gaol.
January 13 :	Gandhiji had brief interview with Smuts, who asked him to await Robertson's arrival in Pretoria; Andrews met Governor-General Gladstone.
January 16 :	Gandhiji had interview with Smuts; presented proposals.
January 20 :	Several women satyagrahis released from Durban Central Gaol.
Before January 21:	Gandhiji received written statement from Pretoria Muslims and Hindus repudiating allegation of split on issue of passive resistance.
January 21 :	Gandhiji met Benjamin Robertson; wrote to Ministry of Interior that passive resistance would not be revived or the Commission's work otherwise hampered.
January 22 :	Andrews saw Smuts provisional settlement between Gandhiji and Smuts arrived at, Government accepting principle of consultation with Indians. Gandhiji left Pretoria for Phoenix; passive resistance suspended.
January 23 :	Arrived in Johannesburg; interviewed by *Rand Daily Mail;* cabled Gokhale reporting provisional

		settlement; set up office at 15, Anderson Street, Johannesburg; several passive resisters released from Durban Gaol.
January 25	:	Gandhiji explained implications of settlement at Durban mass meeting which endorsed it. Attended reception to Andrews by Indian goldsmiths in Durban.
January 26	:	Indian Inquiry Commission held first sitting in Durban.
January 28	:	Reuter reported NIC meeting decision to tender evidence before Inquiry Commission. Several Indian Associations cabled Gokhale approval of 'Provisional Settlement'.
January 29	:	Benjamin Robertson testified before Commission.
January 30	:	Gandhiji, Andrews jointly cabled Gokhale that NIC meeting of January 28 had been engineered and was of no significance. Andrews, Manilal Gandhi arrived at Pietermaritzburg.
January 31	:	Indian mass meeting at Maritzburg honoured Andrews, endorsed Gandhi-Smuts agreement.
February 4	:	Robertson visited Phoenix settlement.
February 6	:	Gandhiji was informed of Government's decision to release Natal and Transvaal passive resistance prisoners.
February 7	:	Indian Women's Sabha inaugurated in Durban; Kasturba, Mrs. Polak elected patrons. Inquiry Commission concluded sitting in Natal.
February 8	:	Indian meeting in Stanger supported Gandhi-Smuts agreement.
February 9	:	HIS conveyed to Robertson resolution demanding settlement of marriage question according to Mahomedan religion.
February 12	:	Andrews addressed public meeting on Tagore at City Hall, Cape Town.
February 17	:	Gokhale left for England.
February 20	:	Andrews addressed University students at Cape Town.
February 21	:	Gandhiji spoke at farewell to Andrews, who later sailed for England.

February 22	:	Miss Valliamma Moonsamy Moodaliar, a passive resister, died of illness contracted in Maritzburg Gaol.
February 24	:	Madras League resolved to depute Gokhale, Srinivasa Sastri and others to present South Africa Indians' case in England.
February 26	:	Smuts requested Gandhiji to postpone meeting him till Inquiry Commission's report was out.
February 27	:	Gandhiji wrote to Gokhale from Cape Town expressing desire to return to India in case of settlement, observe compact of silence for a year and learn at Gokhale's feet.
March 2	:	In letter to Harilal, Gandhiji spoke of ailing Kasturba as "hanging between life and death".
March 4	:	Wrote to Robertson about relief to Indians in regard to specific grievances.
March 7	:	Solomon Commission's report submitted to Government.
March 9	:	Lakshmidas Gandhi passed away at Porbundar.
March 11	:	Gandhiji wrote to Chhaganlal Gandhi how to handle family matters in case of his death. Speaking in the Senate, Smuts observed that Gandhiji was allowed to function in South Africa as he did, "because he never advocated methods of violence to overthrow the State".
March 13	:	In letter to Andrews, Gandhiji wrote : "Mrs. Gandhi was near death's door last week. I have therefore done hardly anything else save nursing her during the last 10 days."
March 16	:	Bombay Committee for South Africa cabled Gandhiji for views on Reuter's forecast about Commission's recommendations, requested him not to commit himself before consulting Committee.
March 17	:	Commission's report presented to Parliament. Robertson left Cape Town for Delagoa Bay en route to India. Viceroy addressed Imperial Legislative Council on subject of Inquiry Commission.

March 19 : Bombay Committee for South Africa expressed satisfaction over Commission's recommendations, hoped passive resistance would not be revived.

March 22 : Transvaal Muslim meeting condemned Solomon Commission's recommendations on question of Muslim marriages ; HIS cabled SSI, others, recommendations violated religion.

March 23 : Smuts announced in Assembly that Government was considering Commission's report and introducing necessary legislation that session.

March 24 : Union Government Gazette published Proclamation requiring publication of banns for Mahommedan and Hebrew marriages.

March 25 : Cape Indians held reception for Kasturba Gandhi, Imam Abdul Kadir Bawazeer, at Hindu Sabha; Gandhiji was presented with set of Cape Town Statutes, also contributions to passive resistance fund. Gandhiji analysed in Indian Opinion recommendations of the Commission's report.

March 26 : Accompanied by Kasturba and Imam Bawazeer, left Cape Town for Phoenix.

March 30 : Arrived at Phoenix. Mr. and Mrs. Polak given farewell by Durban Indian Women's Association.

April 1 : In letter to Gokhale, Gandhiji expressed doubt about Kasturba's survival. Andrews left England for Marseilles en route to India.

April 8 : Gandhiji urged Ministry of Interior to stop deductions for £3 tax from indentured labourers' wages, in view of Commission's recommendations.

April 22 : Telegraphed Ministry to order suspension of forcible tax collections. Smuts replied stating that suspension of prosecutions for tax recommended to Minister of Justice.

Before May 6 : Urged Ministry not to demand photos from Indian women seeking entry to the Transvaal, but accept local proof.

May 6 : Wrote to Gokhale asking whether he and

		Kasturba should meet him in London en route to India, in case of final settlement.
May 16	:	Gladstone forwarded SSC text of Indians' Relief Bill.
May 19	:	Gandhiji inquired of Ministry date of introduction of Bill.
May 20	:	Ministry informed Gandhiji interview with Smuts possible for discussing Bill.
May 22	:	Gandhiji left Phoenix for Cape Town to meet Smuts.
May 23	:	Interviewed by The Transvaal Leader at Johannesburg.
May 27	:	Met Secretary of Interior, received copy of draft Bill.
May 28	:	Indians' Relief Bill published; Polak, interviewed by Reuter at Johannesburg, mentioned Gandhiji's cable that Bill appeared satisfactory.
May 29	:	Polak wrote to *The Star* anticipating end of struggle if administrative measures taken to implement Bill.
June 1	:	Smuts notified Assembly of introduction of Bill next day.
June 2	:	Ficksburg Indian community wired Gandhiji demanding access to Free State.
June 5	:	Gandhiji wrote to Gokhale that he would leave for India by mid-July in event of satisfactory settlement and termination of struggle.
June 8	:	Bill read second time. Anjuman Islam wired Gandhiji to press for acceptance of thumb-prints for identification.
June 9	:	Gandhiji raised with Gorges question of examination by immigration authorities of applicants seeking entry into Natal.
June 11	:	Randeree wired Gandhiji that Bill vested in Government authority to declare 74,000 indentured Indians prohibited immigrants. Gandhiji sought from Gorges reassurance as to interpretation of Bill.
June 15	:	Rustomjee wired Gandhiji for clarification of position of indentured Indians under Bill.

June 17	:	Bill read third time, referred to Senate. In India, Lokamanya Tilak released after 6 years' exile in Burma.
June 18	:	First reading of Bill in Senate.
June 19	:	Second reading of Bill in Senate.
June 20	:	Gandhiji wrote to Campbell denying Indian of position to Bill, refused to believe Bill had effect of making Indians prohibited immigrants. Rustomjee drew Gandhiji's attention to Mercury's interpretation of Bill as adverse to indentured Indians.
June 21	:	Sir David Hunter passed away at Edinburgh.
June 22	:	Gorges informed Gandhiji that Government had no intention to apply Bill adversely to indentured Indians.
After June 22	:	Gandhiji, in open letter, asserted he would fight any injustice from Bill.
June 24	:	Gorges invited Gandhiji for discussions.
June 26	:	Relief Bill read third time in Senate.
June 27	:	Gandhiji had 2-hour interview with Smuts at Cape Town. Addressed European meeting held to felicitate him on passage of Bill.
June 30	:	Wrote to Gorges that "passing of Indians' Relief Bill . . . finally closed the passive resistance struggle which commenced in September of 1906".
July 1	:	Accompanied by Kallenbach and Kasturba, left Cape for Phoenix; broke journey at Kimberley. Relief Act received Governor-General's assent; latter cabled Colonial Office that agreement had been reached on "outstanding administrative points". New Zealand introduced Bill imposing language test to obstruct Asiatic entry.
July 5	:	Gandhiji spoke at Durban reception; stated at farewell banquet that Relief Act was act of justice, urgently needed in Imperial interest.
July 8	:	Was presented with addresses at farewell meeting in Town Hall, Durban.
July 9	:	Gandhiji, Kasturba honoured by Gujaratis, Dheds; addressed sports' meet.

July 10	:	Gandhiji Addressed farewell gathering at Asiatic Location, Pretoria.
July 11	:	Took leave of Phoenix Settlement.
July 12	:	Addressed farewell meeting at Verulam; left for Johannesburg.
July 13	:	Arrived at Johannesburg in evening; taken in procession, addressed mass meeting at Gaiety Theatre.
July 14	:	Given farewell banquet at Masonic Hall, Johannesburg; C.K.T. Naidoo presented him four sons for national service. Gandhiji met European Committee, discussed Provisional Settlement. Interviewed by *The Transvaal Leader.* Section of NIC, HIS protested to *Mercury* that "Gandhi's actions not satisfactory. Relief Bill no settlement".
Before July 15	:	Gandhiji addressed valedictory letter to South Africa Indians.
July 15	:	Paid tributes to Valliamma, Nagappen, passive resisters at memorial unveiling ceremony at Bloemfontein Cemetery. Addressed meetings of TIWA, of Tamils and Muslims.
July 16	:	Arrived at Pretoria at 8 a.m.; spoke at Indian Location; left for Cape Town.
July 17	:	Reached Vereeniging.
July 18	:	Arrived at Cape town; taken in procession from Monument to Docks, received addresses, made farewell speech; interviewed by the Cape Argus. Released valedictory letter to South African Indians; left for England on board s.s. Kinfauns Castle.
July 20	:	Gandhiji's farewell letter published in the Press.
July 22	:	*Indian Opinion* announced plan to issue 'Golden Number' to commemorate struggle.
July 24	:	*Gazette* published regulations regarding registration of marriages under Indians' Relief Act.
July 28	:	Further regulations under Immigration Act gazetted.
August 2	:	Germany violated Belgian neutrality.

August 3	: Phoenix Party for India led by Maganlal Gandhi given send-off at Durban.
August 4	: World War I broke out; Gandhiji received news in English channel; reached London.
August 5	: In India, Viceroy issued war proclamation.
August 7	: In letter to Chhaganlal Gandhi, Gandhiji complained of being ill with 'old leg pain'.
August 8	: Gandhiji given reception at Hotel Cecil, London, by English and Indian friends; Jinnah, Lala Lajpat Rai, Sarojini Naidu were among those present.
August 10	: NIC, Anjuman Islam protested against Government's demand for photographs for identification.
August 13	: Circular signed by Gandhi, Kasturba, Sarojini Naidu affirming resolve to tender unconditional service to Empire, issued for signature by supporters.
August 14	: Gandhiji offered to raise Indian Volunteer Corps for ambulance work.
After August 14:	Indian Volunteer Committee set up with Gandhiji as chairman.
August 24	: Gandhiji inquired of India Office if Kallenbach could join Corps.
Before August 26:	Started attending classes for nursing wounded soldiers.
September 3	: Appeared for First-Aid examination.
September 18	: Met Gokhale in London.
September 22	: Issued general circular appealing for volunteers.
October 1	: Presided over Voluntary Aid Corps meeting, attended among others by the Aga Khan, Kasturba, Sarojini Naidu and Ameer Ali.
October 3	: Indian Ambulance Corps camped at Eastcote. Gandhiji served members "... most remarkable lunch consisting of assorted fruits of superfine quality and nuts of different kinds".
October 6	: Gokhale returned to London after rest-cure at Vichy.
October 13	: In letter to Col. Baker, Gandhiji regretted appointment of Corporals without consulting

		Indian Committee; had motion on like lines passed at meeting.
October 14	:	Forwarded resolution to Col. Baker.
October 23	:	Meeting of Ambulance Corps held.
October 25	:	Gandhiji wrote to Maganlal Gandhi: "I have had to start a satyagraha against India Office." Ill in bed, advised rest.
October 31	:	Col. Baker conceded principle of consultation with Indian Committee. Gandhiji wrote: "The satyagraha is over; we got what we wanted."
November 3	:	Got up first time after illness; started short walks.
November 4	:	Appealed through Press for volunteers for ambulance work. Phoenix Party arrived at Santiniketan from Kangri Gurukul.
November 9	:	Gandhiji's associate and passive resister, Gabriel Isaac, passed away.
Before November 11	:	Gandhiji spent, along with Corps, weekend in camp at Eastcote. *Indian Opinion* reported Gandhiji's name included among nominees to presidentship of Indian National Congress.
November 12	:	Gandhiji received letter from W.W. Pearson regarding Phoenix Party at Santiniketan.
November 13	:	Gokhale arrived in Bombay. Ambulance Corps reported doing nursing work at Metlay Hospital near Southampton.
November 26	:	Gandhiji took ill again; wrote to Gokhale : "I do not want to live on any terms. . . ."
December 1	:	Golden Number of *Indian Opinion* published.
December 4	:	Gandhiji still ill, in bed.
December 18	:	Gave interview to Reuter; given farewell party at Westminster Palace Hotel on eve of departure for India.
December 19	:	Sailed for India, with Kasturba; started learning Bengali on board ship.
December 28-30	:	Indian National Congress in session at Madras.

Chapter Three

Understanding India

1915

January 9	:	Gandhiji and Kasturba landed at Apollo Bunder, Bombay. In interview to The Bombay Chronicle and The Times of India, Gandhiji said he would follow Gokhale's advice and pass some time in India observing and studying.
January 11	:	Reception at Ghatkopar, Bombay.
January 12	:	Public reception at Mount Petit, Bombay, Sir Pherozeshah Mehta presiding.
January 13	:	Welcome by Bombay National Union at Hirabag. B.G. Tilak and Joseph Baptista attended.
January 14	:	Gandhiji entertained by Bombay branch of Servants of India Society. Met Governor of Bombay. Garden party by Gurjar Sabha, Bombay, M.A. Jinnah presided.
January 15	:	Gandhiji left Bombay for visits to Rajkot, Porbunder and other places in Saurashtra.
January 17	:	Rajkot citizens' address. Dewan of Rajkot presided.
January 20	:	Reception by Modh community of Rajkot.
January 22	:	At Darbargarh.
January 25	:	At Porbunder.
January 26	:	In letter, Gandhiji thanked Major Hancock, Administrator of Porbunder, for help during

		satyagraha struggle in South Africa.
January 27	:	Visit to Rasashala Aushadhashram at Gondal.
January	:	Rabindranath Tagore wrote to Gandhiji thanking him for sending Phoenix boys to stay at Shantiniketan.
February 2	:	Gandhiji given reception by citizens of Ahmedabad.
February 4	:	Arrived in Bombay from Ahmedabad.
February 7	:	Speech at Mission School, Bombay.
February 8	:	Arrived in Poona. Held discussions about joining Servants of India Society.
	:	Wrote to Mahatma Munshiram thanking him for hospitality to Phoenix party at Gurukul.
February 11	:	Reception by Deccan Sabha, Poona.
February 12	:	Party by Sarvajanik Sabha, Poona.
February 13	:	Visited Karve's Anath-Balikashram, Fergusson College and Anandashram at Poona. Public meeting at Kirloskar Theatre.
February 14	:	Presided at prize distribution function at Sanatan Dharma Nitishikshan Pravartak Samiti in Bombay.
February 15	:	Spoke at Kapol Hostel, Bombay. Left for Shantiniketan.
February 17	:	Reached Bolpur. Met C. F. Andrews. Was accorded reception in Indian style. Tagore was away.
February 19	:	Gopal Krishna Gokhale passed away at Poona.
February 20	:	Gandhiji spoke at condolence meeting for Gokhale at Shantiniketan. In telegram to Transvaal British Indian Association, suggested universal mourning. Left for Poona.
February 21	:	Lahore Conspiracy unearthed.
February 23	:	Gandhiji wrote letter to Chief Traffic Manager, East Indian Railway, regarding inconveniences during travel.
March 3	:	At Poona meeting to mourn death of Gokhale, Governor of Bombay presiding, Gandhiji moved main resolution. Left for Bombay.
March 4	:	In letter to Maganlal Gandhi, expressed desire to establish an institution at Ahmedabad.

March 5	:	Reached Shantiniketan and met Rabindranath Tagore.
March 13	:	Reception on grounds of Maharaja of Cassimbazar's palace in Calcutta. Harilal Gandhi took final decision to separate.
March 14	:	Gandhiji left Calcutta with Ramdas and Chhaganlal for Rangoon by *S.S. Lanka* to meet Dr. Pranjivan Mehta.
March 17	:	Arrived in Rangoon.
March 18	:	Defence of India Act passed.
March 26	:	Gandhiji left Rangoon for Calcutta by ship.
March 27	:	Traffic Manager, E. I. Railway, replied to Gandhiji's letter of February 23, agreeing to refund excess fare.
March 31	:	Gandhiji advised youth against anarchical crimes at students' meeting at College Square, Calcutta. P. C. Lyons presided.
April 2	:	Had talks with Rabindranath Tagore, C.F. Andrews and teachers at Shantiniketan.
April 5	:	Reached Hardwar from Shantiniketan. Kumbha Fair in progress.
April 6	:	Met Mahatma Munshiram (Swami Shraddhanand) at Gurukul, near Hardwar.
April 7	:	Went to Rishikesh, walked to Lakshman Jhula and visited Swargashram.
April 8	:	Brahmacharis of Gurukul Kangri presented welcome address.
April 9	:	Gandhiji took vow to take only five articles in diet every day.
April 12	:	Arrived in Delhi with Kasturba and others.
April 14	:	Visited Mathura and Vrindavan. Entrained for Madras.
April 17	:	Reached Madras.
April 20	:	Addressed members of Gokhale Club at Madras.
April 21	:	Reception by Indian South African League, Madras. Sir Subramania Aiyar presided.
April 22	:	Gandhiji outlined his future programme of work in India in interview to *The Madras Mail*.

April 23	:	Spoke at Madras Mahajan Sabha meeting and Madras Provincial Congress Committee "At Home". Interview to *Associated Press of India,* explaining how his work in South Africa would be continued.
April 24	:	Muslim League, Madras, was "At Home" to Gandhiji and Kasturba at Lawley Hall.
	:	Gandhiji spoke at Madras Law Dinner.
April 25	:	Spoke at meeting of Social Service League, Madras, at Ranade Hall. Reception by Arya Vaishya Mahasabha.
April 26	:	Reception by Indian Christians at Madras. Gandhiji recalled help by missionaries in South Africa.
April 27	:	Reception by Madras students at Y.M.C.A., V. S. Srinivasa Sastri presiding.
April 29	:	Gandhiji spoke at Lakshmi Memorial Arya Pathshala, Madras. Met Gujarati community of Madras at residence of Lord Govinddas.
April 30	:	Reached Tranquebar from Mayavaram. Reception by South Indian Depressed Classes Society.
May 1	:	Gandhiji spoke on untouchability and swadeshi at Victoria Town Hall, Mayavaram.
May 5-6	:	Attended Madras Provincial Conference session at Nellore.
May 7	:	Spoke on passive resistance in South Africa and thanked G.A. Natesan at meeting of Indian South African League at Madras. League passed resolution dissolving itself and placing balance of money at Gandhiji's disposal.
May 8	:	Gandhiji reached Bangalore. Unveiled portrait of Gokhale at Government High School. Civic reception at Lal Bagh.
May 11	:	Gandhiji returned to Ahmedabad. Drew up estimate of expenditure of Ashram at Ahmedabad.
Before May 20	:	Devised vows and rules for Ashram at Kochrab.
May 20	:	Satyagraha Ashram inaugurated at Kochrab near Ahmedabad.

May 23	:	The Phoenix party (boys and teachers with Maganlal Gandhi) arrived in Ahmedabad from Gurukul Kangri.
June 1	:	Gandhiji fasted at Ahmedabad for a day for 'falsehood among the boys'.
June 3	:	Award of Kaiser-i-Hind medal to Gandhiji for services to British Empire announced in King's birthday honours.
June 16	:	In letter to J. B. Petit, Secretary, South African Indian Fund, Gandhiji gave income and expense account of satyagraha campaign in South Africa up to January 31, 1915.
June 26	:	Received Kaiser-i-Hind medal in Poona.
July 11	:	Attended 15th Bombay Provincial Conference held in Poona. Had two interviews with Lokamanya Tilak.
July	:	Government of India Act, 1915 passed.
September 20	:	Gandhiji received C. F. Andrews and W. W. Pearson in Bombay and left with them for Ahmedabad.
September 23	:	C.F. Andrews and W. W. Pearson sailed for Fiji Islands. In letter to V. S. Srinivasa Sastri, Gandhiji wrote that he might have to live apart from Kasturba in Dhed quarters as a result of admitting an untouchable family in Satyagraha Ashram.
September 26	:	Dudabhai, a Dhed, and his wife joined Satyagraha Ashram. Gandhiji wrote to A. H. West that *Indian Opinion* should be kept up at any cost.
September 30	:	Attended in Bombay meeting of Committee for South African Indian Fund. Proposal for Valliamma Hall was discussed.
October 15	:	In a despatch, Lord Hardinge urged total abolition of indenture system.
October 28	:	Gandhiji spoke on indenture system at Empire Theatre, Bombay. Sir Ibrahim Rahimtullah presided.
November 5	:	Sir Pherozeshah Mehta passed away at Bombay. Gandhiji wrote to A. H. West that proposal for Valliamma Hall be dropped.

November 15 : Moved condolence resolution on death of Sir Pherozeshah Mehta at meeting at Premabhai Hall, Ahmedabad. Sir Chinubhai presided.

November 21 : Gandhiji presided over birth anniversary celebrations of Srimad Rajchandra at Ahmedabad.

November 28 : Spoke at Ahmedabad function held to honour N.C. Mehta for success in I.C.S. examination.

December 1 : Arrived with Ba at Viramgam from Ahmedabad on way to Rajkot.

December 4 : Reached Gondal from Rajkot.

December 8 : Replied to citizens' address at Bhavnagar. Diwan presided. Address from Modh community of Bhavnagar.

December 12 : Gandhiji reached Bagasra via Hadala from Amreli. Assured help to people to abolish customs barrier at Viramgam.

December 24 : Attended session of Industrial Conference at Bombay, Sir Dorab Tata presiding, and supported resolution thanking Viceroy for recommending abolition of indenture system.

December 27-29: Session of Indian National Congress at Bombay under presidentship of S. P. Sinha. Gandhiji moved resolution on 'India and the Colonies'. Congress instructed A.I.C.C. to confer with Muslim League Executive and frame scheme of self-government. Congress constitution amended to allow representatives of political bodies of 2 years' standing. Gandhiji, not eligible for election to Subjects Committee, was nominated by the President.

December 30 : All-India Muslim League met in Bombay under chairmanship of Mazhar-ul-Haq.

1916

January 1 : Gandhiji was presented welcome address at Salej, native place of Pragji Desai.

January 2 : Gandhiji presided over annual celebrations of Arya Samaj at Surat and declared open a temple.

January 3 : Spoke at opening of Jain Students' Library,

		Patidar Youth Association, and Arya Samaj function at Surat. Attended receptions by District Bar Association and Saiyadpura Mohammedan Association and Islamia Library.
January 4	:	Visited Kathor, native place of Dawad Mahomed (President, Natal Indian Congress) in Surat.
January 5	:	Reception by people of Navsari at Seervai Park. Gandhiji extolled services of Koli Fakira and Parsi Rustomjee in South Africa.
January 13	:	In letter to V. S. Srinivasa Sastri, expressed his differences with methods of Servants of India Society.
January 16	:	Appointment of Lord Chelmsford as Viceroy of India announced.
January 17	:	Gandhiji was presented welcome address by Janahitartha Karyalaya at Bavla in Ahmedabad district.
February 4	:	Lord Hardinge, Viceroy of India, laid foundation-stone of Benares Hindu University.
February 5	:	Gandhiji attended anniversary celebrations of Nagari Pracharini Sabha, Kashi and spoke on value of Hindi.
February 6	:	Spoke at Benares University Week meeting under presidentship of Maharaja of Darbhanga. Princes and Mrs. Besant left in protest. Meeting ended abruptly.
February 7	:	In letter to Maharaja of Darbhanga, explained his remarks about Viceroy.
February 9	:	Arrived in Bombay. Interview to Associated Press of India on Benares incident.
February 10	:	Writing in New India on Gandhiji's interview on the Benares incident, Mrs. Annie Besant denied she had suggested to princes to leave and justified her interruptions.
February 14	:	Gandhiji read a paper on swadeshi at Missionary Conference, Madras.
February 16	:	Explained aims of Satyagraha Ashram at Y.M.C.A., Madras. Addressed annual meeting of Social Service League, Madras. *Young India* commented on Benares University incident.

February 17	:	*The Hindu*, Madras, published Gandhiji's letter on Mrs. Besant's denial about Benares University incident. Gandhiji presided over debate at Anderson Hall, Madras.
February 19	:	Reached Poona on invitation from Deccan Sabha and spoke at meeting on death anniversary of G.K. Gokhale at Kirloskar Theatre.
February 23	:	Returned to Ahmedabad. Presided over public lecture delivered by D.K. Karve, founder of Indian Women's University.
February 25	:	In article published in *The Leader*, demanded immediate stoppage of system of indentured labour.
Feburary 26	:	Public reception in Hyderabad (Sind).
February 27	:	Unveiled portrait of G. K. Gokhale in Holmstead Hall, Hyderabad (Sind).
February 28	:	Visited Narishala, Navalrai Hiranand Academy, Nava Vidyalaya High School and Kundanmal Girls' School. Met Gujarati and Deccani residents of Hyderabad in Hirabag. Spoke on vaccination in Holmstead Hall, Hyderabad (Sind).
February 29	:	Welcome by Citizens' Association, Karachi; Gandhiji unveiled portrait of G. K. Gokhale at Khalihdina Hall; address from Gujarati Hindus.
March 2	:	Gandhiji spoke at Karachi Bandhu Mandal reception; gave interview to Parsi Samsar on public life in Sind.
March 4	:	Bonar Law (Colonial Secretary) in despatch to Acting Governor of Fiji agreed to appointment of an Inter-Departmental Committee and continuance of indenture system for another five years.
March 20	:	In Imperial Legislative Council, Madan Mohan Malaviya moved resolution urging abolition of system of Indian indentured labour. Accepting the resolution, Viceroy announced that both Secretary of State and Government had decided on its eventual abolition. Gandhiji spoke at Gurukul anniversary near Hardwar.

March 30	:	Wrote to J. B. Petit regarding details of satyagraha campaign expenses.
April 4	:	Lord Chelmsford, new Viceroy, arrived in Bombay. Demonstrations held. Lord Hardinge left India.
April 19	:	Gandhiji nominated life-member of Gujarat Vernacular Society.
April 21-23	:	Discussions held at A.I.C.C. meeting at Allahabad regarding scheme of self-government for India.
April 23	:	Lokamanya Tilak founded first Home Rule League with headquarters at Poona.
April 29-May 1	:	Sessions of Bombay Provincial Conference at Belgaum. Gandhiji supported resolution on compromise among political parties in the country following amendment of Article XX of Congress constitution in 1915.
April 30	:	Spoke at Belgaum on "The Depressed Classes".
May 7	:	Case against Lokamanya Tilak opened in Poona Magistrate's Court.
May 13	:	Gandhiji sent wheat-powder (as substitute for tea) to students of Bhavnagar Jain Boarding House.
May 28	:	Madras Government demanded security under Press Act from Annie Besant as printer of New India.
June 4	:	Gandhiji spoke on untouchability at Conference of Friendly Associations of Communities, Ahmedabad.
June 5	:	Spoke on Hindu caste system on second day of the Conference.
After June 7	:	Wrote to Vinoba Bhave's father praising the young man's asçeticism.
June 12	:	Annie Besant founded Auxiliary Home Rule League in London.
June 24	:	Gandhiji moved protest resolution against Press Act at Bombay citizens' meeting.
Before July 26	:	Wrote pamphlet in Gujarati on hardships of railway passengers in India.

July 27	:	Explained secret of satyagraha in South Africa at post-prayer meeting at Kochrab Ashram.
August 12	:	Lokamanya Tilak ordered to enter into bond for good behaviour for one year; security given.
September 21	:	Annie Besant founded Home Rule League in Madras.
October 21	:	At Bombay Provincial Conference held at Ahmedabad, Gandhiji proposed election of M.A. Jinnah as President.
October 22	:	At Bombay Provincial Conference, moved resolution protesting against working of Defence of India Act and Government order prohibiting Annie Besant from entering Bombay Presidency.
October 23	:	At Bombay Provincial Conference, moved resolutions urging abolition of indenture system and removal of custom cordon at Viramgam railway station and at other places on Kathiawar frontier.
November 1	:	Annie Besant prohibited from entering Central Provinces.
November 9	:	Gandhiji spoke at Wadhwan (Saurashtra) on birth anniversary of Srimad Rajchandra. Bombay High Court delivered judgment in favour of Lokamanya Tilak in security case.
November 17	:	All-India Congress Committee and Muslim-League held joint conference at Calcutta.
December 12	:	Gandhiji wrote to A. H. West regarding Passive Resistance Fund and Indian Opinion.
December 22	:	Spoke on "Does economic progress clash with real progress?" at Muir Central College Economic Society, Allahabad, Pandit Madan Mohan Malaviya presiding.
December 23	:	Spoke on modern system of education at Allahabad public meeting, Pandit Malaviya presiding.
December 26-30	:	Lucknow session of Indian National Congress under presidentship of Ambika Charan Majumdar. Congress-League Scheme of Reforms adopted; reunion of two wings of the Congress;

Tilak joined after 1907 Surat split; Gandhiji attended and moved resolutions on indentured labour and Defence of India Act. Mrs. Besant, Dr. Rash Bihari Ghose, Surendranath Bannerjea, Mazhar-ul-Haq, M. A. Jinnah, H. S. L. Polak and Lt.-Governor of U. P. attended. Resolutions dealing inter alia with India's loyalty, Arms Act, Volunteering and Commissions in Army, Press Act, Indentured Labour, Indians in Colonies Ryots and Planters in North Bihar passed.

December 27 : New India published Lionel Curtis's letter to "Round Table", London.

December 29 : Gandhiji presided over All-India Common Script and Common Language Conference at Lucknow.

December 31 : At Muslim League session, report of Reforms Committee appointed at Bombay in 1915 was presented. M.A. Jinnah's resolution protesting against treatment of Indians in Colonies was adopted. Gandhiji attended session and spoke on Hindu-Muslim amity.

Chapter Four

Initiation in Freedom Struggle

1917

January 2 : Gandhiji returned to Ahmedabad from Lucknow after Congress session.

Before January 14: Explained, in statement, how Lionel Curtis's letter to Secretary of "Round Table" was discovered.

January 17 : In letter to Narandas Gandhi, conveyed his resolution to set up a national school.

After January 18: Drew up prospectus of the school.

February 4 : Presided over anti-indenture meeting at Ahmedabad. C. F. Andrews and H. S. L. Polak also spoke.

February 7 : While opening session of Imperial Legislative Council, Viceroy explained his refusal to allow Pandit Malaviya's notice to move Bill to abolish indentured emigration entirely.

After February 7: In statement, Gandhiji thanked Viceroy for his assurance on indentured labour.

February 9 : At Bombay public meeting held at Excelsior Theatre under presidentship of Sir Jamsetji Jeejibhoy, spoke in support of resolution demanding immediate abolition of indenture system.

February 11 : Spoke at anti-indenture meeting held under auspices of Home Rule League, Bombay.

February 19 : Arrived in Godhra and presided over public meeting on anniversary of Gokhale's death.

February 26 : At Surat meeting, urged stoppage of recruitment of indentured labour.

March 2 : Spoke at Home Rule League headquarters, Karachi, on passive resistance and austerity. Visited Hardevi Bai Girls' School and met Cutchhi and Gujarati communities at Parsi Theatre. At public meeting, told people to join Defence Forces in "overwhelming numbers". Sir S. P. Sinha presided. At public meeting in Karachi, Gandhiji insisted on abolition of indenture system by May 31, 1917.

March 6 : Reached Calcutta at Maharaja of Cassimbazar's invitation. Declared at public meeting in Town Hall that India could not tolerate indentured emigration "a minute longer than the 31st May".

March 12 : Governor-General-in-Council's decision prohibiting labour emigration from India under Defence of India Act gazetted.

April 8 : Gandhiji attended A.I.C.C. meeting at Calcutta which decided to send eight-member deputation to England for Congress work.

April 10 : With Rajkumar Shukla reached Patna on way to Champaran. Stayed with Mazhar-ul-Haq. Welcomed by J. B. Kripalani and others on arrival at Muzaffarpur, and spent night at students' hostel.

April 11 : Met and explained mission to James Wilson, Secretary, Bihar Planters' Association. In evening, met vakils of Muzaffarpur. In a rejoinder to Ramsay MacDonald regarding report of Public Services Commission, stated, Gokhale would have drawn up "a minority report in conjunction with Mr. Abdul Rahim".

April 12 : Wrote letter seeking interview with L. F. Morshead, Commissioner of Tirhut Division and co-operation of local administration in his mission.

April 13 : Met L. F. Morshead at Muzaffarpur. Later, sent

		him letter restating scope of mission and enclosing statement of local leaders.
April 15	:	In letter to Maganlal Gandhi, described situation in Champaran to be "worse than in Fiji and Natal". Arrived in Motihari.
April 16	:	Left for Jassauli in Champaran; served with notice to leave district by first available train. Returned to Motihari. Conveyed decision to disobey the order in letter to W. B. Heycock, District Magistrate. Conveyed decision to P. S. to Viceroy to return Kaiser-i-Hind medal.
April 18	:	Appeared in District Magistrate's Court, Motihari, and read out statement explaining disobedience of order. Case postponed till April 21.
April 19	:	Executive Committee of Bihar Provincial Association resolved to send protest to Viceroy and Lt.-Governor regarding order against Gandhiji.
April 20	:	Government issued orders for withdrawal of proceedings against Gandhiji and sent instructions to local officials to give him facilities during investigation.
April 21	:	Gandhiji wired thanks to Lt.-Governor, Bihar and Orissa, for withdrawal of proceedings. Issued Press statement. Met Heycock.
April 22	:	Left Motihari for Bettiah.
April 23	:	Had interview with Sub-Divisional Officer, Bettiah.
April 27	:	J. T. Whitty, Manager, Bettiah Raj, wrote to Morshead, protesting against enquiry by Gandhiji and suggested appointment of commission by Government.
April 28	:	Herbert Cox, Honorary Secretary, Bihar Planters' Association, wrote to Morshead protesting against enquiry by Gandhiji. In letter to S.D.O., Bettiah, Gandhiji denied charge of interference with the former's authority.
April	:	Imperial War Conference held in London. Sir S. P. Sinha, Maharaja of Bikaner and Sir James

		Meston represented India. Secretary of State announced decision regarding India's representation at future Imperial Conferences.
May 1	:	Morshead wrote to Chief Secretary, Bihar and Orissa, recommending appointment of enquiry commission. Gandhiji went to Motihari. Olaha outwork of Turkaulia concern in Champaran destroyed by fire.
May 2	:	Government contradicted newspaper report that withdrawal of case against Gandhiji was ordered by Government of India.
May 5	:	Directors of Bihar Planters' Association passed resolution recording emphatic protest against manner of Gandhiji's enquiry.
May 9	:	Gandhiji was warmly welcomed by people on arrival in Patna from Champaran.
	:	W. Maude, Member of Executive Council, met Morshead, Heycock, Lewis and Whitty.
May 10	:	Gandhiji met Maude at Patna and agreed to submit preliminary report of his enquiry.
May 13	:	Wrote report on conditions of Champaran ryots.
May 14	:	Sent copies of report to Maude, McPherson, Morshead and Heycock. May 17: Indian Home Rule League held first annual Conference at Nasik under presidentship of Joseph Baptista. Gandhiji's contradiction of A.P.I. report on his mission and Olaha fire and correspondence with Heycock published.
May 18	:	Kutcherry building of Dhokraha outwork of Loheria factory was burnt down.
May 19	:	Gandhiji wrote to Manager of Loheria concern regarding oppression of raiyats.
May 20	:	In letter to Home Member, Government of India, Lt.-Governor detailed action to be taken against Gandhiji. Bihar Planters' Association wrote to Morshead tracing acts of incendiarism to Gandhiji's mission. Gandhiji wrote to Heycock regarding Belwa and Dhokraha concerns and complained of intimidation by planters.

May 21 : McPherson sought Government of India's approval to remove Gandhiji and his associates from Champaran under Defence of India Rules. Whitty wrote to Maude that Gandhiji had "become the centre of agitation against the European".

May 22 : Gandhiji sent to Heycock another statement about Dhokraha fire. In letter to Morshead, Heycock attributed Dhokraha fire to Gandhiji's visit and described his enquiry as "dangerous to the peace of the district".

May 24 : Viceroy held consultations with his Council. Later, Home Department of Government of India wired to McPherson suggesting appointment of a "strong Committee".

May 26 : In letter to Esther Faering, Gandhiji described condition of Champaran raiyats as "no better than that of slaves".

May 27 : Lt.-Governor-in-Council invited Gandhiji for interview at Ranchi on June 4. In communication to Government of India, McPherson proposed Gandhiji's name as raiyats' representative on the proposed Committee.

May 29 : In Press statement, Gandhiji said any enquiry covering definite issues would meet existing situation if known wrongs were immediately redressed.

May 30 : In letter to McPherson, Gandhiji agreed to meet Lt.-Governor and complained against planters' obstruction in his enquiry.

May : Inter-Departmental Conference held in London to discuss a new assisted system of emigration to British Guiana, Trinidad, Jamaica and Fiji.

June 1 : Planters sent representation to Government.

June 2 : Home Department, Government of India, wrote to Bihar Government that enquiry committee be appointed and investigation started within a month. Gandhiji reached Patna. Met Pandit Malaviya, Rajendra Prasad and others and left for Ranchi.

June 4	:	Gandhiji met Lt.-Governor at Ranchi. In letter to Maharaja of Darbhanga (Member, Executive Council), communicated his terms for enquiry.
June 5	:	Held discussions with Lt.-Governor and saw members of Executive Council. Left for Patna.
June 7	:	Arrived in Patna. Conveyed acceptance of nomination to Enquiry Committee after consulting Pandit Malaviya.
June 8	:	Secretary, European Association, urged removal of Gandhiji from Champaran. Gandhiji returned to Bettiah.
June 10	:	Government resolution announced terms and composition of Champaran Agrarian Enquiry Committee. Gandhiji wrote to McPherson that taking of statements at Bettiah had been stopped.
June 12	:	Went to Motihari. Taking of statements stopped.
June 14	:	Honorary Secretary, Bihar Planters' Association, wrote to McPherson protesting against Gandhiji's inclusion in the Committee.
June 16	:	Madras Government issued internment order on Mrs. Besant, G.S. Arundale and B.P. Wadia.
June 17	:	Gandhiji left Bettiah for Ahmedabad.
June 28	:	Returned to Motihari from Ahmedabad with Dr. Deva, Secretary, Servants of India Society.
June 29	:	In letter to Heycock, proposed sending of volunteers and Dr. Deva for assistance to villagers.
June 30	:	Death of Dadabhai Naoroji. In letter to The Pioneer, Gandhiji refuted criticism of his dress. Wrote to J. B. Petit about internment of Mrs. Besant and others, urging vigorous propaganda in villages despite prohibition.
July	:	Bihar Government issued notice regarding commencement of enquiry by middle of July.
On or After July 3	:	Gandhiji in private circular letter from Motihari detailed expenses and activities of Satyagraha Ashram and appealed for help.
July 7	:	Writing to P. S. to Viceroy from Patna, Gandhiji called internment of Mrs. Besant "a big blunder".

July 9	: Raja Kirtyanand Singh appointed member of Champaran Committee in place of Raja Harihar Prasad Narayan Singh who resigned due to ill-health.
July 11	: Champaran Committee held preliminary meeting to decide procedure and extent of enquiry.
July 12	: In House of Commons, E. S. Montagu, ex-Under Secretary of State for India, in speech on Mesopotamian Commission Report, described Government of India as "too wooden, too iron, too inelastic, too anti-diluvian to be of any use for modern purposes . . ."
July 17	: E. S. Montagu appointed Secretary of State for India. Public sittings of Champaran Committee commenced at Bettiah.
July 19	: Champaran Committee met at Bettiah.
July 25	: Gandhiji wrote to Secretary, Passengers' Grievances Committee, Rangoon, regarding lack of attention to deck passengers of British India Steam Navigation Company. Bihar Planters' Association submitted written statement to Champaran Committee.
July 26	: Champaran Committee met at Motihari and examined W. S. Irwin, Manager of Motihari Ltd.
July 28	: Congress Committee and Muslim League Reform Council held joint conference at Bombay.
July 29	: Gandhiji recorded confidential note on sharahbeshi for circulation among Champaran Committee members.
August	: In a manifesto, prominent Indian leaders, including Congressmen, opposed passive resistance in view of Montagu's proposed visit.
August 8	: Champaran Committee met at Bettiah. Gandhiji's suggestion regarding abwab agreed to.
August 10	: Meeting of Champaran Committee agreed on abolition of tinkathia.
August 11	: Gandhiji discussed sharahbeshi and made proposals at Champaran Committee meeting.

August 12 : Champaran Committee held discussions with planters,

August 13 : Gandhiji wrote to Chairman, Champaran Committee, on sharahbeshi and tinkathia and offered terms of compromise with planters.

August 14 : Champaran Committee discussed Gandhiji's suggestions and adjourned.

August 15 : Gandhiji complained to Manager, Pipra Indigo Concern, against molestation of raiyats.

August 16 : Reached Patna on way to Ahmedabad, leaving behind volunteer camps at Bettiah and Motihari to continue welfare work.

August 20 : In House of Commons, E. S. Montagu declared British Government's policy of "increasing association of Indians in every branch of the administration".

August 24 : Gandhiji addressed meeting of business men held in Ahmedabad to demand release of Mrs. Besant and co-workers.

August 31 : Told Mahadev Desai, "I have got in you the man I wanted" and asked him to join him.

September : In article entitled "Indian Colonial Emigration" in Indian Review, discussed implications of report of Inter-Departmental Conference held in London.

September 1 : Government of India issued resolution embodying report of Inter-Departmental Conference held in London regarding emigration to Colonies. Letter to Shankarlal Banker on satyagraha.

September 2 : Gandhiji took part in Bombay Provincial Congress Committee meeting held to consider passive resistance campaign against coercive measures of Government.

September 4 : Returned to Ahmedabad from Bombay.

September 11 : Left Ahmedabad for Madras.

Before September 13: Drafted petition on behalf of Gujarat Sabha for presentation to Montagu.

September 17 : Mrs. Besant, Wadia and Arundale released. Gandhiji arrived in Poona.

	: Contributed to Provincial Co-operative Conference paper on "Moral Basis of Co-operation".
September 18	: Left Poona for Ranchi.
September 21	: In Imperial Legislative Council, Pandit Madan Mohan Malaviya moved resolution urging holding of I.C.S. examination in India and England simultaneously.
September 22	: Gandhiji reached Ranchi.
September 23	: In interview with Lt.-Governor at Ranchi, discussed sharahbeshi and work of volunteers in Champaran.
September 24-28	: Champaran Committee met in second and last session at Ranchi, Gandhiji participating.
September 25	: Gandhiji wrote letter to Press on third class travelling on railways.
September 27	: Wrote foreword to G.A. Natesan's booklet, *What India Wants: Autonomy within the Empire.*
September 29	: Gandhiji signed agreement with leading planters at Ranchi regarding reduction of sharahbeshi.
October 2	: Mrs. Besant unveiled portrait of Gandhiji in Gokhale Hall, Madras, on his birthday.
October 3	: Gandhiji along with other members of Champaran Committee signed the report.
October 4	: Wrote to Lt.-Governor regarding publication in the regional language of Government's resolution on Committee's report.
October 5	: Reached Patna from Ranchi and left for Allahabad to attend Congress Committee meeting.
October 6	: A.I.C.C. and Council of Muslim League met in joint session at Allahabad and decided to send all-India deputation to Viceroy and Secretary of State in support of Congress-League scheme. Champaran Committee's report was accepted by Lt.-Governor-in- Council.
About October 9	: Gandhiji laid foundation stone for goshala in Bettiah.
October 15	: Presided over Bihar Students' Conference at Bhagalpur.

October 18	:	Government of Bihar and Orissa passed resolution on Champaran Agrarian Enquiry Committee Report which acknowledged "with much pleasure the good sense and moderation shown by Mr. Gandhi, who represented the cause of the tenants on the Committee".
October 19	:	Gandhiji, spoke at reception by merchants at Broach.
October 20	:	Presided over Second Gujarat Educational Conference.
October 21	:	In concluding address at Conference expressed desire to lay down life in country's service. Proposed vote of thanks at Humanitarian League.
October 26	:	All-India deputation, including Gandhiji, Motilal Nehru, Tilak, Jinnah and Sapru, waited on Chelmsford and Montagu.
November 2	:	Gandhiji presided over meeting at Godhra to protest against hardships of third-class railway passengers.
November 3	:	Presided over First Gujarat Political Conference at Godhra.
November 4	:	Announced at Political conference intimation of Government's decision to remove customs levy at Viramgam.
November 5	:	In concluding speech at Conference, exhorted participants to continue propaganda work and obtain signatures on petition to Montagu. Presided over Dhed community meeting.
November 8	:	Arrived at Motihari at night.
November 9	:	Had interview in the morning with J.L. Merriman, District Magistrate.
November 11	:	Addressed public meeting at Dharamshala in Muzaffarpur; appealed for support to Congress-League recommendations. In the evening attended Conference of Hindu and Mahomedan leaders; left for Motihari, at 9 p.m.
November 12	:	Declared open Gokhale Library at Umreth. J.M. Wilson, Secretary of Bihar Planters' Association, published in *The Statesman* opinion of planters' legal adviser.

November 14 : Gandhiji opened school in Bharharwa near Doka, in Champaran; returned to Bettiah.

November 15 : Had interview with J.T. Whitty, Manager of Bettiah Raj.

November 16 : Visited Koeri; went to Amolwa Station, inquired into case of police excesses on labourers.

November 20 : Opened school at Bhitiharwa, near Shrirampur, about two miles from Amolwa.

November 22 : Informed J.L. Merriman of his impending absence from Champaran for over a fortnight and Babu Brijkishore Prasad representing him.

November 26 : Had interview with Chelmsford and Montagu at Delhi.

November 27 : Had interview with Tilak, Montagu.

November 28 : Went to Aligrah; spoke on Hindu-Muslim unity at the Lyall Library Grounds; later, addressed Aligarh College students on "Truth and Thrift". Called on Khwaja Abdul Majid. Left at night for Calcutta by train.

November 29 : Champaran Bill, introduced in Council, referred to Select Committee.

December 4 & 5: Gandhiji held discussion with Ahmedabad millowners about workers' wages.

December 6 : Spoke on "Some Problems of Gujarat" at Dasa Khadayata Wadi in Nadiad. Presided over Committee meetings of First Gujarat Political Conference and Gujarat Stree Kelavani Mandal.

December 10 : Appointment of Rowlatt Committee announced. Gandhiji in letter to Albert West preferred stopping *Indian Opinion* to its removal from Phoenix to the city—Durban.

December 16 : Addressed large public meeting; visited Hindu Orphanage before leaving Nadiad.

December 19 : Communicated views on Champaran Agrarian Bill to Revenue Secretary, Bihar and Orissa Government.

December 26 : Attended 32nd Indian National Congress at Calcutta.

December 27 : Announced adjournment of All-India Social Service Conference in Calcutta.

December 29 : Moved resolution at Congress session concerning disabilities of Indians in South Africa.

December 30 : Proposed, at Indian Social Conference, resolution regarding education and uplift of depressed classes. Spoke at First Bengal Agriculturists' Conference; also at All- India National Language Conference.

December 31 : Addressed session of All-India Muslim League in Calcutta; also meeting held under auspices of Bengal and Bombay Humanitarian League at University Institute. Delivered presidential address at All-India Social Service Conference.

1918

January 1 : Presided over Ahmedabad meeting to protest against defective water supply.

: Gujarat Sabha wrote to Bombay Government for exemption or releif from land revenue payments.

January 4 & 5 : Gandhiji held talks with representatives of Ahmedabad mill-owners and mill-workers.

January 5 : Champaran members of Bihar Planters' Association submitted memorandum against certain provisions of Champaran Agrarian Bill.

January 10 : Gujarat Sabha under Gandhiji's advice asked Kheda farmers to refrain from paying land revenue.

January 12 : Gandhiji returned to Motihari from Ahmedabad.

Before January 13 : Offered jobs to teachers who, having relinquished their work, sought alternative employment.

January 14 : Discussed Champaran Agrarian Bill with L.F. Morshead, Commissioner of Tirhut Division. Kheda Collector in statement criticized Gujarat Sabha's advice to peasants to withhold land revenue, threatened action against defaulters.

January 16 : Government of Bombay issued statement that Collector of Kheda had granted revenue relief in fit cases.

January 21 : Gandhiji wrote to Tagore for his views on adopting Hindi as the lingua franca.

January 24	:	Represented to Revenue Secretary of Bihar and Orissa that material alterations in Champaran Agrarian Bill be made only in consultation with raiyats' representative.
February 4	:	Arrived at Bombay; addressed public meeting on Kheda situation.
February 5	:	Along with Dinshaw Wacha and G.K. Parikh called on Governor Bombay in connection with Kheda situation; later left for Sabarmati.
February 6	:	Reached Ashram, took note of notices issued by Collectors and Mamlatdars.
February 7	:	Wrote to Pratt, Commissioner, Northern Division, protesting against harsh language of Government notices.
February 8	:	Advised Ahmedabad mill-hands to be reasonable in their demands and seek settlement without creating bitterness.
February 12	:	Discussed Kheda situation with Collector and Commissioner.
February 14	:	Along with Shankarlal Banker and Vallabhbhai Patel, represented workers on Arbitration Board to decide wage increase in lieu of Plague Bonus.
February 15	:	Arrived at Sabarmati Ashram; wrote to Pratt to postpone land revenue recovery till his inquiry into Kheda situation was over.
Before February 19	:	Contributed foreword to a translation of Gokhale's speeches.
February 19	:	Explained to mill-hands his responsibility in regard to their trouble. The Servant of India commenced publication on third death anniversary of Gokhale.
February 20	:	Gandhiji presided over annual gathering of Bhagini Samaj in Bombay, spoke on women's education; returned to Nadiad.
February 21	:	Motored to Kheda; interviewed Collector.
February 22	:	Ahmedabad mill-owners declared general lockcut.
February 25	:	Gandhiji returned to Ahmedabad from Nadiad.
February 26	:	Commenced issuing leaflets on mill-hands'

	struggle, also practice of addressing mill-workers daily under babul tree on Sabarmati banks.
February 27	: Addressed prayer meeting at Sabarmati Ashram; interviewed Pratt.
March 1	: Workers' advisers pledged to feed and clothe strikers in need.
March 4	: Bihar and Orissa Legislative Council passed Champaran Agrarian Bill.
March 7	: Gandhiji discussed lock-out situation with coworkers.
March 10	: Presided over annual meeting of Gujarat Sabha at Ahmedabad.
March 11	: Interviewed Collector of Nadiad.
March 12	: Lock-out at mills lifted, strike by mill-workers started.
March 13	: Presided over two meetings addressed by Annie Besant.
March 14	: Mill-workers' reproachful remarks about their plight brought to Gandhiji's knowledge.
March 15	: Declared at workers' meeting decision to fast, to prevent strikers weakening.
March 16	: Returned to Sabarmati Ashram from Anasuyabehn's house.
March 17	: Appealed to Bombay Governor for postponement of land revenue recovery. Explained significance of fast at Ashram prayer meeting.
March 18	: Announced settlement between mill-owners and workers; A.B. Dhruva appointed arbitrator.
March 19	: In leaflet No. 17, last of the series, Gandhiji gave implications of settlement; joined mill-workers' procession.
March 21	: Spoke at public meeting adddressed by C.F. Andrews, who left for Bombay to intercede with Governor on behalf of Kheda peasants.
Before March 22	: Following Governor's rejection of plea for postponement of land revenue recovery, Gandhiji sent ultimatum to Pratt.

March 22	: Inaugurating Kheda Satyagraha, addressed 5,000 peasants in Nadiad. Satyagrahis pledged not to pay land revenue and to face consequences. Left for Delhi in response to Andrews' telegram.
March 25	: Met Private Secretary to Viceroy regarding release of Ali brothers.
March 27	: Returned to Nadiad; wrote to Press on his recent fast. Issued circular on Kheda situation.
March 28	: Issued statement to Press on Kheda situation; left for Indore.
March 29	: Delivered presidential address at Hindi Sahitya Sammelan at Indore.
March 31	: In letter to Press appealed to youths in Madras Presidency to learn Hindi.
April 1	: Commenced Kheda tour; Reached Kathlal. At public meeting in Kathana characterised Government's attitude as unjust.
April 2	: At Limbasi appealed to people not to be scared of Government's oppressive measures.
April 4	: Addressed meeting at Karamsad; Rajendra Prasad and Qureshi were among those present.
April 5	: At Vadathal met Collector; asked people to bear hardships courageously unmindful of consequences.
April 6	: Visitied Uttarsanda with Kasturba, Vallabhbhai Patel and Mahadev Desai . Addressed public meeting of 2 ,0 00 farmers.
April 7	: Over 3,000 agriculturists heard Gandhiji at Navagam.
April 8	: Visited Borsad, addressed gathering of 4,000 people. Left for Ahmedabad by train. At National Education Week inauguration at Gokhale Hall in Madras, Annie Besant read out Gandhiji's message.
April 10	: Gandhiji met District Magistrate, Ahmedabad; spoke at Aklacha on Kheda situation.
April 11	: Met Commissioner at Ahmedabad; spoke at Vadod.
Before April 12	: Issued circular inviting Ahmedabad people to attend Commissioner's meeting on April 12.

April 12	:	Commissioner addressed meeting of about 2,000 agriculturists, convened with Gandhiji's assistance, at Ahmedabad. Gandhiji spoke in order to clear misunderstanding created by Commissioner's speech. Addressed meeting at Nadiad; left for Bombay.
April 13	:	In Bombay met Revenue Board Members regarding Kheda problem.
April 15	:	Wrote from Nadiad letter to *The Bombay Chronicle* dispelling misconceptions created by Commissioner's speech.
April 16	:	Spoke at Od on need to be united in fight against Government.
April 17	:	Issued pamphlet elaborating points in his letter to The Bombay Chronicle on Commissioner's speech. Addressed Satyagrahis at Dantali and Chikhodra.
April 18	:	Visited Ras, in Borsad taluka, addressed agriculturists' meeting.
April 20	:	With Kasturba and others visited Kasar, Ajarpara and Samantha in Anand taluka and addressed meetings of peasants.
April 22	:	Spoke to cultivators at Palaj in Borsad taluka and later at Sunav.
April 23	:	Enroute to Bombay, wrote to Kasturba : "... to be a mother to Maganlal . . . . It is Maganlal if any one, who has so trained himself that he can carry on my work after me." In Bombay add ressed meeting of citizens on Kheda Satyagraha. Tilak moved resolution demanding either immediate suspension of land revenue recovery or impartial inquiry into peasants' grievances.
April 24	:	Gandhiji left Bombay for Delhi. Bombay Government issued Press statement on Kheda trouble.
April 25	:	Orders issued to Mamlatdars in Northern Division not to recover land revenue from those unable to pay. Viceroy opened War Conference in Delhi.
April 26	:	Gandhiji wrote to Sir Claude Hill declining

		invitation to participate in War Conference or any of its committees. Had interview with Viceroy.
April 27	:	Agreed to participate in War Conference after interview with Viceroy. Tilak declined invitation to join War Conference.
April 28	:	Met Sir William Vincent.
April 29	:	Spoke at War Conference supporting resolution on recruitment.
April 30	:	Wrote to Maffey, Private Secretary to Viceroy, offering his services as per his declaration at War Conference.
May 1	:	Left Delhi for Nadiad.
May 3	:	In Bombay attended All-India Congress Committee session; met Annie Besant.
May 5	:	Attended Bombay Provincial Conference and Antyaj Conference at Bijapur.
May 6	:	Issued statement in reply to Bombay Government's Press note on Kheda crisis. Spoke at Bombay Provincial Conference supporting abolition of indenture system; left for Bombay.
May 13	:	Spoke at Dhundakuva on "soul-force v. Coercion".
May 14	:	Was indisposed at Kathal.
May 16	:	Spoke at Sandesar.
May 17	:	Left Ahmedabad for Champaran.
May 18	:	Informed Maffey that he was actively preparing for recruitment campaign.
May 20	:	Arrived at Motihari.
May 24	:	Left Motihari for Ahmedabad via Bankipore after laying foundation-stone of Ashram.
May 25	:	Addressed large public meeting at Patna on India's lingua franca and self-government.
May 27	:	Spoke at Khandhali on significance of satyagraha.
June 2	:	Wrote to The Bombay Chronicle and Sir George Barnes on anti-Indian legislation in South Africa.
June 3	:	Addressed villagers at Uttarsanda and Navagam.
June 6	:	Issued manifesto to people of Kheda signifying end of Kheda satyagraha.

June 8 : Gave evidence in District Magistrate's Court, Nadiad, accepting responsibility for advising accused to remove onions from wrongly forfeited fields; addressed large gathering outside Court exhorting people to adhere to satyagraha.

June 9 : Reached Bombay; wrote to Chief Secretary, Bombay Government, declining to speak at Provincial War Conference.

June 10 : Attended Provincial War Conference at Town Hall.

June 11 : Participated in Servants of India Society celebration in Poona.

June 15 : Had interview with Governor of Bombay.

June 16 : Presided over Bombay public meeting protesting against Lord Willingdon's provocative conduct at Provincial War Conference. Bombay branches of the Home Rule League passed resolutions criticizing Government's attitude.

June 17 : Gandhiji conferred with close associates regarding recruitment in Nadiad.

June 21 : Addressed public meeting, inaugurating recruitment campaign.

June 22 : Issued first leaflet of appeal for enlistment.

June 24 : Spoke at Ahmedabad protesting against Governor's conduct at War Conference; appealed to people to enlist in army.

June 26 : At Ras spoke on need to join army.

June 27 : In Kheda, stressed significance and efficacy of satyagraha at reception to released satyagrahis.

June 28 : Speaking at Kathlal, at meeting to present address to Mohanlal Pandya, leader of the "Onion Satyagraha", on his release, compared satyagraha to kalpavriksha.

June 29 : Received address at meeting to celebrate successful termination of Kheda Satyagraha.

July 8 : Report on Montagu-Chelmsford Constitutional Reforms released.

July 9 : Gandhiji wrote to Jinnah that they should simultaneously work for enlisting in army and

		for amendment of Montagu-Chelmsford Reform Scheme.
July 14	:	Spoke at Karamsad on recruitment.
July 18	:	In response to Sastri's request, set down his views on Montagu-Chelmsford Reform Scheme. Speaking at meeting presided over by Pratt in Nadiad, declared his reluctance to go outside Gujarat for recruitment work, so long as his own people hung back.
July 22	:	Issued second leaflet of appeal for enlistment. Wrote to Govind Malaviya that Montagu-Chelmsford Scheme was good, that its shortcomings could be removed through agitation.
July 27	:	*The Bombay Chronicle* published obituary of Sorabji Shapurji Adajania by Gandhiji.
August 1	:	Gandhiji spoke at Surat, offering condolences to Sorabji Shapurji Adajania's family, and appealing for enlistment in army.
August 6	:	Imperial Conference resolution on India and Dominions.
August 10	:	Gandhiji wrote to Surendranath Banerjea on Montford Reforms and differences among Moderates and Extremists.
August 11	:	Fell seriously ill at Nadiad.
August 12	:	Wrote to B. G. Horniman declining presidentship of Humanitarian Conference.
August 15	:	Wrote on implications of Imperial Conference Resolutions.
August 17	:	Conveyed to Manasukhlal Raojibhai his decision not to attend Congress session and Moderates' Conference. Wrote to Anandshankar Dhruva regarding award in workers' dispute.
August 20	:	Wrote to Samarth that Montford Scheme needed modifications.
August 23	:	Still ill; brought from Nadiad to Ahmedabad. Stayed at Sheth Ambalal's place.
August 25	:	Explained his differences with Congress, Moderate and Extremist leaders in letter to B.

		Chakravarty. Wrote to B. G. Tilak on enlistment of recruits for war.
August 29	:	Special Congress session held in Bombay under presidentship of Syed Hasan Imam. Gandhiji addressed letter to Press on emigration of Indians to Transvaal. Wrote to C. F. Andrews: "I would not have you leave Shantiniketan."
August 31	:	Muslim League met in Bombay under chairmanship of Raja Saheb of Mahmudabad.
September 1	:	Special Congress session accepted resolution on Montford proposals.
September 4	:	Viceroy spoke on Montford Reforms at Imperial Legislative Council, Simla.
September 8	:	Death of Sir Ratan Tata in London.
September 9	:	Madras meeting under presidentship of Justice T. Sadasiva Iyer expressed thankfulness for Gandhiji's recovery. Gandhiji in letter to P. C. Ray reiterated his vow not to take milk or milk-products.
September 17	:	Gandhiji at Sabarmati Ashram; still ill.
September 23	:	Imperial Council discussed Rowlatt Committee Report.
September 29	:	Gandhiji slightly better; attended prayer at Sabarmati.
October 1	:	Replied to birthday felicitations at Sabarmati meeting. Condition became serious. Telegrams sent to Harilal and Devdas.
October 7	:	Victory Day celebrations in India.
October 20	:	Death of Ahmed Mahomed Cachalia, President, B.I.A. (Transvaal). Gandhiji addressed letter to Press recalling Cachalia's services.
October 29	:	Wired to Viceroy Gujarat Sabha's protest against Financial Resolution passed by Imperial Council on September 10.
November 1	:	Moderates' Conference in Bombay.
November 11	:	Armistice between Allies and Germany signed.
November 13	:	S. P. Sinha appointed to represent India at Peace Conference.

November 14 : In message on opening of Gujarat Swadeshi Store, Gandhiji asked people to cultivate swadeshi spirit with religious devotion.

November 16 : First Railway Conference, Nadiad; message from Gandhiji.

November 17 : Gandhiji's portrait unveiled in Shri Ram Free Library, Poona.

November 18 : Gandhiji said in letter to Mahomed Ali: "In the proper solution of the Mahomedan question lies the realization of swaraj."

November 22 : Government cancelled restrictions on Tilak's speeches and public work.

November 30 -December 12: Gandhiji in Matheran (hill station).

December 18 : Meeting in London of War Cabinet members and representatives of India and Dominions.

December 20 : The Servant of India announced that Moderates would attend Congress session.

December 26 : Indian National Congress met for 23rd session in Delhi, Madan Mohan Malaviya presiding.

1919

January 10 : In letter to Maganlal Gandhi, Gandhiji explained how he took to goat's milk.

January 18 : Rowlatt Bills published in Gazette of India. First meeting of Peace Conference at Paris.

January 20 : Gandhiji operated on for piles by Dr. Dalal at Bombay.

January 27 : End of Bombay labour strike announced, Gandhiji explained vow of milk in letter to Narahari Parikh.

January 30 : Wrote to Counsel for Ali 'Brothers assuring action to secure their release.

: Sent good wishes to The Independent, new Allahabad daily.

February 2 : Bombay Home Rule League protest meeting against Rowlatt Bills. Gandhiji's letter to S. G. Banker read out.

February 6 : Viceroy opened session, of Imperial Legislative Council at Delhi. Rowlatt Bills introduced.

		Gandhiji wrote to Swami Satyadev detailing steps for teaching Hindi in Madras Presidency.
February 7	:	Imperial Legislative Council debate on Rowlatt Bill. Bill referred to Select Committee against unanimous Indian opposition.
February 8	:	Gandhiji wrote to Pandit Malaviya suggesting country-wide agitation.
February 9	:	Wrote to V. S. Srinivasa Sastri on civil disobedience campaign against Rowlatt Bills.
February 10	:	Sir W. Vincent announced in Imperial Legislative Council that Rowlatt Act was to be in operation for three years. Second Rowlatt Bill introduced and referred to Select Committee despite unanimous non-official opposition.
February 12	:	Gandhiji wrote to Sir W. Vincent, enquiring about Government's decision regarding Ali Brother.
February 17	:	Spoke at Sabarmati regarding dissatisfaction among Ashramites.
February 20	:	Wrote to P.S. to Viceroy about release of Ali Brothers. Amir Habibullah of Afghanistan assassinated.
February 23	:	Reuter message announced that Tilak had lost his case.
February 24	:	Satyagraha Pledge signed at Sabarmati Ashram meeting, Gandhiji attending.
	:	Gandhiji wired to P.S. to Viceroy conveying satyagraha decision.
February 25	:	In telegram to Pandit Malaviya, informed that he would not go to England in Congress deputation in view of Rowlatt Bills. Wrote letters to C. F. Andrews, K. Natarajan, Stanley Reed and Dinshaw Wachha conveying Satyagraha Pledge. Wrote letter to Press on South African Indians' plight.
February 26	:	Wrote letter to Press on Satyagraha Vow. Committee of the Sabha issued Gandhiji's instructions to volunteers on taking signatures on Satyagraha Pledge. Gandhiji wrote to The Indian Social Reformer elaborating views on

		inter-caste marriages and Patel Marriage Bill.
	:	Sent letter to Press on National School at Sabarmati.
March	:	Issued first "Satyagraha Leaflet" quoting extracts from Thoreau.
March 1	:	Select Committee Report on Rowlatt Bills with dissenting minutes by Indian members presented to Imperial Legislative Council. Executive Committee with Gandhiji as president appointed at meeting of Pledge-signatories under auspices of Satyagraha Sabha at Bombay.
March 2	:	Executive Committee of Satyagraha Sabha appointed sub-committees for collecting funds and propaganda work. Wachha, Banerjea, Sastri, Shafi and others issued manifesto against passive resistance. Many took Satyagraha Vow at Allahabad meeting under presidentship of Motilal Nehru.
March 4	:	Conference of Bengal Nationalists supported Gandhiji and satyagraha.
March 6	:	Gandhiji in Delhi. Interview with Viceroy.
March 7	:	Attended protest meeting at Delhi. Mahadev Desai read out speech. Met Sir James Duboulay, Home Secretary.
March 8	:	Sir W. Vincent presented Select Committee Report on Second Rowlatt Bill. In letter to Srinivasa Sastri, Gandhiji explained decision on satyagraha and differences with others.
March 11	:	Inaugurated satyagraha meeting at Lucknow. Supporters signed Pledge. Gandhiji requested P. S. to Viceroy by wire and letter not to proceed with Rowaltt Bills. Attended satyagraha meeting at Allahabad, Syed Hussain presiding. Mahadev Desai read out speech.
March 12	:	Imperial Council debate on Rowlatt Bills. Motion for consideration of Bill as amended by Select Committee passed. Gandhiji wrote to Sir James Duboulay requesting release of Ali Brothers. Satyagraha Sabha rules published.
March 13	:	Debate in Imperial Legislative Council on

Rowlatt Bill as amended by Select Committee. Non-official amendments rejected.

March 14 : Ganahiji with Swami Shraddhanand attended protest meeting at Bombay. Gandhiji's speech read out.

March 18 : Motion to circulate Second Rowlatt Bill for opinion passed in Imperial Council. Rowlatt Bill passed despite opposition from non-official members. B. N. Sharma resigned in protest. Madras Moderates issued manifesto against satyagraha. Gandhiji reached Madras. Attended protest meeting at Madras. Satyagraha Pledge signed at meeting.

March 19 : Spoke at meeting of Madras Labour Union, B.P. Wadia presiding.

March 20 : Attended protest meeting at Triplicane Beach, Madras, under chairmanship of C. Vijayaraghavachari. Gandhiji's speech read out.

March 21 : Anarchical and Revolutionary Crimes Act, 1919 (Rowlatt Act) received Governor-General's assent Gandhiji spoke at tramway strikers' meeting at Madras.

March 23 : Announced in letter to Press observance of April 6 as day of humiliation and prayer. Wrote to Sir S. Subramania Iyer that satyagraha was not a party movement.

March 24 : Spoke at Tanjore meeting.

March 25 : Spoke at Trichinopoly meeting. Wrote to Counsel for Ali Brothers on satyagraha to secure release.

March 26 : Spoke at Madura meeting.

March 28 : Spoke at Tuticorin meeting.

March 29 : Spoke at labourers' meeting at Nagapatam.

March 30 : Satyagraha Day observed. Riot at Delhi. Mob fired at. Gandhiji left for Bezwada. At Madras Satyagraha Sabha meeting at Triplicane Beach, his speech read out.

March 31 : Delhi in mourning. Military control over city.

April 1 : Gandhiji left Bezwada for Bombay. Day's halt at Secunderabad.

April 2 : Government of India communiqué on Delhi disturbances.

April 3 : Gandhiji arrived in Bombay. Wired congratulations to Swami Shraddhanand on Delhi's opposition to Rowlatt legislation. Wrote letter to Press on Delhi occurrences. Wired V. S. Srinivasa Sastri that fight was against spirit of terrorism.

April 5 : Government communique on Rowlatt legislation Gandhiji wired to Swami Shraddhanand for help to dependants of victims. Wrote to Rabindranath Tagore for a message on the movement.

April 6 : Satyagraha Day observed all over India. Mass meeting at Chowpatty Beach, Bombay, under Gandhiji's presidentship. Jamnadas read out Gandhiji's speech. Prayers at Madhav Baug. Gandhiji addressed meetings of Mahomedans and ladies at Bombay. Appeal to people of Madras. Pandit Malaviya resigned seat in Imperial Council.

April 7 : First issue of Gandhiji's Satyagrahi, priced one pice, came out without registration. Satyagraha Sabha, Bombay, issued note on defying laws governing prohibited literature and registration of newspapers. Sale of proscribed literature by satyagrahis in Bombay.

April 8 : Gandhiji explained in leaflets, vows on swadeshi and Hindu-Muslim unity. Wired to C.R. Das on Satyagraha Day demonstration at Calcutta. Wrote to Police Commissioner, Bombay, denying allegations regarding holding up of tram-cars. Left for Delhi.

April 9 : On way to Delhi at Kosi served with orders restricting entry into Punjab and Delhi. Message to countrymen not to resent arrest or commit violence. Ram Navami Day celebrations. Peaceful processions at Amritsar.

April 10 : Gandhiji elected to disobey prohibition order, put under arrest and sent to Bombay. All-India hartal in protest against arrest. Incendiarism, riot and mob violence at Ahmedabad on hearing news of arrest. Police firing, killing of Europeans and burning of mill and station yard. Arrest and deportation from Amritsar of Drs. Satyapal and Kitchlew. Mob rising and police firing. Several Europeans killed. Police firing at Lahore.

April 11 : Gandhiji brought to Bombay and released. Spoke at mass meeting at Chowpatty Beach, administering warning to satyagrahis. In wire to Swami Shraddhanand, appealed to people to avoid violence. Country-wide hartal continued. Arrests in Bombay. Mob outrage at Ahmedabad. Telegraph and Collector's office burnt down.

April 12 : Rabindranath Tagore wrote to Gandhiji on satyagraha. Gandhiji's interview to Press representatives at Bombay. Attended meeting of cloth merchants at Marwari Chamber.

: Broke down on hearing news of Ahmedabad disturbance. Left for Ahmedabad. Meeting at Badshahi Mosque, Lahore. Firing by troops, derailment and burning of train. Disturbances in Bombay, Viramgam, Nadiad and Amritsar. Riot and bloodshed in Calcutta.

April 13 : Gandhiji reached Ahmedabad with Anasuya Sarabhai. In message to Ahmedabad citizens, implored them to be calm and obey orders. Massacre at mass meeting at Jallianwala Bagh, Amritsar.

April 14 : Hartal, serious disturbances and bombing at Gujranwala. Telegraph wires cut at Lahore, Amritsar and other places. Martial law proclaimed in Punjab. Government of India communiqué on satyagraha movement Gandhiji spoke at mass meeting at Sabarmati Upbraided people for violence, announced three-day penitential fast. Wrote to P. S. to Viceroy on disturbances. Second issue of *Satyagrahi* published.

April 15 : Gandhiji wrote to Collector of Ahmedabad, enquiring about names of English victims to send

		help to their families Visited the wounded at Ahmedabad Civil Hospital. Wrote to Sir I. Rahimtoola ascribing cause of disturbances to his arrest.
April 16	:	Assured help to Government in letter to Commissioner Northern Division (Bombay). In satyagraha leaflet, appealed to people to render help to victims. Arrests at Gujranwala. Wire-cutting and disturbances at several places.
April 17	:	Police firing at Delhi. Deportation of leaders in Punjab. The Amrita Bazar Patrika security forfeited.
April 18	:	Gandhiji announced temporary suspension of civil disobedience.
April 19	:	Attended Hindi Sahitya Sammelan meeting at Bombay under presidentship of Pandit Malaviya.
April 20	:	All-India Congress Committee meeting at Bombay under presidentship of Pandit Malaviya, Gandhiji and Mrs. Besant attending. "Crawling order" issued by General Dyer.
April 21	:	Satyagrahi suspended publication following suspension of Movement. A. I. C. C. passed resolution on Punjab situation. Gandhiji sent telegram to P. S. to Viceroy against whipping in public. Wrote to Collector of Ahmedabad against levy on millhands. Arrived at Ahmedabad from Bombay.
April 24	:	Left for Bombay. Martial Law Commission began work in Punjab.
April 25	:	Gandhiji spoke at satyagraha meeting in Bombay. Issued leaflet explaining significance of satyagraha.
April 26	:	B. G. Horniman served with order to leave India. The Bombay Chronicle suspended publication. Gandhiji issued leaflet on Horniman's deportation advising people against violence and demonstrations.
April 28	:	Congress deputation left for England. Gandhiji wrote to The Times of India correcting report of Ahmedabad speech.

April 29 : Wrote to Crerar, Secretary to Bombay Government on Horniman's deportation and pre-censorship of The Bombay Chronicle.

April 30 : Published in leaflet Horniman's letter from S. S. Takada. Sent Swadeshi Pledge to Sir Stanley Reed and Governor of Bombay. Appealed to Sind satyagrahis to be calm despite prosecutions. Kasur riot case judgment.

May 2 : Gandhiji in a satyagraha leaflet indicated resumption of civil disobedience in July.

May 3 : Wrote to Secretary, Bihar Planters' Association.

May 4 : Wrote to Maulana Abdul Bari praising idea of mixed Hindu-Mahomedan commission for communal unity. Satyagraha Sabha meeting at Bombay decided to observe fast, hartal, etc., on May 11 in protest against Horniman's deportation.

May 5 : Gandhiji sent Swadeshi Pledge to Viceroy. Wrote to District Magistrate, Ahmedabad, on complicity of educated men in Ahmedabad disturbances. Wrote to Maganlal Gandhi asking Ashramites to take up spinning.

May 6 : Called meeting at Bombay to explain observance of hartal.

May 7 : P.S. to Viceroy wrote to Gandhiji seeking help to stabilize Indian opinion in face of Afghan developments. Gandhiji issued message on observance of May 11. *Young India* New Series Vol. I, No. I, issued as a bi-weekly every Wednesday and Saturday, from Bombay under Gandhiji's supervision.

May 8 : Gandhiji spoke at Bombay women's meeting and issued leaflet explaining religious significance of satyagraha.

May 9 : Spoke on Khilafat at special meeting of Anjuman Ziaul Islam at Bombay, M. T. Kadarbhai presiding.

May 10 : Wrote to Annie Besant expressing grief over her accusations.

May 11 : Bombay hartal in honour of Horniman. Annie

		Besant resigned presidentship of Home Rule League. Gandhiji assured help to Viceroy in reply to latter's request of May 7. Sent telegram to District Magistrate, Ahmedabad, on identification of those accused in Ahmedabad disturbances.
May 12	:	Congratulated Bombay citizens on successful observance of hartal.
May 13	:	Explained "pure" and "mixed" swadeshi vows in *Young India*. Names of 47-signatories to swadeshi vow published. Police raid on *The Independent* office.
May 15	:	Southbourough Committee Report published. Gandhiji sent telegram to Viceroy's Private Secretary on arrest of Govardhandas and legal defence of *The Tribune* editor.
May 16	:	Wrote to Viceroy's Private Secretary demanding fullest investigations into disturbances in Punjab.
May 20	:	Addressed letter to satyagrahis of Surat.
May 21	:	Addressed circular letter on Bombay conference of satyagrahis scheduled for May 28.
May 25	:	Wrote to P. S. to Governor of Bombay drawing attention to 1914 amendment of Foreigners Act (1864) regarding orders served on two Kathiawari residents to quit British India.
May 26	:	Sir Edward Maclagan took over as Lt.-Governor of Punjab from Sir M. O'Dwyer.
May 27	:	*The Bombay Chronicle* asked to deposit Rs. 5,000 provisionally.
May 28	:	Gandhiji addressed conference of satyagrahis at Bombay. Wrote foreword to reprint of Indian Home Rule.
May 29	:	Government of India Bill introduced in House of Commons by E. S. Montagu.
May 30	:	Gandhiji wrote to Viceroy's Private Secretary on martial law administration in Punjab.
	:	Wrote to H.S.L. Polak on Rowlatt legislation.
May 31	:	Presided over public meeting held at Bombay to honour B. G. Tilak. Meeting resolved to collect funds to defray Tilak's expenses in England in connection with case against Sir Valentine.

June 1 : Rabindranath Tagore renounced knighthood.

June 3 : Pandit Malaviya re-elected to Viceregal Council.

June 5 : Second reading of Government of India Bill in House of Commons.

June 9 : Gandhiji wrote to P.S. to Viceroy regarding judgment in Kalinath Roy's case. Security of Rs. 10,000 demanded from *The Bombay Chronicle*.

June 10 : Martial law withdrawn from Punjab except from railway lands.

June 11 : In a signed leader in *Young India*, Gandhiji pleaded for immediate release of Kalinath Roy. Appealed to lawyers and journalists and wrote to C.F. Andrews for support in securing release of Roy.

June 12 : Wrote to secretaries of Satyagraha Sabha on resumption of civil disobedience in July.

: Wrote to S. T. Sheppard of *The Times of India* for support in securing release of Kalinath Roy.

June 13 : Mercy petition of Kalinath Roy rejected by Lt.-Governor of Punjab.

June 14 : Gandhiji wrote to E. S. Montagu justifying movement against Rowlatt legislation.

June 15 : Executive Committee of Satyagraha Sabha met at Bombay and decided on resumption of civil disobedience in beginning of July and vested full powers in Gandhiji to guide movement. Protest meeting of Indian Association, Calcutta, against Government of India despatch of March 5.

June 16 : Gandhiji issued second leaflet explaining Swadeshi Vow. Gave evidence before Chief Presidency Magistrate, Bombay, in connection with Dr. Kitchlew's trial before Martial Law Commission.

June 18 : Wrote to P. S. to Viceroy conveying decision to resume civil disobedience in July. Opened shuddha Swadeshi Vastra Bhandar at Bombay.

June 19 : Presided over Swadeshi Sabha meeting at Bombay.

June 20 : Order of pre-censorship on *The Bombay Chronicle* rescinded by Government.

June 24	:	Gandhiji sent cable to Secretary of State for India that he would resume civil disobedience in July unless Rowlatt legislation was withdrawn and a committee was appointed to enquire into Punjab disturbances. Presided at Bombay meeting to protest against Rowlatt legislation and Horniman's deportation.
June 25	:	Wrote letter to G. A. Natesan enclosing instructions on satyagraha campaign.
June 26	:	Wrote to P.S. to Viceroy conveying protest resolution of Satyagraha Sabha against justification of Horniman's deportation by Secretary of State. A.I.C.C. sent cable-to British Prime Minister and Secretary of State requesting suspension of sentences by Martial Law Commission pending enquiry. Government of India declined postponement of sentences.
June 27	:	Gandhiji sent to Viceroy memorial signed by Sir D. E. Wachha, Sir N. G. Chandavarkar and others praying for Kalinath Roy's release. Presided over Bombay meeting under auspices of Satyagraha Sabha. Wrote to S. T. Sheppard regarding anti-Indian legislation in South Africa.
June 28	:	Treaty of Versailles signed. Gandhiji sent reply to letter from P. S. to Viceroy on resumption of civil disobedience. Spoke on swadeshi at meeting in Bombay.
June 29	:	Wrote to Mahomed Ali on Moslem question. Spoke at foundation laying of Vanita Vishram at Ahmedabad.
June 30	:	Wrote to Deputy Superintendent of Police, Ahmedabad that he would give notice to authorities before resuming civil disobedience. Wrote instructions for satyagrahis in terms of Sabha Committee's resolution of June 15. Left Ashram for Bombay.
Before July 1	:	Drafted rules of Swadeshi Sabha.
July 1	:	Interview with Inspector-General and Commissioner of Police, Bombay. In statement said he would not resume civil disobedience

before July 8 and would inform authorities beforehand. Inaugurated Central Swadeshi Sabha at Bombay with branches all over India.

July 2 : Press Association of India sent cable to British Prime Minister and Secretary of State urging repeal of Press Act. Gandhiji thanked S.T. Sheppard for *The Times of India*'s leading article on South African question.

July 3 : Wrote to Press and to Commerce and Industry Member, Government of India, against restrictions on Indians in South Africa. Wrote to R. B. Ewbank seeking his interest in swadeshi movement.

July 4 : Spoke at Bombay meeting under auspices of Swadeshi Sabha.

July 5 : Secretary of State for India cabled Governor of Bombay advising interview with Gandhiji to dissuade him from resuming satyagraha. Gandhiji wrote in Young India on Smuts-Gandhi Agreement. Sent letter to H. S. L. Polak regarding civil disobedience and South African matters.

July 6 : Governor-General-in-Council reduced Kalinath Roy's term of imprisonment from 2 years to 3 months. Gandhiji addressed mass meeting at Nadiad on satyagrahis' duty and spoke on swadeshi at women's meeting.

July 9 : Martial Law Commission delivered judgment in Amritsar Conspiracy Case.

July 10 : Sir N.G. Chandavarkar appealed to Gandhiji through Press not to resume satyagraha.

July 12 : Gandhiji arrived in Poona. Interview with Governor of Bombay. Addressed students at Fergusson College, R.P. Paranjapye presiding. Spoke on swadeshi at citizens' meeting. Swadeshi Association formed under Gandhiji's presidentship. Returned to Bombay. Wrote in Young India on conviction of editor of Pratap.

July 13 : At Home Rule League meeting in Bombay moved protest resolution against anti-Indian legislation in Transvaal.

July 14	:	Wrote letter to R. P. Paranjapye answering his criticism of swadeshi.
July 16	:	Wrote in *Young India* on Paranjapye's observations on swadeshi. Lala Govardhandas sentenced to 3 years R.I. by Special Tribunal.
July 17	:	Gandhiji wrote to A.H. West regarding *Indian Opinion*.
July 18	:	Addressed meeting under auspices of Imperial Citizen ship Association to protest against Asiatic Land and Trading Amendment Act.
July 20	:	A.I.C.C. met at Calcutta.
July 21	:	Gandhiji issued letter to Press announcing postponement of civil disobedience in deference to warning of Viceroy and other friends.
July 23	:	Sir Sankaran Nair resigned office as member of Viceroy's Council. Gandhiji wrote in *Young India* on Lahore Judgment.
July 24	:	Privy Council granted leave to appeal to 21 Indians convicted under martial law for riots in Amritsar.
July 25	:	Lt.-Governor of Punjab reduced term of imprisonment of Radha Krishna, editor of *Pratap*, from 18 to 2 months.
July 26	:	Gandhiji wrote to Commerce and Industry Member, Government of India, on Transvaal Asiatic Law.
July 27	:	Wrote to *The Mahratta* on judge's remarks in Hindwasi case judgment.
July 28	:	Addressed students of Sarvajanik College at Surat and inaugurated Swadeshi Store. Sent cables to V. S. Srinivasa Sastri and Sarojini Naidu on agitation against Rowlatt legislation. Special Bench of Calcutta High Court dismissed appeal of The Amrita Bazar Patrika against forfeiture of security.
July 29	:	Sir Charles Munro's dispatch on India's part in War published in *Gazette*.
July 30	:	Gandhiji wrote in *Young India* on sentence on Jagannath by Martial Law Tribunal.

August 1 : In Kalol, Gandhiji visited handloom factory; spoke on swadeshi.

August 2 : In *Young India* supported appeal of Swami Shraddhanand for Rs. 1.5 lakhs to help victims of martial law atrocities.

August 4 : In Bombay, interviewed by a representative of *The Hindu,* announced intention to resume civil disobedience if Government failed to repeal Rowlatt Act.

August 5 : Presided over Gujaratis' meeting in Bombay in memory of Amritlal Sunderjee.

August 6 : In *Young India* described action of Ahmedabad District Judge as "impudent" in proceeding against barristers who took satyagraha pledge.

August 8 : In Poona, at Deccan Sabha meeting, spoke against anti-Indian legislation in Transvaal; spoke on swadeshi at Gujarati Bandhu Samaj.

August 14 : In Godhra, opened Swadeshi Bhandar; held conference with Collector, local leaders on question of forced labour; visited Stuart Library; spoke on swadeshi at women's meeting and at public meeting.

August 15 : At crowded public meeting, called upon Government to conduct impartial inquiry into Punjab situation, exhorted people to contribute to relief fund.

August 19 : In Bombay, announced at satyagrahis' meeting intention to start Gujarati paper on lines of Young India and to resume satyagraha against Rowlatt Act after petitioning Government.

August 22 : Appealed to Lord Willingdon against proposal to extern Esther Faering from India; pleaded that she might be allowed to join Sabarmati Ashram.

August 25 : Enunciated concept of swadeshi in letter to Cowie and sought Bombay Governor's approval and encouragement for the movement.

August 27 : Wrote to Maulana Abdual Bari that it was inopportune to ask for Ali brothers' release.

August 28 : Deputation led by Surendranath Banerjea wanted on Montagu to protest against Transvaal Trading Act.

August 31	:	In Dohad, Gandhiji spoke on swadeshi at women's meeting; later, exhorted weavers to shed distinctions of caste, community, etc.
September 3	:	Viceroy announced appointment of Commission to go into question of Punjab troubles; referred to Commissions to set right problems regarding South Africa and Fiji.
September 6	:	In Bombay, Gandhiji attended meeting of Swadeshi Sabha and Satyagraha Committee.
September 7	:	Opened Gujarat Swadeshi Store in Girgaum, Bombay; spoke on swadeshi; participated in Swadeshi Sabha meeting. First issue of Navajivan in Gujarati was published.
September 8	:	Government of India telegraphed Bombay, Madras Governments that "existing orders against Gandhiji should be relaxed and all restrictions removed when Lord Hunter arrives in India."
September 12	:	Bombay Government confidentially informed Madras Government that they concur with the Central Government in relaxing restrictions imposed upon Gandhiji.
September 17	:	Gandhiji left Ahmedabad for Bombay.
September 18	:	In Bombay, spoke on Khilafat at public meeting. Indemnity Bill protecting Government servants introduced in Legislative Council, opposed by Malaviya.
September 21	:	Gandhiji opened school for untouchables in Ahmedabad. Public meeting held in Madras and Wardha to celebrate 51st birthday of Gandhiji. Wardha citizens presented purse to be placed at Gandhiji's disposal. Indemnity Bill was passed.
September 25	:	In Rajkot, Gandhiji spoke on swadeshi at meeting in Revashanker Jagjivan's bungalow; spoke to women at Vanik Bhojan Shala in afternoon; later, spoke in Connaught Hall on social service.
September 26	:	Visited schools for untouchables.
September 27	:	Opened Swadeshi Bhandar in Gondal State, Saurashtra; spoke on swadeshi at meetings of men and women.

September 28 : At Moti Marad, presided over Kathiawar Patidar Conference. Spoke on Hindu-Muslim unity at Dhoraji; addressed gathering of Antyajas.

September 29 : On return to Ahmedabad, wired Bombay Government withdrawing apology given by Navajivan publishers for supposed breach of law regarding newspaper publication.

October 1 : In Bombay presided over public meeting at Excelsior Theatre, to celebrate 73rd birthday of Annie Besant; opened Kalbadevi Shuddha Swadeshi Bhandar. Government of India asked Punjab, Delhi and Madras to withdraw restrictions imposed upon Gandhiji from October 15.

October 2 : Gandhiji attended reception at Vanita Vishram Hall of Bhagini Samaj and received purse containing Rs. 20,100; addressed meeting of Muslim students in evening.

October 4 : Wired Madras Governor to expedite granting permission to Miss Faering to join Sabarmati Ashram.

October 6 : Madras Governor's Private Secretary wrote to Gandhiji informing readiness to grant Esther Faering permission to join him, if she would apply in usual way.

October 7 : *Young India* was reported to have been taken over to Ahmedabad. Gandhiji received letter informing Bombay Governor's approval of swadeshi movement.

October 8 : In Baroda, spoke on physical exercise at Manikrao's gymnasium, witnessed demonstration. First issue of Young India under Gandhiji's editorship appeared.

October 9 : Gandhiji spoke at Maharaja Theatre, Baroda; opened Swadeshi Bhandar and visited brush factory and school for untouchables; attended meeting of Stree Samaj in Nyaya Mandir; proceeded to Amreli.

October 10 : Opened spinning-wheel class in Amreli.

October 11 : Reached Bhavnagar at night.

October 12	: Taken in procession, was presented with address by Cloth Merchants' Association; spoke on swadeshi; visited school for untouchables; advocated spinning in spare time at women's meeting; left for Ahmedabad.
October 13	: Presided over farewell to Anandshankar Dhruva at Gujarat College; later spoke to College students at meeting presided over by Robertson, Principal.
October 15	: Restrictions imposed on April 9, 1919, prohibiting Gandhiji's entry into Punjab, were removed. Bombay High Court warned satyagrahi lawyers who took satyagraha pledge.
October 17	: Khilafat Day observed all over India.
October 18	: Registrar, High Court, Bombay, summoned Gandhiji to attend His Lordship's Chamber on October 20 to explain action in publishing private letter of Ahmedabad District Judge.
October 20	: Gandhiji telegraphed Registrar expressing his inability to attend Court on October 20, owing to Punjab tour.
October 22	: Sent Explanation to Registrar from Sabarmati Ashram regarding publication of Ahmedabad District Judge's private letter. Informed Madras Governor of Esther Faering's arrival at Ashram. Participated in function to felicitate Dhruva. Left Ahmedabad for Lahore via Baroda.
October 24	: Lahore citizens accorded warm reception to Gandhiji at station. Government of India, Home Department, informed Bombay Government, Judicial Department, that it had no intention to restrict Gandhiji's movements.
October 27	: Gandhiji had interview with Lt.-Governor Sir Edward Maclagan and Deputy Commissioner.
October 28	: Addressed students at Pandit Rambhuj Dutt Choudhri's house. Left for Delhi with C. F. Andrews to attend Punjab Inquiry Committee meeting. Government of India informed Chief Secretary, Madras State, of withdrawal of restrictions imposed upon Gandhiji with effect from October 15, 1919, and asked latter to do likewise.

October 29	:	Gandhiji attended Punjab Inquiry Committee meeting; met Lord Hunter and other officials. Addressed public meeting under Swami Shraddhanand's chairmanship.
October 31	:	Wired Sabarmati Ashram not to have "peace celebrations" on December 13 and 14 if Khilafat question remained unsettled. Bombay High Court Registrar declared Gandhiji's explanation to be unsatisfactory and demanded publication of apology.
November 1	:	Gandhiji gave interview to Associated Press of India on South African Commission. Attended public meeting of Delhi citizens at Pataudi House, but meeting abandoned due to disorder.
November 2	:	Delhi martyrs meeting was resumed. Gandhiji addressed gathering.
November 3	:	First open session of Punjab Inquiry Committee convened. Gandhiji was reported taking evidence in martial law cases.
November 4	:	At Amritsar Golden Temple, was presented with a turban; spoke on swadeshi at women's meeting; visited Jallianwala Bagh and Khalsa College. Left for Lahore with Andrews.
November 7	:	Telegraphed Registrar, High Court, Bombay for leave till receipt of counsel's opinion.
November 11	:	Held conference with Madan Mohan Malaviya, Motilal Nehru, C.R. Das and Andrews. Malaviya was refused permission to visit Harkishen Lal in jail. Disorders Inquiry Committee arrived at Lahore.
November 15	:	Gandhiji spoke at meeting to bid farewell to Andrews who was proceeding to South Africa.
November 20	:	Visited Gujranwala; addressed public meeting at Gurukul.
November 21	:	Recorded statement from witnesses at Gujranwala; addressed women's meeting.
November 23	:	Spoke at Khilafat Conference at Delhi, attended exclusively by Muslims.
	:	M. A. Jinnah regretted inability to attend.

November 24	:	Gandhiji presided over joint Hindu-Muslim session of Khilafat Congress; spoke in Hindi. Resolution declared Indians' unwillingness to participate in peace celebrations until Khilafat question was settled. Advisory committee against peace celebrations formed; one pice of Gandhiji auctioned for Rs. 501.
November 26	:	Gandhiji visited and spoke at Nizamabad and Kasur.
November 29	:	Visited Akalgarh.
November 30	:	Visited Ramnagar.
December 1	:	Recorded statement at Hafizabad.
December 2	:	Addressed Hafizabad students' and women's meetings.
December 3	:	Reached Sangla Hill in evening, collected evidence; left for Lahore. Indian Reforms Bill discussed In House of Commons.
December 5	:	In Sheikhupura, Gandhiji addressed meeting on Hindu-Muslim unity. Indian Reforms Bill passed third reading in House of Commons.
December 6	:	Gandhiji left Sheikhupura for Chuharkana, spoke on need for discipline when detained by crowd at railway station.
December 7	:	Visited Lyallpur in evening, received statements.
December 8	:	Addressed meeting of women at noon and public meeting in evening. Indian Reforms Bill had first reading in House of Lords.
December 9	:	Gandhiji arrived in Lahore.
December 11	:	Spoke at celebrations of Sabha Mandal. Wrote to Registrar, High Court, Bombay that he "could not conscientiously offer any apology". Registrar's application suo moto for "a rule nisi calling upon Messrs Gandhi and Desai to show cause why they should not be committed or otherwise dealt with according to law for contempt of court" granted.
December 24	:	Reforms Bill received Royal assent; Royal Proclamation announcing clemency to political prisoners issued.

December 28	:	At Amritsar, Gandhiji dissolved All-India Humanitarian Conference on account of disorder.
December 29	:	Attended Indian National Congress session; moved resolution regarding South African Indians' hardships. Attended All-India Muslim League session.
December 30	:	Moved resolution at Indian National Congress session on Punjab and Gujarat disturbances.
December 31	:	Attended Congress session.

Chapter Five

Shaking the Foundations of the Raj

1920

January 1	:	At Congress session supported resolution on swaraj but urged acceptance of Reforms.
January 4	:	In letter from Sabarmati to Registrar, High Court, Bombay asked postponement of date of hearing regarding contempt of Court.
January 5	:	Submitted statement to Disorders Inquiry Committee and informed it of his readiness to give oral testimony.
January 9	:	Appeared before Disorders Inquiry Committee at Ahmedabad.
January 11	:	Invited Lord Hunter and members of Disorders Inquiry Committee to visit Sabarmati Ashram.
January 12	:	Spoke at Arya Samaj; received welcome address at Jalalpur Jattan, spoke to gathering. Proceeded to Sargodha by car. Lord Hunter with members of Disorders Inquiry Committee visited Ashram.
January 15	:	Gandhiji left Ahmedabad for Delhi in connection with Khilafat Deputation.
January 16	:	Reached Delhi.
January 18	:	Met Maulana Abul Kalam Azad.
January 19	:	Had interview with Viceroy, as member of Khilafat Deputation.
January 20	:	Met Motilal Nehru in Allahabad.
January 21	:	Opened Swadeshi Bhandar at Kanpur.

January 22	:	Reached Meerut in morning; spoke at public meeting after reception, procession and addresses by Municipality, Khilafat Committee and general public. Addressed women in connection with Congress Inquiry Committee work on Punjab disorders; en route to Lahore, spoke at Muzaffarpur.
January 23	:	Reached Lahore.
February 1	:	At Lahore, Gandhiji met Dr. Joseph Nunan, Leader of British Guiana deputation visiting India to recruit settlers.
February 3	:	Gandhiji wrote to Chief Secretary, Punjab Government, regarding discharge of political and Martial-Law prisoners.
February 9	:	At Lahore, Gandhiji gave interview to Press on South African Commission.
	:	In Imperial Legislative Council, British Guiana deputation presented their report.
February 13	:	At Sargodha, Gandhiji gave a speech on Punjab atrocities and Hindu-Muslim unity.
February 14	:	Issued appeal for Jallianwala Bagh Memorial Fund.
February 15	:	Wrote to Chief Secretary, Punjab Government, asking for inquirty into atrocities perpetrated by Government officials during recruiting campaign in Sargodha. Completed his tour of the Punjab, commenced on January 23 in connection with the work of Congress Inquiry Committee on the Punjab disorders.
February 18	:	In Imperial Legislative Council, debate was held on change of capital.
February 20	:	Draft of the Congress Report on the Punjab disorders submitted to Motilal Nehru, President of the Congress.
February 21	:	In Banaras, Gandhiji addressed students of Banaras Hindu University.
February 25	:	In Ahmedabad, Gandhiji addressed meeting of mill-hands held to consider formation of Labour Union. Montagu, in interview to Evening Standard, strongly urged retention of

		Constantinople by Turkey. Strike reported at Tata Iron Works, Jamshedpur.
February 26	:	In Ahmedabad, Gandhiji presided at opening ceremony of Night High School under auspices of Marwari Yuvak Mandal. In House of Commons, debate was held on future of Turkey. First Indian Khilafat Deputation arrived in London.
February 27	:	Gandhiji forwarded to Bombay High Court his statement and that of Mahadev Desai in regard to contempt of court case.
February 28	:	Bengal Provincial Khilafat Conference was held at Calcutta.
February 29	:	Gandhiji attended the Khilafat Conference.
March 2	:	In London, Fisher, on behalf of Montagu, received Indian Khilafat Deputation.
March 3	:	At Bombay, Gandhiji appared in High Court regarding contempt of court case against him; judgment was reserved. Spoke at Khilafat meeting.
March 5	:	In Bombay, spoke at a public meeting on abolition of Press Act.
March 6	:	Council of League of Nations passed resolution in favour of Constantinople and Straits coming under control of League of Nations.
March 7	:	*Daily Telegraph* reported decision of British Government to occupy Constantinople. Gandhiji issued Press statement on Khilafat.
March 12	:	Gandhiji and Mahadev Desai were reprimanded by Bombay High Court in contempt of court case.
March 14	:	Police raided offices of Bengal Provincial Khilafat Committee.
March 15	:	At Jamshedpur strikers at Tata Iron Works were fired upon by police and troops.
March 17	:	In London, Lloyd George gave interview to Indian Khilafat Deputation.
March 19	:	Khilafat Day. In Bombay, Gandhiji addressed Khilafat Day meeting.
March 21	:	Labourers in the Sholapur Mills struck work.

March 25 : Congress Sub-committee Report on the Punjab disorders published.

: In House of Commons, Asquith opposed retention of Constantinople by Turkey and recommended vaticanization of Sultan in Constantinople.

March 29 : Government of India affirmed that holy places of Hedjaj would remain under independent Moslem control.

March 31 : Allied Supreme Council offered Mandate for Armenia to League of Nations.

: In Ahmedabad, Gandhiji attended competition held for spinning-wheel prize.

April 2 : At Ahmedabad, Gandhiji and Rabindranath Tagore attended sixth Gujarati Literary Conference; address by Tagore. Gandhiji, in evening, spoke at a meeting on "Literature from Society's Point of View". Bombay Provincial Conference commenced sittings at Sholapur under presidentship of N. C. Kelkar. Rabindranath Tagore stayed at Sabarmati Ashram with Gandhiji.

April 3 : Bombay Provincial Conference demanded inpeachment of Sir Michael O'Dwyer and others and their trial and punishment by judicial tribunal. In Ahmedabad, Gandhiji addressed Gujarati Literary Conference on "Gujarati Literature from People's Point of View". In evening, Rabindranath Tagore addressed public meeting in English; Gandhiji translated speech.

April 4 : Debate in Bombay and Bengal Provincial Conferences on Reforms resolution, with Tilak on one side and Annie Besant taking up a moderate position.

April 6 : Hostilities commenced between the Japanese and the Russians at Nikolsk and Haberovsk. Gandhiji addressed National Week Meeting in Bombay. Issued another appeal for Jallianwala Bagh Memorial Fund.

April 7 : New Cabinet formed in Turkey with Damad

		Ferid, Grand Vizir, Resohib Bey, Minister of Interior, and Mohamed Vid, Minister of Marine and War. Travancore Reformed Council held its first meeting.
April 9	:	In Bombay, Gandhiji spoke at public meeting organized by Central Khilafat Committee in connection with National Week.
April 11	:	Gandhiji, in letter to *The Bombay Chronicle,* again appealed for contributions to Jallianwala Bagh Memorial Fund.
April 13	:	In Bombay, Gandhiji addressed meeting organized by Home Rule League and National Union in connection with National Week. Rabindranath Tagore sent a message to the meeting.
	:	Gandhiji wired to Private Secretary to Viceroy seeking Viceroy's permission to go to England to acquaint Ministers there with Muslim sentiment over Khilafat.
After April 13	:	Gandhiji cabled to Secretary of State for India seeking Government's approval for his visit to England in connection with Khilafat question.
April 15	:	Reforms Committee held its sitting at Simla.
April 17	:	Madras Khilafat Conference commenced its sittings under presidentship of Shaukat Ali.
April 18	:	In Ahmedabad, Gandhiji presided over the second annual meeting of mill workers.
April 22	:	In London, public meeting was held on question of Khilafat with George Lansbury in the chair.
April 24	:	The United States formally recognized independence of Republic of Armenia.
April 25	:	San Remo Conference of Allies entrusted Britain with Mandate for Mesopotamia and Palestine, and France with Mandate for Syria.
April 26	:	Home Rule League meeting held at Ahmedabad to protest against deportation of B. G. Horniman; Gandhiji presided.
April 28	:	Gandhiji joined Home Rule League and became its president. In a statement, advocated non-co-

		operation to express Indian feeling against San Remo decisions regarding Turkey.
May 1	:	Madras Liberal League held its first annual meeting.
May 2	:	Enver Pasha reported to have placed himself at head of Turkish national movement.
May 6	:	In House of Commons, Montagu made statement on General Dyer's forced resignation.
May 7	:	In Ahmedabad, Gandhiji held discussions about having system of arbitration for solving disputes between mill workers and mill-owners.
May 9	:	Gandhiji, writing in Navajivan, appealed for funds for famine relief in Orissa.
May 11	:	In Paris, Turkish treaty was handed to Turkish delegates.
May 12	:	Gandhiji, writing in *Young India,* again appealed for funds for famine relief in Orissa. At Bombay, Gandhiji attended Khilafat Committee meeting.
May 14	:	Turkish Peace Terms published in India along with Viceroy's message to Indian Muslims.
May 15	:	In Turkey, an extraordinary court martial sentenced Mustafa Kamal and his associates to death.
May 16	:	In Ahmedabad, Gandhiji held further discussions about having system of arbitration for settling disputes between mill workers and mill-owners.
May 17	:	Above discussions continued.
May 18	:	Above discussions continued. Gandhiji, in a Press statement, called for revision of peace terms presented to Turkey by Allies.
May 19	:	In Ahmedabad, Gandhiji continued discussions on system of arbitration.
May 20	:	Yakub Hasan resigned his membership of Madras Legislative Council and other official organizations in protest against terms of Turkish Treaty.
May 21	:	Nizam of Hyderabad issued firman prohibiting participation in Khilafat agitation.
May 23	:	In Ahmedabad, Gandhiji addressed meeting of

		mill-hands on settlement of their strike. Tewfik Nessim Pasha formed new Cabinet in Turkey.
May 28	:	Report of Hunter Committee, Government of India Despatch and Montagu's reply published.
May 30	:	All-India Congress Committee met at Banaras to consider non-co-operation programme; Gandhiji was present.
June 1	:	Joint Hindu-Muslim Conference commenced at Allahabad; Gandhiji attended.
June 2	:	Revised draft rules for Provincial Councils, Indian Legislative Assembly and Council of State published in a Gazette of India Extraordinary. Joint Hindu-Muslim Conference continued at Allahabad.
June 3	:	Meeting of All-India Central Khilafat Committee held at Allahabad; Gandhiji spoke on non-co-operation.
June 4	:	In Bombay, Gandhiji performed opening ceremony of Shuddha Khadi Bhandar.
June 5	:	In Nadiad, Gandhiji performed opening ceremony of Swadeshi Bhandar.
June 11	:	In Bombay, Gandhiji attended meeting of Imperial Indian Citizenship Association.
June 13	:	Gandhiji, in a Press statement, opposed scheme of repatriation recommended by South African Enquiry Commission.
June 19	:	The order of externment from Mussoorie passed on Jawaharlal Nehru was withdrawn.
June 21	:	Madras Provincial Conference met at Tinnevelly with S. Srinivasa Iyengar in chair.
June 22	:	In House of Commons, questions asked on the Punjab disorders; Montagu heckled.
	:	Gandhiji, in letter to Viceroy, gave notice of non-co-operation with Government in protest against unjust peace terms presented to Turkey by Allies and forwarded Muslim representation on the subject to Viceroy.
June 25	:	In Bombay, Gandhiji attended meeting of Khilafat Committee.

June 26	:	In Bombay, Gandhiji spoke at public meeting held to protest against Hunter Committee Report.
June 27	:	Turkey submitted counter-proposals to Treaty terms presented by Allies.
June 28	:	Nizam of Hyderabad renounced title of Mohiul-Millat Wad Din.
June 30	:	Gandhiji, in a Press statement, called upon people not to seek election to Legislative Councils under Reforms Act of 1919.
July 1	:	Gandhiji wrote to Press on interim report of South African Commission regarding repatriation of Indians.
July 2	:	Wrote to N. C. Kelkar on draft constitution of Congress. Public meeting held at Bombay to protest against Hunter Report. Sir N. G. Chandavarkar presided.
July 4	:	In *Navajivan* article Gandhiji detailed steps for starting of non-co-operation from August 1.
July 6	:	Churchill announced, in House of Commons, Army Council's conclusion that Gen. Dyer was guilty of error of judgment and that he should not receive any office under Crown.
Before July 7	:	Gandhiji issued Press statement on non-cooperation and sent cable to Mahomed Ali at London. Non-co-operation Committee issued statement on methods and programme on non-co-operation.
July 7	:	In Bombay, Gandhiji spoke at women's meeting. In *Young India* pleaded for boycott of Prince of Wales' visit.
July 8	:	Debate on Hunter Committee Report began in House of Commons.
July 11	:	Gandhiji appealed to Gujaratis in Navajivan article "Gujarat's Duty" to take the lead in non-co-operation. In another article he asked them to contribute money for Shantiniketan. His message on non-co-operation was read out at Rajakiya Mandal meeting, Nadiad. Wrote to Press on South African appellate Court's judgment in favour of Dadoo.

July 13	:	In Bombay, spoke at public meeting to consider Indian situation in East Africa and Fiji.
July 14	:	In article in *Young India,* replied to criticisms of Mrs. Besant and V.S. Srinivasa Sastri.
July 15	:	In Jullundur, spoke at meeting appealing to Hindus and Muslims to support non-co-operation.
July 16	:	In Amritsar, spoke at non-co-operation meeting under auspices of Khilafat Committee.
July 17	:	In Lahore, spoke on khilafat and non-cooperation.
July 18	:	In Lahore, spoke on boycott of reformed councils. All-India Muslim League's Council condemned findings of majority in Hunter Committee Report.
July 19	:	In Rawalpindi, Gandhiji spoke on khilafat. Dyer debate in House of Lords.
July 20	:	In Gujarkhan, Gandhiji spoke on communal unity and khilafat.
July 21	:	Instructions of Central Khilafat Committee, Bombay, for Hartal on August 1 published. In *Young India,* Gandhiji wrote on "The Music of the Spinning-wheel".
July 22	:	In Karachi, spoke at khilafat meeting.
July 23	:	In Hyderabad (Sind), spoke at Khilafat Conference.
July 24	:	Sent telegram to A. V. Thakkar not to go to British Guiana before finishing famine relief work in Orissa. Addressed students at Sind National College. Supported non-co-operation resolution at Khilafat Conference.
On or before July 25	:	Sent telegram to Caliphate Workers' League, Delhi, not to violate Seditious Meetings Act.
July 25	:	In Hyderabad (Sind), delivered public lecture at Citizens' Association.
July 28	:	In *Young India,* replied to Montagu on the khilafat agitation. Gandhiji and Shaukat Ali sent Khilafat Day message to Madras Presidency. In Bombay, Gandhiji addressed non-co-operation meeting.
July 31	:	B.G. Tilak passed away in Bombay. Gandhiji and

Shaukat Ali issued Non-co-operation Committee's directions in a message on observance of Khilafat Day on August 1.

August 1 : Third Khilafat Day—Gandhiji inaugurated nonco- operation movement. Wrote letter to Viceroy renouncing Kaisar-i-Hind and other medals. Addressed meeting in Bombay under auspices of Central Khilafat Committee.

August 2 : Mahomed Ali and other members of khilafat delegation arrived in Bombay; given public reception under Gandhiji's presidentship.

August 4 : In Young India, Gandhiji paid tribute to Tilak and replied to manifesto against non-co-operation by Sir Chandavarkar and others.

August 11 : Left Bombay on tour of South India. Explained non-violent non-co-operation in article, "The Doctrine of the Sword" in *Young India*.

August 12 : Arrived at Madras. Interviewed by *The Madras Mail* representative on non-cooperation. Addressed public meeting at Madras Beach on non-cooperation programme.

August 13 : Spoke on non-co-operation at Juma Mosque, Triplicane, Madras.

August 14 : Visited Ambur and Vellore.

August 15 : Spoke on rights and duties of labour at meeting under auspices of Central Labour Board.

August 16 : Spoke at Kumbakonam. Spoke at Nagore.

August 17 : Spoke at Trichinopoly.

August 18 : Spoke at Calicut.

August 19 : Spoke on non-co-operation at Mangalore.

August 20 : At Salem.

August 21 : In Bangalore, addressed meeting at Idgah.

August 22 : In Madras, addressed students of Law College.

August 23 : In Bezwada spoke at Municipal Travellers' Bungalow compound.

August 25 : Reached Bombay.

August 26 : Reached Ahmedabad.

August 27 : In Ahmedabad spoke at Gujarat Political Conference.

August 28 : Moved resolution on non-co-operation at Gujarat Political Conference.

August 29 : Spoke on boycott at Gujarat Political Conference.

August 31 : Took pledge to wear khadi for life.

September 1 : In *Young India,* replied to Montagu and the Viceroy and wrote on the Gujarat Political Conference.

September 4-9 : Special session of Indian National Congress at Calcutta. Resolutions adopted regarding non-co-operation, Hunter Committee Report and British Cabinet's attitude on Punjab atrocities.

September 5 : At Congress Subjects Committee meeting, Gandhiji moved resolution on non-co-operation.

September 7 : Replied to critics at Subjects Committee meeting.

September 8 : Gandhiji's resolution on non-co-operation carried by majority at Calcutta Congress. All-India Muslim League passed Gandhiji's resolution on non-cooperation.

September 9 : Gandhiji gave interview to Associated Press of India on Indians abroad. Spoke at special A.I.C.C. meeting at Calcutta to consider action on non-co-operation resolution.

September 10 : Interviewed Motilal Ghose, editor of *Amrita Bazar Patrika*.

September 14 : Patel resigned his seat in Viceregal Council.

September 17 : In Shantiniketan, Gandhiji spoke to inmates.

September 22 : A.I.C.C. Sub-Committee consisting of Gandhiji, Motilal Nehru and V. J. Patel issued report on draft instructions for Congress organization.

Before September 25 : All-India Home Rule League with Gandhiji as president issued circular letter for carrying out special Congress resolution on non-co-operation.

September 25 : Gandhiji sent to Chairman, A.I.C.C. draft of Congress Constitution.

: Gandhiji's letter to every voter on duty of voters published.

On or after September 27 : Gandhiji sent message to countrymen in East Africa.

September 28	: In Ahmedabad, addressed students of Gujarat College, on boycott of schools and colleges, V. J. Patel presiding.
September 29	: In Ahmedabad, spoke at teachers' meeting.
October 6	: In Surat, spoke to students and teachers. M. A. Jinnah and 19 others resigned membership of Swarajya Sabha in protest against its new Constitution.
October 8	: Gandhiji spoke at Rohtak. In Bombay, Gandhiji's message to Indian women was read out at Bhagini Samaj meeting celebrating his birthday.
October 11	: In Moradabad, Gandhiji spoke at U.P. Conference
October 12	: In Aligarh, met students.
October 14	: Spoke at Kanpur.
October 15	: Spoke at Lucknow.
October 17	: In Bareilly, spoke in reply to address by municipality.
October 18	: Spoke at Amritsar. Met students of Khalsa College.
October 19	: In Lahore, spoke on non-co-operation.
October 22	: Spoke at Bhiwani Conference.
October 24	: Wrote letter to trustees of Aligarh College. Wrote on All-India Home Rule League reconstituted as "Swarajya Sabha".
October 25	: Wrote to M. A. Jinnah regarding resignation from Swarajya Sabha.
October 27	: *Young India* published Gandhiji's letter "To Every Englishman in India". In Dakor, Gandhiji addressed public meeting and women's meeting.
October 31	: In Ahmedabad, spoke at women's meeting.
November 1	: Spoke at Mehmedabad. In Nadiad, addressed public meeting and met municipal councillors.
November 2	: In Broach, spoke at public meeting. In Ankleshwar, spoke at opening of Lokamanya National School.
November 3	: Wrote in *Young India* on Congress constitution.
November 4	: In Nasik, spoke at meeting, Shrimad Shankaracharya of Karavirpeeth presiding.

November 5	:	In Poona, spoke at meetings in Deccan Gymkhana and Bhavanipeth.
Novemebr 6	:	Addressed women at Poona.
November 7	:	Gandhiji's article "If I am Arrested" and "What to Do on the 16th November" published in *Navajivan*. In Satara, Gandhiji spoke at public meeting.
November 8	:	In telegram congratulated Maulana Mahomed Ali on new Aligarh University. In Nipani and Belgaum, spoke at public meetings.
November 14	:	In Bombay, spoke at student's meeting.
Novemebr 15	:	In Ahmedabad, delivered inaugural speech as chancellor, Gujarat Vidyapeeth.
November 16	:	In Ahmedabad, paid tributes to McSwiney, Lord Mayor of Cork, at condolence meeting. Elections for Legislative councils in Bombay Presidency.
November 19	:	Gandhiji, in letter to *The Bombay Chronicle*, denied report that he favoured adoption of Urdu as national script.
November 20	:	Spoke at public meeting in Jhansi.
November 21	:	Gave interview to Associated Press of India.
November 23	:	At Agra, addressed public meeting and students' meeting.
November 26	:	Spoke to Benares Hindu University students and at public meeting.
November 27	:	Spoke to Benares Hindu University students and at public meeting.
November 28	:	At Allahabad, spoke at public meeting.
Novembar 29	:	Addressed women's meeting at Allahabad. Later, in public meeting, asked Hindus not to suspect the Ali Brothers.
November 30	:	Addressed students' meeting at Allahabad.
December 1	:	In Allahabad, spoke at opening of Tilak Vidyalaya.
December 2	:	Addressed public meetings in Phulwari Shariff and in Patna.
December 3	:	Spoke at students' meeting in Patna.
December 4	:	Spoke at women's meeting in Patna and at public meeting in Arrah.

December 5	:	Spoke at public meeting in Gaya.
December 6	:	Spoke at public meeting in Chapra.
December 8	:	Spoke at Muzaffarpur. At Bettiah, spoke on cow-protection. Writing in Young India, discussed Lord Ronaldshay's comments on Hind Swaraj and defined his conception of swaraj as being synonymous with moksha.
December 9	:	News received that Judicial Committee of Privy Council had rejected Kalinath Roy's appeal against his conviction by Martial Law Court in the Punjab. Gandhiji spoke at Motihari.
December 11	:	Spoke at public meeting in Monghyr, enumerated constituents of non-co-operation.
December 12	:	Spoke at Bhagalpur.
December 13	:	In Calcutta, spoke at opening of National Madrassa and at public meeting.
December 14	:	In Calcutta, spoke at students' meeting.
December 15	:	In Dacca, spoke at public meeting.
December 18	:	In Nagpur, spoke at public meeting.
December 22	:	Dr. Tej Bahadur Sapru assumed charge as Law Member of Viceroy's Executive Council In Nagpur, Gandhiji presided over Weavers' Conference and Antyaj Conference.
December 26	:	Thirty-fifth session of Indian National Congress commenced at Nagpur under the presidentship of C. Vijayaraghavachariar.
December 28	:	Gandhiji moved resolution on new Congress creed in meeting of Subjects Committee. Later, spoke on above resolution in plenary session.
December 29	:	Lord Sinha assumed office as Governor of Bihar and Orissa. Gandhiji, in speech on foreign propaganda at the Congress session at Nagpur, said that the British Committee and the Journal *India* be wound up.
December 30	:	Spoke on non-co-operation resolution in Congress session.
December 31	:	Spoke on Tilak Memorial Swaraj Fund in Congress Session.

1921

January 1 : Surendranath Banerjea knighted. At Nagpur, Gandhiji attended All-India Congress Committee and Working Committee meetings.

January 6 : Gandhiji, in speech at public meeting in Chhindwara, explained Nagpur Congress resolution.

January 9 : Lord Reading's appointment as Viceroy and Governor-General announced.

January 10 : The Duke of Connaught arrived in Madras.

January 12 : Model rules of Provincial Congress Committee, drafted by Gandhiji, published in Young India. In Madras, the Duke of Connaught opened new Legislative Council.

January 13 : Gandhiji spoke to students of Gujarat Mahavidyalaya at Ahmedabad.

January 15 : Col. and Mrs. Wedgwood left Madras for Colombo en route to England.

January 19 : At Nadiad, Gandhiji addressed meetings of students, teachers and merchants.

: At Vadtal, spoke at public meeting and meeting of sadhus In open letter in Young India addressing "Young Bengalis", asked them to practise tolerance and non-co-operation and to take to spinning.

January 20 : In Bombay, spoke at students' meeting.

January 23 : In Calcutta, spoke at students' meeting under presidentship of C. R. Das, and at a women's meeting at the residence of C. R. Das.

January 26 : In Calcutta, spoke at meeting of merchants. Writing on his book Hind Swaraj in Young India, said that just then he was not aiming at the swaraj described therein.

January 27 : Spoke at opening of Tilak National School in Calcutta.

January 28 : The Duke of Connaught arrived in Calcutta.

January 29 : Gandhiji spoke to post-graduate and law students at Calcutta.

January 30 : At Gujranwala, Punjab Students Conference

passed resolution welcoming Congress resolution on non-co-operation. Gandhiji, C. R. Das and Mahomed Ali sent a joint message of congratulations to above conference on their resolution. Gandhiji attended birth anniversary celebrations of Swami Vivekananda at Belur Math, near Calcutta.

February 1 : At Calcutta, the Duke of Connaught inaugurated new Bengal Legislative Council.

: Gandhiji spoke at meetings held in Mirzapur Square and Wellington Square, Calcutta, to express disappointment with Montagu-Chelmsford Reforms.

Before February 2: Gandhiji, in letter to Duke of Gonnaught, explained that non-participation in welcome to him was a demonstration not against him but against the system he had come to uphold and asked him to study and appreciate the view-point of non-co-operation.

February 4 : Spoke at opening of National College in Calcutta.

February 6 : In Patna, spoke at opening ceremony of Bihar National University and National College and at public meeting.

February 10 : At Banaras, spoke at founding of Kashi Vidyapith. Spoke at Fyzabad.

February 13 : At Delhi, spoke at opening ceremony of Tibbia College.

February 15 : At Bhiwani, spoke at Hariana Rural Conference presided over by Lala Lajpat Rai.

February 16 : At Rohtak, addressed Rural Conference, visited Jat School and laid foundation-stone of Vaishya High School.

February 17 : At Calicut, Yakub Hasan and three others were arrested and sentenced to 6 months' imprisonment.

February 19 : Gandhiji spoke at mass meeting in Gujranwala.

February 20 : At Nankana Saheb, near Lahore, 160 Akali Sikhs were massacred on the gurudwara premises by faction led by Mahant Narandas.

February 25	: At Shri, near Lyallpur, Gandhiji spoke on Nankana Sahib tragedy and counselled patience in acquiring control over gurudwaras.
February 26	: In Lucknow, spoke at District Khilafat Conference.
February 28	: The Duke of Connaught left India.
March 3	: Gandhiji along with Shaukat Ali visited gurudwara at Nankana Saheb and appealed to Sikhs to dedicate their bravery to service of the country.
March 4	: Gandhiji addressed message to Lahore Sikhs on Nankana tragedy.
March 5	: Spoke at Multan.
March 8	: At Jullundur, received address from municipality. Spoke at meetings in Hoshiarpur, Hariana and Ambala.
March 16	: In Bombay, spoke at mass meeting and at National College; gave interview to The Daily Herald. Writing in Young India,fixed one crore of rupees as the sum to be collected for Tilak Memorial Swaraj Fund by June 30, 1921.
March 17	: Spoke at Arvi.
March 18	: Spoke at Nagpur mass meeting.
March 19	: Spoke at Amraoti.
March 20	: Discussing the forthcoming Satyagraha Week, in Navajivan, advised people to spend it in pure tapashcharya.
March 23	: Spoke at two meetings in Cuttack. In open letter to Parsis, in Young India, asked them to associate themselves with the temperance movement in the country.
March 24	: In Cuttack, spoke at meeting of Muslims and at mass meeting.
March 29	: In Berhampur, replied-to welcome address presented by municipality and spoke at mass meeting.
March 30	: In Vijayanagaram, spoke at public meeting and pleaded for Hindi being made lingua franca of India. Wrote in *Young India* that the Congress

		Constitution, if honestly worked, could oust Government.
March 31	:	In Bezwada, moved four resolutions at A.I.C.C. meeting.
April 1	:	Lord Reading arrived in Bombay. In Bezwada Gandhiji spoke in reply to address presented by Municipal Council. Later spoke at A.I.C.C. meeting.
April 2	:	Lord Chelmsford left India. In Cocanada, Gandhiji spoke in reply to address of welcome presented by Municipal Council.
April 3	:	Spoke at Rajahmundry and at Ellore.
April 5	:	In Masulipatam, spoke in reply to address presented by municipality.
April 6	:	National Week commenced. Gandhiji spoke at Chirala.
April 7	:	In Nellore, declared open Tilak Vidyalaya; spoke at public meeting.
April 8	:	In Madras, spoke at public meeting and appealed for unity between Brahmins and non-Brahmins.
April 10	:	In Bombay, spoke at public meeting held under auspices of Swarajya Sabha and Central Khilafat Committee.
April 13	:	In article in *Young India,* recommended adoption of a National Flag "to live and die for". In Ahmedabad, in speech at public meeting, declared: "We want swaraj which should be Ramarajya" later, spoke at Suppressed Classes Conference.
April 15	:	Gandhiji addressed public meetings in Ras and Borsad. Reached Godhra at noon.
April 16	:	Presided over Taluka Conference at Halol; was presented with purse. Spoke to farmers in the evening.
April 17	:	Spoke at meeting of Harijans at Kalol. Left for Godhra.
April 18	:	Reached Surat in the morning. Replied to welcome address presented by Surat Municipality, stressing need for introducing

		spinning-wheels and abolishing untouchability. Addressed students of Patidar Vidyarthi Ashram. Spoke to women in the afternoon and received donations from them for Tilak Swaraj Fund. Left for Olpad, taluka town.
April 20	:	Addressed public meeting in Surat in the evening. Spoke at Bulsar.
April 21	:	Accompanied by Vallabhbhai Patel and others arrived at Chikhli in the morning.
	:	Addressed meetings in Sisodra.
April 22	:	Left on Sind tour.
April 24	:	Arrived in Sind. In Hyderabad.
April 26	:	Reached Karachi in the morning; addressed crowded public meeting, received purse of Rs. 25,000. Told municipal councillors of Karachi to resign if they could not nationalize education by teaching Hindi, organizing spinning class, and meeting expenses from municipal fund without requiring Government grant. In interview with members of Karachi Bar advised them to draw lots to decide which pleaders ought to suspend practice. Those on whom chance fell, should non-co-operate, while the rest should subscribe for maintenance of non-co-operators and their families. Riot broke out at Malegaon, Nasik district.
May 1	:	Reached Ahmedabad at night.
May 4	:	Reached Kapadvanj in the morning, addressed public meeting. Spoke at women's meeting in Kathlal. Left for Nadiad at night by car.
May 7	:	Reached Bombay in the morning; addressed Maharashtra Provincial Conference.
May 9	:	Attended marriage of Sarup Kumari Nehru (Vijayalakshmi) with R.S. Pandit.
May 10	:	Received address of welcome from Motilal Nehru on behalf of citizens at Allahabad District Conference which he addressed.
May 11	:	Left Allahabad.
May 12	:	Reached Simla in the afternoon.

May 13 : Had interview with the Viceroy in the afternoon.

May 14 : Had further interview with Viceroy in the morning. Taken in procession and accorded reception; spoke at public meeting. Addressed meeting of ladies exhorting them to take to swadeshi and contribute liberally to Tilak Swaraj Fund, collected cash and gold ornaments.

May 15 : Addressed meeting at Idgah ground, Simla.

May 21 : Addressed meeting at wayside railway station on way to Bhusawal. Reached Bhusawal; spoke at public meeting.

May 22 : Spoke at meeting in Sangamner.

May 23 : Reached Yeola in the night.

May 24 : At meeting in Barsi, urged public to contribute generously to Tilak Swaraj Fund and to take to swadeshi.

May 26 : Reached Sholapur by car early morning. Replied to Municipal address presented at Ripon Hall.

May 27 : Reached Bijapur from Bagalkot in the evening. Addressed women's meeting and later, large public meeting. Addresses presented by Municipality and local Merchants' Association.

May 28 : Left Bijapur.

May 29 : At mass meeting in Bombay, exhorted people to contribute liberally to Tilak Swaraj Fund.

May 30 : Left Bombay for Broach.

June 1 : Spoke at Gujarat Political Conference, Broach. Replied to address presented by Antyaj Conference, Vejalpur.

June 2 : Spoke at Khilafat Conference, Broach.

June 5 : Addressed Gujarat Political Conference.

June 8 : Addressed meetings at Sarkhej, Samod; collected contributions to Tilak Swaraj Fund. Held discussion with lawyers at Ahmedabad.

June 9 : Reached Wadhwan from Ahmedabad by car. Addressed public meeting at residence of Maharaja of Limbdi.

June 12 : Presided over and spoke at public meeting in Ahmedabad.

June 15	:	Accorded warm reception by, or addressed citizens at Ghatkopar, Bombay; purse of Rs. 40,000 presented for Tilak Swaraj Fund on behalf of merchant community.
June 18	:	Addressed Council of Parsi Central Association on non-co-operation. Refused to appear before Military Requirement Committee.
June 19	:	Spoke at public meeting at Vile Parle, Bombay; received purse for Tilak Swaraj Fund.
June 22	:	Inaugurated Lokamanya Rashtriya Kanya Shala—Bombay's first National Girls' School.
June 25	:	Addressed teachers and students of primary schools at Mandvi, Bombay; received purse for Tilak Swaraj Fund.
June 26	:	Addressed public meeting at Santa Cruz; received purse of Rs. 30,000 for Tilak Swaraj Fund.
June 30	:	Addressed meetings of various associations; received contributions to Tilak Swaraj Fund. Received purses from Cotton Association and Parsi Association. Target of one crore fixed at Bezwada Congress for Tilak Swaraj Fund fulfilled.
July 1	:	Spoke on swadeshi at meeting held at Bandra, Bombay.
July 2	:	Addressed meetings organized by Bombay Commission Agents' Association and Lingayat Commission Agents' Association.
July 6	:	Communal riot broke out at Aligarh. Gandhiji issued appeal to mill-owners to conduct business on national and not selfish lines and not to raise price of cloth.
July 7	:	Appealed to cloth merchants to stop import of foreign cloth.
July 10	:	Spoke on swadeshi at meeting of chemists and druggists in Bombay.
July 12	:	Spoke on prohibition to liquor-dealers at meeting organized by Parsi Rajkiya Sabha, Bombay.
July 16	:	Spoke on swadeshi at meeting in Parel, Bombay.

July 17	:	Report of Non-co-operation Committee of Central Khilafat Committee published.
	:	Gandhiji addressed meeting of weavers in Bombay.
July 19	:	Addressed in the afternoon Muslim women's meeting, Bombay. Spoke to Liquor contractors at meeting of Parsi Rajkiya Sabha.
July 20	:	Received address from Poona Municipality. Spoke at inauguration of Tilak Mahavidyalaya, unveiled Tilak's statue. Later addressed public meeting which unanimously resolved to boycott foreign cloth and to use swadeshi.
July 22	:	Addressed two public meetings on swadeshi in Bombay.
July 23	:	Addressed public meeting under auspices of Parsi Rajkiya Sabha, Bombay.
July 24	:	Spoke on swadeshi at Santa Cruz meeting.
July 26	:	Spoke on boycott of foreign cloth at meeting in Marwari Vidyalaya and at Byculla, Bombay.
July 28	:	All-India Congress Committee met in Bombay.
July 30	:	Spoke on swadeshi to crowded meeting of Parsis, held by Parsi Rajkiya Sabha.
July 31	:	Proposed in Working Committee resolution on elections to A.I.C.C. Addressed historic meeting to inaugurate swadeshi campaign with bonfire of foreign cloth, near Elphinstone Mill at Parel, Bombay. Spoke at inauguration of khadi exhibition organized by Rashtriya Stree Sabha, Bombay. Appeared as defence witness in Bombay Court.
August 1	:	Addressed public meeting at Chowpati, in Bombay, on death anniversary of Tilak.
August 3	:	Performed opening ceremony of Khilafat Stores in Bombay.
August 5	:	Arrived at Aligarh.
August 6	:	Arrived at Moradabad; addressed women's meeting and public meeting.
August 7	:	Addressed mammoth public meeting at Aminuddaula Park, Lucknow.

August 8	: Gandhiji and Central Khilafat Committee appealed to Muslims not to slaughter cows on ensuing Bakr-i- Id.
August 9	: Gandhiji arrived at Kanpur; addressed meetings of merchants and women; received address, spoke at public meeting; gave interview to Aaj.
August 10	: Reached Allahabad in the morning and spoke to women on swadeshi. In the evening addressed public meeting at which Motilal Nehru presided.
August 11	: Addressed meeting at Sahasram.
August 12	: Reached Gaya, addressed public meeting at night.
August 13	: Was accorded reception by weavers at Bihar Sharif. Spoke at public meeting at which Municipal address was presented. Attended ladies' meeting at night.
August 15	: Appealed to residents of Simla Hills not to undertake begar for British Government.
August 16	: In Patna.
August 17	: Addressed public meeting in the evening at Mirzapur Park, Calcutta. Received address from Seva Samiti at Sealdah station; left for Assam.
August 19	: Met Congress Workers in the evening at the house of Gopinath Bardoli, Secretary, Assam Provincial Congress Committee.
August 21	: A military proclamation was issued as the Moplahs in Malabar rose in revolt on August 20, set up Khilafat raj and looted Hindu zemindars.
August 22	: In Tezpur, at public meeting, Gandhiji lit bonfire of foreign cloth.
August 24	: In Jorhat, received address from ratepayers' Association and Sarbajanik Sabha.
	: Left for Tinsukia en route to Dibrugarh.
August 25	: In Dibrugarh, addressed women's meeting and public meeting.
August 30	: From Sylhet sent telegram and letter to Vallabhbhai Patel suggesting hartal in protest against visit of Prince of Wales.

August 31 : In Chittagong, spoke giving advice to railway workers on strike and telling them how he had successfully guided strike of forty thousand workers in South Africa.

September 1 : In *Young India,* wrote on "Ethics of Destruction", replying to C. F. Andrews on burning of foreign cloth; also wrote on "National Education" and discussed question of medium of instruction.

September 4 : In *Navajivan,* wrote on "Moplah Outbreak", on "Preparations for Congress" in Ahmedabad and on his experiences of Assam tour.

September 5 : Wrote to Vallabhbhai Patel on postponement of civil disobedience.

September 6 : In Calcutta, met Rabindranath Tagore.

September 7 : Spoke at Punjab Sabha meeting and addressed Marwari merchants.

September 8 : Addressed public meetings on boycott of foreign cloth.

September 10 : Addressed Khilafat volunteers.

September 13 : In Midnapore, addressed a meeting.

September 14 : Mahomed Ali arrested at Waltair on way to Malabar. Gandhiji's message to Bombay citizens on arrest of Mahomed Ali.

After September 14: Addressed circular letter to leaders inviting them to meet in Bombay to consider arrest of Ali Brothers and others.

September 15 : Arrived at Madras. Interviewed by representatives of *Daily Express* and *Madras Mail.* Spoke at public meeting. Appealed to Hindi-lovers to give financial help for spreading Hindi in Madras.

September 16 : In Madras, addressed meetings of women, piecegoods merchants and labourers.

September 17 : In Cuddalore, addressed public meeting. Left for Porto Novo en route to Kumbakonam. Sir Sankaran Nair resigned membership of Council of India.

September 18 : C. R. Das elected President of Congress. In Kumbakonam, Gandhiji spoke at public meeting.

September 19	:	In Trichinopoly, spoke in reply to address by the Municipality and Congress Committee.
September 20	:	In Srirangam, spoke in reply to municipal address and at public meeting.
September 21	:	In Dindigul, spoke in reply to address by Municicipal Council and at public meeting. In Madura, replied to address of welcome.
September 22	:	In Madura, issued message on swadeshi and loin-cloth. In Tiruppathur, spoke at citizens' meeting. Addressed meetings at Kanadukathan, Kottayur and Devakottah.
September 23	:	Interview to *Deshabhimani*. Spoke at Tinnevelly.
September 24	:	Issued appeal to Muslims of India on arrest of Ali Brothers.
September 25	:	In *Navajivan,* wrote on Hindu-Muslim unity. September 26: Trial of Ali Brothers and others commenced at Karachi.
September 27	:	In Salem, Gandhiji spoke in reply to Municipal address and at public meeting.
September 28	:	In Tirupati, spoke in reply to Municipal address.
September 29	:	In *Young India,* wrote, on "Tempering with Loyalty" in reply to Bombay Governor's warning against sedition.
October 1	:	In Bellary, replied to Municipal address.
October 2	:	In *Navajivan,* wrote on "My Loin-cloth". Sent on his birthday a message on swadeshi to the Bhagini Samaj, Bombay.
October 4	:	Issued, with other leaders, Manifesto appealing to soldiers and civilians to sever connection with Government.
October 5	:	In a letter to *The Bombay Chronicle,* appealed to people to remain peaceful in the event of his arrest. Message to workers of the Ceded Districts.
October 6	:	In *Navajivan,* wrote on problems of Indians in East Africa.
October 8	:	In Ahmedabad, spoke at meeting of pupils of workers' schools.
October 9	:	In *Navajivan,* wrote advising observance of strict non-violence, adoption of swadeshi, etc., in the

		event of his arrest. In *Navajivan,* in article "Gujarat's Test", urged Gujarat to set an example by vigorous prosecution of non-co-operation programme.
October 12	:	Spoke on swadeshi at Surat.
October 13	:	"The Great Sentinel", reply to Rabindranath Tagore appeared in *Young India.*
October 16	:	In *Navajivan,* Gandhiji urged Bombay to complete swadeshi programme, to be the first province to start peaceful revolt in the form of civil disobedience. In his notes, in Navajivan, criticized colour bar in Fiji and East Africa and untouchability in India.
October 19	:	Sent telegrams to C. Vijayaraghavachariar and Motilal Nehru on powers of Working Committee and A.I.C.C. president.
October 20	:	In *Young India,* wrote on "The Meaning of the Moplah Rising".
October 23	:	In Ahmedabad, spoke on swadeshi to women. In Navajivan, appealed to Ahmedabad workers to give up drink habit.
October 27	:	*Young India* published Mahomed Ali's letter to Gandhiji from Karachi Jail. In *Young India,* in his article "Honour the Prince" while urging complete boycott of functions, Gandhiji appealed for "forbearance towards those who differ from us". In *Young India* in article "The Secret of It" answered 24 very searching questions.
October 29	:	In Ahmedabad, spoke at bonfire of foreign cloth.
October 31	:	Began vow of spinning—to spin half an hour every day before the second meal, and to forgo the meal in case he failed to do so.
November 4	:	In Delhi, spoke on civil disobedience resolution at the A.I.C.C. meeting.
November 5	:	In Delhi, spoke on resolution regarding renouncing of government service including service in army.
November 9	:	In Lahore, delivered convocation address at National College.

November 10 : In Lahore, spoke at public meeting on conviction of Ali Brothers. In Young India article, "The Momentous Issue", explained conditions for civil disobedience.

November 16 : In Ahmedabad, spoke on birth anniversary of Srimad Rajchandra.

Before November 17: In message to Bombay public meeting, suggested steps to boycott celebrations in honour of Prince of Wales.

November 17 : In Bombay, addressed public meeting urging firm adherence to complete non-violence, swadeshi and Hindu-Muslim unity. Outbreak of riots in Bombay on arrival of Prince of Wales. In *Young India,* in article "Introspection", Gandhiji explained meaning of his threat of suicide if swaraj were not attained by end of December.

November 18 : In "A Deep Stain", condemned riots in Bombay.

November 19 : Commenced fast; appealed to citizens of Bombay for peace and communal amity.

November 20 : Issued appeal to Mavalis of Bombay.

November 21 : Broke fast at a gathering of Hindus, Muslims, Christians and Parsis. In a statement, appealed for communal harmony.

November 22 : His message to co-workers published in *Young India*.

November 25 : District Magistrate of Allahabad issued notices to Congress workers prohibiting meetings regarding civil disobedience.

November 26 : Viceroy declared Government's policy on nonco-operation in course of reply to Punjab Chamber of Commerce deputation. Gandhiji issued appeal to citizens of Bombay on communal amity.

November 27 : Issued letter to Liberals on events in Malabar.

December 2 : Lala Lajpat Rai, K. Santanam and others arrested under Prevention of Seditious Meetings Act.

December 3 : Gandhiji complimented people of Bardoli on removal untouchability.

December 4 : In *Navajivan* article, characterized love as master key of non-co-operation.

December 6 : Motilal Nehru, Jawaharlal Nehru and others arrested at Allahabad under Section 17, Criminal Law Amendment Act.

On or after December 7: Gandhiji congratulated C. R. Das on arrest of his wife and other women of Bengal.

December 10 : George Joseph, editor of *The Independent*, sentenced to 18 months' simple imprisonment. C. R. Das arrested at Calcutta.

December 11 : Harilal Gandhi and other volunteers arrested.

December 15 : Gandhiji, in *Young India* article "A Puzzle and Its Solution", declared "the non-co-operators are at war with the Government". Commenting on the arrest of C. R. Das's wife, appealed to women to take up Government's challenge. Telegraphed to Sri Prakasa congratulations on the arrest of his father, Babu Bhagwandas.

December 17 : Jawaharlal Nehru was sentenced to 6 months' simple imprisonment and a fine of Rs. 100 under Criminal Law Amendment Act.

December 19 : Gandhiji, in telegram to Malaviya, said that round table conference would be abortive unless Government was truly penitent and fulfilled conditions stated by him. In telegram to C. R. Das and Abul Kalam Azad, stated conditions for waiving proposed hartal. S. E. Stokes sentenced to 6 months' simple imprisonment on refusing to furnish security under Sections 124-A and 123-A. Lala Sankarlal sentenced to 4 months' rigorous imprisonment under Criminal Law Amendment Act.

December 20 : At Ahmedabad, Gandhiji gave interview to Associated Press regarding proposed Round Table Conference. At Allahabad, security of the Independent forfeited. Krishnakant Malaviya, Editor of Abhyudaya, and Govind Malaviya arrested while picketing. Jairam Saxena, Secretary, U.P. Congress Committee, sentenced to 18 months' rigorous imprisonment.

: At Hyderabad, Sind, Jairamdas Daulatram, Secretary, Sind Provincial Congress Committee, arrested under Section 124-A, I.P.C.

On or after December 20: In telegram to Malaviya Gandhiji expressed inability to give undertaking to stop non-co-operation pending proposed Round Table Conference.

December 21 : At Calcutta, deputation led by Malaviya met Viceroy. Viceroy, replying to deputation said that it was impossible even to consider convening a conference if "agitation in open and avowed defiance of law" was meanwhile to be continued. C. Rajagopalachari and Arni Subramania Sastri sentenced to 3 months' rigorous imprisonment for civil disobedience of order under Sec. 144. Krishnakant Malaviya, Chanderkant Malaviya and Govind Malaviya fined Rs. 100 each under Criminal Law Amendment Act.

December 22 : First handwritten issue of the Independent appeared.

December 23 : At Ahmedabad, Gandhiji attended Working Committee meeting which selected Hakim Ajmal Khan as President for forthcoming Congress Session, in absence of C. R. Das, President-elect.

December 24 : Mahadev Desai sentenced to one year's rigorous imprisonment for publishing handwritten issue of the Independent. At Ahmedabad, Gandhiji, in interview to Associated Press, regarding Viceroy's speech of December 21, said that Government had to stop its offensive activity aimed at lawful, disciplined non-violent agitation and that there could be no yielding on right of holding public meetings and forming associations.

December 25 : In Subjects Committee meeting at Ahmedabad moved main resolution of session.

December 27 : Spoke at Subjects Committee meeting. Open Session of 36th Indian National Congress commenced at Ahmedabad; Gandhiji attended. Gandhiji attended Khilafat Conference.

December 28 : In morning? spoke at Subjects Committee meeting on proposed Round Table Conference. In open Session, moved resolution on non-violent non-co-operation. Also spoke on Hasrat Mohani's motion on complete independence.

December 29 : Gave interview to Congress delegates from Bengal. In Young India, outlined code of behaviour for non-co-operators in jail.

December 30 : Gave interview to Congress leaders from U.P. Attended Muslim League session.

December 31 : Attended lecture by Paul Richard at Gujarat Vidyapith; also spoke there.

1922

January 4 : Shyam Sunder Chakravarty, editor of the *Servant*, was sentenced to 3 months' simple imprisonment for contempt of court.

January 5 : Writing in *Young India*, Gandhiji described right of free speech and free association as "the immediate issue" before the country.

January 7 : Lajpat Rai and Santanam sentenced to one year's rigorous imprisonment.

January 8 : Writing in *Navajivan*, Gandhiji discussed Khilafat and Muslim League conferences and suggested steps for Hindu-Muslim unity.

January 13 : In Madras, hartal observed on the arrival of Prince of Wales.

Before January 14: At Bombay, Gandhiji gave interview to *The Bombay Chronicle* regarding his participation in forthcoming Leaders' Conference.

January 14 : Leaders' Conference commenced in Bombay under Sir Sankaran Nair's chairmanship; Gandhiji spoke. Conference appointed Committee to frame resolutions.

January 15 : In morning Committee appointed by Conference held meeting; Gandhiji attended. Sir Sankaran Nair walked out. In evening Conference was resumed; Sir M. Visveshwarayya elected chairman instead. Gandhiji agreed to postponement of civil disobedience till January 31, 1922, pending negotiations with Viceroy for Round Table Conference.

January 17 : At Bombay, Congress Working Committee

considered recommendations of Leaders Conference and passed resolution postponing "offensive" civil disobedience till January 31, 1922. Sir Sankaran Nair's letter discussing Leaders' Conference and explaining his standpoint appeared in The *Times of India*. Gandhiji gave interview to The Bombay Chronicle regarding Sir Sankaran Nair's letter to The Times of India.

January 19 : Gandhiji, in article "Worse than Martial Law" in *Young India*, condemned Government's "savage repression". In another article "Hooliganism in Madras" condemned disturbances during hartal on January 13. Babu Bhagwandas released.

January 26 : At Ahmedabad, Gandhiji addressed gathering at Satyagraha Ashram.

January 29 : In Bardoli, spoke at Bardoli Taluka Conference; Conference passed resolution that Bardoli Taluka would immediately commence civil disobedience unless Working Committee decided otherwise or unless Round Table Conference was held. Gandhiji, commenting in *Navajivan* on debate in Central Legislature, declared that position of non-co-operators and that of the Government were "as far apart as the North Pole and the South."

January 30 : In letter to Patels of Bardoli asked them to submit to him letters of resignation from Government service, for use later.

January 31 : At Surat, meeting of Working Committee passed resolution saying that propaganda in foreign countries was absolutely essential. Gandhiji spoke at public meeting at Surat. Lajpat Rai, K. Santanam, Malik Khan and Dr. Gopi Chand released; Lajpat Rai rearrested under the Criminal Law Amendment Act of 1908.

February 1 : Gandhiji, in letter to Viceroy, informed him of Bardoli's decision to commence mass civil disobedience unless Viceroy declared in clear terms policy of absolute non-interference with

		non-violent activities, freed Press from all administrative control and released all non-violent non-co-operation prisoners.
February 4	:	At Chauri Chaura, rioting took place; police station attacked and twenty-one policemen and watchmen killed.
February 5	:	At Bardoli, Gandhiji gave interview to The Bombay. Chronicle on Bardoli's fitness for civil disobedience. Issued first of a series of leaflets in Gujarati, addressed to people of Bardoli.
February 6	:	Government issued communique in reply to Gandhiji's letter of February 1 to Viceroy.
February 7	:	Gandhiji issued to the Press his rejoinder to Government communique.
February 8	:	From Bardoli, sent confidential circular letter to members of Working Committee inviting their opinion on suspension of civil disobedience to be considered at a meeting on February 11. Hardyal Nag, President, Bengal Provincial Congress Committee, was released unconditionally.
February 9	:	Ahmedabad Municipality suspended. Gandhiji, writing in Young India, discussed official lawlessness and declared that defensive civil disobedience "must continue at any cost."
February 10	:	At Bardoli, Gandhiji in a meeting of Congress Workers announced his decision to stop civil disobedience movement immediately.
February 11	:	At Bardoli, meeting of the Working Committee was held.
February 12	:	Gandhiji commenced five-day fast as penance for Chauri Chaura incidents.
	:	Resolution passed at Working Committee meeting that in view of Chauri Chaura incidents civil disobedience be suspended. Writing in *Navajivan,* Gandhiji deplored the Chauri Chaura incidents. In another article, reiterated conditions to be observed by people for obtaining swaraj.
February 14	:	The Prince of Wales arrived in Delhi.
February 15	:	At Bardoli, Gandhiji gave interview to *The*

		Bombay Chronicle on his future programme. In letter to Sir Daniel Hamilton, stressed importance of the spinning-wheel for India.
	:	In England, House of Lords resolved to appoint a Standing Joint Committee of the Lords and Commons on Indian affairs.
February 16	:	In *Young India* Gandhiji wrote on "The Crime of Chauri Chaura".
February 19	:	Wrote to Jawaharlal Nehru explaining Working Committee's resolution suspending civil disobedience.
February 22	:	Wrote to Chairman, A.I.C.C., saying that establishing agency in any foreign country for disseminating news about the political situation in India was undesirable just then.
February 23	:	Sir William Vincent made statement in Assembly on Government's policy regarding Non-co-operation Movement.
February 24	:	At Delhi, A.I.C.C. meeting commenced. Viceroy gave assent to Bill for repeal of Repressive Laws.
February 25	:	At Delhi, A.I.C.C. meeting adopted with modifications Working Committee's resolutions passed at Bardoli on February 12.
February 26	:	At Delhi, Gandhiji gave interview to Press on A.I.C.C. meeting and its resolutions.
March 3	:	Jawaharlal Nehru and six others released from Lucknow Jail before expiry of their term.
March 4	:	Gandhiji in Ahmedabad.
March 5	:	In the afternoon attended Gujarat Provincial Congress Committee meeting presided over by Vallabhbhai Patel.
March 8	:	Left Ahmedabad for Ajmer by evening train.
March 9	:	Attended Ulemas' Conference at Ajmer. Left Ajmer for Ahmedabad. Lajpat Rai sentenced to one year's rigorous imprisonment for breaking ban on addressing public meeting. Resignation of Montagu, Secretary of State for India, accepted.
March 10	:	Gandhiji reached Ahmedabad in the afternoon. Arrested at 10 p.m. and taken to Sabarmati Jail.

March 11 : Charged with promoting disaffection against Government through his writings in Young India before Assistant Magistrate; committed to Sessions. Exhorted Ashram people in parting words to propagate peace and harmony among all communities. Message to country summed up in one word: 'khaddar'.

Before March 18: Lloyd George, British Prime Minister, said in Commons that British supremacy had to be maintained, and repeated that goal of British Policy in India was responsible

: Government, as envisaged in Preamble of the Government of India Act, 1919, but not of the Dominion type.

March 18 : Gandhiji, in jail, gave interview to Manchester Guardian on non-co-operation. Tried by Sessions Court at Circuit House, Shahibagh, sentenced to six years' imprisonment; Shankerlal Banker to one year.

March 20 : At midnight Gandhiji taken from Sabarmati Jail to Yeravda Prison by special train.

March 21 : Arrived at Yeravda Prison at 5.30 p.m.

March 22 : Fasted on being deprived of spinning-wheel, which was restored in the evening.

March 23 : Shuaib Qureshi took over as Editor of *Young India*.

April 1 : Gandhiji visited by C. Rajagopalachari.

April 22 : Had talk with Gangadharrao Deshpande, journalist and Congress leader of Karnatak.

May 6 : Gandhiji informed by Government that his letter to Hakim Ajmal Khan could not be forwarded.

May 12 : Wrote to Hakimji that, in view of Government's action in withholding his last letter, he would stop the quarterly communication permitted by jail rules.

June 1 : C. Rajagopalachari took over editorship of *Young India*.

July 1 : Gandhiji had visit from Maganlal Gandhi.

July 2 : Kasturba, Manilal, Devdas and Mathuradas Trikumji called on Gandhiji.

September 13	:	Gandhiji commenced week's silence.
September 20	:	Went on one week's silence for the second time.
October 4	:	Kasturba, Jamnalal, Ramdas, Punjabhai and Kishorelal called on Gandhiji.
November 11	:	A.I.C.C at Calcutta passed Civil Disobedience resolution.
1923		
January 27	:	Kasturba visited Gandhiji.
February 10	:	Mulshi Peta Satyagrahis in Yeravda Prison flogged for refusing to work.
	:	Gandhiji sought Jail Superintendent's permission to meet Mulshi Peta prisoners.
April 16	:	Devdas met Gandhiji.
April 17	:	Shankerlal Banker released.
April 21	:	Gandhiji indisposed with severe pain in stomach.
May 1	:	Wrote to Jail Superintendent refusing special class treatment denied to other prisoners.
May 5	:	Examined by Col. Maddock, Surgeon-General.
May 15	:	Examined again by Col. Maddock. Visited by Indulal Yagnik.
May 18	:	Transferred to European Ward; Kasturba and others called.
June 27	:	Mulshi Peta satyagrahis commenced fast.
June 29	:	Approached Jail Superintendent for permission to see Mulshi Peta prisoners on their being flogged again. Discussed matter with Col. Dalziel.
July 2	:	In great physical pain at night.
July 9	:	Communicated to Jail Superintendent his decision to fast since his offer to meet Mulshi Peta satyagrahis had been rejected.
July 10	:	Agreed to postpone fast for 48 hours on Superintendent's request.
July 11	:	Received Governor's message through Griffiths.
July 12	:	Informed by Griffiths that he would be allowed to meet Mulshi Peta satyagrahis and that flogging would be restored to only when prisoners

attacked jail officials. Persuaded satyagrahis to give up fast.

July 16 : Kasturba and others met Gandhiji.

August 13 : Discussed with Governor, Sir George Lloyd, classification of prisoners.

September 10 : Devdas, Narandas, and others called on Gandhiji.

October 10 : Kasturba, Avantikabai, Jamnalal and Savatibai saw Gandhiji.

November 26 : Started, writing The History of Satyagraha in South Africa in Gujarati.

December 17 : Visited by Kasturba, Mathuradas and Ramdas.

December 18 : Ramabai Ranade met Gandhiji.

1924

January 2 : Cocanada session of Indian National Congress concluded.

January 5 : C.R. Das elected member of Bengal Legislative Council.

January 8 : Gandhiji had severe stomach pain, passed restless night.

January 12 : Visited by Srinivasa Sastri in Sassoon Hospital.

: Operated on by Col. Maddock for appendicitis.

January 14 : Conveyed thanks to countrymen through Dr. Phatak for deep affection shown him during critical period of health.

January 19 : Gave interview to *The Bombay Chronicle.*

February 2 : In interview to Dilip Kumar Roy, expressed views on music.

February 4 : Order of unconditional release of Gandhiji issued.

Before February 5: Interviewed by editor of *Yug Dharma,* said he contemplated writing autobiography.

February 5 : Release order conveyed at 8 a.m., but continued to remain in Sassoon Hospital.

After February 5: Gave Devdas answers to questions on swaraj from Drew Pearson.

On or before February 6: Sent message to Gujarat Vidyapith that his release was no matter for rejoicing but rather for humility.

Before February 7: In interview to *The Bombay Chronicle,* expressed grief that his release was based on grounds of health.

February 7 : Issued message to nation through Congress President that he was not happy over release.

February 12 : Requested Mahomed Yakub to desist from moving Assembly resolution recommending award of Nobel Peace Prize to him.

February 14 : Issued statement on Class Areas Bill.

February 25 : Issued statement on Jaiton firing.

February 28 : Gave interview to Sind deputation consisting of Jairamdas Doulatram, Kazi Abdul-Rehman, Seth Isserdas and R. K. Sidhwa.

March 1 : Sent message of Sympathy to Poona citizens' meeting, held to protest against ban on Horniman's return to India.

March 4 : Issued statement on Akali Movement.

On or before March 7: In message to Delhi Provincial Political Conference, advised promotion of Hindu-Muslim unity.

March 9 : Interviewed by Associated Press on his talks with Akali deputation.

March 10 : Addressed students of B. J. Medical School, Poona. Left Sassoon Hospital; entrained at night for Bombay.

March 11 : Arrived in Bombay. Stayed at Narottam Morarji's bungalow at Juhu for convalescence.

March 15 : Issued statement on Potti Sriramulu's fast for Harijan entry to temples.

March 17 : Resumed practice of observing silence every Monday.

March 19 : Sent message to Vykom satyagrahis.

March 20 : Issued statement on Government's opium policy.

March 21 : Addressed party of students and teachers from Bombay Rashtriya Shala.

March 23 : Issued second statement on Class Areas Bill.

March 29 : Had discussions regarding 'No-changers' and Swarajists with Madan Mohan Malaviya, Lajpat Rai and Motilal Nehru.

Before March 30: Addressed teachers, members of Managing Committee and guardians of pupils of National School at Vile Parle.

April 2 : Wrote preface to Satyagraha in South Africa.

April 3 : Resumed editorship of *Young India*. Had interview with Dr. Kitchlew.

April 4 : Held talks with Madan Mohan Malaviya, Motilal Nehru and Hakim Ajmal Khan on Hindu-Muslim unity.

April 6 : Resumed editorship of *Navajivan*. Issued third statement on Class Areas Bill.

April 11 : Prepared draft statement in connection with Council-entry.

April 13 : Sent Motilal Nehru copy of draft statement on Council-entry.

April 15 : Expressed views on Vykom Satyagraha in interview to *The Hindu*.

April 23 : Attended Working Committee meeting. Srinivasa Sastri called on Gandhiji.

April 24 : In interview to *The Daily Express*, gave his views on Swaraj.

May 1 : Appealed for Hindu help to starving Moplahs.

Before May 4 : Issued statement on Kathiawar Political Conference.

May 16 : Gandhiji has discussions with representatives of Vykom Satyagraha Committee.

May 17 : Discussions on Vykom satyagraha continued. Gandhiji gave interview to the The Hindu on Vykom satyagraha Council-entry.

May 18 : In first public appearance after release from jail, presided over Buddha Jayanti celebrations in Bombay.

May 20 : Discussions with Vykom Satyagraha Committee representatives concluded.

May 22 : Gandhiji and Swaraj Party leaders issued separate statements on Council-entry.

May 28 : Gandhiji left Bombay for Ahmedabad.

May 29 : Returned to Satyagraha Ashram after absence of 26 months. *Young India* article analysed Hindu-Muslim tension: its cause and cure.

May 30	:	Gandhiji gave interview to *Swatantrya* of Nagpur on Hindu-Muslim question.
May 31	:	Gave inteview to Associated Press of India.
June 3	:	In interview to *The Times of India,* expressed his view of Bengal Provincial Conference's resolution on Gopinath Saha. Sir Michael O'Dwyer awarded damages with costs, in O'Dwyer-Nair case.
June 8	:	Gandhiji gave interview to The Hindu, on Swarajists' programme, Hindu-Muslim tension, and impending A.I.C.C. session.
June 10	:	Delivered annual address at Gujarat Vidyapith.
June 11	:	Sent message to Saurashtra Rajput Conference.
June 19	:	Published in *Young India* four resolutions which he proposed to move at A.I.C.C. meeting.
June 24	:	Gave interview to Associated Press of India.
June 27	:	Moved first of his four resolutions at A.I.C.C. session at Ahmedabad.
June 28	:	Addressed A.I.C.C. on the second day of its session.
June 29	:	Moved his second and third resolutions at A.I.C.C.
June 30	:	Spoke at informal meeting, after conclusion of A.I.C.C. session.
July 1	:	Conveyed his impressions of A.I.C.C. in interview to Associated Press of India.
July 3	:	Made in *Young India* retrospective study of A.I.C.C. proceedings.
July 11	:	Addressed Gujarat Provincial Congress Committee.
July 13	:	Communal riots reported from Nagpur.
July 15	:	Communal riots broke out in Delhi. Sarojini Naidu called on Gandhiji at Sabarmati.
July 17	:	*Young India* article gave analysis of 'an appeal to the nation' issued by D. C. Chatterji and others.
End of July	:	Devastating floods in Malabar.
August 1	:	Gandhiji presided over Ahmedabad Conference of Teachers of National Schools in G0d by Ahmedabad Municipality.

August 28 : In *Young India* in "Gulbarga Gone Mad" appealed for Hindu-Muslim unity.

August 29 : Reached Bombay. Spoke in reply to address presented by Bombay Municipal Corporation.

August 30 : In letter to Motilal Nehru explained the terms of his "full surrender" and proposed measures to improve Congress organization. Participated in the birth anniversary celebrations of Dadabhai Naoroji organized by National Women's Council.

August 31 : In statement on unity explained his attitude of "perfect surrender" to Motilal Nehru. At Excelsior Theatre addressed Parsi Rajakiya Mandal Meeting for Malabar Flood Relief. At Bombay Provincial Congress Committee meeting replied to criticism of Spinning Resolution passed at Ahmedabad.

September 2 : Visited Khadi Bhandar at Princess Street. In the evening gave away prizes at National Medical College. At 9 p.m. spoke at meeting of Bombay Provincial Congress Committee.

September 3 : Left Bombay for Poona by night train.

September 4 : In Poona spoke at Public meeting. Visited Servants of India Society. Spoke at Tilak Mahavidyalaya Convocation. Advised Congress workers to abdicate power and take up hand-spinning.

September 5 : Returned to Bombay en route to Ahmedabad. Visited Surat and addressed mass meeting in the evening.

September 6 : In letter to Motilal Nehru emphasized decision not to divide the Congress. In letter to Rajagopalachari stressed that "we must abdicate power altogether if we have faith in our mission".

September 9-10 : Riots in Kohat; Hindus were evacuated.

September 13 : Gandhiji left Ahmedabad for Delhi in connection with Hindu-Muslim riots.

September 14 : Reached Delhi.

September 15 : In Delhi inaugurated *The Hindustan Times*.

September 17 : Commenced 21-day fast at Mahomed Ali's house.

September 18	:	In a statement released at 2 a.m. described 21-day fast as "penance and prayer".
September 24	:	In statement to the Press on Unity Conference stressed need to evolve "heart-unity" and not just a "patched-up peace".
September 26	:	Unity Conference in Delhi passed resolution requesting Gandhiji to give up fast.
September 27	:	Gandhiji rejected Unity Conference appeal.
October 1	:	Deputation of Bombay women met Gandhiji to persuade him to give up fast. Gandhiji's tribute to Annie Besant on her 78th birthday was read out at a public meeting in Bombay.
Before October 2	:	Gandhiji along with Rabindranath Tagore appealed to International Opium Conference, Geneva, to adopt measures for suppression of opium traffic except for medicinal purposes.
October 8	:	In Delhi at 12 noon, broke his fast after making statement on Hindu-Muslim unity. Mahomed Ali presented Gandhiji with a cow purchased from a butcher for being sent to pinjrapole.
October 9	:	In message to the Press Gandhiji sought "prayer and co-operation of every son and daughter of India" in his endeavour for unity.
October 16	:	In *Young India* reiterated necessity of Spinning Franchise. In a letter sought Viceroy's permission to visit Kohat.
October 20	:	In message asked Transvaal Indians to continue struggle for honourable existence.
October 23	:	In *Young India* in "The Law of Love" asked No-changers to live "on the sufferance of their fellow-workers, the Swarajists and the Liberals".
October 28	:	Viceroy refused permission to Gandhiji to visit Kohat.
October 30	:	In message to U.P. Political Conference, Gorakhpur, Gandhiji condemned repression in Bengal and appealed to people to preserve peace.
November 2	:	Left Delhi for Calcutta.
November 6	:	In joint statement with Swaraj Party leaders announced agreement on concerted action,

suspension of non-co-operation and Spinning Franchise. Spoke in reply to Calcutta Corporation address at Town Hall.

November 7 : Explained during discussions with No-changers implications of agreement with Swaraj Party leaders. Spoke in reply to Howrah Municipality address at Howrah Town Hall. Interview to Associated Press of India on his agreement with Swaraj Party leaders. Left for Delhi.

November 10 : In Delhi, interviewed by Associated Press of India, informed that Calcutta Agreement would be submitted to All-Party Conference, Bombay, for final decision.

November 13 : In *Young India* explained the Calcutta Agreement. In letter informed Romain Rolland of the arrival of Madeleine Slade (Mirabehn) whom he would help "to become a little bridge between West and East". Visited Modern School; addressed students at Ramjas College. Attended funeral of Bi-Amma, mother of Ali Brothers.

November 14 : In a message to World Tomorrow, New York, described non-violence as the greatest living force.

November 16 : Issued statement on Kohat question.

Before November 17:In message to Tamilnad Conference, Tiruvannamalai, said the spirit of non-violence was basis of agreement with Swaraj Party leaders.

November 18 : Left Delhi for Bombay.

November 20 : Reached Bombay.

November 21 : Spoke at Congress Working Committee meeting, Bombay. Moved the first resolution on Bengal Ordinance at All-Party Conference, Bombay. In interview to Associated Press of India refuted reports in local newspapers about withdrawal of Spinning Franchise.

November 22 : Spoke on unity at All-Party Conference.

November 23 : At A.I.C.C. meeting moved resolution approving the Calcutta Agreement. At Chowpatty spoke condoling Bi-Amma's death.

November 25	:	Left Bombay for Ahmedabad.
November 26	:	Reached Ahmedabad.
November 30	:	In Ahmedabad, addressed students of Gujarat National College.
December 4	:	Reached Lahore; conferred with Lajpat Rai and Madan Mohan Malaviya at the former's residence.
December 5	:	Reached Amritsar. In the afternoon spoke at a big diwan in Golden Temple. In the evening, addressed public meeting at Jallianwala Bagh.
December 6	:	At Punjab Provincial Khilafat Conference spoke in reply to Zafar Ali's attack on Hindu leaders.
	:	In Lahore delivered Convocation address at Punjab Qaumi Vidyapith.
December 7	:	Delivered presidential address at Punjab Provincial Conference.
December 8	:	At Gandhiji's instance the representatives of the Khilafat Conference met at Lahore to evolve methods to strengthen Hindu-Muslim unity.
December 9	:	In speech at Rawalpindi Gandhiji advised Hindu refugees not to return to Kohat on Government advice.
December 11	:	Left Rawalpindi in the morning for Ahmedabad; at Lahore Railway Station en route, was interviewed by *The Tribune* on Kohat affairs.
December 13	:	Reached Ahmedabad.
December 14	:	In statement to the Press warned people not to believe unauthenticated reports of his Punjab speeches.
December 18	:	Left Ahmedabad for Belgaum.
December 20	:	Reached Belgaum.
December 21	:	Spoke in reply to welcome address by the Belgaum Municipality and the District Board.
December 23	:	In Belgaum, A.I.C.C. formed itself into Subjects Committee with Gandhiji as president and appointed a subcommittee with 16 members to draft resolution endorsing Calcutta Agreement.
December 24	:	Subjects Committee adopted resolution endorsing Calcutta Agreement and Spinning

		Franchise Khilafat Conference was held in the Congress pandal under the presidentship of Dr. Kitchlew.
December 25	:	In Belgaum at Subjects Committee meeting Gandhiji appealed to No-changers to have faith in Swarajists.
December 26	:	The Indian National Congress began its 39th session under Gandhiji's presidentship. Gandhiji delivered the presidential address and spoke on the resolution endorsing Calcutta Agreement.
December 27	:	Spoke at Fifth All-India Students' Conference in the morning. At the Congress session spoke on various resolutions and on Annie Besant's statement. The Congress session concluded with a moving address by Gandhiji first in Hindi and then in English. Gandhiji Spoke at Untouchability Conference. Attended Hindu Mahasabha session held in Congress pandal.
December 28	:	Delivered the presidential address at Cow-protection Conference.
December 30	:	Spoke at All-India States Conference.
December 31	:	In Bombay at annual session of All-India Muslim League condemned Natal Boroughs Ordinance.

1925

January 1	:	In *Young India,* answered M. N. Roy's criticism of his article "Bolshevism or Discipline?".
January 2	:	Spoke at Dohad and at Godhra.
January 8	:	In Bhavnagar delivered the presidential address at the Third Kathiawar Political Conference.
January 9	:	The Kathiawar Political Conference concluded with a speech by Gandhiji. At Samaldas College Gandhiji spoke on the duty of students.
January 14	:	In Ahmedabad, spoke at Gujarat Provincial Conference meeting. Delivered the convocation address at Gujarat Vidyapith.
January 15	:	In *Young India* summarized instructions regarding working of Spinning Franchise. At Sojitra spoke at Petlad District Cultivators' Conference.
January 16	:	At Sojitra, Gandhiji addressed conference of women and Antyajas. Proceeded to Bardoli.

January 17	:	Addressed mass meeting at Bardoli.
January 18	:	Spoke at Kaliparaj Conference at Vedchhi.
January 19	:	Left Surat for Ahmedabad.
January 20	:	Reached Ahmedabad.
January 23	:	At Delhi, presided over the meeting of the All-Party Conference Committee to consider the appointment of a sub-committee to draw up a plan for swaraj and Hindu-Muslim unity.
January 24	:	A sub-committee with Gandhiji as President and Motilal Nehru as General Secretary was appointed by the All- Party Conference Committee.
January 26	:	The Viceroy disallowed Motilal Nehru's bill to repeal the Bengal Ordinance.
January 27	:	Commenting on the Viceroy's speech, Gandhiji told pressmen at Delhi that Indian opinion was unanimous in condemning the Bengal Ordinance.
February 3	:	Left Delhi for Rawalpindi.
February 4	:	Reached Rawalpindi with Shaukat Ali to enquire into the Kohat disturbances.
February 5	:	At Rawalpindi, addressed the Hindu refugees of Kohat. In the Legislative Assembly, a resolution for the supersession of the Bengal Ordinance by an Act was passed.
February 6	:	At Rawalpindi, Gandhiji examined Ahmed Gul, Khilafat Secretary, and Kamal Jailane, a zamindar, regarding the Kohat riots and recorded their evidence.
February 7	:	Left Rawalpindi.
February 8	:	Reached Delhi. Met leaders.
February 9	:	Reached Ahmedabad.
	:	Sent a wire to the Viceroy, asking for permission to visit Kohat in the beginning of March.
February 10	:	At Sabarmati Ashram, spoke to the inmates on conversions of Hindus in Kohat.
February 11	:	Visited Anklav, Borsad and Bhadran; addressed meetings.
February 12	:	Received a welcome address from the Bhadran Seva Mandal. Spoke at Virsad.

February 13 : Addressed a meeting at Palej. Reached Ahmedabad. The Viceroy sent a telegram disallowing Gandhiji's proposed tour of Kohat.

February 15 : The Kathiawar tour commenced. A special durbar was held at Rajkot to honour Gandhiji. Thakore Saheb Lakhjiraj presented a welcome address on behalf of the Representative Assembly. Gandhiji in reply stressed the programme of khadi and elimination of untouchability. Inaugurated a national school and a Jain hostel at Rajkot.

February 19 : Reached Porbunder from Rajkot. Sent a telegram to the Viceroy repeating his request for permission to visit Kohat in order to assist the Government. Replied to an address of Porbunder citizens. Spoke at a meeting of Antyajas.

February 20 : Reached Wankaner.

February 21 : Reached Wadhwan. Visited an Antyaja enclave. Spoke at public meeting. Inaugurated a Bal Mandir.

February 22 : Reached Ahmedabad. Stressed the need for prohibition in the Kathiawar States in an interview to A.P.I. The Viceroy in a telegram reiterated his decision not to allow Gandhiji to visit Kohat. Acharya Gidwani was released on the suspension of his sentence.

February 23 : Gandhiji sent a congratulatory telegram to Acharya Gidwani. Wrote to Shaukat Ali regarding their differences on Kohat affairs and suggested that the whole matter be examined by Hakim Ajmal Khan or Dr. Ansari.

February 25 : Blessed Dahyabhai Patel and the bride at their marriage at the Ashram.

February 26 : In *Young India* article, criticized the Kohat settlement but ruled out civil resistance.

February 27 : Reached Delhi.

March 1 : Presided over the meeting of the All-Party Conference Comittee's sub-committee on Hindu-Muslim unity at Raisina Hostel, Delhi. The sub-committee adjourned *sine die.*

March 2 : Gandhiji and Motilal Nehru issued a joint statement explaining the reasons for the sub-committee's adjournment. Gandhiji replied to the questions of Sten Konow, a Norwegian Indologist.

March 4 : Lord Reading's visit to England for consultations with the Secretary of State for India announced.

March 5 : Gandhiji reached Bombay on way to Vykom. In interview to Press, said Hindu-Muslim unity was inevitable.

March 7 : Reached Madras. Gave interviews to *Swadesamitran, Free Press of India,* and *Swarajya* representatives. The Madras Corporation presented a welcome address. Spoke at a mass meeting at Tilak Ghat explaining his Vykom mission. Left for Vykom.

March 8 : Reached Ernakulam. Received a welcome address from the Ernakulam Municipal Corporation. Reached Cochin. Addressed a mass meeting on Cochin beach.

March 10 : At Vykom, attended morning prayers with the satyagrahis. Held discussions with the Commissioner of Police Trivandrum, V.V.S. Aiyer of the Tamil Gurukul and the caste Hindu oppositionists. Addressed a public meeting on the Vykom satyagraha; received an address from the Ezhavas of Ambalapuzha.

March 11 : Spoke to the inmates of Satyagraha Ashram on the duty of satyagrahis. Left Vykom. Reached Allepey.

March 12 : Reached Quilon. Spoke on the Vykom satyagraha in reply to a welcome address presented by the Quilon Municipality. Wrote in *Young India* answering Romain Rolland on swadeshi; explained his views on birth-control.

March 13 : At Varkalai, received a welcome address from the Ezhavas and other untouchables at Sivagiri Hall. Reached Trivandrum. Replied to a students' address at the Science College. Met members of the royal family and the Dewan of Travancore.

		Several public bodies presented welcome addresses at a mammoth meeting at the Cantonment Maidan.
March 14	:	The Municipal Council of Trivandrum presented a welcome address at the Victoria Jubilee Town Hall. Gandhiji complimented the Travancore Council on passing resolution on spinning. Addressed students of the Law College, Trivandrum. Visited Cape Comorin and Nagercoil.
March 15	:	Left Trivandrum for Vykom. Reached Kottayam. The Kottayam Municipality and the Hindi students presented welcome addresses.
March 16	:	Gandhiji reached Vykom.
March 17	:	Indanthurithi Nambudiri, a spokesman of the caste Hindus, gave Gandhiji a copy of *Shankara Smriti*. Gandhiji discussed the future of satyagraha with members of the Kerala Provincial Congress Committee. Addressed the Pulayas at Satyagraha Ashram. Left Vykom.
March 18	:	Reached Parur. The citizens of Parur and others presented welcome addresses. At Alwaye, Gandhiji spoke at the Union Christian College and the Advaita Ashram. Reached Trichur at 2 p.m. Addresses were presented by the Trichur Municipality and the Nambudiri Yogakshema Sabha. Gandhiji visited the ex-Maharaja of Cochin. Wrote to the Police Commissioner, Trivandrum, in connection with removal of barriers and the lifting of prohibition order.
Marh 19	:	Reached Podanur. The railway workers presented an address. At Tirupur, Gandhiji received a welcome address from the townsmen and the Municipal Council.
March 21	:	Reached Pudupalayam. Spoke at a villagers' meeting and replied to the welcome address of the Coimbatore District Sengunthar Mahajana Sangham. At Tiruchengode, received an address from the Congress Committee and the Tiruchengode Union.

March 22	:	Reached Madras. Was honoured by the Madras Social Service League. Witnessed a spinning demonstration and spoke at a women's meeting at Triplicane. Unveiled Kasturiranga Iyengar's portrait at the Hindu office.
March 23	:	The Commissioner of Police, Trivandrum, sent a telegram to Gandhiji, agreeing to the withdrawal of prohibitory order from April 7.
March 24	:	Gandhiji conveyed to the Police Commissioner his acceptance of the latter's proposals. Released the correspondence to the Press.
	:	At Madras, the Triplicane Urban Co-operative Society, the Madras Ayurvedic Pharmacy and the Hindi Prachar Samiti presented welcome addresses.
	:	Gandhiji spoke to temperance workers at Gokhale Hall and addressed students of the Women's Christian College.
	:	Several public bodies presented addresses at a public meeting at Tilak Ghat. Yakub Hasan presided.
	:	Gandhiji received a welcome address from the directors and Swarajya.
March 26	:	Reached Bombay. Explained the success of his Vykom mission in an interview to *The Bombay Chronicle*. Addressed a women's meeting; received an address presented by the depressed classes. Witnessed a spinning competition organized by the Bombay Provincial Congress Committee. Opened the Congress House at Girgam. Left for Ahmedabad. *Young India* published the findings of Gandhiji and Shaukat Ali on Kohat riots.
March 29	:	In a manifesto, C.R. Das explained the Swaraj Party's stand on repression, violence and co-operation with the Government. In *Navajivan* article, Gandhiji appealed to people to fast, spin and propagate khadi during the National Week.
April 1	:	Left Ahmedabad for Botad on a tour of Kathiawar.

April 2 : Visited Madhada, Dhasa and Bagasara; spoke at meetings.

April 3 : At Palitana, visited the Jain shrines and replied to an address of welcome. Discussions with Munishri Karpurvijay on spinning by sadhus.

April 5 : Spoke at Lathi.

April 6 : Spoke at a public meeting at Mangrol and replied to objections of orthodox Hindus to sitting with the Antyajas.

April 6-13 : National Week celebrations.

April 9 : In *Young India,* Gandhiji answered a revolutionary's arguments in favour of violence.

April 10 : The Earl of Lytton took charge as acting Viceroy for four months.

April 11 : Gandhiji reached Bombay after the Kathiawar tour. Interview to *The Bombay Chronicle* on dissensions in the Congress.

April 13 : Spoke at a public meeting organized by the Bombay Provincial Congress Committee to observe the Jallianwala Bagh Day.

April 15 : Spoke at meetings in Karadi, Gamdevi and Amalsad.

April 16 : Visited the Gurukul at Supa and addressed the brahmacharis. Reached Navsari. Spoke at a meeting of Parsis. In *Young India* article said he would follow the wishes of the majority in the Congress.

April 18 : The Jambusar Municipality presented him an address of welcome. At Broach, Gandhiji received a welcome by the District Local Board, and addressed a public meeting at the Victoria Memorial Clock Tower.

April 23 : Reached Tithal for convalescence after an attack of malaria.

April 27 : Left Tithal for Bombay. Reached Bombay on way to Calcutta for the Bengal Provincial Conference at Faridpur.

April 28 : At Madhav Bagh spoke at the All-India Cow-Protection Conference where the constitution of

		the All-India Cow-Protection Association was adopted.
April 29	:	Gave interview to the special correspondent of *New India* on the Commonwealth of India Bill. Left Bombay.
April 30	:	Reached Nagpur en route to Calcutta.
May 1	:	Gandhiji arrived in Calcutta. Gave interview to Associated Press of India. Spoke at public meeting in Mirzapur Park.
May 2	:	Inaugurated Industrial Exhibition at Faridpur. Addressed All-India Hindu Sammelan. Spoke at Bengal Provincial Young Men's Conference.
May 3	:	Addressed conference of Muslims. Received addresses from students and Faridpur Municipal Corporation. Spoke at Bengal Provincial Conference, presided over by C.R. Das.
May 4	:	Attended Provincial Conference at Faridpur.
May 5	:	Visited Prabartak Ashram, Chandernagore.
May 6	:	Called on Sir Surendranath Banerjea. Laid foundation-stone of Ashtanga Ayurveda Vidyalaya Hospital building.
May 7	:	Greeted Tagore on birthday eve. Presided over Buddha Jayanti function at Buddh Vihara, Calcutta. Started on tour of East Bengal.
May 8	:	Spoke at Lohagunj (Dacca) and received purse of Rs. 5,000/-. Addressed public meeting at Malikanda.
May 9	:	Visited National School at Dighirpur. Received address from Union Board at public meeting. Addressed workers at Taltola. Spoke at Malkhanagar. Gave interview to Associated Press of India.
May 10	:	Addressed Merchants' Association, Puranbazar. Received addresses and spoke at public meetings at Chandpur. Visited National School, Chandpur.
Before May 12	:	In interview to Hardayal Nag, denied differences on basic issues with Swarajists.
May 12	:	Arrived at Chittagong in the morning. Spoke at public meeting. Discussed Anglo-Indian question with Dr. Moreno.

June 3	:	Arrived in Darjeeling; stayed with C. R. Das.
June 6	:	Spoke to missionary women at Darjeeling.
June 10	:	At Jalpaiguri, exhorted merchants and businessmen to utilize their wealth and talent for country's welfare.
June 11	:	Spoke to students at Nawabganj.
June 12	:	Visited Bijhari school at Upashi (Dist. Nawabganj). At Bhojeswar, addressed meeting.
June 13	:	Addressed public meeting, visited Public Library at Madaripur.
June 14	:	At Barisal addressed public meeting. Visited Oxford Mission weaving shed; said the only supplementary occupation could be spinning, not weaving.
June 16	:	C.R. Das died at Darjeeling.
June 17	:	Gandhiji received at Khulna news of Das's death. Paid tribute to C.R. Das at public meeting.
June 18	:	Attended C.R. Das's funeral in Calcutta.
June 22	:	Issued appeal for Deshbandhu Memorial Fund.
June 23	:	Attended meeting at Municipal Market, Calcutta. Gave interviews to *The Statesman* and *The Searchlight*.
June 24	:	In interview to *The Englishman* denied rift in Swaraj Party. Declared intention to stay in Calcutta a month longer.
June 26	:	Presided at Gujarati residents' meeting to mourn the death of Das.
June 28	:	Appealed through Navajivan for meetings throughout country on July 1, the Shraddha Day of Das, and for taking the spinning pledge.
June 30	:	Presided over condolence meeting at University Institute, Calcutta. Principal S.K. Rudra died.
July 1	:	Gandhiji attended shraddha rites of Das. Spoke at public meeting; at women's meeting received gold bangles and cash for Das Memorial Fund.
July 2	:	Bakr-Id day riots broke out in Kidderpore, Calcutta. Gandhiji, with Abul Kalam Azad, visited trouble spots, pacified both communities.

		In interview to Associated Press of India, put blame on Hindus.
July 4	:	Visited Indian Institute at Kharagpur; later addressed mammoth meeting at Indian Recreation Ground, pleaded for Hindu-Muslim unity.
July 5	:	Resumed publishing his History of Satyagraha in South Africa in Navajivan, interrupted because of fast and other reasons.
July 7	:	At Midnapur, addressed students', women's and public meetings.
July 9	:	At Swarajist Councillors' meeting, urged J. M. Sen Gupta's election as Mayor.
July 12	:	At Rajshahi, visited Public Library, addressed public meeting.
July 16	:	Spoke at Swaraj Party General Council meeting attended by Motilal Nehru and others.
July 17	:	At Swaraj Party General Council meeting said if Swarajists insisted on abolition of spinning franchise he would accede to the demand but would resign from Congress Presidentship.
July 19	:	Wrote to Motilal Nehru, personally absolving him from Belgaum Pact.
Before July 24	:	Addressing Marwari Agarwal Conference at Calcutta, deprecated child-marriage.
July 24	:	Spoke at the University Institute meeting on Kristodas Pal's death anniversary. Addressed European Association meeting at Grand Hotel, Calcutta.
July 27	:	In message to Forward commended spinning and khaddar to honour the memory of Lokamanya Tilak.
July 28	:	Addressed Christian missionaries at Y.M.C.A., Calcutta.
July 29	:	Spoke at meeting of Anglo-Indians at Wellesley Square.
July 31	:	Spoke at Calcutta public meeting.
Before August 1	:	In Calcutta, Gandhiji gave interview to *The Englishman*.

August 1	:	On death-anniversary of Tilak, in a speech exhorted people to work for swaraj through khaddar and spinning.
August 4	:	Spoke at meeting of Indian Christians.
August 6	:	Visited Krishnath College, Behrampur, where he was given an address and purse for Deshbandhu Memorial.
August 7	:	Sir Surendranath Banerjea died at Barrackpore. Gandhiji paid a condolence visit to Sir Surendranath's home.
August 8	:	Addressed gathering of Indians and Europeans at Tata Steel Works, Jamshedpur.
August 9	:	Addressed officers of Tata Steel Works. At a mass meeting of labourers, exhorted them to shun evil of drinking.
August 12	:	In Calcutta, visited offices of *Basumati*. At Chowringhee Branch of Y. M.C.A., spoke on "The Duty of Indian Christian Young Men".
August 14	:	Visited handloom factory at Shreerampur.
August 15	:	Moving condolence resolution at meeting in Calcutta, paid homage to Sir Surendranath Banerjea, and laid emphasis on need for social reforms.
August 18	:	Spoke at Rotary Club meeting in Calcutta on charkha.
August 19	:	In Cuttack, visited Utkal Charmalaya; later addressed public meeting.
August 21	:	Giving interview to *The Englishman,* in Calcutta, explained his stand of Suhrawardy's resignation from Swaraj Party.
August 24	:	Discussed with leaders of both communities riots at Titagarh.
August 25	:	Spoke at meeting of College Branch of Y. M. C.A.
August 26	:	In interview to members of Psycho-analytical Society, discussed factors responsible for Hindu-Muslim problem.
August 27	:	Issued statement to Press regarding forthcoming A.I.C.C. meeting at Patna where changes in Congress constitution were to be discussed.

August 28	:	In Overtoun Hall, Calcutta, spoke of Nationalism.
August 29	:	Addressing students of Ashutosh College, asked them to adopt national outlook. Spoke at meeting of Indian Christians.
September 1	:	Left Calcutta, reaching Bombay on September, 3.
September 3	:	In interview to *The Bombay Chronicle,* gave his impressions of Bengal tour.
September 4	:	Gave interview to *Forward.* Presided over public meeting held to celebrate centenary of Dadabhai Naoroji.
Settember 6	:	At Ahmedabad, addressing Labour Union members, asked them to be courteous, truthful and honest in their work.
September 12	:	Reached Purulia. Received addresses at public meeting. Unveiled portrait of C. R. Das. Attended 16th Bihar Provincial Political Conference.
September 13	:	Spoke at women's meeting; at another meeting of untouchables, called upon them to eradicate evils of drinking and gambling.
September 15	:	At Chakradharpur, addressed students of National School.
September 16	:	Reached Ranchi by car. Received addresses from municipality and untouchables; spoke at women's meeting.
September 17	:	At public meeting declared that charkha alone could feed India's starving millions.
September 18	:	In Hazaribagh, spoke at public meeting. Addressed students of St. Columbus College.
September 21	:	Spoke at meeting in Patna.
September 22	:	Presided over the All-India Congress Committee meeting. Resolution to establish All-India Spinners' Association was passed.
	:	At District Khilafat Conference, Patna, Gandhiji spoke on Hindu-Muslim unity, and appealed to people to take to spinning and khaddar.
September 24	:	Constitution of All-India Spinners' Association finalized. At public meeting, laid emphasis on need of spinning and weaving of khaddar. Laid

fundation stone of National School at Khagaul. Spoke at women's meeting.

September 25 : In Press statement, regretted his inability to complete Bihar tour. At Bikram, addressed public meeting.

September 29 : At meeting, replying to municipal address, pointed out and emphasized duties of civic bodies towards citizens.

October 1 : At Bhagalpur, attended and spoke at Provincial Marwari Conference. Speaking at public meeting, invited members of all communities to join All-India Spinners' Association.

October 7 : Addressed meetings at Giridih.

October 13 : Spoke at meeting inVishanpur.

October 16 : Addressing Ballia District Conference, said that charkha was the only remedy for India's poverty.

October 17 : At students' meeting in Kashi Vidyapith, Banaras, advised them to spin regularly. In Lucknow, addressed two meetings. Replied to address presented by municipality at Sitapur. At another meeting, told Hindus not to bear ill will against Muslims.

October 18 : Attending U. P. Hindi Sahitya Sammelan, declared that Hindi should be national language. At U.P. Political Conference spoke on charkha and evil of untouchability. Addressed Anti-untouchability Conference.

October 21 : In Bombay, before leaving on Kutch tour by steamer, addressed people gathered at Ferry Wharf, Carnac Bunder.

October 22 : At Dwarka, received address from people's deputation on board steamer. Speaking at meeting in Bhuj, said if untouchability among Hindus was not removed, Hinduism would be destroyed.

October 23 : At another meeting in Bhuj, declared that cause of cow-protection suffered through folly of so-called "servants of the cow".

November 2 : Spoke at public meeting at Anjar.

Before November 6: In interview to Press, declared his intention to assist Swarajists in accordance with his promise.

November 22 : Opening "Youth Week" organized by students of Ahmedabad, urged them to be optimistic and imbibe spirit of sacrifice and self-control.

November 22 : In *Navajivan* the 26th Chapter, the last instalment of Gandhiji's book, *Satyagraha in South Africa,* was published.

November 24 : At morning prayer announced fast for 7 days due to moral lapses in the Ashram.

November 26 : Indian deputation left for South Africa.

December 1 : Spoke to students before breaking fast. Issued statement to the Press after breaking fast.

December 5 : Spoke at convocation, Gujarat Vidyapith.

: Unveiled photograph of Acharya Gidwani.

December 6 : Spoke at Dholka.

December 7 : Left Dholka for Ahmedabad and Ahmedabad for Bombay.

December 8 : Spoke at Gujarati National School, Bombay.

December 9 : Left for Wardha.

December 10 : Arrived at Wardha and stayed for 11 days.

December 21 : Spoke to Ashram inmates.

December 22 : Left Wardha for Congress session at Kanpur.

December 23 : Reached Kanpur.

December 24 : Spoke at opening of Swadeshi Exhibition at Kanpur Congress.

: Spoke on franchise resolution at Subjects Committee meeting.

December 26 : Spoke on resolution on South Africa at open session. of the Congress.

December 29 : Interview to Associated Press of India.

1926

January 3 : In Navajivan announced decision voluntarily to retire for one year from public work to 'stay at and attend to the Ashram and to have rest.

January 7 : In *Young India* under "Notes" commended

		Andrews' activities and Bishop Fisher's pamphlet in the cause of South African Indians.
January 9	:	In message to The Bombay Chronicle and in a letter, welcomed Horniman on arrival in India.
January 14	:	In *Young India* wrote on "Vykom Satyagraha", its ultimate objective-temple-entry.
January 19	:	Boro Dada Dwijendranath Tagore passed away.
January 21	:	Issued statement on Gandhi-Smuts Agreement of 1914 to Associated Press of India. Issued appeal to Travancore Government regarding temple-entry.
January 28	:	In *Young India* wrote on the South African question.
February 2	:	Signed Satyagraha Ashram Trust-deed.
February 10	:	Turned down request by North American Newspaper Alliance to write memoirs.
February 11	:	In *Young India* article "From Sweden", Gandhiji explained the significance of his programme of nonviolent non-co-operation and the movement for abolition of untouchability. In *Young India,* described the Asiatic Bill as a "Breach of Faith".
February 14	:	In interview with South-African Deputation in Ahmedabad, assured them of his readiness to go to South Africa if necessary.
February 18	:	In *Young India,* in "Topic of the Hour" and "From Bad to Worse" commented on the injustice of the South-African bill and the remedy of 'self-help' and 'satyagraha'.
February 25	:	In *Young India,* in "Our Humiliation" criticized Viceroy's acceptance of Dr. Malan's proposal that the Government of India place evidence before the Select Committee only through the Paddison Deputation.
February 27	:	Motilal Nehru came to Ahmedabad for discussions with Gandhiji.
March 11	:	Sent message to Swami Shraddhanandji's weekly, *The Liberator.* In letter to Shri Chunilal, sent message to convention on cowprotection.
March 12	:	Sent message on the spinning-wheel to Hindustani, Lahore.

March 15 : In letter to A.A. Paul, explained his attitude regarding invitation to him to visit China.

March 17 : In interview to Katherine Mayo, expressed his views on exploitation by the West, the economics of the spinning-wheel, the blot of untouchability, the injustice of British rule in India, etc., In letter to Dr. Satya Pal, sent message for the "Phulwari" commending the bravery of the Sikh people.

: In letter to Dr. B.C. Roy, sent message to Basanti Devi on opening ceremony by Tagore of Chittaranjan Seva Sadan.

March 18 : In *Young India* article "Difference in Degree", described the racial and colour problem in South Africa as "a tremendous world problem". In letter to J.H. Reinhold, permitted him to translate writings in *Young India*.

March 20 : In letter to Lala Lajpat Rai, explained his attitude to invitations to visit America and Finland.

March 21 : Spoke at annual function of National Music Association, Ahmedabad.

March 26 : In letter to Katherine Mayo, analysing the causes of Indian poverty, underlined the importance of hand-spinning as the remedy therefor.

March 27 : In letter to R.D. Tata, wrote of the latter's promised donation of one lac spindles and taklis during Gandhiji's visit to Jamshedpur.

March 28 : In *Navajivan* article, answered "Some Questions on Religious Issues".

April 1 : In *Young India* article "My Political Programme", emphasized, in reply to American friends, the spinning-wheel as his programme besides unity, and abolition of untouchability and of revenue from drink and drugs. Sent message on abolition of untouchability to a meeting at Trivandrum.

April 4 : In *Navajivan*, wrote on "Brahmacharya", "Satyagraha Week", "Hill Tribes" and "All-India Deshbandhu Memorial".

April 8 : Sent a message to Mysore Lawyers' Conference at Tumkur. Wrote a foreword to Hemendra Babu's *Life of Deshbandhu*.

	: In *Young India* article "Objections Considered", explained the case for the spinning-wheel in reply to Babu Bhagwandas.
April 11	: Wrote a message on Jallianwalabagh Day in response to request from Sarojini Naidu. In letter to G. D. Birla, wrote on the communal riots in Calcutta.
April 13	: In letter to K. T. Paul on the subject of his visit to Y.M.C.A. World Convention in Finland, explained his conditions in the matter of his dress and diet, his preference for "heart to heart conversations" over "speech-making", etc.
April 15	: In *Young India* article "Pandit Nehru and Khaddar', replied to The Times of India which had used "not only insulting" but also "highly misleading" language. In *Young India,* wrote a long review of the book "The Takli Teacher".
April 18	: Issued statement to Press on postponement of Mussoorie visit.
April 20	: In letters to Satis Chandra Das Gupta and Kaka Kalelkar, explained how and why Mussoorie visit was cancelled.
April 21	: Was present at discussions among Motilalji, Jayakar, Kelkar, Aney, Moonje, Lala Lajpat Rai, Sarojini Naidu and others at the conference convened by Pandit Motilal Nehru for framing agreed conditions for responsive co-operation with Government.
April 22	: In *Young India* article "Drink, Drugs and Devil", advocated total prohibition in India. In interview, clarified his attitude to Royal Commission on Agriculture, as a confirmed non-co-operator, while accepting Governor's invitation to discuss problems on agriculture at Mahabaleshwar.
April 23	: Wrote to Romain Rolland, Introducing Jawaharlal and his wife.
April 24	: In letter to S.C. Sen, discussed the process of "the growing revelation of truth". In letter to P. M. Seth, expressed his views on widow-remarriage. In letter to Amritlal, expressed his views on life

		insurance as betraying "a measure of lack of faith in God". In letter to Thakkar Bapa, commended exclusive devotion to the two missions, "the service of Antyajas and Bhils". In letter to Ramu Thakkar, reiterated his faith in Ramanama and charkha.
April 25	:	In *Navajivan* article "Abolish Marriage", in reply to a correspondent, expressed his views in support of marriage against advocates of free love.
April 27	:	In letter to S. Srinivasa Iyengar, expressed confidentially his strong views against Council programme.
April 29	:	In *Young India* article "South Africa", congratulated the Government of India on the diplomatic victory gained in South Africa in the cause of the Indian claim. The Areas Reservation Bill being postponed and a conference agreed upon.
	:	In *Young India* note on "The Good Samaritan", paid a glowing tribute to Andrews for his work in South Africa; and "In the Grip of Untouchability", drew attention to the plight of the untouchables in Cochin State.
May 2	:	In letter to Romain Rolland, explained views on propaganda abroad for the Indian Case.
May 4	:	Attended A.I.C.C. meeting at Gujarat Vidyapith.
May 5	:	Resolution on South Africa was moved by Satyamurti in A.I.C.C. meeting at Sabarmati. Sabarmati Pact between Swarajists, Responsive Co-operationists broke down.
May 6	:	In *Young India* article "From Far-Off America", explained how soul-force was immeasurably superior to brute force.
May 8	:	In letter to Abul Kalam Azad, described the pathetic condition of disunity within the Congress.
May 9	:	Devdas operated on for appendicitis.
May 13	:	Left Ahmedabad for Bombay on way to Mahabaleshwar.

May 14	:	Reached Bombay and visited Devdas.
May 15	:	Visited Mathuradas at Deolali on the way to Mahabaleshwar.
May 16	:	Reached Mahabaleshwar at 5 p.m. and stayed with Sir Chunilal Metha.
May 17	:	Monday, silence day.
May 18	:	Met the acting Governor, Sir Henry Lawrence, and discussed agriculture, charkha and cattle problem.
May 19	:	Continued discussions with the Governor.
May 20	:	Reached Poona, visited Sinhgarh (to meet Kaka Kalelkar) and left for Bombay. In *Young India,* wrote on racial discrimination against Indians in Australia.
May 22	:	Returned to Sabarmati. In letter to K. T. Paul, suggested dropping of his trip to Finland.
May 30	:	In letter to A. A. Paul, in response to an invitation to visit China, agreed to do so. In letter to A. I. Kajee, General Secretary, South African Indian Congress, Durban, gave advice on resolutions for the Annual Conference at Johannesburg on resistance to Colour Bar Bill.
	:	In *Navajivan* advised East African Indians to unify and "cultivate strength for satyagraha" to be able to live with selfrespect.
June 3	:	In *Young India* article "The Bar Sinister", examined and criticized the Colour Bar Bill and the Class Areas Reservation Bill.
June 6	:	In letter to K. T. Paul, cancelled his trip to Finland.
June 8	:	In interview to Press, condemned Colour Bar Bill as "insulting". In letter to Janakdhari Prasad, commented on the tragic drift away from non-co-operation, reiterated his firm faith in it as the way to freedom.
June 10	:	In *Young India,* wrote on "What Is Prayer".
June 14	:	Silence day. Sent message to students of the Gujarat Mahavidyalaya.
June 15	:	Gandhiji in Satyagraha Ashram, Sabarmati.
Before June 19	:	In message to Nellore Adi-Andhra Conference

		asked for spread of charkha and eradication of untouchability.
July 11	:	Anniversary of C.R. Das was observed all over India with meetings and processions.
July 15	:	Hindu-Muslim riots broke out in Calcutta.
July 26	:	On the eve of Lokamanya Tilak's death anniversary Gandhiji sent message to Maharashtra that khadi and charkha were the means of winning swaraj.
August 15	:	Met Natarajan, editor of *Indian Daily Mail* and *Indian Social Reformer,* at the Ashram.
September 18	:	Left Ahmedabad for Bombay to receive South African Delegation.
September 19	:	In Bombay gave interview to *The Natal Advertiser.* Attended Garden Party in honour of South African Delegation. Left for Ahmedabad at night.
September 20	:	Reached Ahmedabad.
September 26	:	Discussed Indian question in South Africa with representatives from South Africa.
October 10	:	Executed his Will.
October 17	:	Gave interview to Associated Press of India on personnel of Indian Delegation to Round Table Conference.
October 24	:	Addressed annual meeting of the Labour Union, Ahmedabad, held at the Ashram.
November 1	:	Left Ahmedabad for Bombay to see Sir Ganga Ram and others.
November 2	:	Returned to Ahmedabad from Bombay.
November 5	:	Gandhiji in Satyagraha Ashram, Sabarmati.
November 21	:	V. S. Srinivasa Sastri met Gandhiji in the afternoon.
November 28	:	Gandhiji spoke at the convocation of Gujarat Vidyapith, Ahmedabad.
December 3	:	Left Ahmedabad for Wardha. Stopped at Surat on the way and visited Vinay Mandir.
December 4	:	Reached Wardha.
December 19	:	Sent message to public meeting, Wardha.
December 20	:	Addressed public meeting at Wardha.

December 21 : Left Wardha for Gauhati. Addressed public meetings at Amraoti and Nagpur. Stayed for a few hours at Gondia.

December 23 : Reached Calcutta. Swami Shraddhanand assassinated.

December 24 : Gandhiji left for Gauhati. Spoke at the A.I.C.C. meeting at Gauhati.

December 25 : Spoke at opening ceremony of Swadeshi Exhibition, Gauhati.

December 26 : Spoke at flag hoisting ceremony at the Congress pandal. Proposed resolutions and spoke on death of Swami Shraddhanand and on status of Indians in South Africa.

December 27 : Spoke in Subjects Committee on desirability of stiffening franchise so that no one who does not wear khaddar should be entitled to vote.

December 28 : Spoke twice on Independence Resolution in the Subjects Committee. Addressed meeting of Municipal Board, Gauhati. In interview to Associated Press, said that his business in the coming year would be to spread message of charkha and khadi. Left Gauhati for Calcutta.

December 31 : Spoke at public meeting held at Maheshwari Bhavan, Barra Bazar, Calcutta.

1927

January 2 : Spoke at gathering of students of sixteen depressed class schools of Calcutta and Howrah.

: Spoke at Chittaranjan Seva Sadan, Calcutta. Laid foundation for memorial to Aswini Kumar Dutt.

: Spoke at opening ceremony of Kalashala of Khadi Pratishthan, at Sodepur.

January 4 : Left for Comilla.

January 5 : Spoke at Abhoy Ashram and public meeting at Comilla.

January 6 : At Comilla gave interview to the Free Press of India on the Khadi resolution. Spoke at a women's meeting, Comilla.

January 9 : In Banaras gave interview to Dr. Bhagwandas on the question of swaraj.

	:	In Banaras delivered speeches at Benares Hindu University, Shraddhanand's Memorial meeting, meeting of untouchables, women's meeting and at public meeting.
January 10	:	Left Banaras for Allahabad.
January 11	:	In Daltenganj.
January 12	:	Spoke at public meeting in Dhanbad.
January 13	:	Addressed meetings at Dhanbad, Katras, Jharia.
January 14	:	Spoke at public meeting in Aurangabad.
January 15	:	Addressed meetings at Gaya and Ramana.
January 16	:	Spoke at women's meeting in Sonepur and at public meetings in Chhapra and Sewan.
January 17	:	Took rest in Rajendra Prasad's house, in Chhapra.
January 18	:	Visited Ekma and Maharajganj.
January 19	:	Visited Darbhanga.
January 20	:	Addressed meetings at Madhubani and Samastipur.
January 21	:	Gandhi in Champaran.
January 22	:	Spoke at Motihari, recalling memories of Champaran struggle.
January 23	:	In letter to Vallabhbhai Patel asked him to accept presidentship of Kathiawar Political Conference.
	:	At Bettiah spoke on including spinning in educational curriculum, on cow-protection and removing untouchability.
January 24	:	In letter to G. D. Birla expressed his views on shuddhi.
January 25	:	At Muzaffarpur visited Provincial Khaddar Depot, Municipal Ayurvedic Dispensary, Ramakrishna Mission and School for Untouchables. In interview to Free Press of India explained non-acceptance of invitations to visit America. Addressed public meeting and student's meeting.
January 26	:	At Begusarai spoke at public meeting.
January 27	:	Spoke at Kharagpur and Jamui.
January 28	:	At Bilaunti and Arrah spoke at public meetings.
January 29	:	Spoke at Sasaram and Mohani.

January 30	:	In Patna delivered convocation address at Bihar Vidyapith.
February 1	:	In Calcutta.
February 2	:	Began tour of Central Provinces and Berar. Spoke at Tumsar.
February 3	:	At Nagpur appealed for Deshbandhu Memorial Fund.
February 4	:	Spoke at Chanda.
February 5	:	At Yeotmal was interviewed by Shapurji Saklatvala. Spoke in reply to municipal address.
February 6	:	Reached Amraoti. At Akola spoke on untouchability
February 8	:	At Khamgaon addressed National School teachers.
February 9	:	At Pachora spoke at public meeting.
February 10	:	At Jalgaon attended spinning demonstration by students; addressed women's meeting, visited pinjrapole and met members of Chaitanya Mandal. Addressed public meeting and meeting of untouchables.
February 11	:	Left Jalgaon by car; reached Bhusaval.
February 12	:	Spoke at Amalner.
February 13	:	At Dhulia addressed six meetings.
February 16	:	Spoke at Nasik.
February 18	:	At Ahmednagar visited Rashtriya Pathashala.
	:	Addressed mass meeting.
February 19	:	At Sholapur spoke in reply to municipal address. Visited the tribal Settlement and the Spinning and Weaving Mills.
February 20	:	Spoke at mass meeting.
February 21	:	Left Sholapur for Gulburga by train.
February 22	:	At Sharana Basappa Temple, Gulburga, addressed Hindus and Muslims.
February 25	:	In Sangli addressed students' meeting at Wellington College.
February 28	:	Spoke at Lanje.
March 1	:	In Ratnagiri spoke at women's meeting.

March 2	: At Mahad.
March 3	: In Sasavane spoke at Vaishya Vidyashram.
March 4	: In Poona spoke at Reay Market. Addressed students about midnight.
March 6	: At Akola attended Manilal-Sushila wedding.
March 7	: Left Akola by train for Ahmedabad.
March 8-14	: At Sabarmati Ashram, Ahmedabad.
March 15	: Spoke at Madhi, Mandvi village.
March 16	: At Vedchhi addressed conference of hillmen.
March 17	: In *Young India* article "No and Yes" replied to Saklatvala's open letter.
March 19	: In Hardwar delivered convocation address at Gurukul Kangri.
March 20	: Addressed National Educational Conference.
March 21	: Left Hardwar for Bombay.
March 23	: Spoke at Santa Cruz.
March 24	: In Poona was interviewed by A.P.I. on Maharashtra tour. In Bombay was interviewed by *The Bombay Chronicle*.
	: At Ghatkopar addressed gathering at Sarvajanik Jivadaya Khata.
March 25	: At Kolhapur addressed seven meetings. Motored to Nipani. Restless at night.
March 26	: Was examined by Dr. Wanless who advised him complete rest.
March 27	: Blood-pressure continued to be high throughout the day.
March 28	: Doctors unanimously decided that the whole hot weather programme must be cancelled.
	: In *Young India* Gandhiji explained conditions for cow-protection.
April 1	: At Belgaum.
April 2	: At Amboli.
April 3	: Was examined by Dr. Jivaraj Mehta who advised him to go to hill station.
April 7	: In *Young India* article "What Shall I do?" declared: "The foundation of satyagraha as of nation-

building is undoubtedly self-purification, self-dedication, selflessness."

April 8 : In letter to Amritlal expressed "no interest in activities other than khadi or similar constructive work".

April 9 : Walked a little.

April 10 : Walked a good distance.

April 14 : In *Young India* article "Faith v. Reason" wrote: "Man is not all body but he is something infinitely higher."

April 17 : Had a talk with the Chief of Savantwadi.

April 18 : Left Amboli for Nandi Hills.

April 19 : Reached Nandi Hills.

April 20 : Had discussion with Inspector-General of Education, Mysore State.

April 21 : In *Young India* article "Truth is One" said: "Independence of each country is a truth in the same sense and to the same extent that independence of each man is."

April 25 : In letter to Satis Chandra Das Gupta wrote that he would "not plunge into active work thoughtlessly or without medical advice".

April 26 : In letter to R.B. Gregg said that living on sun-baked fruits and nuts without using fire would bring animal passions under conscious control.

May 2 : Blood-pressure found to be normal.

May 8 : In *Navajivan* article "Cow v. Buffalo or Cow-cum-Buffalo?" advised "experiments in dairying and tanning from the religious and national point of view in the cities".

May 10 : In letter to Saklatvala said that labour in India was "still extremely unorganized".

May 11 : In letter to Fulchand K. Shah asked him not to offer satyagraha without his permission.

May 12 : In *Young India* in "Notes" under "Evils of Machine-milling" condemned Indians for being "too much obsessed by the glamour of the West".

May 19 : In *Young India* article "Nagpur Satyagraha"

		denied that he ever gave consent for civil disobedience in Nagpur and warned everyone "not to use his name in connection with any movement without getting his permission in writing."
May 22	:	In *Navajivan* article "He Should Be Dismissed" said: "The path of non-violence is neither for the coward nor for the stupid. . . it is for those who are ever vigilant."
May 26	:	In *Young India* in "An Appeal to Indian Humanity" said: "If we want to become a self-respecting and independent nation. . . the honour of the least among our sisters must be as dear to us as that of our blood-sisters."
May 28	:	In letter to G.L. Nanda, described *Bhagavad Gita* as his "only dictionary of reference".
June 5	:	Came down from Nandi Hills. Spoke at Chikballapur. Reached Bangalore.
June 12	:	In letter to Satcowripati Ray said that social reforms were necessary as part of our struggle for freedom.
June 15	:	The debate on the Indian Bills was resumed in South African Union Assembly. In letter to G. L. Nanda Gandhiji said that labour must "better its conditions independently" and negotiate with the mill-owners consistently with "dignity and self-respect".
June 16	:	In Bangalore, where Gandhiji countinued to stay till the end of August
June 19	:	In *Navajivan* article, "Quarrelling in the Name of Religion", wrote: "I do not distinguish between Hindus and Jains. I can establish the unity of Hinduism, that is, the Vedic doctrine, with Jainism, with the help of syadvada itself."
June 25	:	In letter to Sarojini Naidu emphasized that there was no other man than Dr. Ansari who could be the Congress President in 1927 to pilot a Hindu-Muslim pact through the Congress.
June 27	:	The Bills dealing with the Indo-South African Agreement passed the final reading.

July 3	:	In Bangalore, Gandhiji spoke after opening the Khadi Exhibition.
July 8	:	Spoke to Adi Karnataka boys. Spoke at a prize-distribution ceremony in the Khadi Exhibition in Bangalore.
July 9	:	In Mysore, spoke at Amateur Dramatic Association.
July 10	:	In Bangalore, spoke at All-Karnataka Hindi Conference.
July 12	:	I Spoke at Indian Institute of Science.
July 13	:	Spoke at Mahila Samaj.
July 14	:	At Tumkur, spoke in reply to Municipal address; visited the Panchama Boarding School; spoke at Prani Daya Sangha.
July 15	:	At Maddagiri, spoke at public meeting.
July 17	:	In Bangalore, spoke in reply to Municipal address; addressed labourer's meeting.
July 19	:	In Mysore, spoke to students.
July 20	:	Spoke at Hindi Bhasha Seva Samaj. Spoke in reply to welcome address by the Mysore City Municipal Council and others.
July 21	:	Spoke to Adi Karnatakas.
July 23	:	Spoke at farewell meeting.
July 24	:	In Bangalore, spoke at Civic and Social Progress Association.
July 26	:	Spoke at United Theological College and a Mythic Society.
July 29	:	Had a discussion with Christian missionaries.
July 30	:	Spoke at Chamarajendra Sanskrit Pathashala.
August 2	:	At Arsikere Junction spoke to Lambanis.
August 3	:	In Hassan, spoke at Town Hall.
August 4	:	In Bangalore, issued an appeal for funds for Gujarat flood relief.
August 7	:	In Bangalore. Spoke at the Gabbi Theatre.
August 11	:	At Davengere addressed a meeting of women; also a public meeting.
August 12	:	Spoke to Adi Karnatakas.

August 13	: Arrived at Shimoga, addressed a meeting of women; spoke at Harihar.
August 14	: At Shimoga, addressed a public meeting.
August 16	: Reached Sagar; in the evening addressed a meeting of women.
August 17	: At Tirthahalli, spoke at a public meeting. Left Shimoga for Bhadravati.
August 18	: At Bhadravati, addressed the workmen and officers of the Iron Works. Left for Chikmagalur in the evening.
August 19	: At Chikmagalur, addressed a public meeting. Issued an appeal to Tamil Nadu regarding orderly arrangement of his tour.
August 20	: Reached Belur, addressed a pubic meeting in front of the Belur Temple. At Arsikere, addressed a pubic meeting.
August 21	: In Tipur, addressed a meeting at Veerasaivananda Ashram.
August 23	: In Bangalore.
August 24	: Commenced the first stage of Tamil Nadu tour. Visited Hosur. In Krishnagiri, spoke at a meeting.
August 28	: In Bangalore; addressed five meetings.
August 29	: Interview to the Associated Press.
August 30	: At Vellore, spoke at Voorhee's College.
September 1	: At Gudiatham.
September 2	: Spoke at Arni. Also spoke at Arcot.
September 3	: Arrived in Madras; spoke at Provincial Boy Scouts' Association; laid the Madras and Southern Maharatta Railway Employees's Union. At Peravallur, spoke at labourers' meeting. In Madras, spoke to students.
September 4	: Spoke at Y. M.C.A.; addressed a public meeting; spoke on the Gita
September 6	: Delivered speech at Hindi Prachar Sabha. Discussion with Neill Statue volunteers.
September 7	: Concluded discussion with Neill Statue volunteers. Addressed meetings at Pachaiyappa's College and Royapuram.

September 8	:	At Conjeevaram, spoke at a meeting. In Madras, spoke to Arundhatiyas at Perambur; spoke to Gujaratis and Marwaris.
September 9	:	Spoke at a meeting of women; delivered address on C. R. Das; spoke at St. Thomas Mount; interview to *The Hindu*.
September 10	:	Reached Cuddalore; spoke at Y. M. C. A; addressed a public meeting.
September 11	:	At Chidambaram; spoke to Adi Dravidas; addressed a public meeting.
September 12	:	In Mayavaram.
September 13	:	Spoke at a public meeting.
September 14	:	Reached Kumbakonam; addressed a meeting. Had discussion with Pundits.
September 15	:	At Valangaiman, addressed a meeting. Reached Mannargudi; spoke at National High School; delivered speech at Findlay College spoke at a public meeting. In *Young India* article "Drain Inpector's Report", commented on Catherine Mayo's *Mother India*.
September 16	:	Gandhiji continued his khadi tour in South India; speak at Tanjore on Brahmin-Non-Brahmin question.
September 17-20	:	Addressed various meetings at and near Trichinopoly.
September 21	:	Addressed citizens' meeting, Pudukottah.
September 22	:	Visited Nachandipatti, Kadiapatti and Kanadukathan.
September 23	:	Visited Pallathur, Kottayur and Amaravatipur.
September 24	:	Addressed women's meeting. Karaikudi; also spoke at Devakottah.
September 25-26	:	At Karaikudi.
September 27	:	Visited Siravayal, Tirupattur and Paganeri.
September 28	:	Arrived in Madura; received address from Municipal Council and spoke at public meeting.
September 29	:	At Madura; spoke at a meeting of Saurashtra community.
September 30	:	Addressed public meeting at Tirumangalam; conference with Justice Party leaders.

October 1	: At Paramakudi.
October 2	: At Virudhunagar; gave interviews to Rev. J. Himmer-strand and Non-Brahmin Youth League; spoke at public meeting.
October 3	: At Virudhunagar; silence day.
October 4	: At Rajapalayam; spoke at women's meeting and public meeting; opened a khadi vastralaya.
October 5	: At Koilpatti.
October 6	: At Tuticorin; spoke at public meeting.
October 7	: At Tinnevelly; spoke at public meeting.
October 8	: Addressed a meeting at Nagercoil.
October 9-10	: At Trivandrum; met the Maharaja and Maharani of Travancore and discussed the question of the entry of untouchables to the Thiruvarppu temple roads.
October 11	: At Quilon.
October 12	: At Alleppey.
October 13	: At Ernakulam and Cochin; rennounced prize of Rs. 1,000 for the best essay on cow-protection; published an article on the "Neill Statue Satyagraha".
October 14	: At Trichur.
October 15	: At Palghat; had conversation with Shankaracharya of Kamakoti Peetham; spoke at public meeting.
October 16	: At Coimbatore; spoke at public meeting; C. Rajagopalachari announced that Gandhiji would rest at Coimbatore until October 21.
October 17	: At Coimbatore; exchanged telegrams with V.J. Patel on proposed meeting with the Viceroy.
October 18	: Spoke at Pollachi and returned to Coimbatore.
October 19-21	: At Coimbatore; published an article on "Why I Am a Hindu".
October 22-24	: At Tiruppur; spoke at public meeting; accepted Viceroy's invitation to see him on November 2.
October 25	: At Calicut.
October 26	: At Nileshvar, Kasargode and Mangalore; spoke at public meeting at Mangalore.

October 27	:	Left Mangalore by sea for Bombay on way to Delhi to see the Viceroy. Unity conference convened under the auspices of Indian National Congress at Calcutta; Gandhiji did not participate in it.
October 29	:	Arrived in Bombay; gave interview to the Press on the appointment of Assessors on the Royal Commission, and on Hindu-Muslim unity.
October 30	:	Left Bombay for Delhi.
November 1	:	In Delhi; attended meeting of Khadi Pracharak Mandal.
November 2	:	In Delhi met the Viceroy, Lord Irwin; visited Jamia Millia Islamia and spoke to students.
November 3	:	Reached Ahmedabad at night.
November 4	:	At Sabarmati Ashram, Ahmedabad.
November 5	:	Left for Bombay at night.
November 6	:	Arrived in Bombay.
November 7	:	Left for Ceylon on board *s.s. Colaba*.
November 8	:	Viceroy announced personnel of Royal Commission headed by Sir John Simon.
November 12	:	Gandhiji arrived in Colombo at night.
Noveber 13	:	In Colombo; in interview to Press said that Congress was his conscience-keeper regarding his opinion on Simon Commission; spoke at meetings of Chettiar community and Vivekananda Society.
November 14	:	In Colombo; silence day.
November 15	:	In Colombo; received address from municipality; addressed meetings of students, Buddhists and Christians.
November 16	:	In Colombo; spoke to Christian missionaries and labourers.
November 17	:	Left Colombo and visited Paliyagoda, Negombo, Madampe, Chilaw, Kurunegala and Katugastota.
November 18	:	Spoke at public meetings at Matale and Kandy; visited the Dalda Maligawa and saw the Tooth Relic.
November 19	:	At Badulla.

November 20	:	At Nuwara Eliya.
November 21	:	At Kandy; silence day.
November 22	:	Returned to Colombo and spoke at meetings of the Parsis, the Ceylon National Congress and others.
November 23	:	Visited Panadura and Galle.
November 24	:	Spoke at Galle and Matara.
November 25	:	Returned to Colombo and spoke at farewell meetings.
November 26-29	:	At Jaffna; addressed meetings.
November 30	:	Left Ceylon and arrived in Ramnad; addressed public meeting.
December 1	:	Arrived in Madras; gave interview to Associated Press on the Statutory Commission; left for Orissa tour.
December 3	:	Spoke at public meeting at Chicacole.
December 4	:	Visited Ichchapuram, Palasa, Baruva and Kaviti in the morning and spoke at women's meeting, Chicacole. In the evening spoke at Students' meeting at Berhampur.
December 5	:	At Berhampur; silence day.
December 6	:	Addressed public meeting at Berhampur. Also visited Aska, Gohra, Russelkonda; spoke at meetings and then proceeded to Boirani for night's rest.
December 7	:	Visited Purushottampur, Kodala and Khallikote.
December 8	:	At Banpur.
December 9	:	Went to Bolgarh for complete rest on account of rise in blood-pressure.
December 10	:	Spoke at public meeting, Bolgarh.
December 11-12	:	Rest at Bolgarh.
December 13	:	At Begunia, Sakhigopal, and Puri; refrained from visiting Jagannath temple.
December 14	:	Reached Balasore.
December 15-17	:	At Balasore.
December 18	:	Arrived in Cuttack; cancelled all programmes and took rest on account of high blood-pressure.
December 20	:	Gandhiji's speech was read out at a public

meeting in Cuttack.

December 21 : Left Cuttack to attend the Annual Session of Indian National Congress at Madras.

December 23 : Spoke at Hindi and Khadi Exhibition, Madras.

December 23-28: In Madras, had discussions with Congress leaders.

December 26 : Annual Session of the Indian National Congress began in Madras.

December 27 : Gandhiji's draft resolution on Indians in South Africa was adopted unanimously by the Indian National Congress.

December 28 : Gandhiji left for Bombay.

December 29 : Death of Hakim Ajmal Khan.

December 30 : Gandhiji arrived in Bombay; gave interview to Press on Congress resolutions on Hindu-Muslim Unity and Independence.

December 31 : Arrived at Sabarmati.

1928

January 1 to 21 : Gandhiji stayed at Satyagraha Ashram, Sabarmati.

January 7 : Sent message to National Muslim University, Delhi.

January (Second Week) : Friends of the International Fellowship stayed at the Ashram for three days.

January 15 : Gandhiji spoke at the convocation of the Gujarat Vidyapith, Ahmedabad.

January 22 : Spoke at Fourth Kathiawar Political Conference at Porbandar.

January 23 : At Vartej.

January 24 : Laid the foundation-stone of a temple for untouchables at Vartej; also spoke at Morvi.

January 27 : Gandhiji's third son, Ramdas Gandhi, was married at Sabarmati. Gandhiji proposed changes in the constitution of Gujrat Vidyapith.

January 30 : Wished success to hartal against the Simon Commission.

January 31 : Went to stay among the students of the Gujarat Mahavidyalaya.

February 1 : Addressed students of Gujarat Vidyapith at prayer meeting.

February 3 : Statutory Commission under Sir John Simon landed in Bombay. Protest demonstrations and meetings held. Gandhiji sent messages to Ahmedabad and Bombay for success of boycott.

February 5 : Fainted while spinning; doctors advised complete rest.

February 7 : Sent message to Gujarat Vidyapith meeting held to bid farewell to J. B. Kripalani.

Before February 12 : Talked to representatives of Bardoli Taluk and Vallabhbhai Patel regarding Bardoli Satyagraha.

March 17 : Gandhiji was examined by Dr. M.A. Ansari.

March 20 : Gave interview to Alice Schalek. In interview to Associated Press said his visit to Europe was not certain.

March 27 : Spoke at sweepers' meeting, Ahmedabad.

March 31 : Addressed students and teachers of schools run by Ahmedabad Labour Union.

April 4 : Sent message to New India. Spoke at Ashram prayer meeting on Hanuman Jayanti.

April 7 : Sent message for News Sheet of International Fellowship.

Before April 13 : Addressed trainees of Khadi Vidyalaya.

April 18 : Sent message to Students' Conference, Ceylon.

April 22 : After hearing from Romain Rolland decided finally not to visit Europe.

April 23 : Maganlal Gandhi died at Patna.

May 1 : Spoke at opening of creche at Ahmedabad.

May 7 : Conferred with Subhas Chandra Bose at Sabarmati Ashram.

June 11 : Spoke to students of Gujarat Vidyapith.

June 12 : Bardoli Day observed.

June 14 : Draft Constitution of the Satyagraha Ashram was published in Young India.

July 1 : Gandhiji at Sabarmati Ashram, Ahmedabad.

July 6 : Sent message to *The Hindu* on its Golden Jubilee.

July 13 : In letter to Barbara Bauer who requested him

		to resurrect her deceased mother, wrote: "I am but an ordinary mortal . . . as every other human being . . . I possess no extraordinary powers."
July 18	:	Surat Conference between representatives of agriculturists of Bardoli, Vallabhbhai Patel, Abbas Tyabji and the Governor, on conditions for inquiry into "the alleged errors of the official calculations of facts".
July 19	:	In *Young India* article "Non-co-operation or Civil Resistance?" Gandhiji wrote: "My purpose is to distinguish between non-co-operation with attainment of swaraj as its object and civil resistance as that of Bardoli with the redress of a specific grievance as its object."
July 20	:	Interview to the Associated Press representative on Bardoli question.
July 22	:	In *Navajivan* article "Evil Genius of Government" Gandhiji discussed minimum terms of Bardoli Settlement.
July 26	:	Statement on Bardoli question in reply to Governor's speech was published in Young India.
August 2	:	Gandhiji reached Bardoli.
August 4	:	At Sarbhon, addressed patels, talatis and representatives of 25 villages of Sarbhon division.
August 5	:	At Rayam, spoke on discipline.
August 6	:	Bardoli Settlement at Poona. Gandhiji congratulated both the Government of Bombay and people of Bardoli.
August 11	:	At Valod, spoke on the science of satyagraha.
August 12	:	At Bardoli, spoke to volunteers. At Surat, spoke on the occasion of the Bardoli victory celebrations.
August 13	:	Reached Sabarmati.
August 16	:	Welcomed the Nehru Report for its unanimous recommendations. At Ahmedabad spoke on the implications of Bardoli victory.
August 20	:	Spoke at Brahmo Samaj centenary celebrations.
August 28	:	All-Parties Conference met at Lucknow to consider the Nehru Report.

August 30	:	All-Parties Conference endorsed Nehru Committee Report in favour of Dominion self-government for India.
September 7	:	In Ahmedabad, Gandhiji spoke at school for deaf and dumb. Motilal Nehru was elected President of Indian National Congress.
September 10	:	At Ahmedabad Gandhiji delivered speech on birth centenary of Tolstoy.
October 1	:	At Ahmedabad, spoke on Annie Besant's birthday.
October 5	:	Sent a message to Lahore Students' Conference.
October 6	:	The Madras All-Parties Conference met under the presidentship of Dr. Besant.
October 11	:	In *Young India* article "God Is" wrote: " I do dimly perceive that whilst everything around me is ever changing, ever dying, there is underlying all that change a living power that is changeless, that holds all together, that creates, dissolves and recreates. That informing Power or Spirit is God. And since nothing else I see merely through the senses can or will persist, He alone is . . . I have no argument to convince . . . through reason. Faith transcends reason."
October 28	:	In Ahmedabad, spoke at The New Gujarati School.
October 31	:	Lajpat Rai received injury in a fracas between police and Nationalists in Lahore.
November 1	:	Gandhiji gave interview to special correspondent of *The Civil and Military Gazette*.
November 4	:	In *Navajivan* article "Satyagraha Ashram", discussed changes made after renaming the Satyagraha Ashram as Udyoga Mandir.
November 17	:	Lajpat Rai died; Gandhiji gave interview to Associated Press of India on his death.
November 18	:	In Ahmedabad, spoke at Lajpat Rai condolence meeting.
November 21	:	Gave award on the Labour Union subscription.
November 23	:	Left Ahmedabad for Wardha.
November 24	:	Reached Wardha; remained in the Wardha

		Ashram up to December 20.
November 26	:	Issued and endorsed appeal for Lajpat Rai Memorial Fund.
November 29	:	On National Mourning Day for Lajpat Rai addressed Ashram inmates in Wardha.
November 20	:	Left Wardha for Calcutta Congress session. At Nagpur railway station, gave interview to friends.
December 21	:	Arrived at Sambalpur en route to Calcutta.
December 22	:	At Sambalpur; spoke at public meeting in the morning; addressed women's meeting in the evening, and left for Calcutta. The All-Parties Convention met at Calcutta.
December 23	:	Gandhiji arrived in Calcutta in the morning. Met a deputation from the Punjab.
December 26	:	Moved resolution on Nehru Report at the Subjects Committee meeting.
December 27	:	In *Young India* wrote an article on Saunders's assassination.
December 28	:	Moved compromise resolution on Nehru Report in the Subjects Committee meeting.
December 29	:	Annual session of Indian National Congress began in Calcutta. Gandhiji moved resolution on constructive programme at the Subjects Committee meeting. Presided over the Rashtra Bhasha Sammelan in the evening. In *Young India* article "What Is in a Name?", discussed Dominion Status v. Independence.
December 31	:	Moved resolution on Nehru Report in the open session of the Congress.

1929

January 1	:	Opened a khadi bhandar in Calcutta. Moved resolution on constructive programme in the open session of the Congress. Annual session of the Congress concluded. In the All-Parties Convention Gandhiji moved a resolution containing general agreement on communal problems. All-Parties Convention adjourned *sine die*.

January 2	:	Gandhiji gave interview to *The Englishman* and *Daily Telegraph* clarifying his standpoint regarding Congress Resolution on Nehru Report. Inaugurated the new block of Chittaranjan Seva Sadan. Visited Khadi Pratishthan at Sodepur. Visited the Vishwa Kosha Bhawan and met Nagendra Nath Basu.
January 3	:	Left Calcutta at night for Delhi en route to Ahmedabad. Students' strike started in the Gujarat College, Ahmedabad.
January 4	:	Halted at Delhi; met Dr. Zakir Husain.
January 5	:	Reached Ahmedabad at night.
January 9	:	Attended the Arbitration Board's meeting regarding the Gujarat Ginning Mill dispute.
January 10	:	Spoke at the Youth Week celebration.
January 11	:	Presided over the seventh convocation of the Gujarat Vidyapith; spoke at the presentation of khadi purse to J. B. Kripalani.
January 12	:	Sent message to the third gathering of Graduates of the Vidyapith.
January 14	:	Gandhiji attended Arbitration Board's meeting.
January 17	:	In *Young India* article "Then and Now", compared the present Congress programme with that of 1920-21.
January 19	:	An Article "Pran Jaayi Aru Vachan Na Jaayi" written by Gandhiji for *Navajivan* was read at a Gujarat College students' meeting.
January 24	:	*Young India* published articles on "Duty of Resistance" and "Scheme for Boycott of Foreign Cloth through Khadi".
January 30	:	Gandhiji spoke to Gujarat College students.
January 31	:	In *Young India* article "My Apologies", announced the cancellation of his proposed European tour.
February 1	:	Wrote to Jawaharlal Nehru to reorganize the Congress for following year's non-violent non-co-operation campaign.
February 2	:	Left on Sind tour.
February 3	:	Reached Karachi in the afternoon; spoke in reply to the Municipal address at public meeting. Last

		chapter of Autobiography appeared in Navajivan.
February 3	:	Gandhiji arrived at Karachi in the afternoon on a tour of Sind. Last instalment of An Autobiography was published in *Navajivan*.
February 4–6	:	Gandhiji was at Karachi.
February 5	:	Spoke at meetings of untouchables and Depressed Classes.
February 6	:	Spoke at meetings of Parsis and students; left for Jacobabad.
February 7	:	At Jacobabad; spoke at public meeting.
February 8	:	At Shikarpur; spoke at public meeting.
February 9	:	At Larkana.
February 10	:	At Sukkur; spoke at students' meeting.
February 11	:	At Sukkur and Rohri.
February 13	:	At Padidan; reached Hyderabad (Sind) and spoke at public meeting.
February 14	:	At Hyderabad; spoke at meetings of students, Congress, and untouchables. Spoke at Kotri Congress Committee.
February 15	:	Gandhiji addressed public meeting in Mirpurkhas.
	:	Sind tour concluded.

On or after February 15: Issued statement on Sind Congress affairs.

February 17	:	Arrived in Delhi. Attended meeting of Congress Working Committee.
February 19	:	At Delhi. Attended with the Viceroy Vithalbhai Patel's party.
February 21	:	Reached Sabarmati Ashram.
February 28	:	At Ahmedabad, spoke at unveiling of Tilak statue, flag-hoisting ceremony and public meeting.
March 3	:	Arrived in Calcutta.
March 4	:	In a speech in Shraddhanand Park, Calcutta, advised the people to boycott foreign cloth. The speech was followed by bonfire of foreign cloth. Gandhiji was arrested and later released on personal recognizance.

March 5	:	Issued statement to Press on Calcutta's bonfire incident at 2.30 a.m. Left for Rangoon in morning by *s.s. Aronda*.
March 8	:	Arrived in Rangoon. Addressed public meetings. Gave interview to *Free Press of India*.
March 9	:	Spoke at public meeting in Rangoon.
March 10	:	In Rangoon addressed meetings of Gujaratis, Arya Samajists, Indian gate-keepers, Indians and students.
March 12	:	At Moulmein. Addressed Gujaratis' meeting.
March 13	:	Spoke at public meeting, Moulmein.
March 14	:	In Rangoon, spoke at Ramakrishna Mission and women's meeting.
March 15	:	Delivered speeches at Paungde and Prome.
March 18	:	At Mandalay, spoke at public meeting.
March 19	:	At Toungoo, spoke at public meeting.
March 20	:	Spoke at labourers' and students' meetings.
March 22	:	Left Rangoon for Calcutta. Collected more than Rs. 1,50,000.
March 24	:	Arrived in Calcutta.
March 26	:	Gave statement in the course of his trial in the court of the Chief Presidency Magistrate, Calcutta. Left for Delhi.
March 27	:	Reached Delhi. Attended meeting of Congress Working Committee. Left for Ahmedabad.
March 29	:	In Ahmedabad, gave interview to the Associated Press.
March 30	:	At Morvi, addressed Fifth Kathiawar Political Conference held under the Presidentship of Vallabhbhai Patel.
April 1	:	Left Morvi at night.
April 2	:	In Ahmedabad.
April 5	:	Reached Bombay. Spoke at the opening ceremony of the Bombay Provincial Congress Committee's new office. Left Bombay for Andhra Desha.
April 6	:	Reached Andhra Desha. Replied to the joint address presented by the public of Hyderabad (Deccan) and Secunderabad.

April 7	:	In Hyderabad. Visited local schools. Left for Bezwada.
April 8	:	Spent night at Nandigama.
April 9	:	Spoke at Nandigama in the morning. Reached Bezwada.
April 10	:	Addressed Public meeting at Bezwada.
April 11	:	Reached Wuyyur at 8 p.m.
April 12	:	Delivered a speech at Wuyyur.
April 13	:	Delivered speeches at Arundhati Ashram, Andhra Jatiya Kalashala and women's meeting, Masulipatam.
April 17	:	Left Masulipatam for Guntur. Addressed public meetings in Guntur, Kerinchedu and Pedanandipadu.
April 24	:	Laid the foundation stone of Vivekananda Library, Potunooru. Reached Gundukolanu at 8.15 p.m. Stayed there for night.
April 25	:	Spoke at Tadepalligudem.
April 26	:	Spoke at Achanta.
April 27	:	Spent night at Ananda Niketan Ashram, Chagallu.
April 28	:	Reached Vizagapatam at 3 p.m. Spoke at public meeting, Vizagapatam.
May 1	:	Spoke at public meeting, Anakapalli.
May 2	:	Spoke at public meeting, Tuni.
May 3	:	Spoke at public meeting, Pithapuram.
May 5	:	At Palivela.
May 6	:	At Rajole.
May 7	:	Spoke at public meeting, Rajahmundry.
May 8	:	Spoke at public meeting, Sitanagaram.
May 9	:	Spoke at public meeting, Polavaram.
May 10	:	Spoke at Buchireddipalem and Kavali public meetings.
May 13	:	At Nellore.
May 19	:	At Nellore.
May 20	:	At Kurnool.
May 21	:	Spoke at farewell function, Adoni. Left for

		Bombay after visiting 319 villages in Andhra Desha and collecting about Rs. 2,64,400.
May 22	:	Reached Bombay at night.
May 24	:	In Bombay, gave interview to *The Bombay Chronicle.*
May 25	:	Spoke at the A.I.C.C. meeting.
May 28	:	Reached Sabarmati Ashram.
May 31	:	In Sabarmati Ashram.
June 1	:	Gandhiji was in Sabarmati Ashram, Ahmedabad.
June 12	:	Bhagat Singh and Batukeshwar Dutt were sentenced to transportation for life for throwing on April 8 "two bombs in the Assembly".
June 13	:	In Bareilly, at workers' meting, Gandhiji discussed question of Congress reorganization in terms of A.I.C.C. resolution.
June 14	:	At Nainital, spoke on khaddar, communal unity, prohibition and the removal of untouchability.
June 15	:	Visited Bhuwali.
June 16	:	In Tadikhet, spoke at Prem Vidyalaya anniversary celebrations.
June 18	:	At Almora, addressed the Christian community.
June 20	:	In Almora, made a moving reference to Padam Singh's death.
June 21	:	Left Almora for Kausani.
June 27	:	At Kausani, completed introduction to the Gujarati translation of Bhagavad Gita.
July 2	:	Left Kausani.
July 4	:	Reached Kashipur in the morning and left for Delhi in the evening.
July 5	:	In Delhi.
July 6	:	Reached Sabarmati Ashram.
July 23	:	Spoke at Kadi.
July 26	:	Reached Allahabad; attended Working Commitee meeting in Mayo Hall.
July 27	:	In Allahabad, moved compromise resolution on non-violent non-co-operation campaign which was passed by an overwhelming majority in the Working Committee.

July 28	:	Message to Bombay Congress Muslim party meeting at Congress House.
August 2	:	At Sabarmati Ashram, Gandhiji spoke on death anniversary of Tilak.
August 11	:	Arrived in Bombay; attended a conference 'in camera' at M.A. Jinnah's place; discussed "matters of common interest"; left for Ahmedabad in the night.
August 12	:	Returned to Ahmedabad; suffered from dysentery.
August 15	:	Gave up experiment of uncooked food; was under medical treatment.
August 18	:	Elected President of the 44th session of the Congress, Lahore.
August 20	:	Declined Congress Presidentship and suggested instead Jawaharlal Nehru's name.
September 6	:	Left Ahmedabad for Bombay.
September 7	:	In Bombay. Opened Crafts Block at National school, Ville Parle; laid foundation-stone of an ashram for women; presided over meeting at the Vanita Vishram for the blind; visited new building of A.I.S.A. Khadi Bhavan at Kalbadevi.
September 9	:	Associated press released Gandhiji's appeal to mill-workers to keep pending announcement of arbitrators' decision.
September 10	:	At Bhopal, Gandhiji spoke at public meeting; visited Sanchi and left for Agra.
September 11	:	At Agra, spoke at public meeting; addressed women's meeting.
September 13	:	At Agra College, spoke to students.
September 18	:	Visited Dayalbagh.
September 20	:	At Mainpuri.
Septepber 21	:	At Farrukhabad.
September 22	:	In Kanpur, spoke in reply to address by District Board and Municipality; spoke in reply to address by Piecegoods Merchants and Cloth Market Employees' Association.
September 24	:	Spoke at students' meeting.

September 25	: In Banaras, spoke at untouchables' meeting; addressed students of Hindu University.
September 26	: Addressed two women's meetings; spoke at Kashi Vidyapith; spoke at convocation, Kashi Vidyapith; left for Lucknow.
September 27	: In Lucknow, spoke at public meeting.
September 28	: Spoke to Lucknow University students; spoke at A.I.C.C. meeting.
September 29	: Interview to the Free Press of India. Jawaharlal Nehru was elected President for the Lahore Congress session.
October 1	: Gandhiji was at Faizabad.
October 2	: At Jaunpur.
October 3	: At Azamgarh. At Ghazipur.
October 4	: At Gorakhpur.
October 8	: At Basti.
October 9	: Reached Manakpur at 10 a.m.; spoke at Raja Saheb's palace; left for Gonda by car at 3 p.m.
October 10	: At Gonda.
October 11	: Reached Barabanki; at Hardoi addressed political conference.
October 13	: At Moradabad, performed the opening ceremony of the Brijratan Hindu Public Library; spoke at public meeting.
October 14	: Reached Hardwar.
October 15	: At Hardwar.
October 16	: Gandhiji continued his U. P. tour, collecting funds for Lala Lajpat Rai Memorial, U. P. National Service and khadi. At Dehra Dun laid the foundation-stone of the Shraddhanand Abala Ashram; spoke at meetings of students, women, and untouchables.
October 17	: On way to Mussoorie received address composed in Sanskrit by girls at Kanya Gurukul; took part in spinning competition along with Kasturba and Mirabehn; at Rajpur unveiled portrait of Keshav Dev Shastri and planted a tree in his memory.
October 18	: At Mussoorie addressed European Municipal councillors.

October 19 to 23	:	At Mussoorie.
October 24	:	At Mussoorie spoke at public meeting; urged Antyajas to bestir themselves and see to it that the Hindu temple at Mussoorie was made accessible to them.
October 25	:	At Saharanpur.
October 26	:	At Muzaffarnagar.
October 27	:	At Meerut met "Meerut Conspiracy Case" prisoners; spoke at public meeting.
October 28	:	Visited Acharya Kripalani's ashram; spoke at Meerut College.
October 29-30	:	At Asaura.
October 31	:	At Meerut. Viceroy announced Round Table Conference to be convened after Simon Commission submitted its report.
November 1	:	Gandhiji arrived in Delhi; leaders met at Vithalbhai Patel's house to prepare drafts of joint statement; Gandhiji emphasized that Viceroy's offer could not be accepted without fulfilment of conditions.
November 2	:	Conference of prominent leaders at Delhi unanimously issued statement in reply to Viceroy's offer of Round Table Conference. Gandhiji spoke at the Town Hall; received addresses from Congress Committee, Mazdur Sabha and a purse from citizens.
November 3	:	Camped at Khurja.
November 4	:	Arrived in Aligarh; at night addressed students of Aligarh Muslim University and spoke on Hindu-Muslim unity.
November 5	:	At Aligarh; at night addressed students of Aligarh Muslim University and spoke on Hindu-Muslim unity.
November 5	:	At Aligarh; in afternoon spoke at women's meeting and public meeting. House of Lords debated Viceregal announcement; most members questioned its propriety.
November 6	:	Gandhiji arrived at Mathura.
November 7	:	At Brindaban. House of Commons debated

		Viceregal announcement.
November 8	:	Gandhiji reached Hathras.
November 9	:	In Etah district.
November 10	:	In Badaun district.
November 11	:	In Shahjahanpur district; visited American Methodist Mission Girls' School for suppressed classes.
November 12	:	In Pilibhit district.
November 13	:	In Sitapur district; visited Lucknow en route to Rai Bareli.
November 14	:	In Rai Bareli district. Wrote to A. Fenner Brockway that some absolute guarantees from British Government were necessary.
November 15	:	Reached Allahabad.
November 16	:	At Allahabad; in morning visited Dr. Higginbottom's experimental farm and agricultural institute, Mrs. Higginbottom's home for children of lepers, leper asylum conducted by them, Ewing College, Crosthwaite Girls School, Kayastha Pathashala and villages around Allahabad.
November 17	:	First death anniversary of Lala Lajpat Rai. Gandhiji spoke at meeting of students and staff of Allahabad University, Municipal Committee meeting and women's meeting where Indira Nehru presented him cheque for over Rs. 8,000; also spoke at public meeting presided over by Motilal Nehru.
November 18	:	Conference of representative political leaders held at Allahabad adopted resolution to stand by Delhi manifesto and hoped British Government would fully respond. After midnight Congress Working Committee unanimously passed resolution to await response from British Government.
November 19	:	Gandhiji visited Mirzapur and Chunar.
November 20	:	In Fatehpur district.
November 21	:	In Banda district; left for Kulapahar.
November 22	:	In Hamirpur district.

November 23 : In Jhansi and Jalaon districts.

November 24 : At Etawah; completed U.P. tour.

November 25 : Left for Ahmedabad.

November 26 : At Sabarmati executed Navajivan Trust Deed.

November 30 : Had discussion with Jinnah and Vithalbhai Patel at Sabarmati.

December 7 : Reached Wardha in morning; appealed to Ahmedabad labourers to accept arbitrator's award though it had fallen short of their demands.

December 19 : At Wardha.

December 20 : Viceroy telegraphed Gandhiji to meet him along with Motilal Nehru, T. B. Sapru, Vithalbhai Patel and Jinnah on 23rd December afternoon. Gandhiji accepted invitation.

December 21 : Left for Delhi; in letter to Mathuradas Trikumji wrote: "I am not going there with any hopes."

December 22 : The Congress Exhibition at Lahore opened by Dr. P.C. Roy.

December 23 : Attempt was made to blow up Viceroy's special train near New Delhi. Gandhiji reached Delhi; met Viceroy.

December 24 : Reached Lahore; spoke at public meeting; opened Lajpat Rai Memorial Hall; presided over All-India Suppressed Classes Conference.

December 25 : Laid foundation-stone of Lala Lajpat Rai's statue in Golbag (Lahore).

December 26 : Congress Working Committee circulated among members draft resolutions for Congress prepared by Gandhiji in consultation with Motilal Nehru and others.

December 27 : A.I.C.C. meeting commenced at Lahore and continued fro next three days. All-India Hindustani Seva Dal Conference was held at Lahore under presidentship of Srinivasa Iyengar. Gandhiji held discussions with Sikh leaders; moved independence resolution at Subjects Committee Meeting.

December 29 : Indian National Congress session began;

		Jawaharlal Nehru in presidential address advocated complete independence, immediate boycott of legislatures and organization of peaceful mass movement for no-tax campaign. Gandhiji replied to debate on independence resolution.
December 30	:	All-India Students' Convention held at Lahore; Madan Mohan Malaviya presided. Sikh Conference held at Lahore.
	:	Gandhiji's resolutions on autonomy to committees for foreign cloth boycott, for anti-untouchability, for prohibition and on reduction in number of delegates were lost at Subjects Committee meeting.
December 31	:	Gandhiji's resolutions on bomb outrage and Complete Independence adopted at open session.

Chapter Six

On Centrestage of Freedom Movement

1930

January 1	:	At Subjects Committee meeting Gandhiji moved resolution on national debts which stated that financial burdens inherited by free India would be subject to investigation by independent tribunal. Gave special interview to Press before leaving Lahore.
January 2	:	Reached Delhi. Working Committee fixed 26th January as Independence Day.
January 4	:	Earl Russell, Under-Secretary of State for India in speech, said India's Dominion Status would not be like that of Canada, Australia and New Zealand. Mazhar-ul-Haq died.
January 11	:	Gandhiji, in speech at Gujarat Vidyapith Convocation, said Earl Russell's statement on India's Dominion Status meant change to gold chains from iron ones.
January 13	:	Spoke at National Educational Conference.
January 18	:	Rabindranath Tagore visited Sabarmati Ashram and had discussions with Gandhiji.
January 22	:	Gandhiji gave interview to Daily Express about his future plan regarding civil disobedience movement.

January 25	:	Viceroy in statement in Legislative Assembly said Round Table Conference would help prepare guidelines on which Government could prepare drat proposals regarding Dominion Status for consideration of Parliament; Viceroy disapproved of financial resolution of Congress.
January 26	:	Pledge of Independence taken all over India.
February 7	:	Viceroy disapproved of financial resolution of Congress.
February 15	:	Congress Working Committee at Ahmedabad authorized Gandhiji and those who believed in non-violence as an article of faith to launch civil disobedience "as and when they desire and to the extent they decide".
	:	Gandhiji spoke at prayer meeting, Sabarmati, advising Ashram inmates to prepare themselves for the ensuing fight.
February 19	:	All-India Congress Committee adopted civil disobedience programme.
February 27	:	In article "When I am Arrested" Gandhiji wrote: "Not a single believer in non-violence as an article of faith for the purpose of achieving India's goal should find himself free or alive at the end of the effort to submit any longer to the existing slavery."
February 28	:	In letter to G. D. Birla, wrote: "I have little hope of remaining out of jail by the end of March."
March 1	:	Gandhiji was at Sabarmati.
March 2	:	Wrote to the Viceroy explaining his reasons for breaking salt law. Spoke at a wedding ceremony at the Ashram.
March 5	:	Speaking at prayer meeting told women not to accompany him on Dandi March.
March 7	:	Issued statement on Vallabhbhai Patel's arrest and appealed to the people to observe general strike.
March 8	:	Spoke at Ahmedabad meeting exhorting the people to remain peaceful and non-violent during the salt-law campaign.

March 10 : Spoke at prayer meeting, Sabarmati and called for an unlimited supply of volunteers to keep the stream of civil resisters unbroken.

Before March 11: Sent message to Andhra. On or before March 11: Gave interviews to H. D. Rajah and the *Manchester Guardian*.

: Speaking at prayer meeting said "Either we shall win the goal for which we are marching or die in the attempt to win it."

March 11 : At prayer meeting asked people to observe nonviolence if he was arrested.

March 12 : Accompanied by 78 volunteers, left Sabarmati at 6.30 a.m. for Dandi to break salt law and start civil disobedience campaign. At 8.30 a.m. gave parting message at Chandola. Spoke at Aslali.

March 13 : Spoke at Bareja and Navagam.

March 14 : Talked to Press representatives at Navagam. Spoke at Vasana.

March 15 : Spoke at Dabhan and Nadiad.

March 16 : Spoke at Boriavi.

On or after March 16: Spoke to satyagrahis.

March 17 : Spoke at Anand. Talked to volunteers.

March 18 : Addressed public meeting at Borsad.

March 19 : Addressed public meeting at Ras.

March 20 : Spoke at Kareli and Gajera.

March 21 : Spoke at Ankhi.

March 22 : Gave interview to Yusuf Meherally.

March 23 : Spoke at Buva and Samni.

March 25 : A.I.C.C session held at Sabarmati authorized Gandhiji to initiate and control civil disobedience.

: Gandhiji spoke at public meeting, Tralsa.

March 26 : Spoke at Ankleshwar. At Broach spoke on Hindu-Muslim Unity.

March 27 : Sent message to Hindustani Seva Dal. Spoke at Sajod and Mangarol.

March 28 : Spoke at Raima and Umrachhi. Spoke to volunteers.

March 29 : Spoke at Bhatgam emphasizing the need for

		greater self-purification among volunteers and pilgrims of Dandi March.
March 30	:	Spoke at Sandhiyer and Delad.
April 1	:	Spoke at Chhaprabhatha and Surat.
April 2	:	Spoke at Dindoli.
April 3	:	Spoke at Vanjh, Navasari and Dhaman.
April 4	:	Spoke at Vijalpore.
April 5	:	Reached Dandi. Issued statement to Associated Press. Sent message to America. Addressed public meeting at Dandi and advised people not to eat salt supplied by Government.
April 6	:	At Dandi Gandhiji and his party broke salt law.
	:	Salt law was also broken at Ahmedabad, Surat, Broach, Kheda, Bombay and Delhi. At public meeting in the evening Gandhiji advised the people not to eat taxed salt any more.
	:	Civil disobedience was offered throughout the country.
April 7	:	Gandhiji issued statement to the Press on the effects of civil disobedience movement. Spoke to volunteers at Aat. Sent messages to Kathiawar and Gujarat.
April 8	:	Spoke at Aat. Halted at Surat on way to Bhimrad.
April 9	:	Dictated message to the nation on how the people should conduct themselves after his arrest. Spoke at Bhimrad.
April 10	:	At Dandi. Sent message to Bombay Congress Committee and the people of Bombay. At Jalalpur, spoke to volunteers.
	:	Gave interviews to Associated Press of India and *The Hindu.* At public meeting at Abrama, stressed the necessity of complete prohibition and promotion of khadi.
April 11	:	At Jalalpur in a statement to the Associated Press of India, expressed his intention to concentrate on Gujarat.
Before April 12	:	Sent message to Mrs. Hansa Mehta that Bombay women should take up the cause of preventing liquor consumption.

April 13	:	At Dandi. Spoke at Women's conference and stressed his faith in non-violence. Spoke at public meeting. Salt Satyagraha was started at 27 different centres in Bihar. Jawaharlal Nehru and several other Congress leaders were arrested and sentenced to imprisonment.
April 14	:	Gandhiji called upon students to leave schools and colleges.
April 15	:	Spoke at Umber.
April 17	:	At Jalalpur, gave interview to Free Press of India. Spoke to the volunteers.
April 19	:	Spoke at Vejalpore and Bardoli.
April 20	:	At Jalalpur, gave interview to *The Bombay Chronicle*.
April 21	:	At Navasari, gave interview to Associated Press on Chittagong disturbances.
April 22	:	At Surat, appealed to Headmen to take leading part in the constructive work.
April 24	:	At Karadi, gave interview to *The Hindu*.
April 25	:	Spoke at Pannar.
April 26	:	Spoke at Ambheti, Bulsar and Chharwada.
Before April 27	:	Sent message to America.
April 28	:	Gave interview to The Bombay Chronicle.
April 29	:	Spoke at Bilimora. Gave interview to *The Leader*.
April 30	:	At Jalalpur. Issued statement on poisoning of salt-beds. Congratulated Delhi journalists on their decision to stop publication of newspapers and journals in protest against Press Ordinance.
May 1	:	Spoke at Olpad and Rander.
May 4	:	Drafted letter to the Viceroy. Gave interview to J. B. Kripalani. Spoke at Surat.
May 5	:	At Karadi. Was arrested at midnight and taken to Yeravda Prison in a bus. Gave interview to *The Daily Telegraph* at Borivli on way to Poona.
May 12	:	Wrote his first letter to Ashram inmates from Yeravda.
May 18	:	Wrote letter to the Viceroy.
May 20	:	In interview to *Daily Herald*, conveyed his terms of settlement.

May 30	:	Informed Government he would not see his relatives if he was not allowed to see persons equally close to him.
June 30	:	Motilal Nehru, acting Congress President, was arrested at Allahabad.
July 1	:	Gandhiji in Yeravda Prison.
July 8	:	Declined to see relatives unless some others who were as close to him as relatives by blood were also allowed to see him.
July 23	:	Had an interview with Tej Bahadur Sapru and M. R. Jayakar and sent a note for the Nehrus through them.
July 31–August 2	:	Had talks with M. R. Jayakar.
August 14–15	:	T. B. Sapru and M. R. Jayakar had talks with Gandhiji and other Congress leaders—Motilal Nehru, Jawaharlal Nehru, Vallabhbhai Patel, Dr. Syed Mahmud, Jairamdas Doulatram and Sarojini Naidu—in Yeravda Prison.
August 30–31	:	T. B. Sapru and M. R. Jayakar saw Motilal Nehru, Jawaharlal Nehru and Dr. Syed Mahmud in Naini Jail.
September 3–5	:	T. B. Sapru and M. R. Jayakar had talks with Gandhiji and other Congress leaders in Yeravda Prison and received a joint statement signed by Congress leaders and drafted by Gandhiji.
September 12	:	Round Table Conference met in London without Gandhiji.
	:	Gandhiji began series of discourses on the Gita.
December 16	:	Gandhiji was in Yeravda Central Prison from May 5, 1930.
December 21	:	Forty women in Delhi jail went on hunger-strike.
December 23	:	Madan Mohan Malaviya was released.
December 24	:	Viceroy issued two ordinances.
December 25	:	In Bombay over 200 injured in lathi-charge.
December 27	:	Martial Law declared in Smyrna.
December 29	:	Kamala Nehru was arrested.
December 30	:	Volunteer organizations in Meerut declared unlawful.

1931

January 4	:	Mahomed Ali passed away in London, where he had gone to attend the Round Table Conference along with Shaukat Ali, Jinnah and Moonje.
January 5	:	In Ahmedabad Kasturba Gandhi opened Khadi Bhandar.
January 6	:	V. J. Patel, ex-Speaker, Legislative Assembly, was released.
January 7	:	Rabindranath Tagore left London for India.
January 9	:	Dr. Hardikar of Hindustani Seva Dal was convicted.
January 10	:	Bombay gave rousing reception to V. J. Patel.
January 11	:	Bombay High Court quashed conviction of Nariman.
January 12	:	Sholapur prisoners executed.
January 14	:	Assembly session opened.
January 19	:	Plenary session of Round Table Conference. Prime Minister made statement regarding future Constitution of India.
January 21	:	In Allahabad Congress Working Committee met at Swaraj Bhawan to consider statement of Prime Minister. At Borsad a procession of women was lathi-charged; Gangabehn Vaidya received injuries.
January 22	:	Jamnadas Dwarakadas was arrested.
January 23	:	Martial Law withdrawn in Peshawar.
January 25	:	Lord Irwin issued statement releasing Gandhiji and CWC members.
January 26	:	Gandhiji was released from Yeravda Jail at 11 p.m. With Sarojini Naidu, also released on the same day, drove to Chinchwad railway station; interview to A.P.I. on station platform; left for Bombay. Jawaharlal Nehru and other Congress Working Committee members released. First anniversary of Independence Day celebrated; meetings confirmed resolution of independence. In Calcutta, Subhas Chandra Bose, Mayor, was arrested.

January 27	:	Gandhiji reached Bombay at 5.45 a.m.; interview to Press at noon; at Dr. P. S. S. Patil's place met Vithalbhai Patel; visited Congress Hospital. Visited Free Emergency Hospital; left for Allahabad.
January 28	:	Reached Allahabad.
January 31	:	In Allahabad, original and substituted members of Congress Working Committee met at Swaraj Bhawan; Gandhiji spoke twice.
February 1	:	In *Young India,* Gandhiji reiterated his "faith in truth and ahimsa". Interviewed by Reuter's Special Correspondent; addressed public meeting. Wrote to Viceroy on the lathi-charge on women's procession at Borsad.
February 3	:	Spoke to Allahabad Boatmen's Association. Was met by Nawab of Bhopal; returned Nawab's visit. Interview to *The Pioneer.*
February 4	:	Accompanied Motilal Nehru for treatment to Lucknow. Police raided *Young India;* confiscated cyclostyling machine.
February 5	:	In interview to the Press, Gandhiji condemned continuous repression.
February 6	:	In Lucknow Motilal Nehru passed away; body taken to Allahabad. Gandhiji returned to Allahabad; spoke at funeral. V. S. Srinivasa Sastri, M. R. Jayakar, T. B. Sapru and other RTC delegates landed in Bombay.
February 7	:	Gandhiji in message on Motilal Nehru exhorted countrymen to "deserve this hero's sacrifice by each sacrificing . . . to attain freedom".
February 9	:	In Press statement made suggestions on how to observe Shraddha Day of Motilal Nehru. Legislative Assembly adjourned to honour Motilal Nehru.
February 10	:	Spoke to students.
February 12	:	Discussed with commercial magnates "financial safeguards in the proposed constitution".
Before February 13	:	Interviewed by *News Chronicle,* London.
February 13	:	Met Nawab of Bhopal at Sir S. M. Sulaiman's

house; Sastri, Sapru, Jayakar, Dr. Ansari also joined. CWC discussed political situation with some RTC delegates.

February 14 : Talks continued; Gandhiji was authorized "to negotiate settlement with Viceroy." Gandhiji worte to Viceroy; sought appointment for meeting.

February 15 : Addressed public meeting. Rafi Ahmed Kidwai, ex-member of Legislative Assembly and substitute member, CEC, handed over Gandhiji's letter to Viceroy in Delhi. "Motilal Day" observed.

February 16 : Gandhiji left Allahabad by train for Delhi; Mahadev Desai, Mirabehn and Pyarelal accompanied.

February 17 : In London, *The Daily Herald*, 17-2-1931, described Gandhiji as "an optimist and a lover of peace . . . making evey effort . . . whereby co-operation can be offered". Gandhiji detrained at Ghaziabad; after morning walk at Shahdara, drove to Dr. Ansari's house. Spoke to people gathered in the park; received Sastri, Sapru and Jayakar, before meeting Viceroy; RTC terms and scope of Congress participation discussed. Gandhiji held prayer meeting at Dr. Ansari's house in the evening.

February 18 : At 1.40 p.m. before meeting Viceroy spoke to people assembled. Continued talks with Viceroy from 2.30 p.m.

February 19 : Summoned by Viceroy; held consultations with Jawaharlal Nehru, Vallabhbhai Patel, Abul Kalam Azad and other CWC members; communique issued.

February 20 : Gandhiji addressed public meeting.

February 21 : Interviewed by *News Chronicle*, London. Conveyed to CWC meeting result of conversations with Viceroy.

February 22 : Addressed Council of All-India Muslim League.

Before February 24 : In letter to Vithalbhai Patel who was leaving for Vienna, wished speedy recovery.

February 24	:	Viceroy explained to eight RTC delegates summary of talks with Gandhiji. In Delhi Jamnalal Bajaj read out Gandhiji's message at Khaddar Pracharini Sabha meeting.
February 25	:	Gandhiji spoke at Hindu College.
February 26	:	Spoke at Sisganj Gurdwara.
February 27	:	Summoned by Viceroy; no final agreement. CWC met after Gandhi-Irwin talks.
February 28	:	Gandhiji sent note on picketing to Lord Irwin; received from him notes on proposed settlement.
March 1	:	CWC altered draft formula of Gandhi-Irwin agreement without affecting the principle of its terms for truce. Gandhiji met Viceroy at 9 p.m. Talks continued till 12.15 a.m. On return to residence at 1 a.m. informed CWC members about his discussion with Viceroy; at 2 a.m. began his silence day.
March 3	:	Talks with Sir George Schuster commenced at 11 a.m.; agreement reached permitting people on sea coast to pick, manufacture and sell salt; path for Congress participation in Round Table Conference cleared. CWC meeting supported draft formula of Gandhi-Irwin agreement. Gandhiji met Viceroy.
March 4	:	Resumed talks with Viceroy at night; agreement reached. CWC gave unanimous support to Gandhi-Irwin agreement.
March 5	:	At Viceroy's house Lord Irwin and Gandhiji signed the provisional settlement which was officially announced at 5 p.m. CWC passed resolution endorsing the provisional settlement and called for action in accordance with it. Gandhiji issued statement to the Press on the settlement.
March 6	:	Interviewed by S. Hasan Ali Khan on question of zamindars' rights. Interviewed by *Kaiser-i-Hind*. Interviewed by journalists. Addressed public meeting.
March 9	:	Reached Ahmedabad at 9.30 p.m.
March 10	:	Interview to the Press. In speech to Vanaras,

		Gandhiji appealed for boycott of foreign cloth. Addressed public meeting on provisional settlement.
March 11	:	Interviewed by the Press. At Gujarat Vidyapith, addressed Ashram inmates and students and teachers of Gujarat Vidyapith. Spoke to volunteers; spoke at Labour Union.
March 12	:	*Young India* reappeared in print; Gandhiji explained implications of Delhi agreement. Left Ahmedabad for Borsad at 6.15 a.m.; alighted at Navali; advised peasants to pay up the revenue if their economic condition was good; spoke at Borsad, Ras and Sunav.
March 14	:	Reached Navasari in the morning by rail; at Dandi addressed public meeting; returned to Navasari, addressed Navasari Merchants' Maha Mandal; spoke at public meeting. Spoke at Sisora; left for Bardoli. At Jaipur State Banquet Lord Irwin observed; "Throughout conversations with Mr. Gandhi, I felt complete assurance that I could implicitly trust this word."
March 15	:	Gandhiji spoke at Surat.
March 16	:	Reached Bombay at 5 a.m.; broke silence at 8 p.m. Addressed public meeting at Parel and Dadar. Interviewed by Subhas Chandra Bose from 10 p.m. to 2.30 a.m.
March 17	:	At 7 a.m. spoke to Congress volunteers and Desh Sevikas. Met Shaukat Ali in Khilafat House; offered condolences on the death of Mahomed Ali. Interviewed by *Scrutator*. Received deputation of members of Indian Merchants' Chamber headed by Sir Chunilal Mehta. At Azad Maidan addressed mass meeting.
March 18	:	At Vile Parle spoke to Congress workers.
March 19	:	Reached Delhi. Met Viceroy regarding commutation of death sentences of Bhagat Singh, Sukhdev and Rajguru. Met H. W. Emerson, Home Secretary.
March 20	:	Lord Irwin paid tributes to Gandhiji's honesty, sincerity and patriotism at a dinner given by ruling Princes.

March 21 :	Gandhiji gave interview to Press. Viceroy convened conference of ruling Princes for informal exchange of views on framing the new constitution; Gandhiji and Malaviya attended.
Before March 23 :	Gandhiji gave interview to *Chicago Tribune*.
March 23 :	In letter to Lord Irwin appealed for reconsideration of question of commutation of death sentences of Bhagat Singh and others. Issued statement on Bhagat Singh's execution. Left Delhi for Karachi.
Before March 24 :	Gandhiji gave interview to Manchester Guardian, London.
March 24 :	"Day of Mourning".
March 25 :	Reached Karachi. In Kanpur, Ganesh Shankar Vidyarthi, a prominent Congress leader, was killed while pacifying rioters.
March 26 :	In Karachi Gandhiji gave interview to Press. Issued statement on Kanpur riots. Addressed, on behalf of CWC, deputation of Indian Merchants' Association. Inaugural speech at Karachi Congress.
March 27 :	At Subjects Committee meeting Gandhiji spoke on Kanpur riots. Interviewed by Subhas Chandra Bose and Satyamurti on question of release of Bengal detenus and prisoners sentenced during civil disobedience movement. Interviewed by Congress workers on question of Federation. Spoke to deputation of Red Shirts of Navjawan Bharat Sabha.
March 28 :	At Subjects Committee meeting, spoke on resolution on provisional settlement; the resolution was adopted.
March 30 :	Gandhiji spoke at Congress session. Karachi Congress passed resolution endorsing Gandhi-Irwin settlement; authorized Gandhiji to represent the Congress at RTC.
March 31 :	Gandhiji, in reply to the Karachi civic address, congratulated Mayor Jamshed Mehta on excellent arrangements. At Congress session, spoke on resolution on fundamental rights; the resolution

		was adopted.
April 1	:	Gandhiji interviewed by *The Statesman*. At AICC meeting, proposed new CWC members. Addressed Jamiat-ul-Ulema conference. Spoke at Parsi Rajakiya Mandal.
April 2	:	Addressed Sind National Service League.
April 6	:	In Delhi, issued Press statement on communal problem. Interview with H. W. Emerson.
April 7	:	In Delhi at Council Hall, Gandhiji spoke to Federation of Indian Chambers of Commerce and Industry.
April 8	:	At Amritsar, discussed with Sikhs methods of finding solution to communalism. Discussed boycott of foreign cloth and peaceful picketing with deputation of Piece-goods Merchants' Association. Left Amritsar for Ahmedabad.
April 9	:	Passed through Delhi en route to Ahmedabad.
	:	Interviewed by *Tej*.
April 10	:	Reached Ahmedabad. Cancelled Broach trip owing to indisposition.
April 11	:	Delivered convocation address at Gujarat Vidyapith.
April 12	:	At Ambalal Sarabhai's bungalow, where Gandhiji was staying, met J.H. Garrett, Commissioner, Northern Division.
April 13	:	Addressed Gujarat Vidyapith Graduates' conference.
April 14	:	With Kasturba Gandhi, visited Sabarmati Ashram to see Imam Saheb who was very seriously ill and other patients.
April 15	:	Interview to Associated Press of India. Gandhiji left Ahmedabad for Bombay.
April 16	:	Gandhiji arrived in Bombay from Ahmedabad; bade farewell to Lord Irwin; spoke to Congress workers on return of confiscated lands in Gujarat; and discussed scheme of re-export of foreign cloth with mill-owners Sir N. Wadia, H. P. Mody and Ambalal Sarabhai.
April 17	:	Met Governor of Bombay regarding question of

	land revenue and return of the confiscated property of the Gujarat peasants. Also discussed with Sir Geoffrey Corbers, Commerce Member, Government of India, the question of reexport of foreign cloth from India.
April 18	: Spoke in reply to Bombay Corporation address.
	: Lord Willingdon sworn in as Viceroy of India.
April 19	: Gandhiji arrived at Ahmedabad.
April 20	: At Vidyapith; visited Satyagraha Ashram.
April 21	: At Ahmedabad, officiated at wedding of Lakshmi, daughter of a khadi worker; left for Bardoli.
April 22-26	: In Bardoli taluka.
April 23	: Cabled to *The Daily Herald* that present methods of conversion adopted by missionaries should be abandoned.
April 24	: Held discussions with peasants whose confiscated lands had been sold by Government to third parties.
April 25	: In Bardoli, Sir Cowasji Jehangir, Nariman and Sardar Garda met Gandhiji regarding return of confiscated lands. Gandhiji visited Babla.
April 26	: Visited Akoti village.
April 27	: In Bardoli; left for Borsad.
April 28—May 10	: At Borsad.
April 29	: Advised Khatedars of Kaira District that they were not obliged to pay revenue by incurring debt if they had suffered substantially by reason of satyagraha movement.
April 30	: Gave interview to *Fox Movietone News*. Met the peasants of Bardoli.
May 1	: Brother of King of Bhutan met Gandhiji. Gandhiji wired H.W. Emerson, Home Secretary, not to arrest Abdul Ghaffar Khan.
May 2	: In interview to Press, said that Congress workers were faithful to the Gandhi-Irwin Pact.
May 6	: At Bochasan laid the foundation of Vallabh Vidyalaya. Gave interview to the Associated Press of India.

May 8 : Issued statement to Press on Congress workers' picketing of liquor shops and foreign cloth.

May 9 : Met the Congress workers of Kaira District.

May 10 : Gandhiji saw Collector of Kaira.

May 11 : Collector of Kaira met Gandhiji. Gandhiji left Borsad for Simla.

May 13—17 : At Simla.

May 13 : Held talks with Lord Willingdon and H. W. Emerson on the problems arising out of Gandhi-Irwin Pact.

May 14 : Spoke at public meeting and had talks with H. W. Emerson.

May 15—16 : Continued his talks with Viceroy and Home Secretary.

May 16 : Met Sir G. Schuster.

May 17 : Malaviya and Moonje had talks with Gandhiji. Gandhiji had talks with H. W. Emerson. Gave interview to a group of journalists and left for Nainital.

May 18 : Reached Nainital and met Sir Malcolm Hailey, Governor of U.P., to discuss the agrarian question.

May 19 : At Nainital, held talks with the Governor and spoke at public meeting.

May 20 : At Nainital, had interview with the Governor.

May 21 : At Kumaon, spoke at political sufferers' meeting.

May 22 : At Nainital, in an interview to Press, declined to make any statement regarding his plans for going to London.

May 23 : Wired H.S.L. Polak, Srinivasa Sastri and C. F. Andrews that absence of solution to communal question and attitude of some Provincial Governments made his leaving India difficult; reached a compromise with the zamindars regarding remission of land revenue; left Nainital for Bardoli at 4 p.m.

May 25 : Reached Swaraj Ashram, Bardoli.

May 25—June 8 : At Bardoli.

May 27	:	Had prolonged conversation with Subhas Chandra Bose.
May 30	:	Police fired in communal clashes in Kanpur.
June 5	:	Gandhiji visited Surat.
June 6	:	In Bardoli. Abdul Ghaffar Khan met Gandhiji.
June 8	:	Jawaharlal Nehru met Gandhiji. In the evening Gandhiji left for Bombay accompanied by Jawaharlal Nehru and Abdul Ghaffar Khan.
June 9	:	Arrived in Bombay to attend Congress Working Committee meeting which passed resolution that Gandhiji alone should represent the Congress at R.T.C.
June 10	:	In Bombay, addressed Prabhat Pheris, the processionists who came singing to his Bombay residence, Mani Bhuwan.
June 11	:	In Bombay, addressed meeting of Desh Sevikas and the Hindustani Seva Dal.
June 12	:	In Bombay, explained to a deputation of Europeans the attitude of the Congress towards Englishmen; left for Borsad. At Maroli, on way to Borsad, laid the foundation of a Kasturba weaving school started by Mithubehn Petit.
June 13—17	:	At Borsad.
June 18-24	:	Gandhiji continued in Borsad.
June 22	:	Exhorted farmers in Borsad taluka to pay as much land revenue as they could.
June 24	:	Left for Bombay.
June 25	:	Reached Bombay; told Press reporters that he would attend Federal Structure Committee meeting also if he attended Round Table Conference; told mill-owners that they should not use foreign-manufactured yarn in their mills; addressed Young Europeans' Dinner Club.
June 26	:	In Bombay; spoke at women's meeting and later at "Depressed Classes" meeting.
June 27	:	Left Bombay for Borsad; spoke at meeting of Parsis at Udvada.
June 28-July 6	:	In Borsad.

June 29	: Issued statement regarding change of venue of Congress Working Committee meeting from Sachin to Bombay.
June 30	: Sir Ernest Hotson asked Gandhiji on behalf of Viceroy if he was willing to serve on the Federal Structure Committee. Gandhiji appealed to H. W. Emerson for release of Pandit Jagat Ram. In interview to Press, said that he would, if invited, visit Lancashire to place before mill-owners Congress position regarding boycott of foreign cloth.
July 6	: Left for Bombay.
July 7	: In Bombay; attended Congress Working Committee meetings.
July 10	: Spoke at meeting of Gandhi Seva Mandal, Bombay.
July 11	: Viceroy invited Gandhiji for discussion with H.W. Emerson on alleged breaches of Settlement by Government.
July 12	: Gandhiji left for Surat.
July 13	: Reached Surat; left for Simla to have talks with H.W. Emerson.
July 15-22	: In Simla; held discussions with H.W. Emerson on the breaches of Settlement.
July 17	: Held talks with Sir James Crerar, Home Member.
July 18	: Had talks with Viceroy, Lord Willingdon.
July 20	: In interview to Associated Press, said that he might start on August 15 to attend Federal Structure Committee meeting in London.
July 21	: Gave "Charge-sheet" to H.W. Emerson at Simla listing instances of breaches of Settlement. Had second round of talks with Viceroy; in interview to Associated Press, said that talks were inconclusive.
July 22	: Left Simla in afternoon. Attempt on life of Sir Ernest Hotson, Acting Governor of Bombay.
July 24	: Gandhiji reached Bardoli; demanded open impartial enquiry into complaints of forced collection of land revenue and repression of tenants.

July 25	:	In Bardoli; assured H.W. Emerson that no precipitate action would be taken without informing him.
July 27	:	District and Sessions Judge Garlick of Alipore was shot dead in his court-room; Gandhiji left for Borsad.
July 28-31	:	In Borsad.
July 31	:	Left Borsad and arrived in Ahmedabad; gave interview to Associated Press.
August 1-2	:	In Ahmedabad.
August 2	:	opened family temple of Chinubhai Madhavlal to untouchables.
August 3	:	Arrived in Bombay; at night left for Poona.
August 4	:	In Poona, had talks with Governor of Bombay, Sir Ernest Hotson; in evening returned to Bombay.
August 5-14	:	In Bombay.
August 5	:	Congress Working Committee met in Bombay.
August 6	:	Gandhiji spoke at A.I.C.C. meeting.
August 7	:	Spoke at meeting of Parsis.
August 8	:	Laid foundation-stone of an eye hospital; spoke at A.I.C.C. meeting.
August 9	:	Spoke at meeting of Hindustani Seva Dal.
August 11	:	Wired to Viceroy and Bombay Government that Government attitude was not favourable to enable him to proceed to London.
August 13	:	Congress Working Committee passed resolution to continue honouring Delhi Pact, but not to take part in Round Table Conference. Gandhiji spoke to Press representatives.
August 14	:	Gave interview to Press; left Bombay for Ahmedabad at night.
August 15-23	:	In Ahmedabad.
August 18	:	Released correspondence regarding breakdown of negotiations with Government; gave interview to Press.
August 22	:	Interview to Associted Press.
August 23	:	Gandhiji left Ahmedabad for Simla.

August 25	:	Reached Simla at 11 a.m. accompanied by Vallabhbhai Patel, Prabhashankar Pattani, M. A. Ansari and Jawaharlal Nehru; met H. W. Emerson.
August 26	:	Had three hours' talk with Viceroy in morning; announced to Press that he was sailing from Bombay for London on August 29.
August 27	:	Left Simla for Bombay in evening.
August 28	:	Government communique, known as Second Settlement, released.
August 29	:	Gave interview to *The Bombay Chronicle* on train; reached Bombay; addressed public meeting; sailed for London by *S.S. Rajputana* to attend Round Table Conference.
September 2	:	Appealed to Indian people to preserve absolutely non-violent atmosphere during absence and follow constructive programme.
September 3	:	Reached Aden; gave interview to Reuter; was presented address and purse at reception in reply to which he said that free India could be a great force of service to whole of mankind.
September 6	:	Reached Suez.
September 7	:	Silence Day. Gandhiji reached Port Said; in interview to Cairo's Al Ahram, said if Round Table Conference failed consequence would be resumption of civil disobedience movement; urged Egyptian nationalists to fight non-violently; in special interview to The Daily Telegraph, said he would not be a party to any settlement subjugating any community to another in India.
	:	Received Mustafa Nahas Pasha's welcome message inviting him to visit Egypt on his homeward journey.
	:	Expressed disappointment on arrival at Port Said as large number of admirers were prevented by authorities from meeting him.
September 10	:	In interview on board ship said he had prepared no plans, no speeches, no arguments and no programme for his stay in England.

September 11 : Landed at Marseilles; was received by Madeleine Rolland on behalf of her brother, Romain Rolland, who was ill; told Pressmen: "I am going to England to realizc the dream of my life—the freedom of my country."

: In interview to *The New York Times* said he had no intention of visiting the United States as he believed he was "not wanted" there.

: In another interview to Press said he would, provided he was invited to, go to Lancashire even if he was to be lynched. Left at 4.30 p.m. by *P. and O. Express* for Calais.

September 12 : Gandhiji arrived in London. In interview to the Press gave essence of Congress mandate. Spoke at Friends' House, London.

September 13 : In broadcast to America from Columbia Broadcasting Service made an appeal to conscience of the people. Met British Prime Minister and Lord Sankey.

Before September 14 : In message to the *The Times* said that he wanted goodwill of every Englishman and English woman in this mission of peace.

September 14 : Attended Federal Structure Committee meeting but did not speak, it being his Silence Day.

September 15 : At Federal Structure Committee presented national demand of Complete Independence.

September 16 : Speaking at meeting of Labour M.P.s reiterated India's demand for Complete Independence.

September 17 : Gave interview to the *Textile Mercury* and *News Chronicle*.

: Spoke at Federal Structure Committee on elections of members of Federal Legislature.

September 19 : Spoke at Reception at Kingsley Hall.

September 21 : Shifted to 88 Knightsbridge from Kingsley Hall.

September 22 : Had interview with Charlie Chaplin. Spoke at meeting of Federal Structure Committee on Government decision to abandon Gold Standard.

September 23 : Spoke at Guild House Church on "Voluntary Poverty". Speaking at meeting of M.P.s elucidated idea of Complete Independence.

September 24 : Had discussions with Aga Khan and Jinnah. Attended Federal Structure Committee meeting.

September 25 : Called on Lord Irwin.

September 26 : Had talks with representatives of cotton industry at Edgeworth and at Darwen. Received deputation of unemployed workers at Springfield Garden Village.

September 26/27: Spoke on Lancashire's unemployment problem.

September 27 : Spoke at Adult School, West Bradford. Received deputations from unemployed workers and Clitheroe Weavers' Association at West Bradford. Had talks with Press reporters.

September 28 : Attended Minorities Committee meeting.

September 29 : In London. Had discussion with Sir Samuel Hoare.

September 30 : Had inerview with British Prime Minister. Spoke at reception, Indian Chamber of Commerce, London.

October 1 : Had meeting with the Aga Khan and other Muslim leaders at Ritz Hotel. Had discussions with Prime Ministers. Speaking at Minorities Committee meeting, asked for its adjournment for a week.

Before October 2 : Give interview to the *Jewish Chronicle*.

October 2 : Talked to Henry Carter on prohibition. Independent Labour Party, Indian National Congress, League and the Gandhi Society arranged a birthday luncheon for Gandhiji at Westminster Palace rooms.

: At Minorities Conference, London, Gandhiji opposed special representation to Depressed Classes.

: Spoke at women's receiption arranged by Women's Indian Association at Central Y.M.C.A., London.

October 3 : Went to see C.F. Andrews at Canterbury.

October 4 : At Canterbury.

October 5 : Spoke at a meeting of Minorities Conference, London

October 6 : Addressed Fellowship Club. Attended party in honour of Lord Irwin.

October 7 : Spoke at a meeting of Friends of India, London.

October 8 : Presented Congress policy on minority question at Minorities Committee meeting.

: Spoke at a conference of Missionary Societies in Great Britain and Ireland, London.

On or before October 9 : Gave interviews to Madame Montessori and Shaw Desmond.

October 9 : Spoke at Federal Structure Committee meeting.

October 10 : At Chichester.

On or before October 11 : Gave interview to H.N. Brailsford.

October 12 : At National Labour Club said that India was determined to achieve complete Independecne without shedding blood.

October 13 : Explained communal quesion in interview to the Press. Addressed Indian Students' meeting, Gower Street Hostel, Bloomsbury, London.

On or before October 14 : Gave interview to Joseph Bard, Editor, The Island, London.

October 14 : Issued statement to the Press on solution of communal issue. Had talks with Sir Samuel Hoare, Benthal and M.A. Jinnah. spoke at Federal Structure Committee meeting, London.

October 15 : Spoke at meeting of students at International Students' Movement House, Russell Square, London. Had talks with Samuel Hoare, T. B. Sapru, M.R. Jayakar and others.

October 16 : Had discussion with Callender on Mass Production v. Production by the Masses. Spoke at Federal Structure Committee meeting and at Temperance Workers' meeting.

October 17 : Spoke at Nottingham University College, Nottingham.

On or after October 17 : Gave interview to E. Wrench, Editor, *The Spectator,* London.

October 18 : Spoke to Indians at Selly Oak, Birmingham and exhorted them to return to India and serve their countrymen.

	:	Spoke at Woodbrooke Settlement, Selly Oak, Birmingham on India's decision to attain freedom through peaceful means.
October 19	:	Left Birmingham in the morning.
October 20	:	Spoke at federal Structure Committee meeting, London. At meeting held under the auspices of the Royal Institute of International Affairs at Chatham House, London, spoke on "India of Today and Tomorrow".
October 21	:	Called on Lord Irwin and Col. Maddock. Attended Federal Structure Committee meeting.
October 22	:	Gave interview to *The Statesman*. Spoke at Federal Structure Committee meeting, London.
Ocotber 23	:	Gave interview to Reuter. Spoke at Federaal Structure Committee meeting, London.
	:	Had a talk with T.B. Sapru and others. Reached Eton at night. Addressed a gathering of School Boys, Eton. Left Eton in the morning for Oxford.
October 24	:	Spoke at meeting of Indian Majlis, Oxford. Delivered a talk at Oxford.
October 26	:	Attended Federal Structure Committee meeting.
October 27	:	Attended Federal Structure Committee meeting.
October 28	:	Spoke on child education at Montessori Training College, London.
October 29	:	Gave inerview to Charles Petrasch and others.
October 30	:	Spoke at a meeting of Commonwealth of India League, Central Hall, Westminster
October 31	:	Spoke at meeting of Quakers at Friend's House, London.
November 1	:	Spoke at Pembroke Colege, Cambridge, reiterating his faith in a partnerhsip of India and Britain on equal terms. Spoke at Indian Majlis. Reached London.
November 2	:	Submitted written statement at Federal Structure Committee, London.
November 3	:	Spoke at the annual meeting of Children's House, Bow.
November 4	:	Spoke at Federal Structure Committee meeting, London. Spoke at the Indian Medical Association.

November 5	:	Spoke at meeting of Postal Workers' Union.
November 6	:	Mr. & Mrs. George Bernard Shaw called on Gandhiji.
November 7	:	Gandhiji reached Oxford. Had talks with Ramsay MacDonald and Prof. Murray.
November 9	:	Returned to London from Oxford. Declared in Press statement that the had cancelled his continental engagements. Spoke at meeting, organized by fellowship of Reconciliation at Friends' House, London.
November 10	:	Had talks with T.B. Sapru and others. Discussed with J.M. Sen Gupta situation in Bengal. Spoke at London School of Economics.
November 11	:	Gave interview to the Press. Explained his concept of Provinicial autonomy at conference of the Round Table Conference delegates.
November 12	:	Spoke at Commonwealth of India League, London.
November 13	:	Gave inerview to *News Chronicle*. Spoke at Minorities Committee meeting. Spoke at Westminster School.
November 14	:	Called on Lord Irwin. Gave interview to the Press.
November 16	:	Attended Minorities Committee meeting.
November 17	:	Sent a message to F. B. Fisher expressing his inability to visit America. Spoke on defence at the Federal Structure Committee meeting.
November 18	:	Spoke at meeting of Women's Indian Council at Morley College, London.
November 19	:	Spoke on "Commercial Discrimination" at Federal Structure Committee meeting. Addressed London Vegetarian Society.
November 20	:	Atteneded Vegetarians' meeting.
November 24	:	Had discussions with Prime Minister, Lord Sankey, State Secretary, Sapru and Lees-Smith.
November 25	:	Gave interview to *New Leader*. Made two speeches on "Provincial Autonomy" and on "Finance" in Federal structure committee meetings. Met Dr. Ambedkar in the evening.

November 26 : Participated in proceedings of Federal Structure Committee meeting.

November 27 : Participated in Federal Structure Committee meeting.

November 28 : Took part in proceedings of plenary session of Round Table Conference.

Before November 30: Gave interview to the Press, London.

November 30 : Participated in proceedings of plenary session of R.T.C.

December 1 : Delivered concluding speech at plenary session of Round Table Conference. Gave interview to journalists. Released statement to the Press on events in India.

December 2 : Gave interview to Sir Philip Hartog.

December 3 : Gave interview to the Press. Had discussions with J. F. Horrabin, Wrench, Laski, Kingsley Martin, Brailsford and Nevinson.

December 4 : Called on Prime Minister and Secretary of State for India.

Before December 5 : Gave inerview to Edmond Demeter. Issued parting manifesto.

December 5 : Gave farewell messages to Reuter and *Bristol Evening News*. Left Britain for Paris en route to India. Spoke at reception organized by Indians in Paris. Spoke at public meeting in afternoon.

December 6 : Had discussion with Romain Rolland at Villeneuve. Gave interview to the Press.

December 8 : Addressed three meetigs a Lausanne.

December 9 : Had discussions with Romain Rolland in Villeneuve.

December 10 : Spoke at meeting held at Victoria Hall organized by International Women's League for Peace and freedom.

December 10-11: Had discussions with Romain Rolland.

December 11 : Left Villeneuve. In Milan.

December 12 : In Rome visited Vatican city. Called on Mussolini.

December 13 : In Rome, had talk with Sukhotina Tolstoy. Addressed a women's meeting.

December 14	:	In Brindisi. Atttended function organized by History and Art Society.
December 17	:	Gave interview to Reuter at Port Said.
December 24	:	Made statement to the Associated Press of India.
December 25	:	Delivered a talk on Jesus and Christianity on *S.S.Pilsna* at 4.30 in the morning.
December 27	:	Gave interview to Reuter on *S.S. Pilsna*.
December 28	:	Landed in Bombay in the morning. Gave interview to the Press. Spoke at public meeting at Azad Maidan, Bombay. At night spoke at Welfare of India League in Majestic Hotel, Bombay.
December 29	:	Wired to the Viceroy seeking interview to discuss Frontier, U.P. and Bengal Ordinances. Had talks with Subhas Chandra Bose.
December 31	:	Viceroy declined to discuss with Gandhiji Frontier, U.P.and Bengal Ordinances.

1932

January 1	:	Resolution of the Congress Working Committee, drafted by Gandhiji, calling upon the nation to resume civil disobedience was adopted. Gandhiji sent rejoinder to the Government that if the Viceroy refused to discuss with him the Frontier, U.P. and Bengal Ordinances, the nation will resort to civil disobedience. Gandhi-Willingdon corresondence was released.
January 2	:	Gandhiji was interviewed by the Associated Press on the revival of civil disobedience. Had talks with the deputation of Welfare of Indian League. Viceroy rejected Gandhiji's request for an interview.
January 3	:	Gandhiji wired to the Government regretting Government's decision and assuring a non-violent struggle. Sent message to America and to Indian Christians. In an interview to Associated Press of India emphasized the need for the resuming civil disobedience. In an interview to *The Bombay Chronicle* outlined the plan of action to be followed by the nation after

his arrest. Spoke on the 'utility of prayer'.

January 4 : In Bombay, at Mani Bhuvan, Gandhiji was arrested at three in morning. In letter to Vallabhbhai Patel, conveyed message to people. Taken to Yeravda Central Prison, interned with Vallabhbhai Patel. In Patna, Rajendra Prasad, Congress President, was arrested. Dr. M.A. Ansari assumed Presidentship. Jawaharlal Nehru was tried and sentenced to two years' rigorous imprisonment. Four new Ordinances were promulgated; All Congress organizations were declared unlawful; but not the Congress and its flag.

January 5 : Arrests and convictions on large scale in Bombay, Calcutta and Delhi. Gujarat Vidyapith was declared illegal and seized.

January 6 : Hartal in Bombay; lathi-charge in Coimbatore.

January 7 : In Ahmedabad, Mahadev Desai, D.B. Kalelkar were arrested; and in Karachi, Jairamdas Doulatram.

January 8 : In New Delhi, Dr. M. A. Ansari was arrested; Sardul Singh assumed Presidentship of the Congress.

January 9 : Viceroy received Sapru and others. In Madras, C. Rajagopalachari, S. Satyamurti were arrested; foreign-cloth picketers lathi-charged.

January 10 : Kasturba was arrested near Bardoli.

January 11 : In Tirupur lathi-charge Kumaraswami died.

January 12 : Gandhiji obtained permission to write letters.

January 13 : In Allahabad and Madras, police seized Congress offices. In Ahmedabad, "Navajivan" office was locked up.

January 15 : In letter to Sir Samuel Hoare, Secretary of State, Gandhiji said: "The initiative for every step was mine and it was a logical outcome of my creed of satyagraha." At Surat, Kasturba, Manibehn Patel and Mithubehn were convicted. In Calcutta, 30 students, including girls, were arrested.

January 16 : In Bombay, Jamnalal Bajaj and Dr. Hardikar were arrested. Home Department, Bombay, issued

		instructions on privileges to Gandhiji and Vallabhbhai Patel.
January 18	:	Hundred and six religious leaders of U.S.A. appealed to British Premier to release Gandhiji.
January 19	:	In Madras, influential non-Congressmen issued statement protesting against lathi-charges.
January 20	:	In Bombay, J.M. Sen Gupta was arrested on board *S.S. Ganges,* and taken to Yeravda Prison.
January 23	:	Gandhiji wrote to the Bombay Governor to stop repression and make amends.
January 24	:	Gandhiji was allowed an interview per week.
January 25	:	In Legislative Assembly, Lord Willingdon said: "There can be no compromise in resisting the civil disobedience movement. . . . No Government worth the name could hesitate to accept the challenge."
January 26	:	In Ahmedabad, Bombay, Calcutta, Delhi and Lucknow, Independence Day processions led to arrests.
January 27	:	Mirabehn met Gandhiji.
January 28	:	Sir Samuel Hoare, in a broadcast, said: "Our policy . . . is a policy of progress combined with firmness. . . . Though dogs bark, caravan passes on."
January 29	:	In Bombay police firing, one person was killed.
February 2	:	Devdas Gandhi was arrested.
February 5	:	In letter to M. G. Bhandari, Superintendent, Yeravda Central Prison, Gandhiji sought permission to meet fellow-prisoners.
February 6	:	At Calcutta University Convocation, Sir Stanley Jackson, Governor of Bengal, was fired at by a girl student.
February 14	:	Sardul Singh Caveeshar, Acting Congress President, was arrested.
February 17	:	Mirabehn arrested for refusal to leave Bombay, sentenced to three months' rigorous imprisonment and sent to Arthur Road Prison, Bombay.
February 21	:	In letter to Narandas Gandhi, Gandhiji completed

		summary of last chapter of Bhagavad Gita.
February 22	:	In Delhi, Consultative Committee of Round Table Conference reassembled under Chairmanship of Viceroy.
February 24	:	Gandhiji was examined by Civil Surgeon.
February 26	:	In a letter said that health was the chief reason for giving up milk.
February 27	:	Independent Labour Party of U.K. issued manifesto condemning Government's repressive policy in India.
February 28	:	Dr. Moonje and M.C. Rajah, as representatives of Hindu Mahasabha and Depressed Classes, cabled British Premier their agreement for joint electorate system with reservation on population basis.
February 29	:	G.S. Bajpai, I.C.S., appointed to succeed K. V. Reddy as Agent-General in South Africa.
March 1	:	In letter to R. V. Martin, Gandhiji sought early decision on question of meeting fellow-prisoners.
	:	Started writing with left hand as right hand pained.
March 4	:	In Delhi, Consultative Committee of Round Table Conference met.
March 5	:	Gandhiji received orders permitting to see visitors. In letter to Narandas Gandhi, gave instructions about informing Jail Superintendent before anybody visited him. Navajivan Press was returned.
March 6	:	In letter to M. G. Bhandari, Gandhiji sought clarification of term "political" with reference to his visitors.
March 7	:	In letter to D. B. Kalelkar, informed that he was getting up at night to study position of stars.
March 10	:	Was joined by Mahadev Desai, who was transferred from Nasik Jail.
March 11	:	In letter to Sir Samuel Hoare, conveyed intention to resort to fast if proposal to create separate electorate for Depressed Classes was implemented.
March 12	:	Discussed astronomy with Mahadev Desai.

March 13 : In his letter to Gandhiji, Sir Samuel Hoare stated that on question of separate electorate no decision would be taken without considering views of Lothian Committee and Gandhiji's supporters.

: Kasturba was sentenced to six months' imprisonment and fined Rs. 50 or 1 months' imprisonment in default.

March 16 : Home Department, Bombay, passed orders permitting Gandhiji to see fellow-prisoners.

March 25 : In House of Commons, Sir Samuel Hoare made statement on Indian situation.

March 26 : Gandhiji received permission to write to Jamnalal Bajaj and other co-workers in prison.

March 28 : In letter to H. W. Emerson, expressed distress over proposal to "sell out" lands of "recalcitrant" farmers and urged him to desist from such action.

March 29 : Was examined by surgeon.

April 2 : In letter to Dudhibehn Desai, said that there was nothing wrong with his right hand. He was not using it for writing "merely as a measure of precaution".

April 5 : In letter to Maithilisharan Gupta, expressed views on *Saket, Anagh, Panchavati* and *Jhankar*.

April 6 : Government banned Congress session in Delhi.

April 7 : In letter to C. F. Andrews, Gandhiji explained that "fasting unto death is a corrupt expression. . . . It is fasting unto a new life."

April 8 : In letter to Mirabehn, gave an account of his daily schedule of food, work and sleep.

April 11 : In telegram to Kamala Nehru, expressed distress over injury sustained by Swarup Rani Nehru in police assault during National Week at Allahabad. Lothian Committee met at Simla.

April 12 : In letter to Narandas Gandhi, Gandhiji gave instructions to send cable to America to explain Ashram's policy of not claiming any rights over its publication or to grant them to others.

April 15 : In letter, appealed to Shankarrao Deo, a fellow-prisoner, to give up his fast.

April 18 : Government banned Reception Committee of Delhi Congress session.

April 21 : Sarojini Naidu was ordered not to leave Bombay.

April 22 : Sarojini Naidu was arrested in Bombay and M.M. Malaviya in Delhi.

April 24 : In Delhi, police dispersed Congress session presided over by Ranchhodlal Amritlal and arrested him; arrested 400 Congressmen. Gandhiji was awarded service to mankind medal by Community Church of New York.

April 27 : In letter to Harilal Gandhi, said: "I will still not give up hope of your reformation for I have not given up hope about myself."

April 29 : In House of Commons, Sir Samuel Hoare said: "There clearly cannot be any question of co-operation with anyone associated with civil disobedience. If Mr. Gandhi shows a disposition to restore the relations which existed at the Round Table Conference, he will not find the slightest difficulty."

April 30 : Robert Douglas, District Magistrate of Midnapore was fired at and seriously wounded.

May 7 : In letter, Gandhiji requested E.E. Doyle to enquire into missing letters.

May 8 : All-India Depressed Classes Congress was held at Kamptee. In South Africa, Kunwar Maharaj Singh was appointed Indian Agent.

May 10 : In London, it was decided to re-establish London Branch of Indian National Congress.

May 11 : In letter to Devdas Gandhi, Gandhiji stated that he would have to take milk after his release from jail. Lothian, before leaving for U.K., issued farewell message on Indian Constitutional reforms.

May 14 : Hindu-Muslim riot in Bombay.

May 15 : In letter to Fulchand Bapuji, Gandhiji said: "There are no restrictions on food except those which are self-imposed nor on the hours of rest and sleep. Carding and spinning are going on fairly well. . . . And we also read."

May 18	:	In Bombay, Mirabehn was released from Arthur Road Prison. Mirabehn was prohibited from seeing Gandhiji. In letter to E. E. Doyle, Gandhiji wanted Government to reconsider decision regarding Mirabehn and permit her to see him.
May 20	:	Bipin Chandra Pal passed away.
May 21	:	Ranchhodlal was sentenced to nine months' rigorous imprisonment.
May 22	:	Manager, *Navajivan,* and Editor, *Bombay Samachar,* each sentenced to one year's rigorous imprisonment. Gandhiji began to use Gregorian date in correspondence.
May 24	:	In letter to Satyacharan Law, Gandhiji conveyed tributes to P. C. Ray on his 70th birthday.
May 26	:	Meeting of British Socialists presided over by Fenner-Brockway, sent fraternal greetings to Congressmen, especially those in prison.
May 27	:	In letter to Verrier Elwin, Gandhiji communicated decision to sing Gujarati version of "Lead Kindly Light" at 7.40 every Friday evening and believed that the addressee would join him from wherever he was. In letter to Devdas Gandhi, paid generous tribute to Narandas Gandhi for his "firmness, patience, courage, renunciation and good judgement."
May 28	:	Bengal anti-terrorist Ordinance was renewed.
June 1	:	Gandhiji's incarceration in the Yeravda Central Prison continued. Gandhiji wrote to Mirabehn about his decision to decline to see visitors if the Government did not permit her to see him.
	:	Satyagraha Ashram at Wardha seized by police.
June 3	:	Report of the Franchise Committee, under Lord Lothian, published.
June 4	:	Gandhiji received Government's reply refusing permission for Mirabehn seeing him. Gandhiji decided not to see visitors.
June 6	:	Wrote the article "Concerning Titiksha and Yajna" for the inmates of the Ashram.
June 9	:	Wrote to Col. E. E. Doyle concerning his resolve

		not to have visitors unless Government revised its decision about Mirabehn.
June 10	:	Met follow-prisoners—Jethalal Gandhi and Bindu Madhav Gurle.
June 14	:	Col. E. E. Doyle paid a visit.
June 15	:	Gandhiji received a wire about Devdas's illness in Gorakhpur jail.
June 18	:	Wired to Sir Malcolm Hailey requesting Devdas's transfer to Yeravda or Dehradun, and forwarded Mirabehn's letter to Government denying the alleged charges.
June 19	:	Wrote the article " Prayer".
June 24	:	Col. E. E. Doyle paid a visit.
June 25	:	Gandhiji wrote the article " How to Observe Ahimsa".
July 3	:	Wrote the article " How to Observe Truth".
July 5	:	Sent wires of condolence to C. Rajagopalachari and his daughter on the death of Varadachari.
July 6	:	Col. E. E. Doyle paid a visit.
July 8	:	T. B. Sapru and M. R. Jayakar resigned form Consultative Committee.
July 10	:	Gandhiji wrote the article "Education".
July 13	:	In a letter to Col. E.E. Doyle, protested against delay in attending to his correspondence and asked for clarification.
July 17	:	Wrote the article " Individual Prayer".
July 21	:	Received a wire about Devdas's relapse of fever. Met fellow-prisoners—Chhaganlal Joshi, Shankar and Mukund.
July 24	:	Wrote the article "Supervision Is Not Necessary". Wrote to Col. E.E. Doyle regarding his correspondence in Gujarati, Hindi and Urdu.
July 31	:	Wrote the article "Learn the Gita by Heart".
August 3	:	Dr. Pranjivan Mehta died in Rangoon.
August 4	:	Gandhiji sent a wire of condolence to Chhaganlal, son of Dr. Pranjivan Mehta.
August 5	:	Met fellow-prisoners—Jamnadas, Brelvi, Ramdas and Hargovan.

August 6	:	Met two fellow-prisoners who were on fast and persuaded them to give it up.
August 7	:	Paid tribute to Dr Pranjivan Mehta in an article.
August 14	:	Wrote the article "Reading and Reflection—I".
August 17	:	MacDonald's Communal Award announced.
August 18	:	In his letter to Ramsay MacDonald, Gandhiji announced his decision to go on a fast unto death from 20th September unless Communal Award was withdrawn.
August 19	:	Met fellow-prisoners—Gangadharrao, Shanker and Devidas Ghevaria's nephew.
August 21	:	Wrote the article " Reading and Reflection— II".
August 26	:	Col. E.E. Doyle paid a visit and requested Gandhiji to reconsider his decision to undertake a fast.
August 28	:	Gandhiji wrote the article "Action—Thoughtful and Thoughtless".
September 1	:	Gandhiji in Yeravda Jail.
September 9	:	Wrote to Ramsay MacDonald that his decision to fast unto death against Communal Award was final.
September 13	:	Gandhiji's correspondence with Prime Minister and Sir Samuel Hoare regarding fast released for publication.
September 15	:	Gandhiji sent to bombay Government for general release to the Press statement giving reasons for his impending fast. Government announced its decision to release Gandhiji conditionally during his fast.
September 16	:	Gandhiji wired to Government expressing himself against his conditional release. Issued statement to the Press giving reasons of his impending fast.
September 18	:	Deputation of Bombay Hindu leaders consisting of Purushottamdas Thakurdas, Mathuradas Vissanji Khimji, Sir Chunilal Mehta and G.D. Birla met Gandhiji.
September 19	:	Hindu leaders'deputation again met Gandhiji and discussed conditions for his abandoning fast.

September 20 : At noon, Gandhiji commenced his fast unto death against the British Government's announcement regarding separate electorates for Depressed Classes. Called his first Press interview and explained motive of his fast. At night Hindu leaders and Dr. B.R. Ambedkar approved of tentative scheme based on joint electorates.

September 21 : Deputation consisting of M.R. Jayakar, C. Rajagopalachari, Rajendra Prasad and G.D. Birla discussed with Gandhiji scheme based on joint electorates. S.M. Mate, P.N. Rajbhoj and Limaye met Gandhiji in prison. Gandhiji declared that he would break his fast when the British Prime Minister agreed to change Communal Award.

September 23 : Informed Press reporters that his fast was not political move but spiritual effort and penance.

September 24 : Discussed with the correspondents of The Times of India the scope and implication of restorting to fasting by political leaders. Hindu leaders and suppressed class leaders signed the Agreement in the presence of Gandhiji who also gave his assent. The terms of settlement were communicated to the Government of India and the British Premier with the request to expedite revision of Communal Award.

September 25 : Gave interview to Ellen and V.K. Krishna Menon. In his second Press conference announced that he would break his fast only if the Premier accepted the settlement in toto.

September 26 : Fast broken at 5.15 p.m. Gandhiji issued statement to the Press describing the settlement as generous gesture on all sides.

On or before September 27 : Issued statement to the Press on chances of Congress co—operation in work of Round Table Conference.

September 27 : Asked Government not to withdraw facilities extended to him during fast.

September 29 : Gandhiji was informed at 12.30 p.m. that special facilities allowed to him during fast regarding interviews and correspondence had been

	withdrawn. Wrote to M.G. Bhandari strong letter resenting this change.
September 30 :	Wired to K. Kelappan advising him to suspend his fast.
October 1 :	Again wired to K. Kelappan to break his fast.
October 2 :	K. Kelappan broke his fast in the morning.
On or after October 2:	Gandhiji issued statement to the Press on temple-entry.
Octber 17 :	Dr Ambedkar and Sarojini Naidu saw Gandhiji in jail.
October 18 :	Gandhiji wrote to H.F. Hudson, seeking Government's definite reply regarding interviews and correspondence for untouchability work.
October 19 :	Gandhiji was removed to the cell in which he had lived before the fast.
October 20 :	started taking bread.
October 23 :	Punjabhai Shah passed away.
October 24 :	Gandhiji suspended correspondence on untouchability till the Government removed restrictions on correspondence and interviews relating to untouchability work.
October 26 :	Col Doyle saw Gandhiji in jail.
October 31 :	Gandhiji declined to take special food from November 1, as a protest against restrictions on correspondence and interviews relating to untouchability work.
November 1 :	Stopped taking special diet.
November 2 :	Suspended restrictions on diet in response to message from Government.
November 3 :	Government lifted all restrictions on visitors, correspondence and publicity for untouchability work.
November 4 :	Gandhiji issued his first statement to the Press on untouchability.
November 5 :	Issued second statement on untouchability.
Novermber 7 :	Issued third statement on untouchability. Gave interview to Associated Press on temple—entry question.

November 8	:	Issued fourth statement on untouchability.
November 11	:	Dissuaded P. N. Rajbhoj and his friends from starting any satyagraha or fast for temple—entry.
November 12	:	Gave interview to *The Hindu*.
November 13	:	Replied to Lord Sankey's public appeal to him.
November 14	:	Issued fifth statement on untouchability.
November 15	:	Issued sixth statement on untouchability.
November 16	:	Gandhiji issued seventh statement on untouchability. In Foreword to *Hamara Kalank*, exhorted Hindu public to realize implications of untouchability and their duty in the matter.
November 17	:	Issued eighth statement on untouchability.
November 18	:	In letters to E. E. Doyle, requested transfer of Jamnalal Bajaj; also permission to write to Manibehn Patel on progress of her brother's illness.
November 19	:	In letter to M. G. Bhandari, reassured Government about his desire to abide by the undertaking given in regard to facilities permitted to him for doing untouchability work. In discussion with G. K. Devdhar, President, Maharashtra Divisional Board of All-India Anti-untouchability League, stressed need to educate public opinion on removal of untouchability.
November 21	:	In letter to Narandas Gandhi, referred to increase in pressure of work and said his elbows needed rest. In interview to the Press said that all his activities in life sprang from a "passion for vindication of truth and non-violence".
November 22	:	In letter to E.E. Doyle, requested transfer of Jamnalal Bajaj to Yeravda Prison.
November 23	:	In letter to K. Kelappan, informed him that he would join him in his fast as a point of honour.
November 24	:	In letter to Home Secretary, Government of Bombay, requested permission to be granted to Swami Anand to stay with him to help clear arrears of correspondence which had accumulated owing to pain in his hand. In letter to Haribhau Phatak, sent draft manifesto on removal of untouchability.

November 25	:	In interview to Khimji and J. K. Mehta, urged for a vigorous propaganda for removal of untouchability and temple-entry.
November 26	:	Issued ninth statement on untouchability. Jamnalal Bajaj was taken to Yeravda Prison.
	:	In interview to *The Times of India,* Gandhiji denied rumour about his fast for opening all temples in India to untouchables.
November 28	:	In letter to E.E. Doyle, asked Appasaheb Patwardhan to be permitted to do conservancy work in Ratnagiri Jail. In letter to Keshav Gandhi said that he had completely stopped spinning for the time being because of pain in the elbow.
November 29	:	In appeal to public reminded all concerned that people could meet him "only in connection with bonafide untouchability work and no other". In letter to Home Secretary, Government of Bombay, sought permission to meet Jamnalal Bajaj "frequently, of course, subject to restriction as to conversation".
November 30	:	In letter to E. E. Doyle, conveyed decision to do his own conservancy work from December 3, and to resort to complete fast if Appasaheb was not permitted to do conservancy work.
December 2	:	Interview to Depressed Classes leaders.
December 3	:	Received message allowing him to do conservancy work, but was informed that Government would not accept his intervention on behalf of Appasaheb Patwardhan.
	:	Commenced fast; informed E. E. Doyle in letter that he would continue fast till relief was granted to Appasaheb Patwardhan.
December 4	:	Suspended his fast; made statement to Anti-untouchability Committee. In letter to E.E. Doyle, informed him that fast was suspended in order to give Government time to decide.
December 5	:	In interview to the Press said that he was devoting all his time to untouchability work. Was examined by jail doctor.
December 6	:	Issued statement on observing

Antiuntouchability Day on December 18. In telegram asked Appasaheb Patwardhan to suspend fast in order to give Government time to take decision. Appasaheb Patwardhan agreed to suspend his fast in response to Gandhiji's appeal. Interview to Free Press representative.

Before December 7: In interview to Sripad Shankar of Madras said that it was not possible to accept any conditions with regard to temple-entry.

December 7 : Interview to students; interview to Associated Press of India.

December 8 : In letter to E.E. Doyle, sought decision on Patwardhan's case in view of his contemplated fast from January 2, 1933. In letter to P.N. Rajbhoj, told him that proposed fast would be postponed if Guruvayur referendum went against temple-entry.

December 9 : Issued tenth statement on untouchability.

December 14 : Issued eleventh statement on untouchability. Interview to Arya Samaj Deputation.

December 15 : Issued twelfth statement on untouchability. Interview to Untouchables' Deputation.

December 16 : Issued message for Anti-untouchability Day to be observed on December 18. In letter to Home Secretary, Government of Bombay, asked for reply to his letter seeking permission to see Jamnalal Bajaj.

December 18 : In letter to Kotwal, said that it was his "duty to fast with Kelappan" because it was he who had asked Kelappan to suspend fast.

December 21 : In letter to K. Ramunni Menon, said: "My fast was intended to stir Hindus to action, and that, I am glad to say, is happening day after day, although the fast has yet to come."

December 22 : In letter to Mirabehn said that he had eliminated bread and even vegetable and therefore also salt.

: In letter to Kowtha Suryanarayana Row, said that he believed his fast to be spiritual "both in intention and end; intention is to purify Hinduism and end is to secure religious justice

		for those of the Hindus who have been hitherto denied that justice".
December 23	:	Had meeting with sanatanist reformers and shastris.
December 24	:	In letter to Radhakant Malaviya, said that he would not hesitate to postpone fast if referendum was improper.
December 28	:	Guruvayur referendum favoured temple-entry of untouchables.
December 29	:	In letter to Mirabehn, Gandhiji told her that he was continuing saltless diet "without any effect on the elbow". In interview to Associated Press of India announced decision to "postpone the contemplated fast indefinitely".
December 30	:	Issued thirteenth statement on untouchability. In telegram to Private Secretary to Viceroy, sought sanction for introduction of Subbaroyan's Bill in Madras Legislative Assembly. Issued statement on interview to Tarkaratna.

1933

January 2	:	In interview to Associated Press of India observed that his suggestion to keep Guruvayur Temple open during certain hours to Harijans was made by way of compromise.
	:	In interview to *The Hindu,* said that Subbaroyan's Bill was "intended to undo the wrong done by British courts".
January 3	:	Issued fourteenth statement on untouchability.
January 5	:	Interview to Associated Press of India on compromise proposal with regard to temple-entry at Guruvayur.
January 7	:	In statement to the Press, asked Congressmen to decide for themselves whether to work as civil resisters or social reformers.
January 11	:	Gandhiji continued to be in Yeravda Central Prison. Gave interview to Associated Press.
January 12	:	Deonayakacharya, Secretary, All-India Varnashram Swarajya Sangh, and others came for discussion with Gandhiji but returned without meeting him.

January 13 : Gandhiji met Sadashivrao and Shinde.

January 14 : Gave interview to S. Salivati, *The Hindu* correspondent; discussed compromise proposal with K. Kelappan.

January 16 : Telegraphed to M. G. Hallett inquiring about Government's decision on conservancy work in prisons. Met Sir Lallubhai Samaldas. Gave interview to Associated Press.

January 17 : Met Lady Thackersey; had discussion with Dharmadev.

January 18 : Telegraphed to *The Hindu* and its correspondent contradicting distorted report of interview. Gave interview to Associated Press.

: Madan Mohan Malaviya issued statement concerning conference of sanatanists at Allahabad.

January 20 : Gandhiji met, among others, Haribhau Phatak, Smt. Bhatt, Nargisbehn and Shankarrao Thakkar. Had talks with Talegaonkar, Jedhe and others.

January 21 : Met Purushottamdas Trikamdas, Vaze, Devdhar and Patwardhan.

January 22 : Gave interview to Associated Press.

January 23 : Viceroy gave sanction to introduction of Untouchability Abolition Bill by Ranga Iyer in Central Assembly but refused sanction to introduction of Subbaroyan's Temple-entry Bill in Madras Council.

: Gandhiji discussed Madan Mohan Malaviya's proposal with Lakshmanshastri Joshi. Met Macrae, Gopalan and girls from Seva Sadan.

January 24 : Issued statement on Viceregal decision. Met Smt. Gadgil, Lilavati Munshi's daughter, Purushottam and Macrae.

January 25 : Gave interview to Associated Press.

January 26 : Wrote to T. B. Sapru inquiring about his views on Untouchability Abolition and Temple-entry Bills.

January 27 : In interview to Associated Press, advised sanatanists "to join Servants of Untouchables

	Society and . . . work its programme for temporal uplift".
January 28	: Met S. Salivati, Kaka, Paramananda and some Gujarati students.
January 30	: Discussed with C. Rajagopalachari, G. D. Birla and Devdas steps to be taken after Viceregal sanction.
January 31	: Continued discussion with C Rajagopalachari and G. D. Birla. M. R. Jayakar visited Gandhiji.
February 1	: Gandhiji wrote to Viceroy seeking Government's co-operation in expediting consideration of Bills. Had talks with C. Rajagopalachari and G. D. Birla.
February 2	: Gave interview to Associated Press. Met Velankar, Gohil, some students and Ramachandra Shastri.
February 3	: Met Hiralal Shah and Lilavati Munshi.
February 4	: Discussed with Ambedkar two Bills and templeentry issue. Gave interview to Stanley Jones.
February 5	: Sent message to Harijan Conference, Kolaba.
Before February 6	: Issued statement on Harijan.
February 6	: Met Macrae.
February 7	: In interview to Associated Press, commented on Puri Shankaracharya's letter to Ranga Iyer and latter's reply.
February 9	: Wrote to E. E. Doyle on Appasaheb Patwardhan's partial fast. Gave interview to Press.
February 11	: First issue of Harijan published. Gandhiji wrote to Government regarding Appasaheb Patwardhan's fast.
	: Sent message to members of Legislative Assembly urging them to "join in facilitating consideration of the measures" in current session.
	: Met Kodandarao, Janakibai, Shantabai and Gomatibehn.
	: Lakshmanshastri Joshi delivered Madan Mohan Malaviya's letter.

February 13	:	Gandhiji gave interview on receiving news of Appasaheb Patwardhan breaking his fast.
February 14	:	Telegraphed to Madan Mohan Malaviya on necessity of Bills "in terms of the Bombay pledge" and urging him to come for discussion. Had discussion with Kelkar. Gave interview on Ambedkar's statement.
February 16	:	In interview, commenting on News Chronicle's statement, clarified reformers' position.
	:	Received wire from Madan Mohan Malaviya insisting on circulation of Bills and suggesting release of correspondence for publication.
February 17	:	Received Viceroy's letter insisting upon circulation of Bills.
February 18	:	In article "When Is It Possible?" warned reformers against exploiting possibility of another fast by him for abolishing untouchability.
February 19	:	Wrote to M. G. Hallett.
February 20	:	Met fellow-prisoner Jamnalal.
February 23	:	First issue of Harijan Sevak published.
February 24	:	Ramdas, Jamiatsingh, Nargisbehn, Perinbehn, Kamalabehn and Mathuradas met Gandhiji.
	:	In letter to Madan Mohan Malaviya, Gandhiji wrote pledge given in Bombay Resolution could not be honoured without legislation.
February 27	:	Met Kamaladevi Chattopadhyaya.
March 2	:	Gave interview to Associated Press.
March 4	:	In article "Confusing the Issue", stated essence of varnadharma and emphasized untouchability had no connection with varnashrama.
March 6	:	C. Rajagopalachari, Devdas Gandhi and, Shankerlal Banker met Gandhiji in Yeravda Central Prison.
March 8	:	Gandhiji sent message on wedding of Lakshmi—a Harijan girl brought up by Gandhiji—and Maruti.
March 9	:	Prepared Draft Constitution of Harijan Sevak Sangh.

March 12	:	First issue of Gujarati *Harijanbandhu* was released from Poona.
March 17	:	White Paper on Indian Constitutional Reforms was issued.
March 18	:	Gandhiji wrote to Home Secretary, Bombay Government, to reconsider decision to withhold his telegram advising Poonamchand Ranka to break his fast.
March 23	:	Again wrote to Home Secretary, Bombay Government, requesting revision of decision and release of telegram to fasting prisoner on humanitarian grounds as was the practice since 1922.
March 25	:	Polak visited Gandhiji.
March 27	:	Gandhiji in interview with Associated Press emphasized need for opening temples to Harijans.
March 28	:	Wrote again to Home Secretary for permission to establish communication with Poonamchand Ranka. Was interviewed by Associated Press.
April 1	:	Twenty-seventh session of Indian National Congress was held in Calcutta in defiance of Government orders and 600 delegates were arrested.
	:	Gandhiji thanked Home Secretary, Bombay Government, for permission to establish contact with Poonamchand Ranka, but regretted Government's decision to depart from old policy of permitting him to communicate with other prisoners and carry on humanitarian work. Anne Marie Petersen visited Gandhiji.
April 2	:	B. R. Ambedkar consulted Gandhiji in jail regarding revision of Poona Pact.
April 10	:	Gandhiji wired to Poonamchand Ranka to break his fast as it was not proper for satyagrahi to resort to fasting for getting more comforts.
April 12	:	Wrote to Home Secretary, Bombay Government, regretting Government's decision not to permit him to communicate directly with other prisoners for humanitarian work.

On or before April 16: Harijan leaders of Ahmedabad met Gandhiji in jail.

April 18	:	Gandhiji issued appeal for the observance of Harijan Day on April 30.
April 23	:	Gandhiji was in Yeravda Central Prison, Poona.
	:	Interview to Associated Press of India on talks with B.R. Ambedkar.
April 27	:	In *Harijan* article, "Yervada Pact", Gandhiji stated that Ambedkar's suggestion for alteration of panel system was "in no way to the advantage of Harijans".
	:	In letter to P. N. Rajbhoj said that "the yajna started in September . . . is still continuing, it can end only when untouchability is eradicated".
April 29-30	:	At midnight resolved "to go on an unconditional and irrevocable fast for twenty-one days "from May 8" for the purification of self and associates".
April 30	:	Issued statement on fast. In telegram to Home Department intimated decision to fast.
May 1	:	In letter to Raojibhai Patel, said that proposed fast was "intended as punishment for those who believe that they are too weak to fulfil the vow they had taken". Broke silence at noon. Interview to the Press on decision to fast. Gandhiji met co-workers.
May 2	:	Received cable from Gen. Smuts appealing to desist from decision to fast.
May 3	:	Interview to Associated Press of India. Sarojini Naidu came and took charge of Gandhiji.
May 4	:	In telegram to Dr. M. A. Ansari, Gandhiji said: "God would be my invisible medical attendant".
May 5	:	In letter to C. Rajagopalachari, agreed to undergo medical examination which he had rejected the previous day.

On or before May 6: Sent message to Arya Samaj Conference.

May 6	:	In the evening gave message to numerous friends and admirers who had called on him.
Before May 8	:	Interview to the Press on his proposed fast.
May 8	:	Gandhiji commenced 21-day fast at 12 noon;

		issued statement explaining fast. Was released from jail at 6 p.m.; reached Lady Thackersey's bungalow at 9 p.m. Interview to Associated Press of India. Gandhiji advised suspension of civil disobedience movement for one month or six weeks; appealed to Government to withdraw ordinances and release all civil resisters.
May 9	:	M. S. Aney issued statement suspending civil disobedience movement for six weeks. Government of India issued communique on Gandhiji's release.
May 10	:	In telegram, Gandhiji asked Kasturba to "be brave".
May 11	:	In *Harijan,* gave message "To the Reader". Doctors Phatak and Gharpure, by turns, attended on Gandhiji from 9 a.m. to 9 p.m.
May 13	:	Kasturba was released from Sabarmati Jail. Gandhiji began to take 'Vichy' water in order to control acidity.
May 14	:	Kasturba and Harilal visited Gandhiji.
May 18	:	Was examined by Dr. M. A. Ansari who considered condition to be better.
May 20	:	As desired by Gandhiji, Mahadev Desai returned to Sabarmati Ashram. In telegram, Gandhiji advised Senapati Bapat to give up fast. Began taking Sinhagad spring water mixed with soda bicarbonate; it was sweeter than 'Vichy' water and was associated with Shivaji and Tilak.
	:	Medical bulletin from 'Parnakuti' read: "Mahatma Gandhi spent yet another good night. There is no change in his condition which continues to be quite satisfactory. A few of the most important letters were read [out] to him this morning.".
May 21	:	Another 'Parnakuti' bulletin: "Gandhiji passed another good night and enjoyed undisturbed sleep till the morning prayer time. The feeling of nausea has almost entirely disappeared. Since yesterday afternoon he has been drinking water from Sinhagad springs. His general condition

continues to be very satisfactory and his spiritis are calm and cheerful". Senapati Bapat rejected Gandhiji's appeal to give up fast.

May 23 : "Heads I win, tails also" was Gandhiji's reply to Dr. B. C. Roy who asked how he was feeling.

: Medical bulletin on Gandhiji announced: "Gandhiji had good sleep and rest and is well."

May 25 : Dr. B.C. Roy and Dr. M.A. Ansari ware at Gandhiji's bed-side.

May 26 : Discussion with Mahadev about Ashram management.

May 27 : Gandhiji had discussion with Devdas.

May 29 : Gave message which was read out by Mahadev Desai; broke fast.

June 6 : Notice of Devdas-Lakshmi wedding was given to Registrar of Marriages, Poona.

June 10 : Devdas Gandhi and Lakshmi gave declarations under Section 10 of Special Marriages Act.

June 16 : At 'Parnakuti', Poona, Devdas-Lakshmi wedding was performed according to Hindu rites. Gandhiji addressed bride and bridegroom.

June 17 : In message to South Indians, wanted spread of Hindi in every village.

Before June 18 : In a message, wanted Ashram inmates to lead "purer lives than heretofore".

June 21 : Registrar of Marriages, Poona, registered Devdas-Lakshmi marriage under Act III of 1872.

June 25 : In reply to Asaf Ali's open letter, Gandhiji said: ". . . non-violence for me is not a mere experiment. It is a part of my life. . . . I am more convinced that in the complex situation that faces India, there is no other way of gaining freedom."

July 2 : Invited Congressmen for Leaders' Conference to be held on July 12.

: Had discussion with Harijan workers in morning.

July 8 : In *Harijan* wrote "All about the Fast".

July 11 : In Poona, had discussion with M. S. Aney, M.M. Malaviya, C. Rajagopalachari, Bhulabhai Desai, Dr. Alam and Abul Kalam Azad.

July 12 : Spoke at Leaders' Conference. Conference recommended withdrawal of civil disobedience movement. Gandhiji addressed people from balcony of Tilak Memorial Hall, venue of Leaders, Conference.

July 14 : Spoke at concluding session of Leaders' Conference which authorized him to seek interview with Viceroy. In telegram sought interview with Viceroy. Spoke at Tilak Smarak Mandir.

July 17 : Viceroy refused to grant interview; Gandhiji renewed the request which was again turned down.

July 18 : Interview to the Press. Gandhiji reached Bombay en route to Ahmedabad. In Bombay, gave interview to *The Hindu* and *The Bombay Chronicle.*

July 19 : Reached Ahmedabad; stayed at Sheth Ranchhodlal's Amrit Bhuvan; had discussion with Harijans and anti-untouchability workers.

: Interview to Associated Press of India on Sir Samuel Hoare's speech in House of Commons.

: Gandhiji visited Sabarmati Ashram in afternoon.

: Was examined by Ahmedabad doctors; condition considered "good".

July 20 : In interview to representative of *The Times of India,* explained individual civil disobedience.

July 21 : Accompanied by Kasturba, Gandhiji met Mirabehn in Sabarmati Jail.

July 22 : In *Harijan,* published reply to "An American Criticism". In letters to Jamnalal Bajaj and Devdas Gandhi, announced decision to disband Sabarmati Ashram. M. S. Aney issued statement discontinuing mass civil disobedience movement.

July 23 : At Ashram prayer meeting, Mahadev Desai read out Gandhiji's appeal for funds for removal of untouchability; contributions collected on the spot.

July 24 : In letter to Satis Chandra Das Gupta, Gandhiji suggested stopping publication of Bengali

Harijan, if it was not self-supporting, Interview to The Bombay Chronicle on M. S. Aney's statement.

July 25 : Interview to Associated Press of India on decision to disband Sabarmati Ashram.

July 26 : Gandhiji issued statement on M. S. Aney's statement. In letter to Home Secretary, Government of Bombay, conveyed decision to disband Sabarmati Ashram. Interview to Associated Press of India. Interview to *The Hindu* on disbanding of the Ashram.

July 27 : In letter to Rabindranath Tagore, Gandhiji said that "there was no injustice done to Bengal" by Yeravda Pact. Interview to *The Daily Herald* on disbanding of Ashram. Interview to *The Times of India*.

July 28 : Interview to Associated Press of India on disbanding of Ashram.

July 29 : Interview to Associated Press of India on suspension of Congress Committees. Gandhiji visited Sharda Mandir on its foundation day.

July 30 : Issued statement approving the appeal for observance of Sen Gupta Day on August 6. In statement to Associated Press of India, urged Congressmen not to fritter away their energy in debating over decision on civil disobedience; reminded Englishmen that for "real friendship with India, Ordinance Rule is not the way, . . . Congress is the only way". In telegram to Home Secretary, Government of Bombay, conveyed decision to march to Ras. In an appeal to people of Gujarat, announced proposal to leave Ashram on march to Ras with 33 companions on August 1.

August 1 : Along with Kasturba and Mahadev Desai, was arrested after prayers. Bade farewell to Harijans who had gathered on the road, on way to Sabarmati Jail. Gave statement before District Magistrate, Ahmedabad. In letter to Advani, Superintendent, Ahmedabad Central Prison, asked for permission to do Harijan work. Ahmedabad observed hartal.

August 2 : Gandhiji was transferred to Yeravda Prison.

August 3 : In letter to Home Secretary, Government of Bombay, declined to conform to proposed restriction on his movements. In statement before District Magistrate, Poona, referred to his letter to Home Secretary, Government of Bombay, sent earlier in the day.

August 4 : Was released from Yeravda Prison and served with order to quit Yeravda village and confine his movements to Poona city municipal limits.

: Rearrested and sent for trial in Yeravda Prison for disobeying restraint order.

: During trial gave brief statement explaining his "wilful and deliberate breach of order of the Government of Bombay". Was sentenced to one year's simple imprisonment and was allotted 'A' class.

: Mahadev Desai also was sentenced to an equal term of simple imprisonment and was allotted 'B' class.

: In letter to Home Secretary, Government of Bombay, Gandhiji renewed his request for permission to "resume antiuntouchability work" and sought decision before Monday, August 7.

August 5 : In *Harijan* article, "Ethics of Fasting" wrote: "Just as a fast for regaining lost health is neither unnatural nor criminal self-torture, so is not a fast for purification of self or others." In letter to R.V. Martin, refused "to pay for any extra food" and asked Government to extend the same facilities given to him before.

August 6 : In letter to Home Secretary, Government of Bombay, requested expeditious decision on his request for grant of facilities.

August 8 : Thanked Government of Bombay for "limited permission" on some points and asked Government to be equally "considerate in regard to [his] supra-physical needs".

August 10	:	In letter to Home Secretary, Government of Bombay, appealed for a decision on or before Monday, August 14.
August 14	:	In letter to Home Secretary, Government of Bombay, conveyed decision to deny himself all nourishment if demands were not granted before Wednesday, August 16. At Akola, M. S. Aney with 13 companions was arrested while starting on a march.
August 15	:	In letter to R. V. Martin, Gandhiji urged granting of three requests, pending final orders, in order to avert proposed fast.
August 16	:	Commenced fast in the afternoon despite sanction of certain facilities, which he described as having been "grudgingly given".
August 17	:	In letter to R. V. Martin, enumerated points for settlement.
August 19	:	In letter to Home Secretary, Government of Bombay, stated that civil disobedience, "a perfectly lawful activity", was his creed though considered by Government as unlawful.
August 20	:	In *Harijanbandhu,* paid tributes to Hariprasad Desai of Bhavnagar—"A silent worker in the Harijan Cause".
August 21	:	Gandhiji was removed to Sassoon Hospital, Poona, because of serious condition. Andrews and Kasturba visited him. Fearing that he was nearing death, Gandhiji distributed his personal articles of use among Hospital staff attending on him.
August 23	:	Was released unconditionally. Broke fast at 3.45 p.m. by taking a glass of orange-juice; taken to 'Parnakuti' in an ambulance-car; Dr. Dinshaw Mehta took charge of him.
August 24	:	Sarojini Naidu visited Gandhiji; Legislative Assembly decided to hold over "Temple-entry Bill" for one year.
August 25	:	Gandhiji gave interview to the Press. Prabhashankar Pattani visited Gandhiji.
August 28	:	In Legislative Assembly, Viceroy announced that

on question of reforms he had been consistent in his policy "so as to help India towards responsible Government, Home Rule or Dominion Status". Jamshed Mehta visited Gandhiji.

August 30 : In letter to V. S. Srinivasa Sastri, Gandhiji said that he would "gladly retire from Congress and devote myself to the development of civil disobedience".

September 2 : Interview to Associated Press of India. Hallett, Home Secretary, met C. F. Andrews who gave him his impressions of Gandhiji's mind as gathered from daily interviews since his release.

September 3 : In *Harijanbandhu* article, "No Exaggeration", Gandhiji wrote:"Harijan service is the breath of my life and that, therefore, I cannot live for a moment without it".

: In statement to the Press, deplored the assassination of B.E.G. Burge, Magistrate of Midnapore.

September 7 : Issued statement on 'Harijan Day' fixed for September 24, 1933. 1 On p. 393 of the text, Gandhiji mentions the last to have happened on the afternoon of the 24th. But that seems to be a slip of memory. The date given in Mahatma, Vol. III, p. 264, is August 21.

September 9 : In *Harijan* article, "Was it Coercive?", said: "As a great weapon in the armoury of satyagraha, it [fasting] cannot be given up because of its possible abuse."

: In letter to Said: " . . . I do not want power. I look upon it as a privileged service. The moment I feel that I can get out of it to the benefit of the Congress, I will not fail."

September 10 : In *Harijan,* congratulated Harijans and Hindus of Vina on having resolved their differences.

September 10-14: Had discussion with Jawaharlal Nehru.

Before September 11: Sent messages to World Fellowship of Faiths; also to Swadeshi Exhibition organized by Gujarat and Broach All-India Women's Conference.

September 12	:	A Japanese sadhu visited Gandhiji.
September 13	:	In a letter to Gandhiji, Jawaharlal Nehru pointed out that "Fundamental Rights and Economic Policy" Resolution adopted at Karachi Congress "gave the direction in which we should move".
September 14	:	In letter to Jawaharlal Nehru, Gandhiji said: "I can go the whole length with you and say that 'We should range ourselves with the progressive forces of the world'. But ". . . though there is such an agreement between you and me in the enunciation of ideals, there are temperamental differences between us."
September 15	:	Left Poona for Bombay.
September 16	:	Gandhiji continued to stay at Bombay. Conferred with Jawaharlal Nehru, Sarojini Naidu, G. D. Birla and Cowasji Jehangir.
September 19	:	Had discussion with representatives of Millowners' Association and labourers.
September 20	:	Annie Besant died; Gandhiji paid tribute to her.
	:	Left for Ahmedabad.
September 21	:	At Ahmedabad; unveiled statue of Chinubhai; laid foundation stone of Maneklal Jethalal Library. Left for Bombay at night.
September 22	:	In Bombay
September 23	:	Arrived in Wardha.
September 24	:	Third 'Harijan Day' observed.
September 29	:	Sent condolences on K. Madhavan Nair's death.
September 30	:	In letter to G. D. Birla proposed to hand over Satyagraha Ashram to Servants of Untouchables Society.
October 4	:	Gave interviews to Rev. Fuji and Rev. Okitsu.
October 8	:	At public meeting reiterated his decision to devote himself to Harijan work till August 3, 1934.
October 9	:	Met N.S. Hardikar and Kamaladevi Chattopadhyaya.
October 14	:	Sent message on fiftieth anniversary of Swami Dayananda's death.

October 18	:	Spoke at wedding of Prabhudas Gandhi.
October 22	:	Gave interview to *Unati*. Vithalbhai Patel died in Geneva.
October 24	:	In interview to Associated Press Gandhiji paid tribute to Vithalbhai Patel.
October 31	:	Met K. F. Nariman.
November 2	:	Wrote to Governor of Bengal on inhuman treatment meted out to civil resisters in Hijli jail.
Before November 7	:	Addressed Harijans at Nalwadi.
November 7	:	Commenced Harijan tour. Visited Rama Mandir of Wardha and Lakshminarayana temple. At Selu opened temple to Harijans; addressed public meeting. At Wardha spoke at public meeting in evening.
November 8	:	Arrived in Nagpur in morning. Spoke at Lendra and Dhantoli. Addressed meeting at sweepers's quarters, opened well for them. Visited various Harijan institutions; inaugurated Harijan Mahila Ashram. Visited Katol, Mopa, Kalameshwar and Dorli. At Nagpur addressed public meeting in evening.
November 9	:	Gave interview to the Press in morning. Visited Khadi Vastralaya, Untkhana Boarding, Navi Shukravari and Anath Vidyarthi Griha; opened well to Harijans. Addressed Harijan workers' meeting and University students' meeting. Visited Kamptee, Kanan, Ramtek, Dumbri Khurd and Saoner during day.
November 10	:	Gave interview to the Press. Reached Tumsar, addressed public meeting. At Bhandara addressed meeting, opened Lakshminarayana temple. Visited Mohali, Shihora, and Lakhni. At Gondia, addressed public meeting. Left for Wardha.
November 11	:	Arrived in Wardha at 7 a.m. Gave interview to the Press. At Deoli addressed public meeting.
November 12	:	At Wardha.
November 13	:	Left Wardha for Hinganghat. At Hinganghat visited Harijan quarters, addressed public

		meeting in evening. Reached Chanda at night.
November 14	:	Visited Mool, opened two wells to Harijans. At Saoli visited Khadi Karyalaya and weavers' quarters; spoke at public meeting. At Chanda spoke at public meeting in evening.
November 15	:	Addressed public meetings at Warora and Wun in morning. Visited Brany and Umani. Reached Yeotmal in evening. Visited Chokhamela Harijan Boarding and other institutions. Addressed workers' meeting and public meeting.
November 16	:	Left Yeotmal for Amraoti in morning. Visited Dhamangaon, Chandur. Arrived in Amraoti at 11 a.m. Addressed Children's meeting, women's meeting and Harijans' meeting in afternoon. Visited Harijan quarters. Spoke at Hanuman Vyayamshala and public meeting in evening.
November 17	:	Visited Kamargaon, Loni, Karanjia, Murtazapur, Balapur, Wadegaon, Wallaya and Shegaon. At Lasura opened Shiva temple. At Khamgaon visited Harijan quarters and Harijan hostel. Spoke at Anjuman Mufid-ul-Islam, public meeting and workers' meeting.
November 18	:	Arrived in Akola at 10 a.m. Visited National School, Saraswati School, Saraswati Mandir and Harijan quarters. Had interview with harijans. Had discussion with sanatanist Swami Lalnath. Addressed public meeting and Harijan workers' meeting. Gave interview to the Press.
November 19	:	Left Akola in morning. Visited Ugwa, Keliveli, Akot,Anjangaon and Pathrot. Reached Chikalda.
November 20	:	At Chikalda; silence day.
November 21	:	Left Chikalda. At Ellichpur addressed two public meetings. Visited Utkhed and Chandur Bazaar. At Morsi spoke at public meeting. Arrived in Badnera at night, addressed public meeting. Gave message to people of Berar.
November 22	:	Arrived in Drug. Visited house of a sweeper, Municipal school, Arya Samaj Girls' School, Khadi Centre and Harijan quarters. Addressed public meeting. Visited Kumhari. Reached Raipur at night.

November 23	:	Had interviews with Harijans and sanatanists in morning. Spoke in reply to addresses. Visited Harijan quarters, Khadi Bhandar, Hindu Anathalaya and Sanatani Ashram. Opened All–India Swadeshi Exhibition in evening.
November 24	:	At Dhamtari, addressed–women's meeting and public meeting; visited Harijan quarters. Visited Rajim. At Raipur opened Hanuman temple and two wells to Harijans; addressed public meeting in evening.
November 25	:	At Baloda Bazaar opened Gopalji temple to Harijans; addressed public meeting. Visited Bhatapara and Sakti. At Baitalpur visited Clare Leper Asylum. At Bilaspur spoke at women's meeting, public meeting and railway workers' meeting. Returned to Raipur.
November 26	:	At Raipur.
November 27	:	Addressed women's meeting in afternoon. Spoke at Chhattisgarh Harijan workers' meeting and Rajkumar College in evening. Left for Amgaon.
November 28	:	Reached Amgaon at 1 a.m., addressed villagers' meeting. At Risama opened Ganesh temple. At Lanji visited Harijan quarters; addressed meeting. Visited Kirnapur. At Balaghat addressed women's meeting and public meeting; visited Harijan quarters. Visited Waraseoni. Arrived in Seoni.
November 29	:	Addressed women's meeting and public meeting. Had interview with sanatanists. At Chhindwara addressed workers' meeting and public meeting; visited Harijan quarters. Visited Kherwani and Multapi. Reached Betul.
November 30	:	Visited Khedi, Savaligarh and Baraling. At Betul spoke at public meeting; visited Harijan quarters. At Itarsi addressed public meeting.
December 1	:	At Kareli addressed public meeting. At Deori opened Shri Muralidhar temple; addressed public meeting. Visited injured Harijan girl in hospital.
	:	At Anantpur spoke at public meeting; visited

Khadi Nivas and villagers' houses; conferred with khadi workers.

December 2 : Left Anantpur. Visited Garhakota. At Damoh, laid foundation–stone of temple for Harijans; addressed public meeting; visited Harijan quarters. Reached Sagar at 4 p.m.; addressed women's meeting and public meeting; laid foundation–stone of temple to be built by Harijans for all Hindus. Left for Katni at night.

December 3 : At Katni addressed public meeting. Visited Sihora, Burhagar and Panagar. Reached Jabalpur at 4 p.m., spoke at public meeting.

December 4 : At Jabalpur; silence day; met Dr. M. A. Ansari.

December 5 : Conferred with Jawaharlal Nehru, Dr. Ansari, S. Mahmud, K.F. Nariman and Jamnalal Bajaj.

December 6 : Spoke at Harijan workers' meeting. Visited Mandla; addressed public meeting. Returned to Jabalpur; visited Narayanganj, Barela and Beoharji's temple; inspected night school for Harijans. At Jabalpur spoke at Gujaratis' meeting.

December 7 : Conferred with Harijan leaders and workers. Visited Swadeshi Museum and Harijan quarters. At Khadi Bhandar sold khadi; opened Lakshminarayana temple to Harijans. Spoke at women's meeting and Leonard Theological College. Left Jabalpur by train. Arrived at Sohagpur. Visited Babai.

December 8 : Reached Harda in morning; addressed public meeting. Spoke at public meetings at Khandwa and Burhanpur. Left for Jhansi.

December 9 : Arrived at Bhopal, spoke at public meeting. Visited Bhilsa and Basoda. At Jhansi addressed women's meeting and public meeting. Left for Delhi.

December 10 : Arrived in Delhi in morning; addressed labourers' meeting. Visited Harijan quarters, Khadi Bhandar and Jamia Millia Islamia. Had discussion with Harijans.

December 11 : At Delhi; silence day.

December 12 : Conferred with Congress leaders.

December 13 : Had discussion with sanatanists. In morning visited Alipur and spoke at public meeting. Attended meeting of Central Board of Harijan Sevak Sangh. Addressed students' meeting and unveiled portrait of Motilal Nehru. In statement to the Press categorically refuted charges made by Mohammed Iqbal. Met members of Japanese Delegation. Continued talks with Congress leaders. At night conferred with Congress workers.

December 14 : Continued discussion with Abul Kalam Azad, Jawaharlal Nehru, J.B. Kripalani, Jamnalal Bajaj and Syed Mahmud. Addressed Harijans' and women's meetings. Left for Bezwada at 4 p.m.

December 15 : In train.

Before December 16 : Had discussion with sanatanists.

December 16 : Arrived in Bezwada at 3 a.m. Visited Padamata, Padamatalanka, Mogalrajapuram and Idupugallu. At Bezwada visited Harijan quarters; addressed women's meeting, Andhra Harijan workers' meeting and public meeting.

December 17 : At Mudunuru opened two temples to Harijans in morning. At Gudivada, spoke at public meeting. At Siddhantam opened temple to Harijans; gave interview to *The Hindu* in afternoon. Visited Angaluru, Gudlavalleru, Kavutaram and Pedanna. Reached Masulipatam; addressed public meeting. Paid visit to Challapalle.

December 18 : At Masulipatam; silence day.

December 19 : In evening visited Kankipadu, Pamaru, and Bhatlapenumarru. Returned to Bezwada. Left for Madras.

December 20 : Arrived in Madras in morning. Spoke in reply to civic address; opened All–India Swadeshi Exhibition. Addressed South India Chamber of Commerce, two women's meetings, students' meeting and public meeting.

December 21 : Visited Harijan cheries. At Robinson Park, Royapuram, spoke at Harijans' meeting. At

Perambur addressed M.S.M. Railway labourers' meeting and public meeting. Spoke at Bharat Sabha at Vellala Teynampet. At Wadia park addressed Labour Union meeting and unveiled Annie Besant's portrait. At Choolai spoke at public meeting.

December 22 : Gave interview to S. Satyamurti. Addressed public meeting, Vaishya Association and Gujarati, Marwari and Sindhi residents at Jain Mandir. Unveiled portrait of Nageswara Rao Pantulu at Andhra Maha Sabha. Visited slums in Triplicane. Presided over Hindi Prachar Sabha Convocation. Met Depressed Classes Deputation; gave interviews to *Madras Mail* and *The Hindu*. Sent message to Tamil Lovers' Conference. Left for Guntur.

December 23 : Reached Guntur in morning. Paid visit to Konda Venkatappayya's ailing wife. Renamed a temple; addressed public meeting. Visited Chebrole, Munipalle, Manchalla; Vellalur and Ponnur.

: At Nidubrole, spoke at public meeting; declared open institution for adult education and library.

: At Thalapalem, opened Free Ayurvedic Kuteeram and laid foundation–stone of Atma Vilas Ashram building; addressed Harijan's meeting.

: At Kavur; laid foundation of Vinay Ashram building, opened temple to Harijans, addressed public meeting.

: At Ithananagarampadu opened temple to Harijans. Visited Bhattiprolu and Repalli. Reached Tenali; spoke at public meeting.

December 24 : Arrived at Samalkot at 10.40 a.m.. At Peddapuram, spoke at public meeting. At Cocanada addressed women's meeting and public meeting. Visited Gollapalem. At Ramchandrapuram, visited Valmiki Ashram, addressed public meeting. Reached Rajahmundry at 7.30 p.m., addressed public meeting. Met Harijan leaders' deputation at night. Spent night in launch.

December 25	:	Reached Sitanagaram in morning; silence day.
December 26	:	Visited Vangalpadu, opened Sitaramaswami temple, Sitanagaram Harijan Ashram and two temples of Ramalingeshwara and Kodandam. Reached Tallapudi by steam launch. Visited Malakapalli, Dharmavaram, and Nidadavole. Arrived in Tanuku.
December 27	:	At Tanuku spoke at public meeting, visited Eletipadu, Kavitam, Poduru, Vedangi and Jinnunur. At Palakollu, spoke at public meeting, laid foundation of Harijan Ashram. Paid visit to Ballipadu. Addressed public meetings at Bhimavaram and Tadepalligudem. Reached Ellore at 5 p.m. and addressed public meeting and Arya Andhra Sangha, unveiled Lajpatrai's portrait; visited Harijan quarters.
December 28	:	Met Congress workers. Left Ellore. Reached Vizagapatam in afternoon. Visited Harijan workers; opened Swadeshi Store; spoke at women's meeting and public meeting. At Bimlipatam opened Ramamandiram. At Vizianagaram met Harijan leaders.
December 29	:	At Vizianagaram visited Harijan quarters; spoke at public meeting. At Anakapalle, spoke in reply to civic address. Reached Bitragunta.
December 30	:	Addressed public meetings at Kavali and Allur. At Gandavaram; opened temple to Harijans; spoke at public meeting. Visited Yellayapalem. At Buchireddipalem; addressed women's meeting and public meeting. At Nellore; visited Harijan quarters, opened reading–room for Harijans; addressed women's meeting and public meeting. At Gadur; spoke at public meeting. Arrived in Venkatagiri.
December 31	:	Visited Harijan quarters; laid foundation stone of reading–room for Harijans; spoke at public meeting. At Tirupati, addressed public meeting. Visited Renigunta. Reached Cuddapah.

1934

January 1 : At Cuddapah; silence day.

January 2 : Had an interview with Harijan workers. Opened Cuddapah Swadeshi Emporium. Visited Harijan quarters; addressed public meeting.

January 3 : Reached Peddavadugur at 4.30 a.m.; addressed public meeting. Visited Gooty. At Guntakkal visited tannery and Harijan quarters; spoke at public meeting. Visited Konakondla, Vajrakarur and Uravakonda. At Anantapur, visited Harijan quarters, addressed public meeting. Arrived in Hindupur.

January 4 : Left Hindupur. Visited Goribidnur. At Doddaballapur spoke at public meeting. At Tumkur had talk with local workers; visited Harijan quarters; addressed public meeting. Visited Tyamagondlu and Nelamangala. Arrived in Bangalore at 4.45 p.m.; opened branch of All–India Spinners' Association; addressed women's meeting, public meeting and Marwaris' meeting visited Harijan quarters. Reached Mysore.

January 5 : Visited Tagadur, Badanvall and Nanjangud. At Mysore visited Harijan quarters; addressed Harijan workers' meeting, women's meeting and public meeting..

January 6 : Visited Mandya, Sakoor, Maddur, Besagrahalli, Shivapuram, Somanhalli, Chennapatna, Closepet, Kankanhalli, Bidali and Kengeri. Returned to Bangalore; addressed students' meeting.

January 7 : At Bangalore, visited Narasimharaya Adi–Karnataka Hostel, Deena Seva–sangha, Adi–Karnataka Girls' Home and Harijan quarters.

: Addressed Malleswaram women's meeting, co–operators' meeting at Apex Bank, Temperance Federation, women's meeting, public meeting and Harijan workers' meeting; spoke at civic reception.

January 8 : At Bangalore; silence day.

January 9 : Gave message to people of Mysore. Left

		Bangalore.
January 10	:	Reached Olavakkote; visited Shabari Ashram. At Palghat addressed public meeting and women's meeting. Visited Chittur, Koduvayur, Thenkurissi and Veliyanchathanur. At Kuzhalmannam addressed Nayadis' meeting. Visited Karimpuzha, Cherpulasseri, Ananganadi, and Ottapalam. Reached Guruvayur at 10 p.m.
January 11	:	At Guruvayur addressed public meeting. Visited Kunnamkulam. At Akikav laid foundation of free dispensary for Harijans. At Pattambi spoke at public meeting. Arrived in Cannanore.
January 12	:	At Payyanur; visited Shree Narayan Harijan Ashram, khadi depot; addressed public meeting. Returned to Cannanore; spoke at Harijan workers' meeting and public meeting. Reached Tellicherry.
January 13	:	At Tellicherry spoke at public meeting. Addressed public meetings at Mahe and Badagara. At Pakkanarpuram opened Balakrishna Memorial Ayurvedic Dispensary. Visited Quilandy. Arrived in Calicut. Addressed women's meeting, public meeting and students' meeting; unveiled portraits of K. Madhavan Nair at Town Hall and Mathrubhumi office.
January 14	:	Visited Kalpetta; opened Harijan colony; spoke at public meeting, Harijan workers' meeting; visited Harijan quarters.
January 15	:	At Calicut; silence day.
January 16	:	At Calicut, Gandhiji met the Zamorin and discussed with him question of temple-entry. Left Calicut in evening for a tour of Cochin.
January 17	:	At Trichur. Visited Harijan Colony. Spoke at public meetings at Trichur, Kurukkancheri and Alwaye. Visited Perruvanam, Irinjalakuda and Chalakudi. Went to Ernakulam in evening.
January 18	:	Spoke at public meetings at Palluruthi, Thuravoor, Ernakulam and Alleppey. Visited Tripunittura, Chalavennur and Nedumudi.
January 19	:	Spoke at public meeting, Kottayam. Opened

		Anand-ashram, Changanacherry. Visited Odur and Panamanna.
January 20	:	Spoke at public meetings at Panamanna, Quilon and Trivandrum. Gave interview on Travancore Government communique declaring open tanks and wells to all castes. Visited Sivagiri and Varkala.
January 21	:	At Trivandrum. Visited Harijan Hostel. Visited Neyyattinkara, Pappanam Amaravilai, Kuzhuthorai, Takkalai — Nagarcoil.
January 22	:	Reached Cape Comorin (Kanyakumari).
January 23	:	Gave interview to Members of Self Respect Party at Cape Comorin. Visited Nanganeri and Velliyur. Reached Tinnevelly.
January 24	:	At public meetings at Tinnevelly and Tuticorin, exhorted people to donate generously for Bihar Earthquake Relief Fund and to banish untouchability. Visited Palamcottah and Tenkasi.
January 25	:	Spoke at public meeting, Rajapalayam. Visited Tuticorin, Ettaiyapuram, Koilpatti, Sankarankoil, Sivakasi, Virudhunagar, Kalligudi.
January 26	:	At Madura, appealed to merchants for Bihar Earthquake Relief. Spoke at Municipal Council meeting, public meeting, women's meeting, Hindi Pracharak Sabha and at meeting of labourers.
January 27	:	Appealed to Karaikudi Municipal Council for better treatment of Harijans. Spoke at public meetings at Karaikudi and Devakottah and exhorted people to contribute generously for Bihar Earthquake Relief Fund. Visited Therukutheru, Kilaour, Chittanoor, Tiruppattur, Paganeri, Sivaganga and Manamadurai.
January 28	:	Laid foundation stone for Harijan School, Devakottah. Spoke at Harijan cheri, Chitthanur. Had talks with Nattars at Devacottah. Gave interview to *The Hindu* on Nattar-Harijan problem. Visited Pollachi and Podanur.
January 29	:	At Mettupalayam and Coonoor.
January 30	:	At Coonoor.

January 31	:	Laid foundation stone of Harijan school, Ramnagar.
February 1	:	Gave interview to Adi-Dravida Jan Sabha, Coonoor.
February 2	:	Spoke at a public meeting, Kotagiri. Issued appeal to foreign countries on behalf of earthquakeaffected people of Bihar.
February 3	:	Visited two Harijan cheries—Ottupatrai and Thandakaramcheri. Spoke on untouchability at public meeting, Coonoor.
February 4	:	Visited Ramakrishna Ashram, Dakshinamoorti Ashram and Om Prakash Mutt, Ottacamund. Gave interview to the Adi-Hindu Deputation.
February 5	:	At Coonoor.
February 6	:	Addressed public meetings at Erode, Chokkampalayam, Tirupur, Coimbatore and Podanur.
February 7	:	Addressed public meetings at Pollachi, Palni and Dindigul. Visited Pondar, Udamalpet and Vannivalasi.
February 8	:	Visited Batlagundu, Vadugapatti.
February 9	:	Spoke at public meeting and women's meeting, Thevaram. Visited Cumbum, Bodinayakanur and Theni. Left for Trichinopoly by train.
February 10	:	Spoke at public meeting, Srirangam. Gave interview to Harijans, Srirangam.
	:	Spoke at the National College and at a public meeting, Trichinopoly. Visited Manachanalloor, Samayapuram and Chintamani.
February 11	:	Spoke at public meetings at Karur, Erode and Tiruchengodu. Visited Kulittalai, Mayanur, Kodumudi, Bhavani and Pudupalayam.
February 12	:	Spoke at public meeting, Pudupalayam. Jawaharlal Nehru was arrested in Allahabad.
February 14	:	Gandhiji spoke at public meetings at Namakkal and Salem. Visited Sendamangalam.
February 15	:	Spoke at public meetings at Tanjore, Kumbakonam and Negapatam.
February 16	:	Addressed students of Annamalai University, Chidambaram, and public meetings at Karaikal,

		Shiyali and Cuddalore. Jawaharlal Nehru was sentenced to two years' imprisonment. Gandhiji visited Nagore, Tillaiyadi and Mayavaram.
February 17	:	Spoke at public meeting, Pondicherry. Visited Gandhi Kuppam, Tiruvannamalai and Vellore.
	:	Kaka Kalelkar was sentenced to two years' imprisonment.
February 18	:	Gandhiji spoke at public meeting, Vellore. Visited Katpadi and Ambur. Spoke at Christkula Ashram, Tiruppattur.
February 19	:	At Madras.
February 20	:	At Madras. Gave interview to *The Hindu*.
February 21	:	Spoke at public meetings at Conjeevaram, Arni, Arkonam. Visited Chingleput, Walajapet, Ranipet, and Arcot.
February 22	:	Left Mysore for Coorg by car. Spoke at public meetings at Hudekeri and Pannampet.
February 23	:	Spoke at public meetings at Virajpet and Mercara. Visited Bellur, Somwarpet and Gundukutti.
February 24	:	Spoke at public meeting at Puttur; Jnanodaya Samaj, women's meeting, public meeting, Mangalore. Visited Mercara, Sampaje, Sulya Uppingadi, Vithal-Gabka, Kannadka, Panemangalore and Bantval.
February 25	:	Spoke at students' meeting, Mangalore, public meetings, Mulki, Udipi, Kundapur.
February 26	:	At Kundapur.
February 27	:	Visited Bhatkal, Honavar, Tadri and Karwar.
February 28	:	Spoke at public meeting at Sirsi. Visited Karwar, Binaga, Chandia, Ankola, Hiregutti, Madangeri, Kumata, Aminpalli and Hegde.
March 1	:	Spoke at public meeting, Siddapur. Visited Kanasur, Dasankop, Islur, Ekambi, Samasji, Alur, Devihosur, Haveri, Byadagi, Moti-Benur and Murgimath.
March 2	:	Visited Haveri, Ranibennur, Harihar, Davangere, Duggathi, Bemipalli, Harpanahalli, Kotturu, Kudilgi, Kanivihalli and Sandur.
March 3	:	Spoke at public meeting, Bellary. Visited Hospet,

		Bhanapur, Gadag and Jakkali and Hubli.
March 4	:	Spoke at Railwaymen's meeting, Hubli. Visited Dharwar, Marewadi, Aminbhavi, Morah, Harobidhongal, Uppin-Betgeri, Hireullegiri, Saundatti, Guruhosur, Hosur, Bailhongal, Sampagaon, Bagewadi and Belgaum.
March 5	:	At Belgaum answered Harijan workers' questions.
March 6	:	Visited Tondikatti.
March 7	:	Addressed Mercantile Association, Nipani. Visited Yamkanmardi, Vantimuri, Hukeri, Gokak, Sankeshvar, Gad-Hinglaj and Hat Kanagle, Bhoj, Navlihal, Kothali, Dholgarwadi, Chikodi, Ankali and Shedbal.
March 8	:	Visited Mangsuli, Banhatti, Athni, Honwad, Tikota, Torvi, Bijapur, Ilkal and Jorapur.
March 9	:	Addressed women's meeting and public meeting, Hyderabad and public meeting at Secundrabad. Gave interview to the Associated Press of India, Hyderabad.
March 11	:	At Allahabad. Met Kamala Nehru and Swarup Rani Nehru. Reached Patna at night.
March 12	:	At Patna. Wrote his message to afflicted Bihar in earthquake bulletin.
March 14	:	Toured the affected area and visited Hajipur, Chatro, Lalganj and Motihari.
March 15	:	At Motihari spoke at public meeting. Gave interview to the Middle-class Deputation of Motihari and Relief Workers of Champaran.
March 16	:	Spoke at public meeting, Muzaffarpur. At Patna, gave interview to *The Searchlight*. Visited Chapra.
March 18	:	Addressed meeting of Bihar Central Relief Committee, Patna.
March 20	:	Spoke at public meeting, Patna.
March 21	:	Spoke at meeting of Representatives of Relief Societies, Patna.
March 22	:	Spoke at Dinapore. Advised the Ashram inmates to stop courting imprisonment.
March 23	:	In message to the Press, laid down some rules

		for guidance of relief workers.
March 24	:	At Patna. Visited Dinapore.
March 27	:	Addressed public meeting and meeting of relief workers, Chapra. Visited Sonepur, Sarava, Parasurampur and Panapur.
March 28	:	Spoke at meetings at Hajipur and Sonepur. Visited Chapra, Muzaffarpur and Baulghat.
March 29	:	Addressed public meetings at Bhartua Chaur and Sitamarhi. Visited Muzaffarpur, Bedaul, Belsand, and Chandauli.
March 30	:	Spoke at workers' meeting and prayer meeting, Sitamarhi. Visited Kamtaul, Koriapira, Sursand and Puri.
March 31	:	Addressed public meetings at Darbhanga and Madhubani. Had talks with relief workers, Darbhanga. Reached Rajnagar.
April 1	:	Visited Nirmali and Saharsa.
April 2	:	From Saharsa issued statement to the Press, advising suspension of satyagraha by others but himself retaining right of starting of individual satyagraha. Visited Bihpur and Bhagalpur.
April 3	:	At Monghyr. Spoke at public meeting.
April 4	:	At Patna. Had talks with Congress leaders including Dr. Ansari, Dr. B. Ç. Roy and Bhulabhai Desai on revival of Swaraj party to take part in elections to Central Assembly. Visited Jamalpur, Mokamah, Punarek, Barh and Bakhtiyarpur.
April 5	:	Wrote to Dr. Ansari approving revival of Swaraj Party.
April 6	:	At Patna gave interview to *The Hindu* on Bihar earthquake.
April 7	:	In interview to *The Hindu* said that he would, consistent with his views on Council-entry, render all the assistance to Swaraj Party.
April 8	:	Visited Katihar, Forbesganj, Fulkana and Araria.
April 9	:	Addressed public meeting, Purnea. Bihar tour ended. Left for Assam Harijan tour.
April 10	:	At midnight reached Assam.

April 11	:	At public meeting at Rupsi appealed to the people to efface untouchability. Addressed meetings at Dhubri, Barpeta. Visited Gauripur, Bansbari, Chaprakata, Sorbhog, Howli and Sorupeta.
April 12	:	Visited Goreswar, Tangla, Udalguri, Bindukuri Rangapada. Spoke at public meetings at Tejpur. Left Tejpur for Gauhati by steamer.
April 13	:	Reached Gauhati. Spoke at public meeting. Inaugurated Seva Ashram. Visited Leper Asylum and Harijan quarters.
April 14	:	Addressed women's meeting and Marwaris' meeting, Gauhati. Visited Chaparmukh, Khetri, Nowgong and Furkating.
April 15	:	Addressed public meeting, Golaghat. Visited Ganakpukhari, Dergaon and Jorhat.
April 16 & 17	:	At Jorhat.
April 18	:	At Jorhat. Gave interview to Harijan leaders. Gave interview to American Missionary. Gave interview to the Press on the role of Swaraj Party. Visited Charing and Sibsagar.
April 19	:	At Dibrugarh gave interview to the Associated Press. Visited Dimu, Sapon, Kwang and Dihing.
April 20	:	Visited Chabua. At Tinsukhia issued statement to the Associated Press on untouchability. Addressed public meeting. Left Tinsukhia by train for Bihar.
April 21	:	At Gauhati.
April 22	:	Addressed public meeting, Katihar. Reached Muzaffarpur.
April 23	:	At Muzaffarpur. Opened Gokhalepuri—a settlement for displaced persons on account of earthquake.
April 24	:	Left Muzaffarpur. Reached Patna.
April 25	:	Visited Kulharia, Jamira, Arrah. Addressed public meeting, Buxar. In Jasidih sanatanists attacked Gandhiji's car with lathis and stones.
April 26	:	Gandhiji spoke at public meeting, Deoghar. Reached Gaya.

April 27	:	Visited Chapra and Hazaribagh.
April 28	:	Spoke at public meeting, Gumia. Visited Bermo and Jharia.
April 29	:	Visited Purulia and Ranchi.
April 30	:	At Ranchi.
May 1	:	Conferred with Swarajist leaders, Ranchi.
May 4	:	In interview to the Press at Jamshedpur discussed the results of his Harijan campaign. Addressed public meeting, Jamshedpur.
May 5	:	Visited Leper Asylum, Sambalpur.
May 6	:	Addressed public meeting, Angul. Visited Bamur, Meramandeli, Banurpal, Hindol, Sadashivpur and Cuttack.
May 8	:	From Puri issued statement to the Press announcing his decision to complete tour on foot. Addressed public meeting, Puri.
May 9	:	Commenced his walking tour. Addresssed meeting at Harekrishnapur and Chandanpur. Visited Gopinathpur.
May 10	:	Visited Virgovindpur and Sakhigopal Kadua.
May 11	:	Visited Dandmukund, Pipli and Balasore.
May 12	:	Visited Seola and Balkati.
May 13	:	Visited Satyabhamapur, Balianta and Pipli.
May 14	:	At Balianta.
May 15	:	Spoke at opening of Kunjabihari temple, Balianta. Addressed meeting at Telangapeth.
May 16	:	Spoke at Kajipatna. At Cuttack. Gave interview to the Press. Addressed public meeting, Cuttack. Kasturba Gandhi was released. Gandhiji left Cuttack for Patna by train.
May 17	:	Reached Patna at night.
May 18	:	In Patna, Gandhiji spoke at A.I.C.C. meeting.
May 19	:	Spoke at A.I.C.C. after moving resolution on Council-entry.
May 20	:	Left Patna; interview to *The Hindu*.
May 21	:	Reached Byree is morning and walked to Gandhi Seva Ashram, Champapurhat; interview to *The Hindustan Times*.

May 22	:	At Champapurhat, spoke on need for educating people on hygiene and sanitation.
May 23	:	Spoke at Gopinathpur.
May 25	:	Had discussion with M.R. Masani and N. R. Malkani; spoke at Patpur, Nishchintkoili.
May 26	:	Spoke at Kaktia and Salar.
May 27	:	Spoke at Kendrapara.
May 29	:	In letter to Masani, gave opinion on Socialist programme; spoke at Kendrapada; interview to Associated Press of India.
May 30	:	Interview to Utkal workers.
May 31	:	Spoke at Bari, Neola and Sahaspur.
June 1	:	Spoke at Purushottampur and Budhaghat; due to rain stayed for night in Budhaghat.
June 2	:	At Jajpur, spoke at public meeting.
June 3	:	Spoke at Bhandaripokhari and Todang.
June 5	:	Reached Garadpur Ashram, Bhadrak.
June 7	:	At Garadpur Ashram, addressed Harijan workers.
June 8	:	Cancelled walking tour due to rain; reached Kharagpur by train; in railway station speech, characterized the Calcutta Mayoral election dispute as "unseemly" fight among Congressmen in Calcutta Corporation. At Balasore, interview to Associated Press of India; spoke on removal of untouchability.
June 9	:	At Nagpur railway station, spoke to textile workers; reached Wardha in evening; walked to Ashram.
June 12	:	In Wardha, Congress Working Committee met after lapse of two and a half years.
June 13	:	Gandhiji left for Bombay.
June 14	:	In Bombay, interview to members of Harijan Sevak Sangh and Gandhi Seva Sena.
June 15	:	Spoke at women's meeting.
June 16	:	Interview to B.R. Ambedkar; spoke at meeting of Congress Parliamentary Board; addressed public meeting at Azad Maidan.

June 17 : Interview to members of All-India Swadeshi League.

June 19 : In Poona, interview to workers of Indian States' Peoples' Movement, led by N.C. Kelkar.

June 20 : Interview to Congress constructive workers.

June 21 : Spoke at Mahila Ashram; addressed students.

June 22 : Visited Christ Seva Sangh; interview to national education workers.

June 23 : At Maharashtra Mandal, a physical culture institute, advised need for moral and spiritual development along with physical culture; visited khadi bhandar and Tarachand Ayurvedic Hospital; spoke at meeting commemorating the Prophet's death.

June 24 : Spoke in reply to District Board address; interview to Harijans; addressed a public meeting.

June 25 : Escaped attempt on his life; gave statement on bomb incident; visited Seva Sadan; left for Bombay.

June 26 : In Bombay, interview to Associated Press of India; left for Ahmedabad; spoke at Baroda railway station.

June 27 : In Ahmedabad, had discussion with Harijan workers; spoke at women's meeting; in message to Associated Press of India, thanked authors of numerous telegrams on his narrow escape at Poona.

June 28 : Visited Harijan quarters; had discussion with Gujarati Swadeshi Sangh workers.

June 29 : Spoke at mill-workers' meeting; addressed Jyoti Sangh members and public meeting.

June 30 : Spoke at Congress Socialists' meeting.

July 1 : At Bhavnagar, attended reception at Sanatana Dharma High School; had discussion with Kathiawar youths; spoke to Harijans; addressed a public meeting.

July 2 : At a joint session of Kathiawar Harijan Sevak Sangh and Kathiawar Political Conference Harijan Samiti, advised members of both

		organizations to come under the All- India Harijan Sevak Sangh, Delhi.
July 3	:	Visited Thakkar Bapa Harijan Ashram and Khadi Bhawan; interview to Harijans; addressed public meeting; spoke on State goshala; left for Ajmer by train.
July 4	:	En route to Ajmer, spoke at Mehsana and Palanpur.
July 5	:	At Ajmer, addressed women's meeting; met Harijan sevaks; spoke at public meeting.
July 6	:	Early in morning, went by car to Beawar; visited Harijan quarters; received address from Jain sadhus; left for Karachi by train.
July 7	:	En route to Karachi, spoke at Hyderabad. In Karachi, spoke in reply to civic address.
July 8	:	Addressed Congress workers; spoke to Sind Harijan sevaks; laid foundation-stone of Karachi Indian Merchants' Association building; visited Harijan quarters; addressed public meeting.
July 10	:	Issued statement on fast; interview to Harijan leaders; spoke at Dayaram Jethamal Sind College.
July 11	:	Interviewed by Sind journalists; advised members of Provincial Harijan Sevak Sangh to make independent collection from year to year and not to meet current expenditure from the collections made during his current visit, which should be reserved for backward areas; visited Harijan Handicrafts Institute; spoke to Parsis; left for Lahore.
July 12	:	On train, interviewed by The Tribune representative.
July 13	:	At Lahore, interview to Provincial Congress leaders; also to Harijan deputation; spoke at students' meeting.
July 14	:	Spoke at women students' meeting; addressed women's meeting.
July 15	:	Interview to Akali and Khalsa Durbar deputation; also to Punjab Hindus' and Sikhs' deputation; addressed public meeting.

July 17 : Spoke at prayer meeting; interview to volunteers; also to Frontier leaders; addressed Punjab nationalist workers; also khadi workers; interview to journalists; spoke at Gulabdevi Tuberculosis Hospital; also at Model Town; interview to Associated Press of India; left for Calcutta.

July 18 : At New Delhi Station en route to Calcutta, interview to Associated Press of India.

July 19 : In Calcutta, issued statement to the Press; was examined by Dr. S. Nilratan Sircar, and Dr. B. C. Roy; attended women's meeting at Albert Hall; was called on by Rabindranath Tagore.

July 20 : Was examined by Drs. Sircar and Roy.

July 21 : Spoke at Chittaranjan Seva Sadan and laid foundation-stone for its children's wing; had discussion with students; spoke at Town Hall; addressed a public meeting; left for Kanpur; on train interview to Associated Press of India.

July 22 : In Kanpur, spoke at civic reception; addressed public meeting.

July 24 : Spoke at opening of Tilak Hall; had discussion with sanatanists; addressed U. P. Harijan workers; spoke to students and Harijans; interview to Rashtra Bhasha deputation.

July 25 : Went to Lucknow for two hours; spoke at women's meeting, Zenana Park; visited Charkha Sangh Khadi Bhandar; addressed public meeting.

: Returned to Kanpur; spoke at Arya Samaj; interview to zamindars.

July 26 : Discussion with Congress, Harijan and khadi workers; addressed women's meeting; visited Harijan quarters; left for Benares.

July 27 : In Benares, discussion with Socialists.

July 29 : Drafted manifesto of Congress Parliamentary Board; spoke on manifesto of Congress Parliamentary Board; spoke at Central Board meeting of Harijan Sevak Sangh and at Kashi Vidyapith on national education.

July 30	:	Issued statement on fast.
July 31	:	Refused to obey warrant sent by Lalnath to appear before the Kotwal; addressed a public meeting.
August 1	:	Spoke at Benares Hindu University; also at Harijans' meeting.
August 2	:	Spoke at women's meeting; left for Patna.
August 3	:	In Patna, spoke to Bihar Central Relief Committee and moved resolution recording its confidence in the Managing Committee; interview to the Press.
August 4	:	Left for Wardha; interview at Jabalpur.
August 5	:	Had talk with Jamnalal Bajaj on purifying every institution; advised him to go to Bombay for an operation and offered to look after purification week in Ashram.
August 6	:	Issued statement on fast.
August 7	:	After morning prayer and last meal at 5.30 a. m., began fast at 6 a. m.; spoke on significance of fast.
August 14	:	Broke fast at 6 a. m. by taking a glass of hot water and honey.
After August 14	:	In discussion, exhorted Gujarat Vidyapith teachers to go to villages and "be a peripatetic Vidyapith".
August 15	:	Was examined by doctors.
August 16	:	Interview to the Press.
On or before August 23	:	Issued statement to the Press on Communal Award Resolution of the Congress Working Committee.
On or before August 24	:	Interview to khadi workers.
August 26/27	:	In letter to Vallabhbhai Patel, informed him of discussion he had with Rajagopalachari on his "intention of leaving the Congress".
September 5	:	In statement to the Press said that no final decision has been taken about his relinquishing Congress Party leadership.
September 16	:	Gandhiji was at Wardha.

September 17 : Issued statement to Press explaining his decision to resign from Congress.

September 20 : Gandhiji and M.S. Aney issued joint statement to Press.

September 23 : Gandhiji wrote introduction to Varnavyavastha.

September25-28: Had discussion with C. F. Andrews, Rajendra Prasad and Vallabhbhai Patel.

October 5 : Gandhiji's 66th birthday according to Gujarati calendar celebrated.

October 6 : In statement to Press, Gandhiji acknowledged messages received on his birthday.

Before October 10: Sent message to Madras electors urging them "to choose Congress representatives".

October 12 : Paid tribute to Raja of Kalakanker through *Harijan*.

October 15 : Issued statement to Press regarding amendment to Congress constitution and other resolutions he proposed to move at forthcoming Congress session.

October 20 : Reached Bombay in morning.

October 22 : In public meeting, paid tributes to Vithalbhai Patel on his death anniversary.

October 23 : Spoke at Congress Subjects Committee meeting.

October 24 : At Subjects Committee meeting, moved his resolution on All-India Village Industries Association.

October 26 : Addressing Subjects Committee members, urged them to adopt amended constitution.

October 27 : Continued his speech on amendments at Subjects Committee meeting.

: Sub-committee appointed to study amendments.

October 28 : Gandhiji presided over anniversary celebration of Shoorji Vallabhdas Swadeshi Bazaar, in morning.

: Presented at Subjects Committee meeting Sub-committee's report on amendments and draft resolution on Indian States. Gandhiji's resolution on amendment of Congress constitution passed

		at open session. Congress session concluded. Gandhiji gave message to nation in interview to Associated Press.
October 29	:	Issued statement to Press urging people to vote for Congress candidates. Gave statement on silk yarn. Left for Wardha in evening.
October 30	:	Reached Wardha. In statement to Press spelled out changes in Congress constitution and explained his retirement from Congress. Resigned from Congress.
November 8	:	Issued statement to Press regarding A.I.V.I.A.
November 9	:	Gave interview to Nirmal Kumar Bose.
November 10	:	Interview to Nirmal Kumar Bose continued.
November 11	:	Gandhiji had discussion with B. Shiva Rao and J.C. Kumarappa.
November 15	:	Wrote to Viceroy on his contemplated visit to North-West Frontier Province. Gave interview to *The Manchester Guardian*.
November 22	:	Joint Parliamentary Committee's report published. In interview to Associated Press, Gandhiji refused to comment on it.
November 25	:	Private Secretary to Viceroy wrote to Gandhiji that it was not desirable for him to visit Frontier Province at "the present time".
November 26	:	Gandhiji released to Press his correspondence with Sir George Schuster regarding salt concession.
November 28	:	Wrote to Viceroy in reply to Government's stand not allowing Gandhiji to visit Frontier Province.
On or before November 30:		Spoke at annual session of Gandhi Seva Sangh.
December 1	:	V. P. Madhava Rao died.
December 7	:	Gandhiji sent telegram to Viceroy seeking permission to publish correspondence. Abdul Ghaffar Khan arrested.
December 9	:	In statement to Press Gandhiji warned public against believing unauthorized reports of his correspondence with Viceroy.
December 11	:	Released to Press his correspondence with

Government.

December 14 : Paid tributes to V. P. Madhava Rao through Harijan. All-India Village Industries Association formed.

On or before December 15: Mary Chesley met Gandhiji.

December 15 : Gandhiji issued constitution of A.I.V.I.A. through statement to Press.

December 16 : Gandhiji was at Wardha.

December 20 : Released bye-laws of A.I.V.I.A. to the Press.

December 29 : Reached Delhi in the morning. Gave interview to Associated Press.

December 30 : Spoke at Harijan Industries Exhibition, Delhi.

1935

January 1 : Gave interview to *The Hindustan Times.*

January 2 : Had discussions about new Constitution of Harijan Sevak Sangh. Laid foundation-stone of Harijan Colony, Delhi. Opened Harijan Conference at Narela.

January 3 : In letter to Carl Heath enumerated his objections to Joint Parliamentary Committee Report.

January 4 : Received deputation led by Raghubir Narain Singh who pointed out difficulties in reviving village industries. Had talks with deputation of Chamars who had been ill-treated by zamindar of their village.

January 5 : Attended meeting of Central Board of All-India Harijan Sevak Sangh.

January 8 : Had discussions with deputation of Ahmedabad Mill-owners' Association. Gave interview to C. Kuttan Nair.

January 9 : Gave interview to Halide Edib Hanum.

January 10 : Had discussion with Socialists. Gave interview to the Press regarding Government's circular on rural development.

January 11 : Had discussion with Ahmedabad mill-owners and workers.

January 12 : Visited cattle-breeding farm, Delhi. Discussed Harijan uplift work with G.D. Birla and others.

January 13	:	Settled dispute between Ahmedabad mill-owners and workers.
January 14	:	Wrote Foreword to *Two Servants of God.*
January 15	:	Visited Modern High School, Delhi. Had discussions with Rajendra Prasad and C. Rajagopalachari.
January 16	:	Had discussions with members of Congress Working Committee.
January 17	:	Attended meeting of Congress Parliamentary Party as invitee.
January 18	:	Attended first meeting of Congress Assembly Party.
January 19	:	Presided over le0cture by Halide Edib Hanum at Jamia Millia. Spoke at Sansis' Basti.
January 21	:	Gave interview to United Press.
January 23	:	Started his three-day village tour around Delhi accompanied by Kasturba Gandhi, Dr. Zakir Husain, Krishnan Nair and others. Visited Narela and Bakhnir.
January 24	:	Visited villages of Thud, Sultanpur, Buwana.
January 25	:	Visited Humayunpur, Munirka and Ramtal.
January 27	:	Spoke at M.L.A.s' meeting, Delhi.
January 28	:	Left Delhi for Wardha.
January 29	:	En route to Wardha, advised Congressmen at Nagpur station on need for industrial education for girls.
February 4	:	Attended meeting of A.I.V.I.A. at Wardha.
February 9	:	Had discussion with Edith Howe-Martyn.
February 11	:	Spoke at Lakshmi Narayan Temple, Wardha.
February 22	:	Spoke at kitchen meeting, Wardha.
February 23	:	Opened Itwari Khadi Bhandar, Nagpur. Spoke at opening of Sitabuldi Khadi Bhandar, Nagpur. Spoke at meeting of village workers, Nagpur. Addressed public meeting, Nagpur.
February 24	:	Returned to Wardha.
March 10	:	Held consultations with members of All-India Spinners' Association at Wardha.
March 11-12	:	Had talks with V. S. Srinivasa Sastri.

March 16-18 : Spoke at A.I.V.I.A. Board meeting. Had discussions with members of A.I.V.I.A.

March 22 : Commenced his four-week silence.

March 23 : Sent message on death of T.A.K. Sherwani.

April 10 : Had discussion with J. P. Bhansali.

April 19 : Broke his four weeks' silence. Spoke at prayer meeting Wardha Left for Indore in the evening.

April 20 : Spoke at Hindi Sahitya Sammelan, Indore.

: Spoke at opening of village industries exhibition, Indore.

April 23 : At Indore. Addressed Hindi Sahitya Sammelan. Spoke at public meeting, meeting of Gujaratis, and at Harijan School.

April 25 : Gandhiji was at Wardha.

April 26 : In letter to F. Mary Barr, who was T.B. patient, offered to meet the cost of expenses for her treatment.

Before April 27: Had discussions with J. P. Bhansali.

Before May 11 : Interview to missionary nurse.

On or before May 21 : Discussion with a Christian student.

May 21 : Left Wardha by train for Bombay. On train had discussion with Pierre Ceresole.

May 22 : In Bombay, interview to *The Bombay Chronicle;* spoke at prayer meeting.

On or after May 23: At Borsad village, addressed several meetings.

May 25 : In *Harijan,* appealed for collection of one lakh rupees for Harijan Wells Fund.

May 31 : At Nadiad, spoke at opening of Vithal Kanya Vidyalaya; also at inauguration of Bal Mandir in Memory of Fulchand Shah.

: At Ahmedabad, met Khan Abdul Ghaffar Khan in Sabarmati Jail. Interview to the Press. Answered questions by members of Jyoti Sangh.

June 1 : At Borsad, visited Arya Kanya Vidyalaya.

June 3 : Returned to Wardha.

June 6 : Statement on Quetta Earthquake.

June 13 : Discussed Quetta situation with Congress President, Rajendra Prasad.

Before June 15 : Talk with Harijan Sevak.

Before June 16 : Message on opening Memorial to C.R. Das.

June 18 : Issued award on dispute between the employers and the employees of Khadi Bhandar, Bombay.

June 19-21 : Attended A.I.V.I.A. session.

Before June 22 : Discussion with a visitor from Quetta on utility of prayer. In discussion, explained that the village industries movement was not meant to oust all machinery.

July 13 : In *Harijan* article, "Need for a Standard Wage", suggested "eight annas for eight hours' strenuous work".

Before July 20 : At Wardha Ashram, spoke on the occasion of Keisho's departure to Calcutta.

July 20 : In *Harijan* article, "Meaning of Non-violence", defended his argument in favour of advocacy of self-defence as "the only honourable course where there is unreadiness for self-immolation"

On or before August 1: In message to Council of League of Nations, said: "I can only pray and hope for peace." In statement on Italo-Abyssinian crisis, contradicted rumours about his appeal for raising a volunteer corps of Indians for Red Cross service in Abyssinia.

August 1 : In statement to the Press, contradicted Lord Zetland's reply to Lord Forrington in the House of Commons on impounding of M. R. Masani's passport.

August 5 : In message to Hansa, said "A monthly of this kind is badly needed if Hindi or Hindustani is to become the national language."

Before August 10: Discussion with Congress Working Committee members on reorganizing khadi production.

August 22-23 : Discussion with Management Board of A.I.V.I.A. on minimum living wage.

August 30 : In telegram to Viceroy, appealed for Jawaharlal Nehru's unconditional release in view of Kamala Nehru's serious illness.

September 2 : Jawaharlal Nehru was released from Almora Jail.

Before September 7: At Wardha, Gandhiji had discussion with Swami Yogananda.

Before September 14: Discussion with khadi workers on minimum living wage.

On or after September 24: Discussion on celebration of his sixtyseventh birthday.

September 28	:	In *Harijan* article, "About Conversion", commented on propositions of A.A. Paul of the Federation of
October 1	:	Gandhiji was in Wardha.
October 2	:	Gandhiji's sixty-seventh birthday celebrated. Italy invaded Abyssinia.
October 5-6	:	Gandhiji discussed acceptance of office with Congress leaders.
October 11	:	Sent message for Indian immigrants of Suriname. Presided over A.I.S.A. Council meeting. Discussed spinners' wages.
October 12	:	Attended A.I.S.A. Council meeting.
October 13	:	Attended A.I.S.A. Council meeting. Assured Rabindranath Tagore that he would "strain every nerve" to collect necessary funds for Santiniketan.
October 14	:	B.R. Ambedkar advised Harijans to renounce Hinduism and embrace any other religion which guaranteed equal status.
October 15	:	Through Press, Gandhiji urged B.R. Ambedkar "to assuage his wrath and reconsider the position".
October 20	:	Gave interview to a delegation consisting of Patitpawandas, D.K. Bhagat, T.A. Purohit and D.S. Shende.
October 22	:	Addressed village workers.
October 24	:	Wrote foreword to Shrimadrajachandra.
November 7-8	:	Attended meeting of A.I.V.I.A.
November 10	:	Spoke on Rajachandra anniversary.
November 16	:	G.K. Deodhar died.

Before November 23 : Gandhiji had talk with professors and students of Wardha.

November 23	:	In *Harijan* paid tribute to G.K. Deodhar.

November 24 : Issued appeal to Gujaratis to donate for Gujarat Harijan Sevak Sangh.
December 3 : Gave interview to Margaret Sanger.
December 4 : Sent message on Vidyagauri Nilkanth's sixtieth birthday.
: Gave interview to Margaret Sanger.
December 7 : Suddenly Gandhiji took ill and was advised rest.
December 13 : Met Rajendra Prasad.
Before December 27 : Wrote Foreword to *Satyagraha in Gandhiji's Own Words*.
Before December 28 : Sent message to Indian National Congress Jubilee Sammelan.
December 31 : Met members of International Federation of Fellowship.

1936

January 7 : Met Muriel Lester, Dr. Tomiko Koro and Mrs. Tyace.
January 9 : Had some teeth extracted. Mahadev Desai informed Associated Press that "Gandhiji had been having high blood-pressure during the past few weeks, but there was a distinct though slow improvement."
Before January 11 : Gandhiji gave interview to Yone Noguchi.
Before January 17 : Sent message to Bihar Political Conference.
January 17 : Reached Bombay.
January 19 : Had some more teeth extracted.
January 20 : King George V died.
January 21 : Gandhiji cabled condolence to Queen Mary.
January 22 : Reached Ahmedabad.
February 1 : Jawaharlal Nehru elected Congress President.
February 9 : Gandhiji met Muriel Lester.
February 12 : Met Prabhashankar Pattani.
February 16 : Visited Harijan Ashram and spoke to inmates.
February 18 : Dinshaw Wacha passed away.
February 19 : Gandhiji addressed students of Gujarat Vidyapith. Paid tribute to Dinshaw Wacha.
February 21 : Reached Bardoli en route to Wardha.

	:	Interviewed by American Negro Delegation.
February 22	:	Spoke at village workers' meeting.
February 23	:	Reached Wardha.
February 28	:	Kamala Nehru passed away. Through Press Gandhiji paid tribute to Kamala Nehru, sent condolence to Vijayalakshmi Pandit. Left for Savli.
February 29	:	At Savli spoke at Gandhi Seva Sangh meetings.
	:	Opened A.I.V.I.A. Exhibition.
March 1, 3 and 4 123	:	Addressed Gandhi Seva Sangh meetings.
March 5	:	Attended marriage of Krishnadas Gandhi and Manojna. Spoke at Gandhi Seva Sangh meeting.
March 6	:	Addressed Gandhi Seva Sangh meeting. Left Savli.
March 7	:	At Wardha en route to Delhi.
March 8	:	Arrived in Delhi. Stayed in Harijan Colony.
Before March 9	:	Sent message to Gurukul convocation.
March 9	:	Began practice of silence between 10 a.m. and 5 p.m.
March 10	:	Jawaharlal Nehru returned to India.
March 16	:	Gandhiji ended the practice of silence between 10 a.m. and 5 p.m.
March 17	:	Met Jawaharlal Nehru.
March 19	:	In note to Jamnalal Bajaj explained his 'idea of living in a village'.
March 21	:	Congress Working Committee began deliberations.
March 22	:	Gandhiji gave interview to M.C. Rajah. Attended Harijan Sevak Sangh meeting.
March 25	:	Discussed with Rabindranath Tagore finances of Santi-niketan.
March 27	:	Sent draft for Rs. 60,000 to Rabindranath Tagore. Had discussion with Harijan workers.
March 28	:	Arrived in Lucknow. Opened Khadi and Village Industries Exhibition.
March 30	:	In statement to the Press contradicted report that Lord Halifax was arranging an interview between Lord Linlithgow and himself.

April 4	: Arrived in Allahabad.
April 5	: Bhavani Dayal, South African Delegate to Congress session, met Gandhiji. Opened library and museum of Hindi Sahitya Sammelan.
April 6	: Gandhiji visited Harijan Colony. T.B. Sapru met Gandhiji.
April 7	: Gandhiji attended Congress Working Committee meeting. Left Allahabad.
April 8	: Reached Lucknow. Subhas Chandra Bose was arrested on his return to India.
April 12	: Gandhiji spoke at Khadi Exhibition.
April 13	: Observed fast on Jallianwala Bagh Day. Congress rejected new Constitution.
April 14	: Gandhiji addressed All-India Depressed Classes Conference.
April 15	: Addressed public meeting in Congress pandal in evening.
Before April 16	: Had discussion with two foreign ladies.
April 16	: Left Lucknow.
April 17	: Reached Wardha in afternoon.
After April 17	: Visited Segaon and in a speech to villagers explained his decision to settle there.
April 18	: Linlithgow assumed office as Viceroy.
April 23	: Gandhiji left Wardha in evening.
April 24	: At Nagpur. Presided over Akhil Bharatiya Sahitya Parishad in morning.
April 26	: Harilal met Gandhiji at Nagpur. Gandhiji arrived at Wardha at night.
April 27	: Congress Working Committee met at Wardha.
April 28	: Gandhiji attended C.W.C. meeting.
April 30	: Moved to Segaon early in the morning.
May 1	: Met B.R. Ambedkar and Walchand Hirachand.
May 3	: At Wardha, inaugurated Exhibition of A.I.V.I.A.
May 4	: At Segaon.
May 6	: At Paunar, spoke at Khadi Yatra.
May 7	: At Wardha, addressed annual general meeting of A.I.V.I.A.

May 8 : At Wardha, spoke at Training School for village workers. Left for Bangalore in evening.

May 9 : Reached Madras in morning en route to Bangalore. In interview to Associated Press declined to comment on "Indian or world politics".

May 10 : Reached Nandi Hills. Dr. M.A. Ansari died.

On or after May 10 : Gandhiji gave interview to Sir C.V. Raman and Professor Rahm.

May 11 : Telegraphed condolence to Begum Ansari. Issued to Associated Press message on Dr. M.A. Ansari's death.

May 14 : Met Captain C. Oommen.

May 15 : News reached Gandhiji that Mary Chesley had died at Rishikesh.

May 29 : Harilal Gandhi embraced Islam, assuming name Abdulla.

Before May 31 : Gandhiji met Sir C.V. Raman and Lady Raman. Had discussion with Dr. Erika Deussen Rosenthal.

May 31 : Left Nandi Hills for Bangalore in morning. Visited Chickballapur, Chintamani, Kolar and Bowringpet and addressed meetings. Spoke at Labourers' meeting at Kolar Gold Fields. At Bangalore visited Municipal colony.

June 2,1936 : Bangalore, Gandhiji issued public appeal to Muslim friends in connection with Harilal Gandhi's conversion to Islam.

June 9 : Abbas Tyabji died in Mussoorie.

June 10 : Gandhiji gave interview to Adi-Karnataka Sangh Deputation. In the evening addressed Harijan Workers' Conference at Kengeri.

June 11 : Had interview with M.V. Jambunathan.

June 12 : Addressed Harijan Workers' Conference, Kengeri. Presided over Hindi Prachar Sabha. Visited Institute of Science, Bangalore. Left Bangalore.

June 13 : Arrived in Madras en route to Wardha. Visited Hindi Prachar Sabha Bhavan under construction.

June 14	: Reached Wardha in the morning.
June 16	: Arrived at Segaon.
June 27	: Congress Working Committee met at Wardha. Gandhiji arrived in Wardha but did not attend the meeting.
June 29-30	: At Wardha. Had discussions with Jawaharlal Nehru.
June 30-July 4	: At Wardha.
July 5	: At Wardha, presided over Bharatiya Sahitya Parishad. Returned to Segaon in the evening.
July 15	: Public meeting in Calcutta with Tagore in chair proposed amendment of Communal Award.
July 17	: Gandhiji gave message to khadi workers.
July 19	: Met students of Village Workers' Training School.
July 30	: Endorsed appeal for funds for Harijan Sevak Sangh.
August 2	: Abdul Ghaffar Khan released.
August 4	: Dharmanand Kosambi and Abdul Gaffar Khan called on Gandhiji.
August 11	: C. Rajagopalachari resigned from Congress.
August 16	: C. Rajagopalachari and Jawaharlal Nehru called on Gandhiji.
August 27	: Gandhiji attended A.I.S.A. meeting. Had talks with Jawaharlal Nehru.
August 28	: Attended A.I.S.A. meeting. Had talks with C. Rajagopalachari.
August 30	: Jayaprakash Narayan called on Gandhiji. Harilal as Abdulla preached Islam.
August 31	: Gandhiji had an attack of malaria.
September 2	: Sent a message to World Peace Conference.
September 3-11	: In hospital at Wardha.
September 12	: Returned to Segaon.
September 17	: Harilal fined in Madras for drunkenness.
September 21	: Gandhiji sent blessings to Zohra Ansari on her wedding.
September 24	: Wrote Preface to *Gitapadarthkosha*.
October 3	: Received Jawaharlal Nehru, Vallabhbhai Patel and Rajendra Prasad.

October 7 : A.I.V.I.A meeting.

October 12 : Gandhiji had talks with students and teachers of Maganwadi Vidyalaya, Wardha.

October 23 : Left Segaon for Banaras.

October 24 : Arrived in Banaras.

October 25 : Banaras. Performed the opening ceremony of Bharat Mata Mandir. Presented a commemoration volume to Maithilisharan Gupta on his golden jubilee.

: Visited Kalabhavan and Nagari Pracharini Sabha.

October 27 : Arrived in Delhi.

: Met Mrs. Ansari and ailing mother of Brijkrishna Chandiwala.

: Left for Ahmedabad.

October 28 : Arrived in Ahmedabad.

October 29 : Arrived in Rajkot. Met his cousin Khushalchand Gandhi.

: Addressed a meeting of Harijan Workers.

October 30 : At Nadiad. Spoke at the inauguration of Vithal Kanya Vidyalaya Hostel. Arrived in Ahmedabad. Inaugurated the building of Municipal Girls' School.

October 31 : Spoke at the Labourers' Meeting. Visited Art Exhibition.

: Presided over Twelfth Gujarati Sahitya Parishad.

November 1 : Presided over the convocation of Gujarat Vidyapith. Attended meeting of the Gujarati Sahitya Parishad.

November 2 : Addressed the concluding session of the Twelfth Gujarati Sahitya Parishad. Left for Baroda on his way to Segaon.

: At Baroda, called on the Tyabji family.

November 3, 1936: Gandhiji left Baroda for Surat on his way to Segaon.

November 4 : Reached Segaon.

November 9 : CF. Andrews arrived in Segaon to meet Gandhiji.

November 12 : Maharaja of Travancore issued Proclamation declaring open temples tc all Hindus.

November 17	:	At Segaon Gandhiji issued statement to the Press congratulating Travancore Maharaja for throwing open temples to Harijans.
December 2-4	:	Had discussions with Mill-owners of Ahmedabad and representatives of Labour Union.
December 4	:	Issued statement to the Press regarding Ahmedabad mill industry wage dispute.
December 5	:	C.F. Andrews, Agatha Harrison and Carl Heath arrived in Segaon.
December 6	:	Gandhiji gave interview to students of Village Workers' Training School, Wardha.
December 19	:	Left Segaon for Faizpur to attend Congress session.
December 20	:	Arrived in Faizpur.
December 21	:	Addressed meeting of Congress volunteers.
December 22	:	Addressed public meeting at Kiroda.
December 24	:	Resigned from Presidentship of All-India Cowprotection League and issued statement to the Press explaining the step.
December 25	:	Spoke at inauguration of Khadi and Village Industries Exhibition, Faizpur.
December 26	:	Gave Award on Ahmedabad mill industry wage dispute. Sent message to Students' Conference.
December 27	:	Addressed public meeting at Exhibition grounds. Spoke at A.I.C.C. meeting.
December 28	:	Sent message to Rashtrabhasha Sammelan held at Faizpur.
December 29	:	Had talks with Congress volunteers.
	:	Left Faizpur for Segaon.
December 31	:	Arrived at Segaon.

1937

January 3	:	Henry Polak and Agatha Harrison arrived.
January 6	:	Gandhiji left Segaon for Poona to meet G.D. Madgavkar, Umpire in Ahmedabad Mill Industry Wage Dispute.
January 7	:	Arrived in Poona. Had discussions with Ahmedabad Mill-owners and labourers.

January 8	: Discussions continued.
January 9	: Discussions continued.
January 10	: Gandhiji attended reception at Justice Madgavkar's residence. Left Poona for Madras en route to Trivandrum.
January 11	: Arrived in Madras. Left for Trivandrum.
January 12	: Arrived in Trivandrum. Addressed public meeting, Trivandrum.
January 13	: Trivandrum. Presided over convocation of Dakshina Bharat Hindi Prachar Sabha. Visited Padmanabha temple. Addressed public meeting.
January 14	: Addressed public meetings on Travancore Proclamation at Neyattinkarai, Venganoor, Tecklai, Thiruvattar and Nagercoil. Arrived in Cape Comorin.
January 15	: Left Cape Comorin. Arrived in Trivandrum.
January 16	: Addressed public meetings at Varakalla, Paripalli and Quilon advising people to fulfil spirit of Travancore Proclamation.
January 17	: Addressed meeting at Thatharampalli advising people to learn Hindi. Spoke at Haripad on essence of Hinduism.
January 18	: Addressed public meetings at Sherthalai and Vaikom. Gave interview to temple trustee, Vaikom. Visited Thakzi.
January 19	: Addressed public meeting at Etamanoor, Kumaranelloor, Thiruvarppu, Kottayam. At Kottayam had discussion with Bishop Moore, Bishop Abraham and others.
January 20	: Addressed public meetings at Kottayam, Changanacheri, Thiruvalla, Chenganoor, Aranmula, Elanthoor and Pandalam.
January 21	: Kottarakarai. Threw open private temple to Harijans. Addressed public meeting. Left for Madras.
January 22	: Arrived in Madras. Spoke to students of Harijan Industrial School, Kodambakkam. Addressed prayer meeting. Gave intervew to an Egyptian.
January 23	: Visited cyclone-affected areas of Guntur, and

		Bezwada. Also collected funds for victims. Left for Segaon.
January 24	:	Arrived in Segaon.
February 26	:	Jawaharlal Nehru and other Congress Leaders arrived.
February 27-28	:	Gandhiji attended Congress Working Committee Meeting at Wardha.
March 3	:	Had talk with an Egyptian Deputation on Indo-Egyptian relations.
March 15	:	Gandhiji arrived in Delhi.
March 16	:	Attended A.I.C.C. meeting, which passed resolution on office-acceptance.
March 17	:	In Calcutta, Subhas Chandra Bose was released from prison.
March 19-20	:	In Delhi, convention of newly elected Congress members of Legislatures and other A.I.C.C. members was held to take oath of national independence and allegiance to Indian people.
On or before March 22	:	Gandhiji gave interview to leaders of Jamiat-ul-Ulema-i-Hind. Visited Industrial Training School.
March 22	:	Left for Segaon.
March 25	:	Left for Madras, accompanied by Kasturba, Manubehn Mashruwala, Kanu Gandhi (Junior), Mahadev Desai and Pyarelal.
March 26	:	In Madras, spoke at Hindi Prachar Sabha Convocation.
March 27-28	:	Spoke at Bharatiya Sahitya Parishad.
March 28	:	Interview to The Hindu.
March 30	:	In statement to the press, Gandhiji declared that British Government "had broken to the heart what it had promised to the ear" by refusing to grant assurances required from Governors. Left for Segaon.
March 31	:	Reached Segaon.
April 8	:	Cabled to Agatha Harrison that legal opinion supported demand for assurances and condemned existing Ministries as illegal.

April 10 : In statement on political impasse, suggested appointment of judicial tribunal to decide whether it was competent for Governors to give assurances demanded by Congress.

April 14 : Left for Hudli.

April 15 : At Kalyan and Poona, interview to Associated Press of India.

April 16-17 : At Hudli, Gandhiji spoke at Gandhi Seva Sangh meeting.

April 18 : Spoke to newly married couples; gave advice to brahmacharis at thread ceremony.

April 20 : Spoke at Gandhi Seva Sangh meeting.

April 22 : At Poona, en route to Segaon, interview to *The Hindu*. In interview to the Press, Gandhiji described Cochin Maharaja's order, which prohibited devotees from entering Cochin temples after their visit to Travancore temples, as "unsurpassed in irreligiousness".

April 23 : Reached Segaon.

April 25 : Left for Allahabad to attend Congress Working Committee meeting. At Nagpur, interview to the Press.

April 26 : At Allahabad, interview to Associated Press of India.

April 30 : On the train, interview to *The Bombay Chronicle*.

May 1 : Gandhiji reached Segaon.

May 9 : Left for Tithal (Bulsar).

May 10 : Reached Bardoli.

May 11 : Had discussion with Congress workers on choice of Haripura as venue for Congress session.

May 12 : Reached Tithal. In statement to the Press, observed that Congress demand was "perfectly constitutional and equally honourable for both parties".

May 15 : Interview to Associated Press of India on Bombay Governor's speech.

May 22 : Gandhiji addressed teachers of Gujarat National Schools.

June 1	:	In interview to *The Times of India,* said that Congress was awaiting a move from Government on constitutional deadlock.
June 10	:	Left for Segaon.
June 11	:	Reached Wardha.
June 12	:	At Segaon, spoke to villagers.
June 21	:	Viceroy made statement.
June 22	:	Interview to Associated Press of India.
June 22	:	In letter to Lord Lothian, Gandhiji explained that he had no faith in the "possibility of the existing Act to expand into an instrument of complete freedom" and that "the sooner it was replaced by something of Indian design the better".
July 6	:	Spoke at Congress Working Committee meeting.
July 7	:	Congress Working Committee meeting resolved that "Congressmen be permitted to accept office where they may be invited thereto". Gandhiji spoke at opening of Hindi Pracharaks' Training School.
July 8	:	Interview to *The Hindu*.
July 9	:	Gandhiji had discussion with Abul Kalam Azad on choice of Muslim Ministers in Provinces. Vallabhbhai Patel issued statement on controversy between Nariman and himself.
July 11	:	Gandhiji attended marriage of Madalasa and Shriman Narayan.
July 17	:	Breaking his self-imposed restriction, published in *Harijan* his atricle "Congress Ministries". Congress Working Committee stated in a resolution that fresh election would have been held had Vallabhbhai Patel been found guilty of allegations levelled against him by Nariman.
July 27	:	Gandhiji wrote to Viceroy accepting invitation to meet him in Delhi on August 4.
August 1	:	Gandhiji was at Segaon.
August 3	:	Left for Delhi.
August 4	:	Reached Delhi. Had interview with Viceroy regarding question of lifting ban on Abdul Ghaffar Khan's entry into Frontier Province.

August 5 : Reached Segaon.

August 11 : Had discussion with D.K. Mehta and P.B. Gole.

August 12 : Discussion with D.K. Mehta and P.B. Gole continued. In statement to Press repudiated Bombay Sentinel report on his interview with Viceroy.

On or after August 16: In telegram to Rabindranath Tagore stated that he would do his utmost to end crisis arising from Andamans prisoners' hunger-strike.

August 20 : In statement to Press on Nariman-Sardar controversy invited evidence from witnesses.

Before August 24: Sent message to Travancore Women's conference, Quilon.

August 27 : Through telegram appealed to Andamans prisoners to abandon hunger-strike.

August 29 : All but seven Andamans prisoners suspended hunger strike.

August 31 : Releasing to Press his correspondence with Andamans prisoners, Gandhiji expressed hope that they would be discharged unconditionally.

September 1 : Received news of Chhotelal Jain's suicide; paid tribute to him through Harijan.

September 3 : Sent telegram urging Andamans political prisoners to give up hunger-strike.

September 8 : Telegraphed another appeal to Andamans prisoners. Wrote to Viceroy regarding Andamans prisoners. Sent message to Tiruchengodu Taluk Political Conference.

Before September 11: Had discussion with Ravishankar Shukla, Owen, De Silva and other educationists.

September 11 : In telegram urged Andamans prisoners to "end national anxiety by suspending strike".

Before September 13: Gave interview to William B. Benton.

September 14 : Telegraphed Nilratan Sarkar to keep him informed about Rabindranath Tagore's health.

September 15 : In statement to Press appealed to Government for release of Andamans prisoners. Met Justice Madgaonkar.

Before September 24: Sent message to Karnataka Unification League, Belgaum. Andamans prisoners suspended hunger-strike.

September 25 : Gandhiji issued appeal in *Harijan* for flood-relief in Orissa.

October 1 : Gandhiji's birthday according to Vikram calendar celebrated.

October 2 : On his 69th birthday Gandhiji sent message to Friends of India Society, London.

October 6 : Acknowledged birthday greetings through Press.

October 14 : D. N. Bahaduriji visited Segaon with his judgement on Nariman-Sardar case. Gandhiji wrote concurring note on it.

October 16 : Issued statement to Press on Nariman-Sardar case.

October 17 : In statement to Press appealed to Andamans prisoners not to resort to hunger-strike. Paid tribute in *Harijan* to Manilal Kothari.

October 22 : At Wardha presided over Educational Conference. Met Acharya P.C. Ray.

Before October 23: Sent message to Shop Assistants' Conference.

October 23 : Spoke at Educational Conference.

October 25 : Left Segaon.

October 26 : Arrived in Calcutta in morning. Attended Congress Working Committee meeting in afternoon. Met Rabindranath Tagore and discussed communal tension in Bengal.

October 27 : C.W.C. meeting continued. Gandhiji had discussion with Bengal Premier and three of his ministers about release of detenus and Andamans prisoners.

October 28 : Met N. R. Sarkar. C.W.C. issued statement on "Vandemataram".

October 29 : Gandhiji gave interview to deputation of political sufferers from Bengal and Punjab.

October 30 : Met Andamans prisoners in Alipore Central Jail.

November 1 : Issued statement to Press on negotiations for release of Andamans prisoners. On medical

		advice cancelled departure for Wardha.
November 2	:	C.W.C. passed resolution on Nariman-Sardar case and released it to Press.
November 4	:	Gandhiji postponed Frontier tour and informed Abdul Ghaffar Khan through telegram.
November 7	:	Had discussion with ex-detenus in evening.
November 9	:	Had interview with Governor at Barrackpore in afternoon. Gave statement to Press.
November 11	:	Met N.R. Sarkar in morning.
November 12	:	Met internees from Deoli in Presidency Jail.
November 16	:	Had discussion with Fazlul Huq, Khwaja Nazimuddin, B.P. Singh Roy, Nawab Habibullah of Dacca, H. S. Suhrawardy and N.R. Sarkar in afternoon.
November 17	:	Met Sir George Campbell and Arthur Moore in morning. Continued discussion with Khwaja Nazimuddin, N.R. Sarkar and B.P. Singh Roy. Left Calcutta at 12.50 p. m. Reached Kharagpur at 4 p. m. At 5 p. m. visited Hijli Detention Camp. In Interview to 'United Press' declined to comment on his negotiations with Bengal Government.
November 18	:	Arrived in Wardha in evening.
November 21	:	Issued statement to Press on Bengal Government's communique.
November 27	:	Wrote Foreword to Acharya-Kripalanina Lekho.
December 6	:	Left Segaon for Bombay on medical advice.
December 7	:	Reached Bombay; stayed at Juhu.
December 14	:	Met Aga Khan and his son.
December 21	:	Met Maharaja of Rewa.

1938

January 2 and 3	:	Had discussions with Congress Working Committee.
January 5	:	Had discussion with Rajendra Prasad.
January 7	:	Met C. Rajagopalachari. Gave interview to Press at Victoria Terminus Station before departure from Bombay in evening.

January 8 : Reached Segaon.

January 10 : Saruprani Nehru died. Gandhiji telegraphed condolence to Jawaharlal Nehru.

January 11 : Sent telegram to political prisoners in Punjab jail to give up hunger-strike.

January 14 : Through Press issued appeal to Punjab prisoners to abandon hunger-strike.

Before January 15: Had discussion with Dr. Zilliacus and other members of New Education Fellowship Delegation.

January 18 to 20: Had discussion with Lord Lothian. Gave message for "Lord Lothian and Responsible Statesmen".

January 23 : Sent telegram welcoming Subhas Chandra Bose on his arrival at Karachi from London.

January 24 : Had discussion with B.C. Roy and N.R. Sarkar.

February 2 : Had discussion with Subhas Chandra Bose.

February 3 to 5 : Attended Congress Working Committee which met at Wardha.

On or before February 8: Had discussion with John De Boer.

February 8 : Left Segaon for Congress session at Haripura.

February 9 : Arrived in Haripura. Offered condolences to Lakshmibai, widow of N.M. Khare.

February 10 : Opened Khadi and Village Industries Exhibition.

February 11 : Addresed sanitation volunteers.

February 12 : Visited exhibition.

February 13 : Visited exhibition pertaining to cattle-breeding and dairy-keeping.

February 15 : Gave interview to Amin, General Secretary of East African Indian Delegation. Addressed volunteers. Bihar and U.P. Ministries resigned.

February 16 : Gandhiji spoke at Khadi and Village Industries Exhibition. Issued statement to Press on Ministerial crisis.

February 17 : Had interview with Tushar Kanti Ghosh.

Before February 18: Drafted resolution on resignation of Ministries.

February 18 : Congress Working Committee discussed resolution on resignations. Gandhiji gave interviews to *The Daily Herald* and *The Times*.

February 19 : Attended Congress session.

February 20 : Through letter to Shamlal urged Punjab prisoners to abandon hunger-strike.

February 21 : Congress session concluded.

February 22 : Gandhiji addressed volunteers. Governor-General issued statement on resignations of Ministries.

February 23 : Gandhiji reached Segaon. Issued statement to Press in reply to Governor-General's statement.

February 24 : Invited M. A. Jinnah for personal discussion.

On or before March 4: Through telegram to Shamlal congratulated Punjab prisoners on their decision to give up hunger-strike.

March 4 : Met Shantikumar Morarjee and Gaganvihari Mehta.

March 8 : Wrote to M. A. Jinnah agreeing to meet him in Bombay.

March 11 and 12: Had discussion with Vallabhbhai Patel.

March 15 : Left Segaon.

March 16 : Arrived in Calcutta in morning.

March 18 : Met Vernon Bartlett of *News Chronicle*. Talked with Harijan members of Bengal legislature. Had discussion with Khwaja Nazimuddin from 2 p.m. to 5.25 p.m.

March 19 : Had discussion with Subhas Chandra Bose and Abul Kalam Azad. Met Krishak Proja Party members in afternoon.

March 20 : Met leader of Independent Praja Party. Had discussion with Bengal Congress leaders. Met Khwaja Nazimuddin at 3 p. m.

March 22 : Met Governor regarding release of political prisoners. Met Rabindranath Tagore in evening. Wrote article on Allahabad riots asking Congressmen to analyse their non-violence and urging them to "put forth a non-violent army of volunteers".

March 23 : Met Lord Bishop of Calcutta in evening.

March 24 : Wrote Foreword to *The Sayings of Muhammad.*

	: Issued appeal to public and political prisoners for restraint while negotiations for release were going on. Left Calcutta at 8 p. m.
March 25	: Arrived in Delang. Addressed fourth annual session of Gandhi Seva Sangh. Opened Gandhi Seva Sangh Exhibition.
March 26	: Spoke at Gandhi Seva Sangh meeting.
March 27	: At Gandhi Seva Sangh spoke on resolution regarding methods to be adopted to counteract communal riots.
March 28	: Addressed Gandhi Seva Sangh. Kasturba, Durga Desai and others visited temple at Puri.
March 29	: High Priest of Puri called on Gandhiji. Gandhiji presided at Council of All-India Spinners' Association in evening.
March 30	: At Gandhi Seva Sangh spoke on Kasturba's visit to Puri Temple.
On or before March 31	: Gave interview to Press on appointment of Acting Governors in provinces.
March 31	: Gave interview to Raja of Parlakimedi.
April 1, 1938	: Gandhiji arrived in Calcutta. Congress Working committee met.
April 2	: Gandhiji attended Congress Working Committee meeting. Maharaja of Darbhanga and Arthur Moore, editor of The Statesman, called on Gandhiji. Gandhiji had discussions with Khwaja Nazimuddin regarding release of detenus and political prisoners.
April 3	: Issued Press statement on talk with Khwaja Nazimuddin. Congress Working Committee meeting continued.
April 7	: Gandhiji had discussion with Lord Brabourne, Governor of Bengal, regarding release of political prisoners. Met Maulana Azad and Tusharkanti Ghosh, editor of *Amrita Bazar Patrika*.
April 8	: Had talk with political prisoners of Presidency Jail.
April 9	: Had discussions with Khwaja Nazimuddin. Met political prisoners in Alipur Jail.

April 10	:	Met political prisoners in Alipur Jail. Visited Khadi Pratishthan, Sodepur. Called on Khwaja Nazimuddin to discuss release of political prisoners.
April 11	:	Met political prisoners in Dum Dum and Alipur Jails.
April 12	:	Called on Khwaja Nazimuddin. Visited women political prisoners in Presidency Jail. Sent message to Gurukul, Kangri.
April 13	:	Observed Jallianwala Bagh Day by fasting. Issued Press statement about his negotiations with Government of Bengal regarding release of political prisoners and appealed for suspension of agitation while negotiations continued. Had discussions with Bengal Congressmen. Left Calcutta at night for Delhi.
April 14	:	Arrived in Delhi.
April 15	:	Had interview with Viceroy. Left Delhi for Wardha.
April 16	:	Arrived in Wardha, Segaon.
April 17 to 20	:	At Segaon.
April 21	:	Spoke at Vidyamandir Training School, Wardha.
April 24	:	Addressed meeting of Hindustani Talimi Sangh, Wardha.
April 27	:	Left Segaon for Bombay.
April 28	:	Arrived in Bombay. Had discussions with M.A. Jinnah. M.A. Jinnah and Gandhiji issued joint statement.
April 29	:	Gandhiji issued Press statements on Mysore firing and on appointment of Dain as acting Governor of Orissa. Had discussions with Sardar Vallabhbhai Patel and Purushottamdas Thakurdas. Left Bombay for Peshawar.
May 1	:	Reached Nowshera. Arrived in Peshawar by car.
May 4	:	Had interview with Governor of N. W. F. P. Addressed students of Islamia College. Met local Congress socialists.
May 5	:	Visited Khyber Pass and Torkham.
May 6	:	Visited Kulashabeg, Saudzai, Shabkadar and

		Tangi. Addressed meeting at Charsadda. Arrived in Utmanzai.
May 7	:	Addressed public meetings at Mardan and Kalukhan.
May 8	:	Returned to Peshawar in morning. Addressed Political Conference.
May 9	:	Left Peshawar for Bombay in morning.
May 11	:	Arrived in Bombay.
May 18	:	Met Sardar Prithvi Singh. Had discussions with Congress leaders.
May 19	:	Wrote to District Magistrate, Bombay, that Sardar Prithvi Singh of Lahore Conspiracy Case had surrendered himself. Had discussions with Jawaharlal Nehru.
May 20	:	Called on M. A. Jinnah. Sardar Prithvi Singh was arrested. Gandhiji issued Press statement of Prithvi Singh's arrest. Gave interview to James A. Mills of American Associated Press. Left Bombay for Segaon.
May 21	:	Arrived in Segaon.
May 28	:	Wrote foreword to Basic National Education.
June 6	:	Sent message to Indians in South Africa.
June 12	:	Received Dr. N. B. Khare at Segaon.
June 18	:	Met Bhulabhai Desai.
June 21	:	Had discussions with trainees under Wardha Scheme of Education.
June 22-23	:	Had discussions with Congress leaders about Bengal political prisoners and Hindu-Muslim unity.
June 28-29	:	Had talks with Dr. N. B. Khare.
July 6	:	Talked to trainees under Wardha Scheme of Edcuation.
July 25	:	Dr. N. B. Khare resigned. The Governor dismissed the other Ministers. Gandhiji had talks with Dr. N. B. Khare on C. P. ministerial crisis.
July 30	:	Issued statement to the Press regarding ministerial crisis in C. P.
July 31	:	Cholera broke out in Segaon.

August 18	:	Gandhiji took silence for indefinite period to recoup health.
August 21	:	Had talks with Nagpur Students's Deputation who had come to protest against Working Committee's resolution condemning Dr. N. B. Khare.
August 27	:	Had discussions with Harijan satyagrahis who were fasting to press their demand for inclusion of a Harijan in C.P. Cabinet.
August 29	:	Appealed to Harijan satyagrahis to give up fast.
September 5	:	Issued Press statement in reply to Dr. N. B. Khare's.
September 6	:	Issued Press statement demanding inquiry into police firings in Travancore.
September 19	:	Left Segaon for Delhi.
September 20	:	Arrived in Delhi. Called on ailing Begum Ansari.
September 21-22	:	Discussed (in writing) with Congress Working Committee his scheme of "Non-violent Militia".
September 23	:	Spoke at Working Committee on necessity of observing truth and non-violence.
September 24	:	Attended meeting of Congress Working Committee. Gave interview to F. S. Young, Inspector-General of Police, Jaipur State.
September 25	:	Congrees Working Committee passed resolution censuring Dr. N. B. Khare.
October 2	:	Congress Working Committee expelled Dr. N. B. Khare from Congress Party.
October 3	:	Gandhiji issued Press statement on Travancore situation.
October 4	:	Issued Press statement regarding release of polticial prisoners. Left Delhi for N.W.F.P.
October 5	:	Arrived in Peshawar.
October 9	:	Arrived in Utmanzai.
October 14	:	Visited industrial school for Khudai Khidmatgars at Kaimatang.
October 15, 1938	:	Gandhiji was at Utmanzai. Returned to Peshawar.
October 16	:	Addressed meetings of Khudai Khidmatgars at Nowshera and Hoti Mardan.

October 17	:	Mardan. Issued statement to the Press condemning students' rowdyism in Travancore.
	:	Visited Swabi and addressed meeting of Khudai Khidmatgars.
October 18	:	Returned to Utmanzai.
October 19/20	:	Had discussions with Khan Abdul Ghaffar Khan.
October 21	:	Returned to Peshawar. Arrived in Kohat.
October 22	:	Addressed public meeting at Kohat.
October 23	:	At Hungoo. Had talk with Khudai Khidmatgars.
October 24	:	At Bannu.
October 25	:	At Bannu. Addressed public meeting.
October 26	:	At Bannu. Issued statement to the Press Congratulating Maharaja and Dewan of Travancore for granting amnesty to satyagrahi prisoners in the State. Visited Lakki. Addressed public meeting. Had talk with Khudai Khidmatgars.
October 27	:	Arrived in Dera Ismail Khan.
October 28	:	At Dera Ismail Khan. Addressed public meeting.
October 30	:	Visited Kulachi. Returned to Dera Ismail Khan.
October 31	:	Tonk. Addressed public meeting. Had talk with Khudai Khidmatgars. Returned to Dera Ismail Khan.
November 1	:	Had talk with Khudai Khidmatgars at Paniala.
	:	Arrived in Mirakhel.
November 2	:	At Mirakhel. Visited Ahmedbandh. Reached Peshawar in the evening.
November 3	:	At Peshawar. Inaugurated khadi exhibition.
November 4	:	At Peshawar.
November 5	:	At Peshawar. Addressed meeting of the Bar Association.
November 6	:	At Peshawar. Visited Bibhuti, Punja Saheb and Haripur.
November 7	:	At Haripur, Abbottabad. Had talk with Khudai Khidmatgars.
November 8	:	At Abbottabad. Reached Mansherra. Addressed public meeting. Returned to Abbottabad. Received Minorities' Deputation. Addressed

		public meeting.
November 9	:	At Abbottabad. Visited Taxila. Left for Delhi.
November 10	:	Arrived in Delhi. Called on Begum Ansari. Left for Segaon.
November 11	:	Arrived in Segaon.
November 14	:	Had discussion with Vallabhbhai Patel about Rajkot satyagraha.
November 15	:	Had discussion with Deputation of Travancore State Congress.
November 16	:	Continued discussion.
November 21	:	Received Jawaharlal Nehru.
November 27	:	Had discussion with leaders of Aundh State.
November 29	:	Had discussion with Appasaheb Pant on Aundh Constitution.
November 30	:	Started drafting constitution for Aundh State.
December 1	:	Had discussion with Appasaheb Pant.
December 3	:	Discussed with Ruikar strike in Rajanandgaon Mill and State policy towards it.
December 15	:	Had discussion with members of Congress Working Committee.
December 22	:	Addressed Scouts rally.
December 23	:	Dr. Radhakrishnan called on Gandhiji and suggested his persuading Rajaji not to make Hindi compulsory in Madras State.
December 24	:	Gandhiji arrived in Wardha. Inaugurated Magan Sangrahalaya and Udyog Bhavan. Had discussion with the economists who attended Economic Conference at Nagpur. Had discussion with Frydman. Returned to Segaon.
December 31	:	Gave Interview to Timothy Ling Fang Lew, member of Chinese delegation to Missionary Conference at Tambaram.

1939

January 1	:	Gave interview to Ling Fang Lew and P.C. Hsu, members of Chinese delegation to Missionary Conference at Tambaram. Gave interview to Rev. S. S. Temo of D. R. Mission, Johannesburg. Left for Bardoli.

January 2	:	Arrived in Bardoli.
January 3	:	Had discussion with U.N. Dhebar about Rajkot satyagraha.
January 4	:	Had talk with Jamnalal Bajaj concerning Jaipur satyagraha.
January 11-14	:	Attended Congress Working Committee meeting.
January 15	:	Had talk with Toyohiko Kagawa. Had discussion with the Aga Khan about minority community and communal unity.
January 17	:	Received B. G. Kher.
January 23	:	Vallabhbhai Patel arrived in Bardoli to discuss Rajkot affairs with Gandhiji.
January 24	:	Gandhiji had talk with Pattabhi Sitaramayya.
January 26	:	Addressed meeting of peasants on emancipation day.
January 28	:	Had discussion with representatives of Municipalities and Local Boards.
January 29	:	Addressed meeting of peasants held on occasion of restoration of confiscated lands.
January 31	:	Issued statements to the Press on election of Subhas Chandra Bose as Congress President and on Rajkot and Jaipur satyagrahas.
February 1	:	Left for Segaon.
February 2	:	Arrived in Segaon.
February 3-4	:	At Wardha. Had talk with teachers undergoing training under Wardha scheme of education.
February 5	:	At Segaon.
February 8	:	Issued statement to the Press on Jamnalal Bajaj's arrest.
February 9	:	Issued statement to the Press on Rajkot and Jaipur satyagraha.
February 13	:	Had discussion with Dr. Chesterton of English Baptist Mission.
February 14	:	Subhas Chandra Bose arrived in Segaon to have discussion with Gandhiji.
February 15	:	Discussion continued.
February 21	:	Gandhiji had talk with delegates of Hyderabad State Congress.

February 23 : Issued statements to the Press on strike in Annamalai University and Rajkot satyagraha.

February 24 : Had talk with Ashram inmates about his decision to go to Rajkot.

February 25 : Issued statement to the Press on Rajkot satyagraha. Left for Bombay en route to Rajkot.

February 26 : Arrived in Bombay.

February 27 : Arrived in Rajkot. Gave interview to Associated Press and *The Hindu*.

February 28 : Had separate discussions with representatives of Muslim Council of Action and deputation of Garasia Mandal. Gave interview to *The Hindu*.

March 1 : Gandhiji was in Rajkot; interview to Associated Press of India.

March 2 : In statement to the Press, Gandhiji announced decision to go on fast if his request to Thakore Saheb was not complied with.

March 3 : Commenced fast; issued statement to the Press and released letter to Thakore Saheb; had discussion with Fateh Mohammed Khan.

March 4 : In statement to the Press, appealed to Congressmen "to make supreme efforts to clean the Congress house of proved corruption and impurities".

March 6 : Had discussion with Agatha Harrison.

March 7 : Broke fast; issued statement to the Press.

March 8 : Had talk with Agatha Harrison.

March 9 : In telegram to Jawaharlal Nehru and Subhas Chandra Bose, emphasized need for resolution "to rid Congress of internal corruption". Appealed to people of Rajkot to become worthy of "responsible government".

March 11 : In statement to the Press, declined "to give a decisive opinion" on question of revival of civil resistance in Travancore.

March 14 : Had discussion with Haribhau Upadhyaya and others on Jaipur Satyagraha.

March 15 : In Delhi had two-hour meeting with Viceroy; in Delhi Jail persuaded prisoners to give up

		hunger-strike.
March 16	:	Had another meeting with Viceroy; interview to Gobind Bihari Lal; Gandhiji had discussion with Hyderabad Aryasamaj leaders on Hyderabad Satyagraha.
March 18	:	Spoke at opening ceremony of Lakshmi Narayan Temple and Buddha Vihara.
March 19	:	Asked Jaipur Satyagraha Council to postpone despatch of satyagrahis to Jaipur.
March 20	:	In statement to the Press, condemned action of Travancore Dewan in arresting Pattom Thanu Pillai and other Congress leaders. Had separate discussions with Travancore Satyagrahis and Jaipur satyagrahis.
Before March 23	:	Interview to *The New York Times*.
March 23	:	Gandhiji issued statement advising suspension of Travancore Satyagraha.
March 24	:	In Allahabad, called on Abul Kalam Azad; left for Delhi.
March 25	:	In telegram to R. K. Jha, confirmed that statement suspending Travancore Satyagraha contemplated similar action in Nandgaon State.
March 26	:	In *Harijan*, commended Bombay Government's decision to introduce prohibition from August 1, 1939.
March 29/30	:	Had discussion with Agatha Harrison.
March 30	:	In letter to Subhas Chandra Bose gave permission to publish their correspondence.
March 31	:	Had discussion with inmates of Birla House on communal situation in Allahabad.
April 3	:	Sir Maurice Gwyer gave verdict in favour of Vallabhbhai Patel.
April 4	:	Gandhiji issued statement to the Press on Bombay prohibition programme; in another statement condemned repression in Travancore.
April 6	:	Had meeting with Viceroy.
April 7	:	Left for Rajkot.
April 9	:	Reached Rajkot.

April 11	:	Met E. C. Gibson.
April 12	:	Bhayats and Muslims met Gandhiji.
April 14	:	On behalf of Vallabhbhai Patel, Gandhiji wrote to Dharmendrasinh suggesting seven names for Reforms Committee.
April 15	:	Issued statement to the Press regarding nomination of seven names for Reforms Committee.
April 16	:	Muslims and Garasias staged a demonstration at prayer; Gandhiji issued statement.
April 17	:	In telegram to Satyamurti disapproved observing of 'Kenya Day' on May 14.
April 18	:	In telegram to Lord Linlithgow, reminded him of 20,000 Talcher refugees.
April 19	:	Suffered from gastric flu.
April 20	:	Met Gibson with "the sporting offer" namely, "Parishad should withdraw from the proposed Committee altogether and that the Thakore Saheb should nominate his own Committee" in terms of December 26 Settlement.
April 22	:	Met Virawala; gave statement to Associated Press of India.
April 23	:	In letter informed Gibson of Virawala's rejection of "sporting offer"; addressed meeting of Praja Parishad workers.
April 24	:	Left for Bombay; issued statement to the Press on his defeat in Rajkot.
April 25	:	Reached Bombay; left for Calcutta.
April 27	:	On train, between Kharagpur and Calcutta, interview to *The Statesman*.
April 29	:	In letter to Subhas Bose Gandhiji said:". . . knowing how you and most of the members differ on fundamentals . . . you are free to choose your own Committee".
	:	Subhas Bose resigned from Congress Presidentship after reading out Gandhiji's letter at A.I.C.C. meeting.
May 1	:	Gandhiji left for Brindaban (Bihar).

May 3	:	Spoke at opening of Village Industries Exhibition.
May 4	:	Spoke at Teachers' Training Camp.
May 5	:	Answered questions at Gandhi Seva Sangh meeting.
May 6	:	Answered questions at Gandhi Seva Sangh meeting.
May 7	:	Answered questions at Gandhi Seva Sangh meeting; addressed All-India Village Industries Board; also addressed public meeting.
May 8	:	Left for Benares to see Madan Mohan Malaviya.
May 11	:	In Bombay, interview to the Press.
May 12	:	Gandhiji reached Rajkot; spoke at meeting of Praja Parishad workers.
	:	In interview to A.P.I., regretted anti-Asiatic policy of South Africa Union Government.
	:	In a personal letter to Virawala mentioned "the double game" he was playing.
On or after May 12	:	In talk to Praja Parishad workers confessed his "impatience" in attitude to problem of Bhayats and Mussalmans.
May 13/14	:	Interview to Travancore National Congress delegation.
May 15	:	In talk to Praja Parishad workers Gandhiji expressed desire to renounce Gwyer Award.
May 17	:	In statement to the Press, renounced Gwyer Award. Had discussion with Mahadev Desai.
After May 17	:	Had talks with co-workers on his decision to give up the Award; interview to Steel of *The New York Times*.
May 18	:	Gandhiji had discussion with Kasturba Gandhi.
May 20	:	Attended Durbar at Rajkot Palace.
On or after May 20	:	Had talk with co-workers who remonstrated with Gandhiji for attending the Rajkot Durbar.
May 23	:	In message, advised South Africa Indians to fight unitedly the Union Government's "policy of progressive stringency in their anti-Asiatic drive"; addressed public meeting.
May 31	:	Spoke at Executive Committee Meeting of

Kathiawar Political Conference.

June 1 : Accompanied by Kasturba Gandhi, Mahadev Desai, Pyarelal and Dr. Sushila Nayyar, Gandhiji left Rajkot for Bombay by Kathiawar Mail. On train, had discussion with Travancore State Congress deputation.

June 2 : Reached Bombay. Interview to Bombay Victuallers' Association representatives, which was followed by Parsi deputation led by Cowasji Jehangir.

June 4 : Gandhiji issued statement explaining his new technique of action in Travancore.

June 6 : Interview to deputation of Kolhapur Praja Parishad.

June 7 : Left Bombay for Segaon.

June 11 : In *Harijan* article "Meaning of Prohibition", replied to letter from Archbishop of Bombay.

June 13 : Interview to Mysore Congress representatives.

June 20 : Accompanied by Mahadev Desai, Pyarelal and Dr. Sushila Nayyar, Gandhiji left Segaon for Bombay.

June 23 : In Bombay, drafted resolutions for the All-India Congress Committee.

June 27 : In *Harijan,* wrote on "The National Flag".

July 4 : Visited Chemical Industrial and Pharmaceutical Laboratories.

July 5 : At Bombay Central, before leaving for Frontier Province, received *Aim of Japan's Expansion in China* from Chinese monks.

: Before boarding Frontier Mail, received from S.K. Bole, who had led group of forty Bhandaris, petition to Premier of Bombay and assured him that they "will not be allowed to starve".

: Left for Peshawar. Mahadev Desai accompanied him. Kasturba Gandhi, Pyarelal and Dr. Sushila Nayyar stayed back.

July 7 : Gandhiji reached Abbottabad in the evening.

July 8 : In statement to the Press urged Bengal political prisoners "not to take to hunger-strike".

: Meenakshi Temple in Madurai was thrown open to Harijans.

July 9 : Interview to L. W. Jardine of M. R. A.

July 10 : Gandhiji had discussion with Jayaprakash Narayan, who spoke about Kisan Sabha and Congress in Bihar and also about Socialist Party's attitude towards Forward Bloc.

July 13 : In statement, Gandhiji expressed regret over Subhas Chandra Bose's opposition to Bombay prohibition scheme.

July 14 : Kasturba Gandhi, Pyarelal and Dr. Sushila Nayyar reached Abbottabad.

July 15 : In statement to the Press, Gandhiji urged Bengal Government to release the political prisoners.

July 16 : Gandhiji was in Abbottabad since July 7.

July 17 : In letter to Sikandar Hyat Khan, expressed inability to agree with his alternative scheme of Federation.

July 22 : In statement to the Press, announced cancellation of his visit to Kashmir. Interview to Provincial Congress Committee members.

July 23 : Message to Bombay Government Prohibition Board on decision to promulgate prohibition in Bombay from August. In letter to Adolf Hitler, Gandhiji appealed to him as "the one person in the world who can prevent a war which may reduce humanity to the savage state".

: Spoke at Abbottabad.

On or before July 26: Discussion with Dr. Charles Fabri.

July 26 : Gandhiji left Abbottabad for Wardha. Kasturba Gandhi, Mahadev Desai, Pyarelal and Dr. Sushila Nayyar accompanied him.

July 27 : At Ghaziabad Station in the morning, Gandhiji got down and proceeded to Delhi in motorcar.

: At about 10.30 a.m., at Harijan Colony presided over first convocation of Harijan Industrial Home and gave away certificates to students.

: In afternoon, interview to Ghanshyamsingh Gupta, Speaker, Central Provinces Legislative

Assembly, Vinayak Rao of Arya Samaj Satyagraha in Hyderabad State, and Deshbandhu Gupta, who places before him correspondence between Ghanshyamsingh Gupta and Akbar Hydari regarding reforms. Gandhiji advised Himalayan States Peoples' Conference deputation to meet Jawaharlal Nehru, their President, in connection with firing in Dhami.

: Left Delhi for Wardha by Grand Trunk Express.

July 31 : S.K. Bole in his letter to Gandhiji said that "the signatories to the memorial acted bona fide and they never intended to offer any threat to the Bombay Ministry".

August 1 : In telegram to Viceroy, Gandhiji regretted his inability to see him in Delhi on August 5.

August 3 : Bengal political prisoners decided to suspend hunger-strike.

Before August 4 : In letter to president, Tanzeem-ul-Mominin, Gandhiji advised withdrawal of civil disobedience started by Shias in early June as a result of the Shia-Sunni dispute.

August 5 : In discussion, persuaded V. V. Sathe, a satyagrahi, to postpone his proposed fast to seek redress of grievances against Bombay Government.

August 7 : Rajagopalachari introduced in Madras Legislative Council Temple-entry Authorization and Indemnity Bill as passed by Madras Legislative Assembly.

August 8 : "Arya Satyagraha" was called off.

August 11 : The Congress Working Committee passed resolution disqualifying Subhas Chandra Bose from being President of Bengal Provincial Congress Committee for three years from August 30.

August 23 : In statement to the Press, Gandhiji replied to criticisms against two resolutions of Congress Working Committee—one disqualifying Subhas Chandra Bose and other on war.

August 27 : In statement to the Press on international crisis, declared: "I cannot emphasize my belief more

		forcibly than by saying that I personally would not purchase my own country's freedom by violence even if such a thing were a possibility."
Before August 30	:	In message to Poles, sent "good wishes and blessings".
August 31	:	In telegram to G. D. Birla, advised commercial community to "remain silent" on international crisis till "actual result is known".
September 2	:	Left for Simla in response to invitation from Viceroy.
September 3	:	England and France declared war on Germany.
September 4	:	Interview with Viceroy.
September 5	:	Gandhiji left for Wardha. Issued statement on Simla visit. Sabarmati Ashram was officially declared as 'Harijan Ashram'.
September 8	:	Congress Working Committee meeting began in Wardha.
September 11	:	Viceroy addressed Legislative Assembly; announced postponement of Federation.
September 15	:	Gandhiji gave statement to the Press on Congress Working Committee's Manifesto.
	:	Congress Working Committee concluded its meeting.
September 20	:	Gandhiji issued statement suggesting mode of action by the Ministries in view of Congress Working Committee Manifesto.
September 23 and 24	:	Discussion with members of Oxford Group.
September 24	:	Gandhiji left for Simla on being invited by Viceroy for second round of talks.
September 26	:	In Simla, interview with Viceroy.
September 27	:	Gandhiji left for Segaon.
September 28	:	At Nagpur railway station, answered questions on interview with Viceroy. In statement to the Press, appealed to Lord Zetland to "forget the old language of imperialists and open a new chapter for all those who have been held under imperial bondage".
October 2	:	In Delhi, discussion with Rajendra Prasad and

		Jawaharlal Nehru before their meeting with Viceroy.
October 3	:	In message to British people through *The Manchester Guardian,* Gandhiji appealed for Britain's sincerity in "professions about democracy".
October 5	:	Interview with Viceroy.
October 6	:	Gandhiji reached Segaon.
October 7–10	:	In Wardha attended Congress Working Committee meeting.
October 10	:	A.I.C.C. passed Working Committee resolution on war. In *Harijan* article "On Trial", Gandhiji observed that "Congressmen are unprepared for non-violent defence against armed invasion" and he declared, "it is better for India to discard violence altogether even for defending her borders".
October 12	:	In letter to Dr. B. C. Roy, declined to shoulder burden of leading Congress and suggested to have Jawaharlal Nehru for that post.
October 13	:	In statement, described A.I.C.C. resolution on war as "moderate and wise" and appealed to Congressmen "to desist from any action that would savour of indiscipline or defiance".
October 17	:	Viceroy made declaration of India's political future and her attitude to war.
October 18	:	In statement to the Press, Gandhiji characterized Viceroy's declaration as "profoundly disappointing".
October 19	:	At Wardha, in conference of Central Provinces and Berar Local Bodies' representatives, spoke on the Basic Education Scheme.
October 20	:	At Segaon, interview to *The Times of India*.
October 22	:	In note to Police Superintendent and Deputy Commissioner, Gandhiji declined their offer to arrange for his protection.
	:	Congress Working Committee passed resolution calling upon "Congress Ministries to tender their resignations".

October 23	:	In cable to world Press, Gandhiji declared: "Congress has left the door open to Britain to mend the mistake".
October 25–26	:	Discussion with members of Gandhi Seva Sangh.
October 27	:	In statement to the Press, Gandhiji appreciated conciliatory tone of Sir Samuel Hoare's speech in House of Commons but criticized his plea for protection of minorities in rejecting the Congress demand. Madras Ministry tendered resignation.
October 28	:	Message to Basic Education Conference, Poona.
October 31	:	Gandhiji left for Delhi to meet Viceroy.
	:	In *Harijan* article "The Congressmen", said, "for decisive action, the whole Congress has to move forward in confidence and with one mind."
November 1	:	During his journey to Delhi wrote to Chinese Premier and children of China, expressing sympathy in their hardship caused by Japanese aggression. In Delhi, along with Rajendra Prasad and M. A. Jinnah, had joint conference with Viceroy. Continued talks with Jinnah at the latter's residence.
November 2	:	Spoke at opening ceremony of Prayer Hall in Harijan Nivas.
November 4	:	Interview with Viceroy. In interview to The Manchester Guardian, Gandhiji said 'he was shocked at Lord Zetland's suggestion that the Congress is a Hindu organization.'
November 5	:	At Nagpur, interview to the Press. Viceroy, in a broadcast, declared that his "disappointment" at the leaders' refusal to agree to his proposal to expand Governor-General's Executive Council to include representatives of the Congress and the Muslim League was not "final" and that he would not "abandon the efforts. . . to bring about a friendly adjustment".
November 7	:	In *Harijan* article "Opinions Differ", Gandhiji expressed hope that talks between Jinnah and Jawaharlal Nehru would result in producing "a basis for a lasting solution of the communal tangle".

November 8 : In statement to the Press, referred to Viceroy's broadcast and Press statement and urged Britain to free India from bondage.

November 14 : Cabled statement to *The News Chronicle*, London.

November 18 : Left for Allahabad.

November 19 : In *Harijan* article "The Only Way", said, "the Constituent Assembly provides the easiest method of arriving at a just solution of the communal problem."

: At Allahabad, attended Congress Working Committee meeting; laid foundation-stone for Kamala Nehru Memorial Hospital and addressed a large gathering.

November 22 : Congress Working Committee considered Gandhiji's draft resolution on political situation in India.

November 23 : Gandhiji gave testimonial to Munnilal, a barber.

: Congress Working Committee passed Gandhiji's resolution.

: In letter addressed to Subhas Chandra Bose, Gandhiji explained that he was party to ban imposed on Bose. Discussion with U. P. Congress workers.

November 24 : In letter to people of Mysore, Gandhiji disapproved of Forest Satyagraha.

November 25 : Reached Wardha.

November 27 : In *Harijan* article, "Swaraj through Women", exhorted women to take up spinning.

December 1 : Gandhiji was at Segaon.

December 2 : In cable to Agatha Harrison stated that "no progress possible without unequivocal declaration independence".

December 3 : Sent message to The Hindu on its diamond jubilee. Had discussion with C. Rajagopalachari.

December 4 : Sent cable to The News Chronicle stating that declaration of British policy about India was a purely moral issue.

December 6 : M.A. Jinnah issued statement calling upon Mussalmans to observe December 22 as "Day of Deliverance" from Congress Ministries.

December 7 : Sir Stafford Cripps arrived at Karachi.

December 8 : Gandhiji met Hirday Nath Kunzru.

December 9 : In statement to Press appealed to M. A. Jinnah to desist from observing "Day of Deliverance" in view of unity talks and await Viceroy's and Governor's opinion on allegations made by Muslim League against Congress. Sir Daniel Hamilton died in Scotland.

Before December 10 : Gandhiji sent message to Jabalpore District Political Conference.

December 10 : Sent condolences to Lady Hamilton.

December 17 : Through Harijan appealed to correspondents and message-seekers to spare him.

December 18 : Attended Congress Working Committee meeting.

December 19 : Congress Working Committee meeting continued. Sir Stafford Cripps called on Gandhiji.

December 20 : Gandhiji continued discussion with Sir Stafford Cripps.

Before December 22 : Congress Working Committee passed resolution on Independence Day Pledge.

December 22 : Gandhiji sent telegram to Rabindranath Tagore intimating Working Committee's inability to lift ban against Subhas Chandra Bose.

: Congress Working Committee session concluded.

: Muslim League observed "Day of Deliverance".

December 27 : Gandhiji addressed Nagpur Provincial Congress Workers at Wardha.

1940

On or before January 2 : Sent cable to Ismet Inonu expressing sympathy on earthquake in Turkey.

Before January 6 : Had discussion with Christian missionaries.

Before January 7 : Gave interview to an English reporter.

On or before January 8 : Sent condolences on Lala Shamlal's death. Sent condolences to Hirday Nath Kunzru on Venkatasubbiah's death.

January 8 : In *Harijan* paid tribute to Venkatasubbiah.

January 9 and 10 : Had discussion with Bhai Paramanand.

January 13 : Met C. Rajagopalachari.

January 14 : Wrote to Lord Linlithgow regarding his Bombay speech and expressed willingness to see him if so desired.

Before January 15 : Had discussion with English Pacifists.

January 15 : Had discussion with Rajendra Prasad and C. Rajagopalachari.

: In *Harijan* congratulated M.A. Jinnah on forming pact with other political parties.

January 17 : Expressed doubt in letter to Lord Linlithgow whether time had "arrived for our meeting" in view of interviews the Viceroy had with Bhulabhai Desai, K. M. Munshi and B. G. Kher.

January 19 : Attended Congress Working Committee meeting.

January 20 : Had discussion with Bengal leaders. C.W.C. meeting continued.

January 21 : C.W.C. session concluded.

January 22 : Gandhiji had discussion with Subhas Chandra Bose.

January 23 : Wrote to Lord Linlithgow that he could reach Delhi any day after February 4.

January 25 : Through Press issued warning against sale and purchase of uncertified khadi.

January 26 : Independence Day celebrated.

Before January 27 : Gandhiji sent message to All-India Women's Conference.

January 31 : Gave interview to Holmes Smith.

February 3 : Left Wardha for Delhi. En route gave interview to Associated Press at Nagpur.

February 4 : Reached Delhi. Met Sir Sikandar Hayat Khan.

February 5 : Had interview with Viceroy at 11 a.m. Government communique on interview issued in evening.

February 6 : Gave statement to Press about difference between Congress demand and Viceregal offer. Left Delhi for Wardha. En route gave interview to Press at Jhansi.

February 7	:	Sent cable to *The News Chronicle.* Cabled statement to *The Daily Herald,* London. Sent message to mill-workers, Ahmedabad.
February 8	:	Had discussion with Gulzarilal Nanda.
February 9	:	Gave interview to Harbans Singh.
February 14	:	Iussed statement to Press on Zetland's interview to *The Sunday Times.*
February 15	:	Left Wardha in evening.
February 17	:	Reached Calcutta in morning : later proceeded to Santiniketan.
	:	At Santiniketan spoke in reply to address in afternoon.
February 18	:	Visited Sriniketan. Had discussion with Rabindranath Tagore. Attended dramatic performance of "Chandalika".

On or before February 19 : Had discussion with Pacifists.

February 19	:	Left Santiniketan. Reached Calcutta in afternoon. Visited C.F. Andrews at Presidency General Hospital. Called on N. R. Sarkar. Left Calcutta at night.
February 20	:	Reached Malikanda. Opened Khadi and Village Industries Exhibition; visited injured volunteers at hospital. Made will in favour of "Navajivan" about copyrights of his writings.
February 21	:	Addressed Gandhi Seva Sangh and advised it to give up politics.
February 22	:	Spoke at Gandhi Seva Sangh meeting.
	:	Gandhi Seva Sangh passed resolution eschewing politics and confining itself to constructive programme.
February 24	:	Spoke at Bengal Worker's Conference. Addressed Bengal women workers.
February 25	:	Spoke at public meeting. Left Malikanda.
February 26	:	Reached Calcutta.

Before February 27 : Sent message to people of Manipur.

February 27	:	Gave message to Press for Bengal. Left for Patna.
February 28	:	Reached Patna. Attended Congress Working Committee meeting. Had discussion with Socialists.

February 29 : C.W.C. meeting continued. Bengal Provincial Congress Committee suspended.

March 1 : Gandhiji attended C.W.C. meeting. Met Scheduled Caste representatives.

: C.W.C. approved resolution to launch civil disobedience as soon as organization was considered fit enough or "in case circumstances so shaped themselves as to precipitate a crisis" and recommended it for Congress session at Ramgarh.

March 2 : Gandhiji reached Calcutta. Issued statement to Press on Patna Resolution clarifying that Congress had not closed door on negotiation but it could not be on Zetland's terms.

March 3 : Arrived in Segaon.

March 5 : Notified in Harijan change of name from 'Segaon' to 'Sevagram'.

March 7 : Jayaprakash Narayan was arrested.

Before March 12 : Gandhiji had discussion with a missionary.

March 12 : Had discussion with Christian missionaries. Left for Ramgarh in evening.

March 13 : Sir Michael O'Dwyer shot dead and Zetland, Lamington and Sir Louis Dane wounded in London.

March 14 : At Ramgarh Gandhiji opened Khadi and Village Industries Exhibition.

: Issued statement to Press condemning Michael O'Dwyer's assassination. Sent condolences to Michael O'Dwyer's family.

March 15 and 16 : Attended Congress Working Committee meeting.

March 17 : Attended Subject Committee meeting.

March 18 : Addressed Subjects Committee. Spoke at Exhibition.

March 19 : At Ranchi opended Thakkar Bhavan and Industrial Home for Harijans and Aborigines in morning. Returned to Ramgarh. Gave interview to Associated Press.

March 20 : Spoke at Congress session. Gave interview to Ceylonese National Congress delegation. Patna

		Resolution passed.
March 21	:	On way to Wardha.
March 22	:	Arrived at Wardha in morning. At All-India Muslim League's session at Lahore M. A. Jinnah suggested division of India "into autonomous national States".
March 26	:	In *Harijan* Gandhiji refuted M. A. Jinnah's allegation that Congress was a Hindu organization.
March 30	:	Spoke at Khadi Yatra.
March 31	:	Had discussion with delegates of Khadi Yatra.
April 1	:	Had discussion with Gandhi Seva Sangh Committee.
April 3	:	Met Ghanshyamsingh Gupta.
April 5	:	C. F. Andrews died. In statement to Press Gandhiji paid tribute to C. F. Andrews.
Before April 7	:	Had discussion with a Chinese visitor.
April 12	:	Telegraphed congratulations to Jamnalal Bajaj on settlement between Jaipur State and Jaipur Rajya Praja Mandal.
April 15	:	Attended Congress Working Committee meeting.
April 16	:	Sevagram. Gandhiji attended Congress Working Committee meeting at Wardha.
April 17	:	Attended Congress Working Committee meeting at Wardha. Had discussion with Jawaharlal Nehru.
April 20	:	Had discussion with Maulana Azad.
April 24	:	K. M. Munshi called on Gandhiji.
May 3	:	Gandhiji attended All-India Education Conference. Had discussion with R.S. Pandit about Congress Volunteer Corps.
May 9	:	In an interview to *The Times of India* said that he would "welcome a settlement which ensures peace with honour".
May 16	:	Received a delegation of Red Shirts ; Jawaharlal Nehru was present.
May 17	:	Gandhiji had discussion with Jawaharlal Nehru.
May 18	:	Wrote Foreword to Maulana Abul Kalam Azad.

May 24 : Took silence for indefinite period from 7.30 a.m. In an interview to Associated Press refused to comment on Amery's statement in House of Commons.

June 2 : There was a theft of a pen and some letters in Ashram.

June 3 : Announced his intention to fast from June 8 if theft was not traced.

June 8 : Gave up proposed fast over theft incident as all Ashram inmates were against it.

June 17-19 : Attended meetings of the Congress Working Committee at Wardha.

June 20 : Sevagram. Maulana Azad called in the morning.

: Gandhiji had discussion with Subhas Chandra Bose.

June 21 : Attended joint meeting of Gandhi Seva Sangh and Charkha Sangh at Wardha.

: The Congress Working Committee passed resolution absolving Gandhiji from responsibility of future programme and policies of the Congress.

June 22 : Gandhiji addressed a joint meeting of Gandhi Seva Sangh and Charkha Sangh at Wardha.

: Was present at the meeting of Rashtrabhasha Seva Sangh, Wardha.

: Had long discussion with Pattabhi Sitaramayya, Rajagopalachari, Rajendra Prassad and Jamnalal Bajaj.

June 27 : Left for Delhi en route to Simla accompanied by Jamnalal Bajaj, Mahadev Desai, Pyarelal and others.

June 28 : Arrived in Delhi. Had discussion with Asaf Ali. Left for Simla.

June 29 : At Simla. Met the Viceroy. Left for New Delhi.

June 30 : New Delhi. Attended public prayer at Harijan colony.

July 2 : New Delhi. Issued appeal " To Every Briton' to fight Nazism with 'non-violent arms'.

July 3	:	Attended meeting of the Congress Working Committee on special invitation and reported to the Committee on his interview with the Viceroy.
July 4 and 5	:	Attended meetings of the Congress Working Committee.
July 6	:	Attended meeting of the Congress Working Committee. Discussed political situation with Aney.
July 7	:	The Congress Working Committee passed resolution stating that Britain should immediately make in unequivocal declaration according complete inde pendence to India. Left New Delhi for Wardha.
July 8	:	Reached Wardha and then proceeded to Sevagram. Declared copyright on translations of all his articles.
July 10	:	Had discussion with Rajagopalachari.
July 13	:	At Wardha attended the wedding of Uma, youngest daughter of Jamnalal Bajaj.
July 20	:	Emily Kinnaird called on Gandhiji to persuade him to adopt Christianty.
July 21	:	Gandhiji had long meeting with Pandit Kunzru. Kodanda Rao meet Gandhiji.
July 23	:	Dr. Profulla Chandra Ghosh met Gandhiji.
July 24	:	Gandhiji had a long discussion with Maulana Azad, Rajendra Prasad and Profulla Chandra Ghosh.
July 30	:	Rajagopalachari, Profulla Chandra Ghosh and Gopinath Bardoloi met Gandhiji.
August 1	:	Gandhiji had a long talk with Rajagopalachari.
August 2	:	Maulana Azad met Gandhiji in the morning.
August 10	:	Gandhiji had discussion with Jamnalal Bajaj about Jaipur affairs.
August 17	:	Maulana Azad arrived for discussion.
August 18	:	Gandhiji had long discussion with Maulana Azad. Attended Congress Working Committee meeting at Wardha.

August 19 : Attended Congress Working Committee meeting at Wardha.

August 20 : Attended afternoon session of Congress Working Committee meeting at Wardha.

August 21 : Attended afternoon session of Congress Working Committee meeting at Wardha.

August 22 : Attended afternoon session of Congress Working Committee meeting at Wardha.

August 23 : Sardar Patel, Nehru and Maulana Azad met Gandhiji.

August 24 : Gandhiji had discussion with Maulana Azad in the morning. Later other Congress leaders also came. Attended meeting of National Planning Committee at Wardha.

August 25 : Went to Wardha to have discussion with the Congress leaders.

September 5 : Attended meeting of Congress Working Committee at Wardha.

September 6 : Sevagram: Attended wedding of Dakshayani and Velayudhan.

September 8 : Attended the Bullocks festival.

September 10 : Syed Mahmud and Abdul Ghaffar Khan arrived for talks with Gandhiji.

September 11 : Gandhiji had meeting with Abdul Ghafar Khan.

: Left for Bombay accompained by Kasturba, Abdul Ghaffar Khan and Syed Mahmud.

September 12 : Gandhiji arrived in Bombay; had informal discussions with Abul Kalam Azad, Sardar Patel, Pandit Nehru and other members of the Congress Working Committee.

September 13 : Attended Congress Working Committee meeting.

September 15 and 16: Addressed A.I.C.C. meeting.

September 17 : Attended Congress Working Committee meeting.

September 18 : Attended Congress Working Committee meeting; left for Wardha.

September 19 : Reached Wardha; walked to Sevagram.

September 20 : C. Rajagopalachari arrived in Wardha to discuss with Gandhi the future programme of the

		Congress in the light of the A.I.C.C. resolution.
September 25	:	Gandhiji left for Simla accompanied by Mahadev Desai and Pyarelal.
September 26	:	Arrived in Delhi in the morning; left for Simla in the evening.
September 27	:	At Simla, had a meeting with the Viceroy.
September 29	:	Met Harijan leaders.
September 30	:	Interview with the Viceroy; left for Delhi.
October 1	:	In Delhi, had long talk with Bhulabhai Desai and J.B. Kripalani; attended a function at Harijan Colony to celebrate his 72nd birthday; left for Wardha.
October 2	:	In Sevagram, addressed meeting to celebrate his birthday.
October 10	:	Had discussion with Profulla Chandra Ghosh.
October 11	:	Attended the Congress Working Committee meeting.
October 12 and 13	:	Attended Congress Working Committee meeting.
October 13	:	The Congress Working Committee approved Gandhiji's plan for individual civil disobedience. Gandhiji went to Paunar for discussion with Vinoba Bhave.
October 15	:	In Sevagram, issued statement that Vinoba Bhave would be the first satyagrahi to start individual civil disobedience.
October 17	:	At Paunar, Vinoba Bhave began the individual satyagraha by delivering anti-war speech.
October 18	:	The District Magistrate, Poona, served notice on the Editors of *Harijan,* and allied weeklies directing them to submit to the Chief Press Adviser in Delhi all the news regarding Vinoba Bhave's satyagraha before publication.
October 21	:	Vinoba Bhave was arrested under the Defence of India Act.
	:	Gandhiji issued a statement advising Congressmen not to be impatient about the next step.
October 24	:	Announced the temporary suspension of *Harijan, Harijanbandhu* and *Harijan Sevak.*

October 30 : Had seven hours' discussion with Jawaharlal Nehru.

November 4 : Informed the Viceroy of his proposal to fast.

November 5 : At Wardha, attended Congress Working Committee meeting.

November 6 : Attended Congress Working Committee meeting. Gave up his proposed fast as Congress agreed to an extension of individual satyagraha.

November 7 : Gave away Dr. Soundaram in marriage to G. Ramachandran. Attended Congress Working Committee meeting.

November 8 : Attended Congress Working Committee meeting. Attended wedding of Sharad Parnerkar.

November 13 : Drafted a list of nearly 1,500 individual satyagrahis.

Novembtr 15 : Interview to Senanayake, Ceylonese Minister.

November 16 : In telegram to Amtussalaam, said that he was "stopping civil disobedience [in] Sind".

November 17 : Vallabhbhai Patel was arrested.

November 18 : Arthur Moore of *The Statesman* met Gandhiji.

November 23 : Gandhiji had discussion with Tai Chi-Tao, President of Examination Yuan of Chinese Government.

Before November 24:Interview to M. L. Shah, General Secretary, All-India Students' Federation.

November 29 : In statement to the Press, Gandhiji exhorted students to express their national sympathy in a disciplined manner and not by resorting to strikes.

Before December 3: In telegram, instructed Rajendra Prasad to prevent demonstration in connection with civil disobedience movement.

December 5 : Subhas Chandra Bose was released.

On or before December 6: In telegram to Barada Prasanna Pain, Gandhiji regretted his inability to recommend withdrawal of ban on Subhas Chandra Bose and Sarat Chandra Bose.

December 6 : In statement to the Press, explained that Sampuran Singh's example was a warning to people that "empty and meaningless discipline" had no value.

December 7 : In statement to the Press, appealed to people of Bombay "to revise their sporting code and erase from it communal matches".

Before December 16: In letter to Hansraj Radhar, a political worker from Jind, prohibited the State Congress from "civil disobedience, individual or mass".

December 17 : Gave instructions for suspension of satyagraha from December 24 to January 4.

December 20 : In statement to the Press, called for suspension of "final judgment about Sardar Sampuran Singh's conduct".

December 21 : Interview to Madras Delegation to All-India Students' Conference.

December 24 : In letter to Hitler, Gandhiji appealed to him "in the name of humanity to stop the war".

Before December 25: In letter to Dunichand, laid down conditions for eligibility to offer satyagraha.

December 27 : Invited Master Tara Singh, a prominent Akali leader, to meet him at Sevagram. (The invitee had resigned from the Congress following lengthy correspondence between him and Gandhiji on the question of non-violence.)

December 29 : In letter to Subhas Chandra Bose, said: "As for your Bloc joining civil disobedience, I think, with the fundamental differences between you and me, it is not possible."

Chapter Seven

Towards Freedom

1941

January 5 : Satyagraha was resumed after a break from December 24 to January 4.

January 10 : In Sevagram, Gandhiji gave instructions to satyagrahis "that even as a resister courts imprisonment, he is expected to court any other form of punishment, i.e., fines".

On or after January 10: In message, asked the Punjab Congressmen to develop "a living faith in the virtue of non-violence for being chosen for civil disobedience".

January 11 : Gave instructions for suspension of civil disobedience on 'Independence Day', i.e., January 26.

: Interview to Prof. R. Coupland.

On or before January 12: In letter to Abdul Ghaffar Khan, Gandhiji permitted 'Red Shirts' to offer satyagraha in the Frontier Province.

January 12 : In instructions to satyagrahis, announced that there would be no successor to Abul Kalam Azad and said: ". . . everyone who . . . gets a short term should know that on every release, he has to repeat civil disobedience till the end of the struggle".

January 17 : In Sevagram, blessed Vinoba Bhave, who offered

civil disobedience for the second time after he was released on January 15.

: Subhas Chandra Bose disappeared from his house in Elgin Road, Calcultta.

Before January 23: In message to Gujarat College students, Gandhiji said that they had every right to resort to strike if they failed to obtain justice through negotiations.

January 24 : Exhorted Congressmen to observe rules of conduct even in matters "too trifling for attention".

January 28 : In letter to newspaper editors, appealed to the Press "not to succumb to the gag but to assert its independence by publishing all the satyagraha news in its fullness".

Before February 1: In letter to Manoranjan Chaudhuri, declined to lead satyagraha movement against Muslim League Ministry of Bengal, as suggested by Bengal Hindu Mahasabha leaders.

February 4 : Had discussion with Sarojini Naidu and J. B. Kripalani.

February 9 : In letter to T. B. Sapru, refused to write to M.A. Jinnah unless the latter wanted "to come to some settlement".

February 10 : In letter to *The Times of India,* said: "In spite of your disbelief, I must adhere to my faith in the possibility of the most debased human nature to respond to non-violence."

February 13 : In message to Punjab Congressmen, stressed importance of constructive work.

February 16 : In letter to Mukundalal Sircar, described differences with Subhas Chandra Bose as "vital and fundamental", and said: "Independence secured through violence would have contents different from that secured through non-violent means." In letter to T. B. Sapru, expressed inability to meet M. A Jinnah.

On or before February 20: In letter to P. V. Naidu, said that question of Congress partaking "in the reorganization of Central Government . . . would not arise so long as the Congress demand remained unconceded".

On or after February 24: Interview to Calcutta satyagrahis.

February 26 : Gandhiji disallowed Maharajkumar of Vizianagaram to offer satyagraha as he did not fulfil all conditions of Satyagraha Pledge.

February 27 : In Allahabad, put up at Anand Bhavan.

February 28 : Visited Harijan Ashram; opened Kamala Nehru Memorial Hospital; had discussion with Bengal Congress leaders on withdrawal of Bengal Congress Party from the Legislature; received deputation on behalf of Garhwal Harijans.

: With Mahadev Desai called on T. B. Sapru at 8 p.m.; later met Madan Mohan Malaviya.

March 1 : Addressed U. P. Provincial Students' Federation. Called on Vijayalakshmi Pandit and Abul Kalam Azad in Naini Central Jail; at 11 a.m. left for Wardha.

March 2 : Reached Sevagram.

March 4 : Interview to Shankaran, Secretary, Tamil Nadu Provincial Congress Committee.

March 6 : In statement to the Press, Gandhiji warned people against 'journalistic flights of imagination" about his meeting with T. B. Sapru and others in Allahabad.

March 7 : In letter to Sir T.B. Sapru, agreed to suggestion to meet M.A. Jinnah, but expressed apprehension that time for communal settlement had not come.

: In Sind, Khan Bahadur Allah Baksh was sworn in as Premier.

Before March 10: Gandhiji instructed Andhra and Tamil Nadu Congress Committees not to take persons from districts into Madras city for offering satyagraha.

Before March 11: In telegram, urged Shibbanlal Saxena, satyagrahi prisoner in Benares Central Jail, to give up hunger-strike.

March 13-16 : In Bombay, Non-Party Leaders' Conference was held under Presidentship of T. B. Sapru.

March 16 : In Foreword to Jawaharlal Nehru's article, "The Parting of the Ways", Gandhiji said that the

		author had led the reader to the inevitable conclusion that independence could not be achieved without non-violence.
March 18	:	Appeal to C. F. Andrews Memorial Fund.
March 21	:	In appeal to Congress workers, hoped that they would devote their time to constructive programme during the National Week in April.
Before March 23:		In message to M. R. Jayakar, said that while he was always ready "to meet old friends ... he could not, without consultation with the members of the Working Committee, give them any assurance".
March 29	:	Proposal to resume publication of *Harijan* was countermanded on account of letter from the Government.
	:	In *Sarvodaya,* Gandhiji reiterated his conviction that "in this long and arduous struggle, quality alone will count, never quantity".
April 1	:	In Sevagram, introduced practice of keeping personal diaries by inmates.
April 6	:	In message to Delhi Basic Education Conference, said:"our experiment to be thorough has to be at least some-where made without alloy and without outside interference?'.
April 7	:	In message to Mysore Congress, said that constructive programme "is the truest foundation for the swaraj for millions based on non-violence". T. B. Sapru met Viceroy in Delhi.
April 8	:	In statement to the Press, Gandhiji said that report of his interview with Ruikar and Sircar was "a mischievous distortion of a friendly conversation".
April 16	:	Gandhiji was at Sevagram.
April 18	:	Riots broke out at Ahmedabad.
April 19	:	Gandhiji gave statement to *The Times of India.*
April 25	:	Issued statement to Press on L. S. Amery's speech.
April 27	:	Broke three days' fast.
May 1	:	Wrote to Editor of *The Times of India.*

May 2 : Attended funeral of J. P. Trivedi.

May 4 : Appealed to Congressmen to do their duty during riots.

May 7 : Issued statement to Press on riots in Bihar.

May 15 : Wrote on *Khadi Jagat*.

May 19 : Srinivasa Iyengar died.

May 18 to May 21: Gandhiji had discussions with Mridula Sarabhai and Gulzarilal Nanda.

May 22 : Gave interview to *The Hindu*.

May 23 : Spoke at National Youths' Training Camp at Wardha.

June 9 : In statement to Press denounced murder of a Muslim family in Bihar.

June 12 : Had discussion with K. M. Munshi, Rajendra Prasad and Gopichand Bhargava.

June 13 : Discussion continued.

June 15 : In statement to Press stated reasons why he had advised K. M. Munshi to resign from Congress.

July 6 : Gave statement to Press.

July 12 : Had discussion with Abdul Ghaffar Khan.

July 22 : Gave interview to The Hindu on Government communique.

July 23 : Gave interview to A. S. N. Murti.

July 31 : Wrote to *The Times of India*.

August 1 : Opened Khadi Vidyalaya at Wardha.

August 4 : Gave statement to Press.

August 5 : Gave statement to Press.

August 7 : Rabindranath Tagore died. Gandhiji paid tribute to Rabindranath Tagore.

August 12 : Issued statement to Press on shraddha day of Rabindranath Tagore.

August 24 : Wrote foreword to A Discipline for Non-violence. Gave statement to Press on Indo-Burman Immigration Agreeement.

August 29 : Attended A.I.V.I.A. meeting.

August 30 : In *Sarvodaya* paid homage to Rabindranath Tagore.

August 31	:	Wrote foreword to Practical Non-violence.
September 1	:	Telegraphed condolence on Fulchand Kasturchand Shah's death.
September 5	:	Gave interview to H. V. Kamath.
September 11	:	Gave interview to *The Hindu*.
September 14	:	Met Allah Bux, R. K. Sidhwa and deputation from Burma.
September 16	:	Met Allah Bux and R. K. Sidhwa.
September 18	:	Gandhiji's birthday celebrated according to Vikram era. Gandhiji addressed meeting at Sevagram and participated in spinning. Sent message for people of Ahmedabad.
September 24	:	In statement to Press cautioned public against uncertified khadi dealers.
September 30	:	At Nalwadi, addressed meeting of Goseva Sangh.
October 1	:	Sent message to States' people.
October 2	:	Gandhiji's birthday celebrated. Gandhiji spoke at meeting.
October 7	:	Presided at A.I.S.A. meeting.
October 10	:	At Sevagram.
October 11	:	Gandhiji was at Sevagram. Met Hancock and S. Satyamurti.
October 12	:	Received yarn and money collected by Nagpur, Berar and Mahakoshal Provincial Congress Committees and addressed them.
October 15	:	Met Asaf Ali and Rajendra Prasad.
October 21	:	Gave statement to Press on Government communique regarding Jayaprakash Narayan's alleged attempt to smuggle some papers from Deoli Camp.
October 22	:	After prayer spoke on ideal village community.
October 23	:	Met Khan Bahadur Alla Bux.
October 28	:	In statement to Press reviewed satyagraha movement and issued instructions for guidance of satyagrahis.
October 30	:	Issued statement to Press on hunger-strike by detenus in Deoli Camp and Government communique thereon.

November 11 : Issued statement on Indo-Ceylonese Pact.

November 12 : Sent telegram to Jayaprakash Narayan advising discontinuance of hunger-strike.

: In statement to Press discountenanced move to press Government to release satyagrahi prisoners.

November 14 : Through Press urged Government to grant demands of Deoli detenus.

November 15 : Granted permission to S. Satyamurti to publish whole correspondence.

November 19 : Telegraphed to Home Member seeking permission for Mahadev Desai to meet Deoli detenus.

Before Novemebr 20 : Sent message to Frontier people.

November 27 : In statement to Press expressed relief at discontinuance of hunger-strike by Deoli detenus and appealed to Government to give better treatment to detenus and political prisoners.

: Sent message to Majoor Mahajan, Ahmedabad, on its 25th anniversary.

November 28 : Gave interview to *The Daily Herald* on L. S. Amery's speech.

December 4 : Gave interview to Press on Government communique regarding release of political prisoners.

December 7 : Through Press announced that civil disobedience would continue until Bombay Resolution was reversed by Congress.

December 9 : Gave statement to Press on Khudai Khidmatgars' camp held in N.W.F.P.

: Left Sevagram.

December 10 : Reached Bardoli.

On or before December 13 : Completed Constructive Programme : Its Meaning and Place.

December 17 : Addressed A.I.S.A. meeting.

December 18 and 19 : Attended A.I.S.A. meeting. Through Press appealed to people not to be scared in face of approaching war but act bravely.

December 20 : Sent message to Bhagini Samaj, Bombay, on its

Silver Jubilee. Gave statement to Press on America's entry in war.

December 23 to 26 : Attended Congress Working Committee meeting.

December 27 : Attended Congress Working Committee meeting. Through Press appealed to Bihar Government to lift ban on Hindu Mahasabha.

December 28 : Attended Congress Working Committee meeting.

Before December 29 : Sent message to All-India Women's Conference.

December 29 : Attended Congress Working Committee meeting.

December 30 : Wrote to Congress President to relieve him of responsibility laid upon him by Bombay Resolution. C.W.C. passed a resolution relieving Gandhiji. C.W.C. passed another resolution reiterating its demand and restated the Congress position and attitude in regard to war.

: Gandhiji gave statement to *The Hindu* on Congress resolution.

1942

January 4 : Addressed Gujarat Provincial Congress Committee meeting.

January 7 : Through Press stated his intention to restart three weeklies and suggested constructive programme as "best preparation to face danger".

January 8 : Opened Gujarat Khadi Vidyalaya.

: Had discussion with Harijan workers.

Sir Akbar Hydari died.

On or before January 9 : Gandhiji addressed khadi workers. Left Bardoli.

January 10 : Reached Sevagram.

January 14 : In *Harijan* paid tribute to Sir Akbar Hydari.

January 15 : At A.I.C.C. meeting spoke on Bardoli Resolution.

January 16 : Attended C.W.C. and A.I.C.C. meetings. A.I.C.C. session concluded.

January 17 : Gandhiji attended C.W.C. meeting.

: Addressed members of Provincial Congress Committees and C.W.C.

January 18	:	*Harijan, Harijanbandhu* and *Harijan Sevak* resumed publication.
January 19	:	Gandhiji left for Benares.
January 20	:	Reached Benares.
January 21	:	Spoke at Silver Jubilee Convocation of Benares Hindu University.
January 22	:	Addressed Congress workers of U.P.
January 24	:	En route to Wardha halted at Nagpur. Spoke at Chokhamela Boarding House. Visited Hitavada office and Servants of India Society. Reached Sevagram.
January 29	:	Addressed students of Khadi Vidyalaya.
February 1	:	Inaugurated All-India Goseva Sangh Conference.
February 3	:	Spoke at All-India Goseva Sangh Conference.
Before February 8	:	Had discussion with Dr. John.
February 8	:	Wrote to Lord Linlithgow requesting that A.I.S.A. may be exempted from liability to pay income-tax.
February 9	:	Marshal and Madame Chiang Kai-shek arrived in New Delhi.
February 11	:	Jamnalal Bajaj died. Gandhiji attended funeral. After prayer paid tribute to Jamnalal Bajaj.
February 12	:	Had talk with members of Bajaj family.
February 14	:	Sent letters inviting Jamnalal Bajaj's friends to a meeting on February 20.
February 17	:	Left for Calcutta. At Gondia, gave statement to Press on Hare Krushna Mahtab's arrest.
February 18	:	Reached Calcutta. Met Chiang Kai-shek and wife. Left for Wardha.
February 19	:	En route at Nagpur gave interview to Press.
February 20	:	At Wardha addressed Jamnalal Bajaj's friends.
February 21	:	Spoke to Jamnalal Bajaj's friends.
February 26	:	Wrote message for Marathi *Harijan*.
Before March 1	:	After prayer addressed members of Mahila Ashram.
March 1	:	Marathi *Harijan* started.
March 11	:	Gandhiji addressed students of Khadi Vidyalaya

		on the occasion of Jamnalal Bajaj's masika shraddha.
March 16 and 17	:	Attended Congress Working Committee meeting.
March 18	:	Wrote foreword to The Medium of Instruction.
March 23	:	Stafford Cripps arrived in India.
March 25	:	In reply to Stafford Cripps's invitation for meeting in New Delhi, Gandhiji telegraphed his consent.
March 26	:	Left for Delhi.
March 27	:	Arrived in Delhi. Met Stafford Cripps.
Before March 29	:	Gave interview to Eve Curie.
March 29	:	Attended Congress Working Committee meeting. Telegraphed condolence to Prabhavati Devi Bose on reported death of Subhas Chandra Bose.
March 30	:	Sent telegram to Prabhavati Devi Bose expressing relief at contradiction of the news. British War Cabinet't proposals released to Press. Congress Working Committee meeting continued.
March 31	:	Congress Working Committee meeting continued.
April 1	:	Gandhiji attended meeting of Congress Working Committee in New Delhi.
April 5	:	Left Delhi for Sevagram.
April 6	:	Arrived in Sevagram.
April 10	:	Congress Working Committee rejected Cripps proposals.
April 11	:	Gandhiji inaugurated Swarajya Bhandar at Wardha.
May 1	:	Congress Working Committee passed resolution defining attitude to war and foreign soldiers.
May 9	:	Gandhiji left Sevagram for Bombay to collect funds for Andrews Memorial.
May 10	:	Arrived in Bombay.
May 17	:	Left Bombay for Sevagram.
May 18	:	Arrived in Sevagram.
May 27	:	Had discussions with Jawaharlal Nehru.
May 28	:	Met the members of the Rashtriya Yuvak Sangh, C. P.

June 2	:	Mridula Sarabhai and U. N. Dhebar called on Gandhiji.
June 4 and 5	:	Gandhiji gave interview to Louis Fischer.
June 6	:	Gave interviews to Chaplin of International News Service and Belden of *Time* and *Life* and Louis Fischer.
June 7-9	:	Had talks with Jawaharlal Nehru. Gave interview to Louis Fischer.
June 19	:	Gave interview to United Press of London on Cripps statement.
June 26	:	Had discussion with workers of Charkha Sangh.
	:	Spoke to students of Khadi Vidyalaya, Wardha.
June 29 and 30	:	Had discussions with C. Rajagopalachari.
July 3	:	Had discussions with Rajendra Prasad and Dr. Profulla Chandra Ghosh.
July 4	:	Had discussions with Rajendra Prasad and Jawaharlal Nehru.
July 5	:	In letter to Rajagopalachari advised him to resign from Congress and Assembly.
July 6	:	Attended meeting of Congress Working Committee.
July 8-11	:	Attended meeting of Congress Working Committee.
July 14	:	Congress Working Committee passed resolution asking British Government to withdraw from India.
July 26	:	Gandhiji had talks with Vinoba Bhave, Kishorelal Mashruwala and others.
August 1	:	Spoke at opening of Hindustani Talimi Sangh Bhawan.
August 2	:	Left Sevagram for Bombay.
August 3	:	Arrived in Bombay.
August 4	:	Attended meeting of Congress Working Committee and All-India Congress Committee.
August 8	:	Spoke at meeting of A. I. C. C. A. I. C. C. passed "Quit India" resolution.
August 9	:	Gandhiji was arrested early in morning and was taken to Aga Khan Palace, Poona. Members of

		Working Committee were also arrested and all Congress Committees declared illegal.
August 15	:	Mahadev Desai died in Aga Khan Palace.
August 16	:	Rioting broke out in Chimur when police opened fire on procession taken out to protest against arrests of leaders.
August 20	:	Gandhiji took silence.
August 24	:	Broke silence after 91 hours.
November 12	:	C. Rajagopalachari's request to be allowed to see Gandhiji in jail was turned down by Viceroy.
	:	J. P. Bhansali went on fast demanding enquiry into Chimur excesses.
November 30	:	Gandhiji was refused permission to communicate with Bhansali.
December 18	:	In Aga Khan Palace, Poona, Gandhiji who was in detention from August 9, 1942, completed revision of his book, *Key to Health,* originally written in Gujarati.
December 31	:	In letter to Lord Linlithgow, conveyed New Year greetings and said: "Convince me of my error or errors and I shall make amends."

1943

January 12	:	Jaikrishna P. Bhansali gave up fast following agreement with the Central Provinces Government.
January 26	:	On the occasion of Independence Day, Gandhiji repledged himself.
January 29	:	In letter to Lord Linlithgow, conveyed his intention to go on "fast according to capacity after the early morning breakfast on February 9".
February 7	:	In letter to Sir John Gilbert Laithwaite, suggested that his entire correspondence with Government, beginning with his letter dated August 14, should be published.
February 8	:	In letter to Viceroy, declined Government's offer to release him for the duration of his proposed fast.

February 10	:	Began his 21-day fast.
February 21	:	Interview to S. A. Brelvi.
February 23	:	Discussion with Horace G. Alexander.
March 3	:	Gandhiji broke the fast at 9.34 a.m.
May 4	:	In letter to M. A. Jinnah, thanked him for his reported invitation to write to him and suggested "meeting face to face rather than talking through correspondence".
May 27	:	In letter to Sir Richard Tottenham, expressed regret over Government's refusal to forward his letter to M.A. Jinnah.
July 15	:	Handed to Superintendent, Detention Camp, detailed reply to Government publication, Congress Responsibility for the Disturbances, 1942-43.
July 16	:	In letter to Sir Richard Tottenham, refuted rumours that he had written to Viceroy withdrawing A.I.C.C. resolution of August 8, 1942.
September 27	:	In letter to Lord Linlithgow, said: "Of all the high functionaries I have had the honour of knowing, none had been the cause of such deep sorrow to me as you have been."
October 26	:	In letter to Sir Richard Tottenham, said that a tribunal should go into the charges against Congress.
November 18	:	Talk with Mirabehn about dangerous animals, snakes, etc.
December 7	:	Talk with Nirmala and Devdas Gandhi.
December 9	:	Talk with Devdas Gandhi, Manorama Mashruwala, Ramabehn Parekh and Madhavdas Kapadia.
December 29	:	In letter to Agatha Harrison, Gandhiji said:"... I am the same man as you have known me.... Truth and non-violence remain my sheet-anchor as never before."

1944

After January 14: In message to Vijayalakshmi Pandit, asked her

		"to remember that henceforth Mr. Pandit would live in her actions".
January 24	:	In letter to Secretary, Home Department, Government of Bombay, exercised his "right to make representation" against detention order served on him.
January 26	:	Talk with Devdas Gandhi regarding Ayurvedic treatment for Kasturba Gandhi. Chhaganlal Gandhi, Jaisukhlal Gandhi and Ramdas Gandhi with his daughter met Gandhiji.
January 27	:	In letter to Secretary, Home Department, Government of India, Gandhiji asked for Dr. Dinshaw Mehta's treatment and Kanu Gandhi's nursing for Kasturba Gandhi.
January 28	:	Talk with Ramdas Gandhi.
February 11	:	In a note to Inspector-General of Prisons, Gandhiji absolved the Government from responsibility for any untoward result following the change over to Ayurvedic treatment for Kasturba Gandhi.
February 14	:	In letter to Inspector-General of Prisons, sought permission for Vaidyaraj Shiv Sharma's stay in Aga Khan Palace.
February 16	:	In letter to Inspector-General of Prisons, proposed three alternatives: (i) to permit Vaidyaraj Shiv Sharma to stay in the Palace, (ii) to release Kasturba Gandhi on parole, (iii) if neither was accepted, to transfer him elsewhere.
February 21	:	In cable to Shirinbai Jalbhoy Rustomjee, Durban, informed that Kasturba was "slowly going" and that Manilal and Sushila should "continue their work".
February 22	:	Kasturba Gandhi passed away at 7.35 p.m. Gandhiji dictated instructions to Inspector-General of Prisons for Kasturba Gandhi's funeral at 8.07 p.m.
March 4	:	In letter to Additional Secretary, Home Department, Government of India, wanted to "be removed to any regular prison" in order to save expenses which came from ... taxes collected

from the dumb millions of India".

: In letter to Additional Secretary, Home Department, Government of India, refuted Butler's statement in the House of Commons about facilities afforded for Kasturba Gandhi's treatment and her funeral rites.

March 9 : In letter to Lord Wavell, criticized his speech to Legislature on February 17.

March 16 : In letter to Ardeshir E. Kateli, refused to avail himself of the restricted facility to reply to condolence messages.

April 1 : In letter to Additional Secretary, Home Department, Government of India, disproved Government's claim that "they did everything possible" for Kasturba Gandhi.

April 2 : In letter to Additional Secretary, Home Department, Government of India, rebutted Home Secretary's statement in the Council of State that request for Vaidyaraj Shiv Sharma's services was made on February 9.

April 9 : In letter to Lord Wavell, appealed for Government's co-operation "with the people of India through their elected representatives".

May 3 : In letter to Secretary, Home Department, Government of India, said, he would deny himself the pleasure of meeting people "so long as the Government restrict the permission only to relatives".

May 6 : Prior to his release from detention, asked Secretary, Home Department, Government of Bombay, to acquire the plot where Mahadev Desai and Kasturba Gandhi were cremated.

: Was discharged from detention at 8 a.m.

: As the car drove to Parnakuti, thought of Kasturba Gandhi and Mahadev Desai: "She had been so eager to get out of prison, yet I know she could not have had a better death. Both she and Mahadev Desai . . . have become immortal." Commenced evening prayer meetings where collections were accepted for Harijan Welfare Fund.

May 10	:	Accepted Presidentship of Kasturba Gandhi National Memorial Trust.
May 11	:	In Juhu, at Jehangir Patel's shack, attended prayer meeting. Adhered to restrictions on interviews, meetings, etc., on medical advice.
May 14	:	Commenced fortnight's silence.
Before May 15	:	In telegram, informed Inayatullah Khan, readiness for talks with Jinnah.
May 17	:	Listened to Manohar Barve's music.
May 19	:	Visited dock area which was damaged by explosion. Called on Mangaldas Pakvasa, who was ill.
May 20	:	In letter to V. S. Srinivasa Sastri, offered condolence on death of V. S. Ramaswami Sastri.
	:	In letter to M. R. Jayakar, said: "The country expects much from me. . . . I cannot withdraw the August resolution. . . ."
May 23	:	Called on G. L. Mehta's daughter who was ill.
May 25	:	Gave message to China through a group of Chinese.
May 26	:	In the afternoon, listened to Bade Gulam Ali Khan's rendering of bhajans.
May 28	:	Gave message in writing to Christians who offered prayers at his place.
May 29	:	Broke silence at 3 p m.
May 30	:	Observed partial silence; called on Yusuf Meherally.
June 8	:	In Juhu, appealed to people who had gate-crashed into the compound to disperse quietly.
June 9	:	In letter to T. B. Sapru, assured him that he would not make any hasty statement. In letter, advised Aruna Asaf Ali to come out and surrender herself and not to die underground. In letter to Annada Babu Chowdhary, said: "Secrecy is a sin and symptom of violence . . . all underground activity is taboo." Discussion with H. P. Mody.
June 10	:	Gandhiji distributed to friends copies of his correspondence with Government, as also his reply to Congress Responsibility for the

Disturbances, 1942-43.

June 11 : Discussion with H. P. Mody.

June 12 : Gandhiji gave message in writing to Bombay Keraleeya Samaj, whose members offered prayers at his place and presented him with a purse of Rs. 501. Silent interview to journalists.

June 15 : After observing silence for a couple of hours, Gandhiji left for Juhu at 7.55 a.m.; boarded Poona Express at a level crossing between Kurla and Sion, accompanied by Dr. Sushila Nayyar, Dr. Gajjar, Dr. Gilder and Mayor Nagindas T. Master. In Poona, put up at Dr. Mehta's nature-cure clinic.

June 17 : In letter to Viceroy, renewed request for permission to meet Working Committee members; also expressed willingness to meet the addressee anywhere at his convenience.

June 20 : Interview to Stuart Gelder of *News Chronicle*.

June 22 : Viceroy turned down Gandhiji's request; consented for publication of correspondence between them.

June 29 : Gandhiji spoke in Hindustani to Maharashtra Congress representatives.

June 30 : With Gandhiji's approval, C. Rajagopalachari telegraphically informed Jinnah of the decision to publish his Formula and the latter's rejection of it. He, however, appealed to Jinnah to reconsider the decision.

July 4-6 : Gandhiji gave interview to Stuart Gelder.

July 12 : In telegram to Sadanand, apologized for publication of unauthorized report of interview to Gelder.

: Issued statement on interview to Gelder along with two notes giving details about discussions.

July 13 : In interview to the Press, declared that he had never said that August resolution had lapsed.

July 14 : In answer to a question, expressed willingness to resume publication of Harijan without any restraint.

: In interview to the Press, appealed for fair

		treatment to detenus who were released; answered criticisms of some Congressmen.
July 15	:	In letter to Editor, *Free Press Journal*, protested against publication of complaint against him without consulting him.
	:	In interview to the Press, explained difference between Cripps Plan and his own.
July 16	:	In statement to the Press, declared that restrictions on detenus were "degrading".
July 17	:	In letter to Jinnah, asked for time for their meeting.
	:	In letter to Winston Churchill, said: "I . . . ask you to trust and use me for the sake of your people and mine and through them those of the world."
July 19	:	In interview to the Press, expressed confidence that independence was a certainty.
July 20	:	In interview to the Press, answered questions of Cavalcade.
July 22	:	In interview to United Press of India, elucidated his view that military control may remain in the hands of the Viceroy and the Commander-in-Chief.
	:	Pacified a few excited Hindus of the Hindu Rashtra Dal who staged black-flag demonstration at prayer meeting.
July 23	:	In interview to the Press, denied Sind Home Minister's allegation that "subversive movement had been restarted throughout India".
July 24	:	Jinnah invited Gandhiji for talks at his residence in Bombay in mid-August.
July 26	:	Gandhiji gave interview to the Press on Lord Munster's speech in the House of Commons.
July 27	:	In letter to Lord Wavell, said that Lord Munster's speech "may serve as a basis for mutual friendly discussion". Discussion with Panchagani citizens.
July 28	:	In statement to the Press, Gandhiji explained views against sabotage and secrecy.
	:	In the House of Commons, Amery said that

Gandhiji's proposals "do not form even the starting point for a profitable discussion".

July 29/30 : Gandhiji had discussion with Bombay Congress leaders about August 9 celebrations.

July 30 : In letter to P. C. Joshi, asked for further clarifications. Interview to *News Chronicle* on Amery's statement. Interview to the Press on debate in the House of Commons.

August 1 : Gandhiji left Panchgani after a month's stay.

August 2 : In Bombay; gave interview to *Daily Worker.*

August 3 : Reached Sevagram.

August 5 : Issued statement to Press on how to celebrate 9th of August. Gave interview to Shyama Prasad Mookerjee.

August 7 : Gave interview to United Press of India.

August 8 : Issued statement to Press.

August 9 : Inaugurated 60-minute mass spinning in connection with August 9 celebrations in Sevagram. Had discussion with T. B. Sapru.

August 10 : Discussed Rajaji Formula with Bengal Congressmen.

August 15 : Gave interview to Duty Society Deputation.

Before August 17: Gave interview to Peggy Durdin.

August 18 : Gave interview to Associated Press of India on his correspondence with Viceroy.

August 30 : Sent message for All-India Students' Federation.

August 31 : In statement to press appealed to people to pray for success of his talks with M. A. Jinnah.

September 1 : Addressed A.I.S.A. meeting.

September 2 : Addressed A.I.S.A. meeting.

September 3 : Gave statement to Press. Addressed A.I.S.A. meeting.

September 5 : Presided at A.I.V.I.A. meeting.

September 6 : All-India Hindu Students' Federation delegation picketed Gandhiji's hut in Sevagram to protest against his meeting M. A. Jinnah. Gandhiji assured them that he would not do anything without consulting Bengal.

September 9 : Reached Bombay.
: Met M. A. Jinnah; talks began.

September 11 : Discussion continued. Gandhiji spoke at prayer meeting.

September 12 to 15: Talks with Jinnah continued.

September 16 : Talks continued. Gandhiji addressed prayer meeting.

September 17 and 18: Talks with Jinnah continued.

September 19 : Talks continued. In prayer speech Gandhiji warned people against speculations both in Indian and foreign Press.

September 20 to 23: Talks with Jinnah continued.

September 24 : Talks continued. Gandhiji in statement to Press rejected rumours regarding disbandment of Sevagram Ashram.

September 25 and 26: Talks with Jinnah continued.

September 27 : At prayer meeting Gandhiji announced breakdown of talks with Jinnah.

September 28 : Gave statement to Press on breakdown of talks.

September 29 : Gave interview to *News Chronicle* on failure of talks.

September 30 : In afternoon left for Sevagram.

October 1 : Reached Sevagram.

October 2 : Gandhiji's birthday celebrated. Gandhiji addressed Kasturba National Memorial Trust meeting; received purse of Rs. 80 lakhs.

October 7 : Started discussion with Shrikrishnadas Jaju regarding reorientation of All-India Spinners' Association.

October 8 : Discussion continued.

October 10 : Discussion continued. Gandhiji sent congratulations to Raja of Phaltan on introduction of full responsible government.

October 11 : Through Press acknowledged birthday greetings. Discussion with Shrikrishnadas Jaju continued.

October 12 : Discussion continued.

October 13 : Gandhiji had discussion with Shrikrishnadas Jaju.

October 14 : Concluded discussion with Shrikrishnadas Jaju.

October 16 : Wrote foreword to *The Gandhian Plan of Economic Development for India*.

October 22 : Wrote "Hints for Workers on Constructive Programme" for conference of Congressmen to be held at Bombay on October 28.

: Issued statement to Press regarding Syed Mahmud's release and his correspondence with Viceroy and appealed to Congressmen not to ostracize him.

: On or after October 22: Had discussion with friends about his proposed fast.

October 23 : Gave statement to Press on proposed fast.

October 25 : In letter to T. B. Sapru suggested convening of conference to examine "Pakistan issue".

October 26 : Had talk with Mridula Sarabhai on proposed fast.

Before October 27: Had discussion with representatives of Hindustani Talimi Sangh.

October 29 : In statement to Press said that fast would be unnecessary if exploitation and injustice were destroyed. Gave interview to N. G. Ranga.

On or before November 2: Had discussion with H. J. Khandekar.

November 7 : Blessed marriage of Abha and Kanu Gandhi.

Before November 9: In talk with Gulzarilal Nanda stated: "If everyone does his duty it is possible that fast may not come."

November 10 : Addressed Hindustani Talimi Sangh meeting.

November 12 : Sent message for Jawaharlal Nehru's birthday celebration in London.

November 17 : Sent message for "Majur Din" of Ahmedabad.

November 19 : Inaugurated Basic Education Teachers' Training Camp.

November 27 : In statement clarified objects and work of Hindustani Prachar Sabha.

November 28 : Gave interview to N. G. Ranga.

Before November 29: Sent message to Allahabad Students' Conference.

November 30 : Felt fatigued and weak, decided to take rest.

December 1 : Addressed trustees of A.I.S.A. Through Press conveyed his decision to take complete rest and "discontinue all public activities" from 4th to 31st December.

December 2 : Attended A.I.S.A. meeting.

December 3 : Attended A.I.S.A. meeting.

December 11 : Visited samadhi of Jamnalal Bajaj.

December 12 : Visited Leper Ashram.

December 25 : Sent message on Christmas Day.

December 30 : Romain Rolland died in Switzerland.

1945

January 5 : Gandhiji met Bhulabhai Desai.

January 11 : Attended Hindustani Talimi Sangh Conference. His speech was read out.

January 17 : Gandhiji gave interviews to Prahlad Mehta and T. V. Kunhi Krishnan.

January 23 : Met Profulla Chandra Ghosh. Sent message for Independence Day celebrations in London.

January 26 : In speech at prayer meeting, condemned police interference with village-cleaning programme of workers that morning in front of Ashram and praised workers' dignified and firm attitude.

January 31 : Had discussion with Anugraha Narayan Singh.

February 10 : Kasturba's death anniversary, according to Indian calendar, celebrated. Gandhiji participated in spinning yajna. Samagra Gramseva Shibir concluded. Gandhiji addressed volunteers. Advised T. N. Jagadisan of Madras and M. R. G. Cochrane of Vellore regarding leprosy relief work. Met Gopinath Bardoloi.

February 12 : Gave interview to Govind Sahay.

February 15 : Addressed secretaries of Provincial Committees of Kasturba Gandhi Memorial Fund.

February 17 : In statement to Press condemned Government's action in arresting Congressmen in Bihar and rearresting of Purushottamdas Tandon and appealed to Government to stop practice of torture and ill-treatment of prisoners

February 18	:	Wrote foreword to *Amaran Ba*.
February 19	:	Gave interview to deputation from N. W. F. P.
February 22	:	Kasturba's death anniversary, according to Gregorian calendar.
February 23	:	Gandhiji spoke at prayer meeting.
February 26	:	Answered T.B. Sapru's questionnaire regarding former's talks and correspondence with M.A. Jinnah.
	:	Presided at Hindustani Prachar Sabha conference.
February 27	:	Spoke at Hindustani Prachar Sabha conference.
March 3	:	Met C. Rajagopalachari.
March 5	:	Gave interview to Orient Press.
March 7	:	Wrote forewords to *Gandhiji's Correspondence with the Government, 1942-1944,* and *Ahar ane Poshan.*
March 9	:	Gave interview to Andhra deputation.
March 11	:	Issued statement to Press on ban imposed on Congress workers' conference in Akola.
March 17	:	Announced Vinoba Bhave and Kishorelal Mashruwala as his successors in Ashram.
March 20	:	Commenting on L. S. Emery's statement in interview to The Bombay Chronicle declared that 'all talk of resolution of the present deadlock' was useless as long as members of Working Committee were under detention.
March 24	:	Spoke at A. I. S. A. meeting.
March 25	:	Hermann Kallenbach died in Johannesburg. Through Press Gandhiji paid tribute to Hermann Kallenbach. Spoke at A. I. S. A. meeting.
March 28	:	Presided at A. I. V. I. A. meeting.
March 31	:	Reached Bombay. Issued statement to Press on National Week. In statement to Press on rejection of Ashti and Chimur prisoners' petition said that impending hangings could be prevented if there was united voice of India against them. Called on ailing Purshottamdas Thakurdas.
April 2	:	Issued appeal to observe hartal on April 3, for Chimur and Ashti prisoners.

April 4	:	Attended meeting of the Kasturba Memorial Trust.
April 6	:	Spoke at prayer meeting.
April 8	:	Gave interview to B.E.S.T. Workers' Deputation.
April 10	:	Gave interview to *The Times of India*.
April 11	:	Spoke at the Borivli Camp. Addressed prayer meeting at Borivli.
April 12	:	Attended meeting of Kasturba Memorial Trust.
April 14	:	Visited Kasturba Memorial Trust Office.
	:	Met Manilal who had come from South Africa.
April 15	:	Addressed prayer meeting.
April 16	:	Sent condolence message on the death of President Roosevelt.
April 17	:	Issued statement to Press on San Francisco Conference.
April 18	:	Sent message to Indians in South Africa.
April 19	:	Spoke at prayer meeting.
April 20	:	Arrived in Poona.
April 21	:	Arrived at Mahabaleshwar. Spoke at prayer meeting.
April 22	:	In telegram to A. P. I., denied having written to Bhulabhai Desai as alleged by the *Morning Standard*.
April 27	:	Gandhiji, in message from Mahabaleshwar where he had been staying from April 21, exhorted people of Ceylon "to understand the message of the charkha and the constructive programme".
May 1	:	In Foreword to *Rashtrabhasha Vishe Vichar*, said that Hindustani, "a happy amalgam of Hindi and Urdu", was "the perfect national language".
May 2	:	Visited apiaries and appreciated their scientific method and swadeshi spirit.
May 3	:	In answer to D. N. Balavenkataram, confirmed report that he would not enter Mahabaleshwar temples, as long as their "doors are not open to Harijans".
May 4	:	In statement to the Press replied to "remarks attributed to Sir Feroz Khan Noon as having been

made by him at San Fransisco Conference".

May 6 : In Press statement condemned big merchants, capitalists and industrialists who outwardly spoke and wrote against Government but in action conformed to its will.

May 8 : In telegram, gave blessings to G. D. Birla, who along with J. R. D. Tata and Kasturbhai was proceeding in industrial delegation to England. At prayer meeting paid tributes to Rabindranath Tagore on his eighty-fifth birth anniversary.

May 11/12 : Had discussion with C. Rajagopalachari.

May 13 : In letter to Dunichand, regretted his error of mistaken indentity in sending condolence to Mrs. Dunichand.

May 21 : In *Gramodyog Patrika* article, distinguished khadi from other village industries by comparing the former to the sun and the latter to planets.

May 22 : Spoke at Hindustan Scout Association training camp.

May 27 : In letter, requested Government to protect and preserve piece of ground having samadhis of Kasturba Gandhi and Mahadev Desai as consecrated place for use by their friends and relatives.

On or before May 30: Gave interview to Denton J. Brooks Jr.

May 31 : Reached Panchgani; put up at 'Dilkhush' of Nanji Kalidas.

June 1 : Had discussion with Harekrushna Mahtab.

June 2 : In answer to Shriman Narayan, stressed need to demonstrate economic fallacy behind sanction for use of foreign goods.

On or after June 3: In statement to Orient Press, said that Muslims should speak as Indians.

June 7 : In letter, requested Bhulabhai Desai "to see to it that Chimur-Ashti prisoners are not hanged".

June 9 : In message, wished Rajani Palme Dutt success in election campaign against L. S. Amery in Sparkbrook Constituency of Birmingham.

June 10 : Addressed members of Wai Rashtra Seva Dal.

June 11 : In silence-day note, cautioned Bhulabhai Desai against possible danger in agreement with Muslim League, and said that nothing could be done until Working Committee members were free to express their opinion.

June 13 : In letter to Purushottamdas Tandon, said that his leaving Hindi Sahitya Sammelan was intended to serve it better.

June 14 : In broadcast, Viceroy announced release of Working Committee members and summoning of conference of leaders of political parties.

: In telegram, Gandhiji informed Viceroy that he would not like to attend Simla Conference as Congress representative.

June 15 : Congress leaders were released and ban on Congress Working Committee was lifted.

June 16 : In letter to Viceroy, Gandhiji conveyed his willingness to be present at Simla Conference "with no official position" and if "Working Committee wished likewise".

June 18 : In telegram to Viceroy, reiterated his rejection of parity between Muslims and caste Hindus and reaffirmed his advice that Congress should not participate in formation of Executive Council on those grounds.

: Released to the Press, text of letter he had written to Winston Churchill on July 17, 1944.

June 19 : At Poona, visited samadhis of Mahadev Desai and Kasturba Gandhi.

June 20 : In Bombay.

June 21 : In statement to Press appealed to authorities to remove Sarat Chandra Bose to health resort with facilities to receive relatives.

June 21 and 22: Attended Congress Working Committee meeting.

June 23 : Halted at Delhi on way to Simla.

June 24 : Reached Simla; met Viceroy in afternoon.

June 26 : Released to Press names of members for

: Literature Board of All-India Hindustani Prachar Sabha.

June 27	:	At prayer meeting, explained significance of prayer.
June 28	:	In letter, appealed to Viceroy that all "hangings—an aftermath of the disturbances of 1942 . . . be commuted to life sentences".
June 29	:	Gave interview to Preston Grover of Associated Press of America.
June 30	:	In interview to A. S. Bharatan of Associated Press of India, explained Congress stand on issue of parity of representation between caste Hindus and Muslims.
July 2	:	At prayer meeting, explained new rule of A.I.S.A. which required payment for khadi to be made partly in yarn.
July 3 and 4	:	Attended Congress Working Committee meeting.
July 7	:	Congress list for proposed Executive Council was sent to Viceroy by Abul Kalam Azad after discussion with Gandhiji.
July 9	:	Jinnah refused to send his names for proposed Executive Council.
July 12	:	At prayer meeting, Gandhiji rebuked gathering for unruly behaviour.
July 14	:	Gave interview to Francis Sayer of the United Nations Relief and Rehabilitation Administration.
	:	Viceroy announced failure of Simla Conference which Jinnah had called "a snare".
July 16	:	Gandhiji left Simla for Wardha.
July 17	:	Gandhiji arrived in Delhi. Visited Satyavati and Shaukat Ansari. En route to Wardha addressed the crowd assembled at Agra Cantt. Station. Gave interview to *People's War.*
July 18	:	Reached Sevagram. Issued statement to Press.
July 25	:	Resigned from Hindi Sahitya Sammelan.

On or before July 28: Gave interview to *The Hindu*.

August 3	:	Gave statement to Press.
August 4	:	Issued statement to Press. Gave interview to *The Hindu*.
August 6	:	Hiroshima atom-bombed.

August 8 : Gandhiji issued statement on appeal for funds for Dakshin Bharat Hindi Prachar Sabha.

August 9 : Nagasaki atom-bombed.

August 10 : Japan surrendered.

August 11 : Gandhiji issued statement on death sentence of Mahendra Chowdhary.

Before August 14: Had discussion with B. S. Murthy.

August 14 : Addressed Central Board meeting of Harijan Sevak Sangh.

August 16 : Death sentences of Ashti-Chimur prisoners commuted to life imprisonment.

August 19 : Gandhiji attended meeting of Kasturba National Memorial Trust. Left Sevagram for Bombay.

August 20 : At Bombay.

August 21 : Arrived in Poona.

August 29 : Sent message to U. S. A.

Before September 2: Had discussion with Narendra Dev and Suraj Prasad Awasthi.

September 12 and 13: Attended Congress Working Committee meeting.

September 14 : Attended C. W. C. meeting. Spoke at prayer meeting.

September 15 : Attended C. W. C. meeting.

September 16 : Attended C. W. C.meeting. Sent condolence letter to Nawab of Bhopal.

September 17 to 20: Attended C. W. C. meeting.

September 21 : Arrived in Bombay; had mild attack of influenza, was advised complete rest; could not attend A.I.C.C. Spoke at prayer meeting.

September 22 to 23: Attended C. W. C. meeting.

September 24 : Attended C. W. C. meeting, Bombay. Returned to Poona.

October 5 : Laid foundation-stone of Kasturba Goshala.

October 8 : Acknowledged birthday-greetings through Press.

October 31 : At Poona.

November 1 : Gandhiji was at Poona.

November 8 : In Poona, Attended metting of Hindustani Prachar Sabha.

November 10	:	Mahendra Gope was hanged in Bhagalpur jail.
November 12	:	Jawaharlal Nehru called on Gandhiji.
November 15	:	Gandhiji visited Khadakvasala.
November 19	:	Left Poona for Bombay.
November 20	:	Left Bombay for Wardha.
November 21	:	Arrived in Sevagram.
November 22	:	Addressed students of Samagra Gram Vidyalaya.
November 23-25	:	Attended meetings of Kasturba Memorial Trust.
November 26	:	Had talk with members of Hyderabad State Congress.
November 27-28	:	Presided over meeting of the Charkha Sangh.
November 30	:	Spoke at Mahila Ashram Wardha. Left for Calcutta.
December 1	:	Arrived in Calcutta. Put up at Sodepur Ashram. Met R. G. Casey, Governor of Bengal.
December 3	:	Met R. G. Casey.
December 10	:	Had discussion with Lord Wavell.
December 12	:	Dr. N. B. Khare called on Gandhiji.
December 18	:	Gandhiji arrived in Santiniketan.
December 19	:	Laid foundation of C. F. Andrews Memorial Hospital.
December 20	:	Left Santiniketan.
December 21	:	Arrived in Sodepur.
December 22	:	Called on R.G. Casey.
December 23	:	Had discussion with members of Bengal Provincial Congress Committee and kindred organizations.
December 24	:	Left for Midnapore District.
December 25	:	Arrived in Mahishadal.
December 30	:	Left Mahishadal for Contai.
December 31	:	Arrived in Contai.

1946

January 1	:	Had discussion with local Congress workers.
January 2	:	Addressed volunteers' rally. Had discussion with Midnapore political workers.
January 3	:	Left Contai for Sodepur.

January 4	: Arrived in Sodepur.
January 5	: Addressed Conference of Congress workers.
January 6	: Addressed Conference of Congress Workers.
January 8	: Left Sodepur for Assam.
January 9	: Visited Amingaon, Saulkuchi. Arrived in Gauhati.
January 10	: In Gauhati.
January 12	: Addressed Conference of political workers.
January 13	: Left Gauhati for Dhubri.
January 14	: Arrived in Sodepur.
January 15	: Visited Alipur Jail.
January 17	: Visited Dum Dum Jail.
January 19	: Left Sodepur for Madras.
January 20	: Gandhiji was proceeding to Madras (from Sodepur) to inaugurate the Silver Jubilee celebrations of Dakshin Bharat Hindi Prachar Sabha. In train, wrote Foreword to *My Master Gokhale* and *The Gospel of Selfless Action* or *The "Gita" According to Gandhi*. Addressed people at Cuttack, Berhampur, etc.; in message to people of Andhra, regretted his inability to stay with them.
January 21	: In train, wrote Foreword to *Hindustani-Gujarati Kosha;* in Madras, was put up at bungalow adjacent to Hindi Prachar Sabha office.
January 22	: Called on V. S. Srinivasa Sastri at General Hospital; in the evening, addressed prayer gathering.
January 23	: Informed V. V. Giri that Trade Union red flag could be used along with the Congress tri-colour; after prayer meeting, received Parliamentary Delegation.
January 24	: Inaugurated Constructive Workers' Conference; urged members of Parliamentary Delegation need for release of political prisoners; addressed prayer meeting.
January 25	: In message, asked students of Pachaiyappa's College going in procession to observe perfect discipline and non-violence.

January 26 : Answered questions at the Constructive Workers' Conference; spoke at convention of Harijans, organized by Dakshina Bharat Hindi Prachar Sabha; after prayer meeting, exhorted deputation of Nationalist Muslims to cultivate love and good-will towards their neighbours.

January 27 : Answered questions at Constructive Workers' Conference; spoke at twenty-third convocation of Dakshina Bharat Hindi Prachar Sabha; received deputation of Harijans.

January 29 : Addressed Constructive Workers' Conference; spoke at Women's Convention; addressed Nayee Talim Convocation and distributed certificates to teachers trained in Wardha Basic Education Course.

January 30 : At meeting with staff and members of Hindi Prachar Sabha invited questions; later attended convention of teachers and students; exhorted Congress workers to throw off slavery to foreign language; called on Srinivasa Sastri.

January 31 : Spoke to volunteers and members of mess committe; addressed Andhra Pradesh workers of Kasturba Fund; blessed tablets to be laid for new buildings of Andhra Mahila Sabha; appealed to workers to learn Hindustani.

February 1 : Laid foundation stone for Harijan Industrial School, which he suggested could be named after Thakkar Bapa; at Harijan Industrial School, Kodambakkam, expressed hope that some Harijans would aspire to become Sanskrit pundits.

February 2 : In *Harijan,* explained why the weekly was revived; left for Madura; en route spoke at Acharapakkam, Ariyalur, Lalgudi, Golden Rock and Manapparai.

February 3 : At Madurai, visited Meenakshi Temple;; at Palni, visited the temple and wrote in Visitors' Book.

February 4 : Returned to Madras; during short interval before boarding train to Wardha, called on Srinivasa Sastri.

February 5 : At Vijayawada, blessed the foundation-stone of Hindustani Bhavan; in speech, dispelled rumours that he came to set up Rajagopalachari as Premier; appealed to people not to waste their time on language differences; reached Wardha late in the night.

February 6 : Addressed prayer meeting.

February 7 : In reply to U. P. I. representative, denied report of his having admitted that Bengal famine was not man-made.

February 8 : In *Harijan,* answered questions of Golden Rock workers.

February 10 : Rajendra Prasad met Gandhiji before latter began his silence; *Harijan* weeklies resumed publication.

: In letter to Viceroy, Gandhiji regretted inability to accept his invitation to go to Delhi and discuss food situation with him.

Feburary 11 : Viceroy's Private Secretary G. E. B. Abell called on Gandhiji for discussion on food crisis. Gandhiji wrote down his answers. Aruna Asaf Ali called on Gandhiji after prayer meeting.

February 12 : At Wardha, Gandhiji spoke at second Goseva Sangh Conference. In statement on his talks with Abell, reiterated stand that Viceroy should invite Abul Kalam Azad so far as Congress policy was concerned.

February 14 : In *Harijan,* suggested guidelines for facing foods crisis.

February 15 and 16 : Attended Hindustani Prachar Sabha meeting.

February 16 : Advised Zakir Hussain and some other members of Talimi Sangh that, in addition to their educational activity, they should become instruments for increasing food production.

February 17 : Spoke to teacher-trainees on Basic Education; left for Poona.

February 18 : In Bombay, addressed prayer meeting.

February 19 : In *Harijan,* dissuaded public servants from misusing for personal ends trust reposed in them by the public.

February 20 : Reached Poona.

February 21 : In message to British people, said : "My life is a message."

February 22 : In Press statement, condemned coercive fasts. Presided over the meeting of All-India Nature Cure Foundation Trustees.

February 23 : In Press statement, condemened mutiny in the navy.

February 25 and 26 : The Aga Khan and Nawab of Bhopal met Gandhiji.

February 26 : In Press statement, Gandhiji said that Aruna Asaf Ali betrayed "want of foresight to disbelieve British declarations".

February 27 : Warned Manchershaw Awari against fast.

February 28 : In telegram to Awari, Gandhiji reiterated his advice to give up fast, and suggested that he should refer his grievances to Congress Working Committee and A.I.C.C.

March 1 : In telegram, again advised Awari to abandon fast and agitate for redress of grievances, if any.

March 3 : In *Harijan,* Gandhiji answered Aruna Asaf Ali's criticism of his call to R.I.N. men to resign, if their condition was humiliating.

March 4 : In letter to Dr. Dinshaw K. Mehta, repented for "the blunder" in having expensive premises for Nature Cure Clinic.

March 6 : In *Harijan,* confessed his mistake in attempting to practice nature cure in Poona instead of in a village.

: Recommended formation of satyagraha brigades in every village and every block of building in cities, to help prevent looting.

March 7 : In *Harijan,* deplored practice of communal discrimination in sale of Hindu and Mussalman tea, etc., allowed by railways.

: In letter to J. P. Bhansali, desired that none should undertake fast without his prior permission.

: In All-India Nature Cure Foundation Trustees' meeting, emphasized importance of Ramanama as basis of nature cure.

On or after March 8 : Drafted memorandum to be presented to Viceroy by deputation of South Africa Indians.

March 11 : Left Poona at 7.30 a.m.; reached Bombay for the Congress Working Committee meeting.

March 12 and 13 : At Birla House, advised Shah Nawaz Khan and P.K. Sehgal of I.N.A. to absorb themselves in constructive work as it was derogatory for a soldier to live upon charity.

March 14 : At Shivaji Park, in prayer meeting, explained the way of living and dying in satyagraha.

March 15 : In *Harijan,* described reported worship of his image in temple erected for him as insult and "gross form of idolatory"; suggested the place be converted into a spinning centre. At prayer meeting, explained significance of Rananama in nature cure.

March 16 : In statement to the Press, commended Potti Sriramulu's service for the cause of Harijans at Nellore.

March 17 : In *Harijan* and *Hrijanbandhu,* explained the disadvantages of the decimal coniage system and appealed to Central Legislative Assembly to reject Bill for its implementation. Gave interview to H. N. Brailsford.

March 18 : Condoled with Viceroy on the death of his son-in-law at Quetta in an accident.

March 19 : In letters to Amritlal V. Thakkar and Vallabhbhai Patel, expressed his desire to put up in Bhangi quarters during visits to Bombay and Delhi.

March 21 : At prayer meeting, announced decision to go to Uruli-Kanchan in order to make nature cure available to the poor.

March 22 : At Uruli-Kanchan, at prayer meeting, announced that he would receive patients for nature cure treatment from the following day.

March 23 : In letter to G.D. Birla, reaffirmed his decision to stay in Bhangi quarters wherever he went.

March 25 : In *Harijan,* explained reasons behind decision to put up in Bhangi quarters.

March 28 to 30 : At two independent meetings, spoke to Agents and Executive Committee of the Kasturba Smarak Trust.

March 30 : In *Harijan,* announced that there was "strong evidence to counteract the feeling" that Subhas Bose was dead. Opened library named after Kasturba. At prayer meeting, advised people to lead healthy lives and turn the place into a model village.

March 31 : Left for Delhi in response to Viceroy's invitation.

April 1 : In Delhi, met Cabinet Ministers in the evening; spoke at prayer meeting.

April 3 : In letter to Lord Pethick-Lawrence, pleaded for abolition of salt tax and release of prisoners.

April 4 : Appealed to the Press to excuse him from answering questions on Cabinet Mission.

: At Delhi Cantonment, met I.N.A. men.

April 5 : At prayer meeting, paid tributes to I.N.A. men and Subhas Chandra Bose.

April 6 : In *Harijan,* reminded Ministers that they were "servants of the people" and that payments were meant only for those who could not "easily afford to render free service."

: At prayer meeting, explained the origin and significance of the National Week observed from April 6 to 13.

April 8 : In letter to G. E. B. Abell, asked for an interview with Viceroy.

April 11 : Visited I.N.A. men detained in Red Fort.

On or before April 13 : Had discussion with Woodrow Wyatt.

April 13 : At Prayer meeting, commended Government gesture in releasing I.N.A. men, Jayaprakash Narayan and Ram Manohar Lohia.

April 14 : Gandhiji was in New Delhi at the invitation of Viceroy and Cabinet Mission. Congress Working Committee met.

April 15 : Gandhiji advised T. Prakasam not to contest election for Chief Ministership of Madras. Spoke at prayer meeting.

Before April 16	:	Sent message for Indian National Army. Spoke at prayer meeting.
April 16	:	Spoke at prayer meeting.
April 17	:	Spoke at prayer meeting. Congress Working Committee met. V. S. Srinivasa Sastri died.
April 18	:	In *Harijan* Gandhiji paid tribute to V. S. Srinivasa Sastri. Called on Madan Mohan Malaviya and Pethick-Lawrence. Spoke at prayer meeting.
April 19	:	Spoke at prayer meeting.
Before April 20	:	Met S. A. Ayer.
April 20	:	Visited Kasturba Balika Ashram and Jamia Millia. Gave statement to Press regarding T. Prakasam.
Before April 23	:	Had talk with a zamindar and missionaries.
April 23	:	Spoke at prayer meeting.
April 24	:	Had interview with Herbert Hoover. Spoke at prayer meeting.
April 25	:	Met Archibald Rowlands; sent to him draft and note on proposed proclamation on salt. Spoke at prayer meeting.
April 26	:	Gave statement to Press regarding Herbert Hoover's visit. Spoke at prayer meeting. Stafford Cripps called on Gandhiji.
April 27	:	Gandhiji met Jayaprakash Narayan. Spoke at prayer meeting. Cabinet Mission invited representatives of Congress and Muslim League for negotiations at Simla.
April 28	:	Gandhiji addressed volunteers at flag-hoisting ceremony. Spoke at prayer meeting. Congress Working Committee met.
April 29	:	Gandhiji called on Madan Mohan Malaviya. Congress Working Committee concluded its session.
April 30	:	Stafford Cripps called on Gandhiji.
May 2	:	Gandhiji arrived in Simla in response to Cabinet Mission's invitation. Spoke at prayer meeting.
May 3	:	Had talk with Agatha Harrison.
May 4	:	In statement to Press explained reason for sending his party back to Delhi.

May 5	:	Spoke at prayer meeting. Conference with Cabinet Mission began.
May 6	:	Bhulabhai Desai died in Bombay. Gandhiji telegraphed condolence to Dhirubhai B. Desai; through Press paid tribute to Bhulabhai Desai. Met Viceroy and Cabinet Mission. Spoke at prayer meeting.
May 7	:	Speaking at prayer meeting, denounced tendency of speculation and asked people and Press to desist from spreading rumours. Met Viceroy and Stafford Cripps.
May 8	:	At prayer meeting paid tribute to Rabindranath Tagore.
May 9	:	Had discussion with Stafford Cripps.
May 10	:	Spoke at prayer meeting.
May 11	:	Met Viceroy. Spoke at prayer meeting.
May 12	:	At prayer meeting asked people not to be disappointed even if Conference failed and reiterated his faith in Cabinet Mission. Met Viceroy. Conference ended in a breakdown.
May 13	:	Gandhiji sent condolence to Seth Govinddas. In message at prayer meeting stated that there was no need for depression at the failure of Conference.
May 14	:	Left Simla for Delhi.
May 15	:	At prayer meeting warned people against speculation on impending statement of Cabinet Mission. Met H. N. Brailsford and his wife.
May 16	:	In message expressed his conviction that Indians in South Africa must not submit to Land Tenure Legislation. At prayer meeting asked people not to be led away by prejudice but to study statement carefully. Cabinet Mission's Statement released to Press.
May 17	:	Gandhiji attended Congress Wroking Committee meeting. Welcoming Statement at prayer meeting placed his interpretation before people.
May 18	:	At prayer meeting expressed hope that Statement would be honoured in letter and in spirit.

: Congress Working Committee meeting continued.

May 19 : Gandhiji had discussion with Pethick-Lawrence. Spoke at prayer meeting.

May 20 : In *Harijan* analysed Cabinet Mission's Statement. Attended prayer meeting; written message was read out. Attended Congress Working Committee meeting.

May 21 : Attended Congress Working Committee meeting. Spoke at prayer meeting.

May 22 : Addressed I.N.A. officers. Attended Congress Working Committee meeting. Spoke at prayer meeting.

May 23 : Attended Congress Working Committee meeting. Spoke at prayer meeting.

May 24 : Attended Congress Working Committee meeting. Spoke at prayer meeting.

: Congress Working Committee passed resolution expressing its inability "to give a final opinion at this stage on the proposals".

May 25 : Gandhiji spoke at prayer meeting.

May 26 : In *Harijan* disucssed "vital defects" of official interpretation of Statement. Spoke at prayer meeting.

May 27 : Referring to riots, at prayer meeting asked people not "to encourage them by word, deed or thought".

May 28 : Reached Mussoorie for rest on medical advice.

May 29 : At prayer meeting reminded the rich of the misery of rickshaw-coolies and advised them to build dharmashala for the poor.

May 31 : Gave interview to Norman Cliff. At prayer meeting, again appealed for building dharmashalas for the poor and Harijans. Met Abul Kalam Azad.

June 2 : Addressed Azad Hind Dal volunteers. At prayer meeting spoke of deplorable living conditions of labourers in Mussoorie and emphasized need for sanitation.

June 3 : At prayer meeting, through written message, welcomed move for building dharmashala.

On or before June 5 : At prayer meeting deplored the custom of rickshaw-pulling.

On or before June 6 : Spoke at prayer meeting.

June 6 : Muslim League Council passed resolution accepting Cabinet Mission's proposals.

June 7 : Gandhiji spoke at prayer meeting.

June 8 : At prayer meeting spoke about work done in connection with dharmashala. Left Mussoorie; reached New Delhi.

June 9 : Attended Congress Working Committee meeting. At prayer meeting advised people to pray and rely on God.

June 10 : Attended prayer meeting; written message was read out. Attended Congress Working Committee meeting.

June 11 : At prayer meeting, regretting inability to give any definite news, pleaded for patience. Had interview with Viceroy.

June 12 : Attended Congress Working Committee meeting.

: At prayer meeting, appealed to Europeans to abstain from participation in Constituent Assembly. Had interview with Pethick-Lawrence.

June 13 : Attended Congress Working Committee meeting. Spoke at prayer meeting.

June 14 : Congress President wrote to Viceroy rejecting proposal for formation of Interim Government.

: At prayer meeting Gandhiji spoke of Cabinet Mission's efforts to bring Congress and Muslim Leauge together.

June 16 : Had interview with Pethick-Lawrence. Viceroy's statement inviting 14 individuals to serve as members of Interim Government, issued.

: At prayer meeting, Gandhiji referred to Viceregal statement and asked people, in spite of his misgivings, to look at bright side and trust in the bonafides of Mission.

June 17 : Attended Congress Working Committee meeting.

June 18	:	Congress Working Committee meeting continued. Gandhiji spoke at prayer meeting.
June 19	:	Spoke at Congress Working Committee meeting. At prayer meeting deprecated irresponsible reports appearing in Press.
June 20	:	In interview with Stafford Cripps, reiterated that Mission must choose between Congress and Muslim League.
	:	Jawaharlal Nehru arrested following defiance of ban on his entry into Kashmir. Gandhiji spoke at prayer meeting.
June 21	:	Spoke at Congress Working Committee meeting. Spoke at prayer meeting. Jawaharlal Nehru released.
June 22	:	At prayer meeting, Gandhiji spoke on satyagraha against Segregation Act in Sough Africa.
June 23	:	At Congress Working Committee meeting advised Congress to keep out of Interim Government. Spoke at prayer meeting.
June 24	:	Had interview with Cabinet Delegation in morning.
	:	Expressed his misgivings before Congress Working Comitee at morning and afternoon sessions.
	:	After ending silence at 8 p.m. again had interview with Cabinet Delegation and Viceroy.
June 25	:	At Congress Working Committee meeting in morning, voiced his doubts and advised it not to accept longterm proposition without its being connected with Interim Government.
	:	Attended afternoon session of Congress Working Committee meeting.
	:	Congress President communicated to Viceroy Congress Working Committee's decision to reject proposal for Interim Government and to accept long-term proposal relating to Constituent Assembly.
	:	At prayer meeting, referring to Congress Working Committee's decision, Gandhiji asked people "to

follow the lead given by the Working Committee".

June 26 : Congress Working Committee passed resolution rejecting Interim Government proposal and accepting long-term arrangement; concluded its session. Gandhiji gave interview to Louis Fischer. Spoke at prayer meeting. Viceroy and Cabinet Mission announced that a temporary caretaker government of officials would be set up.

June 27 : At prayer meeting, Gandhiji asked people to pray for Indian satyagrahis in South Africa.

June 28 : At prayer meeting paid tribute to courage of satyagrahis in South Africa.

June 29 : En route to Poona gave interview to Norman Cliff on train. Between Karjat and Neral, his train met with an accident at night. Cabinet Mission left for England.

June 30 : Gandhiji reached Poona. At prayer meeting spoke of his providential escape in train accident.

July 1 : Communal riots broke out in Ahmedabad. Gandhiji wrote to Morarji Desai in this connection. At prayer meeting condemned hooliganism of white men in South Africa.

July 2 : At prayer meeting expressed sorrow and shame at communal riots.

July 3 : At prayer rmeeting, paid tribute to courage of satyagrahis in South Africa and told people to pray to God to give strength to satyagrahis.

: Gave interview to Joachim Dias and Chandrakant Kakodkar.

July 5 : Reached Bombay. Attended Congress Working Committee meeting.

July 6 : Newly elected All India Congress Committee met under presidentship of Jawaharlal Nehru. Gandhiji attended A.I.C.C. meeting.

July 7 : Addressed A.I.C.C. meeting. A.I.C.C. passed two resolutions, one ratifying Congress Working Committee's resolution passed at Delhi, and another supporting Indian satyagraha in South

Africa. Gandhiji spoke at prayer meeting.

On or before July 8 : Gave interview to *Daily Herald.*

July 8 : Through Press acknowledged congratulatory messages on his provindential escape. At prayer meeting spoke of insanitary conditions of chawls.

July 9 : Left Bombay; reached Poona.

July 10 : Attended Kasturba Memorial Trust meeting. At prayer meeting strongly condemned persecution of Indian satyagrahis by whites.

July 11 : Attended meetings of Kasturba Memorial Trust and All-India Spinners' Association. Spoke at prayer meeting.

July 12 : At prayer meeting spoke about conditions of Indians in Ceylon.

July 13 : Reached Panchgani. Spoke at prayer meeting.

July 14 : Had discussion with Nimbalkar of Indian National Army. Spoke at prayer meeting.

July 16 : Gandhiji was at Panchgani.

July 17-18 : Gave interview to Louis Fischer.

July 20 : Had talks with members of Harijan Sevak Sangh and the Raja of Aundh. Representatives of East Africa called.

July 21 : Opened Dharmashala at Panchgani. Nawab of Wai called on Gandhiji.

July 22-27 : A. G. Tendulkar, President of Goa Congress Committee called on Gandhiji.

July 28 : At Poona. Gandhiji addressed meeting of Deccan Princes.

July 29 : Gandhiji addressed Education Ministers' Conference. Muslim League passed Direct Action resolution.

July 31 : Gandhiji addressed Industries Ministers' Conference.

August 6 : Gandhiji arrived at Sevagram.

August 8 : Attended meeting of Congress Working Committee.

August 9-12 : At Wardha. Addressed Seksaria College of Commerce. The Working Committee meeting

		continued.
August 13	:	At Sevagram. Raja Mahendra Pratap called on Gandhiji.
August 16	:	Four days rioting started in Calcutta as the consequence of Direct Action call by Muslim League.
August 18	:	Gandhiji spoke at the meeting of Doctors.
August 21	:	Gandhiji addressed Hindustani Prachar Trainees.
August 23	:	Addressed Trainees of Basic Teachers' Camp.
August 25	:	Left Sevagram for Delhi.
August 26	:	Arrived in New Delhi.
August 27	:	In New Delhi. Gandhi, accompanied by Jawaharlal Nehru, called on Viceroy. Attended Working Committee meeting.
August 28-30	:	The Working Committee Meeting Continued.
September 1	:	Communal riots broke out in Bombay.
September 2	:	Interim Government took office. Congress Ministers before taking oath called on Gandhiji.
September 11	:	Charkha class introduced at Bhangi Colony.
September 16	:	Gandhiji had talk with Christian Missionary.
September 24	:	Gandhiji had talks with American and English journalists.
September 25	:	Attended A. I. C. C. meeting.
September 26	:	Met viceroy.
September 29	:	Had discussion with Hridaya Nath Kunzru, Hindustan Boy Scouts Association and Nawab of Bhopal.
October 2	:	Had discussion with Nawab of Bhopal.
October 8	:	Had discussion with members of A. I. S. A. and Nawab of Bhopal.
October 10	:	Communal violence broke out in Noakhali and Tippera.
October 15	:	Muslim League announced its decision to join Interim Government.
October 16	:	Gandhiji had talk with Assam Deputation.
October 18	:	Had discussion with co-workers.
October 21	:	In interview to Preston Grover, Gandhiji announced that he would visit Bengal after

		meeting Jawaharlal Nehru and other leaders. Spoke at prayer meeting.
October 24	:	Spoke at prayer meeting.
October 25	:	Spoke at prayer meeting.
October 26	:	Spoke at prayer meeting.
October 27	:	In the evening spoke at prayer meeting.
Before October 28	:	Left by train for Calcutta.
October 29	:	At Sodepur. Addressed prayer meeting.
October 30	:	Had discussions with Governor and Prime Minister of Bengal. Spoke at prayer meeting.
October 31	:	Addressing prayer gathering said that he was hopeful of peace between Hindus and Muslims.
November 1	:	Spoke at prayer meeting.
November 2	:	Spoke at prayer meeting.
November 3	:	In telegram to Jawaharlal Nehru, expressed concern over reported violence by Hindus in Bihar. At prayer gathering, referred to Bihar riots and exhorted the Hindus not to indulge in revenge.
November 4	:	Spoke at prayer meeting.
November 5	:	In letter to Jawaharlal Nehru, expressed distress over Bihar events and hinted that he might have to undertake a fast. At prayer meeting, reiterated his strong wish that Hindus should not "succumb to the temptation of retort".
November 6	:	In open letter to Bihar Hindus in Harijan said his "low diet will become a fast unto death" if the situation in Bihar did not improve. Gave interview to the United Press of India. Left for Noakhali; spoke at Kushtia and Goalundu en route.
November 7	:	At Chandpur. Addressed relief workers and Muslim League leaders. At Chaumuhani, spoke at prayer meeting.
November 8	:	Had discussion with Muslim League leaders.
November 9	:	Reached Dattapara; spoke at prayer meeting.
November 11	:	Spoke at prayer meeting.
November 12	:	Madan Mohan Malviya died. Gandhiji spoke at

		prayer meeting.
November 13	:	Had discussion with co-workers.
November 14	:	At Shahpur. Expressed disinclination for any police escort. At Kazirkhil, addressed prayer meeting.
November 15	:	Spoke at prayer meeting.
November 16	:	At Kazirkhil. Abdul Goffran, Minister for Civil Supplies, Ahmed Hussain, Agriculture Minister and a number of Parliamentary Sacretaries and Muslim League workers met Gandhiji in the evening to discuss rehabilitation proposals of the Government. At prayer meeting, Gandhiji expressed desire to live with a Muslim League member.
November 17	:	In the morning, visited Dashgharia; spoke to women. At Kazirkhil, addressed prayer meeting.
November 19	:	Resumed regular diet after the fast started on November 6; at 7.30 a. m. visited a Muslim house and talked about Koran to the inmates. At Madhupur, addressed prayer meeting. Gave interview to *The Hindu*.
November 20	:	Reached Srirampur with Nirmal Kumar Bose and Parasuram. In statement, declared decision to suspend correspondence including work for Harijan and the allied weeklies. In interview to *The Hindu,* explained his programme of activity in the village. At prayer meeting, explained the distribution of work.
November 21	:	Gave interview to Hindu political workers.
November 22	:	In interview to Nalini Mitra and Rashamoy Sur, warned : ". . . transfer of population ... would be suicidal for the whole country." In the evening, at Conference of Hindu-Muslim representatives, approved of the formation of Peace Committees and said that their success would depend upon right persons being put on the Committees.
November 23	:	54th session of Indian National Congress opened at Meerut.
November 24	:	Had discussion with Sarat Chandra Bose and his co-workers.

November 25	:	At Ramgunj. Spoke at Peace Committee meeting in the evening.
November 26	:	Gave interview to members of Communist Party and Students' Federation in the morning. Met visitors from Gita Press, Gorakhpur. Spoke at Prayer meeting.
November 27	:	In interview to the Press asserted that migration was no remedy.
November 28	:	Spoke at prayer meeting.
November 29	:	Spoke at prayer meeting.
November 30	:	Gave interview to United Press Representative who was staying with him near his cottage. In the evening, addressed prayer meeting.
December 2	:	Spoke at prayer meeting.
December 3	:	In letter to Suhrawardy, expressed misgivings about the functioning of Peace Committees. In statement, suggested solution of the deadlock over Constituent Assembly. Spoke at prayer meeting.
December 4	:	Gave interview to Amiya Chakravarty. Addressed prayer meeting.
December 5	:	In letter to Suhrawardy, suggested that "there should be an impartial commission appointed with the consent of the two Governments, to go into the disturbances, both in Noakhali and Bihar".
	:	Had discussion with Hindu Mahasabha leaders.
December 6	:	Spoke at prayer meeting.
December 7	:	Spoke at prayer meeting.
December 9	:	Deobhankar and other Congress leaders met Gandhiji.
December 10	:	Gandhiji spoke at prayer meeting.
December 11	:	Wrote to V.A. Sundaram about collection and distribution of funds for Malaviya Memorial. At prayer meeting, announced plan to undertake walking tour through villages.
December 12	:	Addressed prayer gathering.
December 14	:	At Madhupur. Opened Indian Medical Association Hospital. Addressed prayer meeting.

December 15 : In interview, advised Assam Congressmen that Assam "should lodge its protest and retire from the Constituent Assembly".

December 16 : At workers' meeting, advised them to learn the art of selfless service. At prayer meeting, recommended Jawaharlal Nehru's Resolution on the objectives of Constituent Assembly.

December 17 : Asaf Ali met Gandhiji. Gandhiji spoke at prayer meeting.

December 18 : At prayer meeting, expressed regret for exaggerated reports in the newspapers.

Before December 19 : Advised Sikhs to "never agree to grouping in any shape or form".

December 20 : Gave interview to Raymond Cartier. Spoke at prayer meeting.

December 21 : Spoke at prayer meeting.

December 23 : Dissuaded Nandigram refugees from hungerstrike. Spoke at prayer meeting.

December 24 : Spoke at prayer meeting.

December 25 : In message to the Secretary, Andhra Harijan Sevak Sangh, conveyed blessings to the temple-entry movement.

December 26 : Spoke at prayer meeting.

December 27 : Devnath Das of the Indian National Army and Dr. Pavitra Mohan Ray met Gandhiji. Gandhiji spoke at prayer meeting.

December 28 : At prayer meeting, introduced Jawaharlal Nehru and other Congress leaders.

December 29 : Had a talk with Gopinath Bardoloi on question of Assam's going into Sections.

December 30 : Sent blessings to Kashi Vidyapith on its silver jubilee celeberations.

December 31 : Spoke at prayer meeting.

1947

January 1 : Advised local weavers to use hand-spun yarn to get over difficulties in getting yarn. Spoke to people of Sambalpore who apprehended that the Hirakund project would be harmful to them. Spoke at prayer meeting.

January 2	:	Left Srirampur at 7.30 and reached Chandipur at 9 a. m. Addressed prayer meeting.
January 3	:	Advised women to "depend on God and on their own strength and not on others". Addressed prayer meeting.
January 4	:	Opened school at Chandirgaon village in the morning.
	:	Had discussion with members of Chandipur-Chandirgaon Gram Seva Sangh.
	:	At prayer meeting, advised the evacuees "to return home in the face of all possible dangers and difficulties".
January 5	:	Spoke at prayer meeting.
January 6	:	Spoke at prayer meeting.
January 7	:	Left Chandipur on village-to-village walking tour. At Masimpur, addressed Masimpur-Meroa Gram Seva Sangh. Had discussions with A. Zaman and Annada Choudhury. Addressed prayer meeting.
January 8	:	At Fatehpur. Had discussion with some Muslims. Spoke at prayer meeting.
January 9	:	In letter to H. S. Suhrawardy, asked for removal of police or military protection. At Daspara, addressed prayer meeting.
January 10	:	At Jagatpur. Addressed prayer meeting.
January 11	:	At Lamchar prayer meeting, advised evacuees to return home.
January 12	:	At Karpara.
January 14	:	At Bhatialpur. Addressed women.
January 15	:	At Narayanpur. Spoke at Gram Seva Sangh meeting in the afternoon. Addressed prayer meeting. Had discussion with members of American Friends' Service Unit and Sucheta Kripalani.
January 16	:	At Randebpur. Addressed prayer meeting.
January 17	:	At Parkote. Addressed women in the afternoon.
	:	Spoke to Gram Seva Sangh volunteers. Addressed prayer meeting.

January 18 : On way to Badalkote, talked to journalists. Addressed prayer meeting.

January 19 : In a note, reiterated his firm conviction that the "four-anna membership should go" and that the membership of the Congress should be "the whole of the population".

January 20 : At Sirhandi. After discussion with local Muslims prepared a draft pledge for their signatures and thereby succeeded in persuading Amtussalaam to give up fast. Amtussalaam broke 25 days' fast by taking orange-juice from Gandhiji's hands.

January 21 : At Kheturi. In statement to the Press, Gandhiji warned the country against adopting Roman script in place of Nagari and Persian. Spoke at prayer meeting.

January 22 : At Paniala. In letter, exhorted Harilal to "turn over a new leaf".

: At prayer meeting, advised Muslims to make amends for the wrongs done and not to depend on the Government.

January 23 : At Dalta. Addressed prayer meeting.

January 24 : At Muriyam. Gave interview to representatives of Krishak Samiti. Addressed prayer meeting.

January 26 : In letter to M. M. Tayabullah said that "A.I.C.C. resolution will not compel Assam to act against the wishes of the people". Addressed prayer meeting.

January 28 : At Panchgaon. Gave interview to Muslim deputation led by Mujibur Rehman.

January 29 : At Jayag. Spoke at prayer meeting.

January 30 : At prayer meeting, suggested construction of comfortable cottages for refugees.

January 31 : At Nabagram. Addressed women's meeting and prayer meeting.

February 1 : Stayed overnight at Nabagram. Gave interview to *The Hindu*. Reached Amishapara at 8.30 a. m. Met some British Army officers.

February 2 : Visited ruined houses on the way. At Satgharia.

February 3 : At Sadhurkhil. In prayer speech, referred to

		Muslim League's resolution on Constituent Assembly.
February 4	:	At Sadhurkhil. Addressed prayer meeting.
February 5	:	At Srinagar. Spoke at prayer meeting.
February 6	:	At Dharampur. Spoke at prayer meeting.
February 7	:	At Prasadpur. Met A. V. Thakkar, Satis Chandra Das Gupta, Hemprabha Devi, Shah Nawaz Khan, Niranjan Singh Gill, Haridas Bose and Bela Bose. Had talk with E. F. McInerny and A. Zaman about relief measures for refugees. Spoke at prayer meeting.
February 8	:	At Nandigram. Met Surendra Ghosh, Lavanyaprabha, Sushila Pai, Sucheta Kripalani. Wrote preface to *Ashram Bhajanavali*. At prayer meeting, answered questions.
February 9	:	At Vijaynagar. Commenced silence; his written answers to workers' questions were read out at prayer meeting.
February 10	:	Spoke at prayer meeting.
February 11	:	At Hamchandi. Met Satis Chandra Das Gupta and, Hemprabha Devi. At prayer meeting, answered questions on proposed Bargadars Bill.
February 12	:	At Kafilatali. Spoke at prayer meeting.
February 13	:	At East Keroa. Spoke at prayer meeting.
February 14	:	At West Keroa. Spoke at prayer meeting.
February 15	:	At Raipura. Visited ailing Imam Saheb. Answered questions at prayer meeting.
February 16	:	At Raipura, attended community dinner, visited mosque, met Muslim leaders. At prayer meeting, answering Fazlul Huq's reported speech, expressed doubts about its authenticity.
February 17	:	At Devipur. Admonished workers for elaborate reception arrangements. Spoke at prayer meeting.
February 18	:	At Alunia. Met Khaksars. Answered questions at prayer meeting. Visited ailing old man.
February 19	:	At Chardhukhia. Met E. W. Aryanayakum. Spoke at prayer meeting. Kasturba Gandhi's death anniversary according to Vikram Calendar observed.

February 20	:	At Char Larua. Had discussion with Amiya Chakravarty. Answered questions at prayer meeting.
February 21	:	Gandhiji was on a walking tour in Noakhali, covering "a village a day". Left Char Larua and reached Kamalapur at 9 a. m. Had talk with E. W. Aryanayakum. Met Satis Chandra Das Gupta and Niranjan Singh Gill. Spoke at prayer meeting.
February 22	:	Left Kamalapur at 7.35 a. m. Reached Char Krishnapur. Met A. V. Thakkar, Shardeshananda and other workers. At prayer meeting answered questions.
February 23	:	Left Char Krishnapur at 7.30 a. m. Reached Char Soladi at 8.30 a. m. At prayer meeting answered questions.
February 24	:	Left Char Soladi at 7.25 a. m. Visited Ramakrishna Mission Ashram on way.
	:	Reached Haimchar, the last stage of second part of walking tour. Had discussion with A. V. Thakkar. In letter to Jawaharlal Nehru, expressed views on Clement Attlee's statement. Spoke at prayer meeting.
February 25	:	Had talk with Deb Nath Das. Addressed public meeting in afternoon. Spoke at prayer meeting.
February 26	:	In statement to Press denounced South African Government's refusal of passports and impounding of identity certificates of Y. M. Dadoo and G. M. Naicker.
	:	At prayer meeting described his Ramarajya or Khudai Raj as Kingdom of God on earth.
February 27	:	Had discussion with Fazlul Huq. Answered questions at prayer meeting.
February 28	:	In statement to Press endorsed boycott by Asiatics and Africans of celebrations in connection with Royal visit to South Africa.
	:	Spoke at prayer meeting.
March 1	:	Gave interview to World Youth Delegation. Spoke at prayer meeting.
March 2	:	Left Haimchar. Reached Chandpur at 3.40 p.m. Addressed prayer meeting. Commenced silence.

	:	Boarded steamer at 10 p.m., left Chandpur. Had talk with Jiwan Singh.
March 3	:	Reached Goalando at 2.30 p.m. Boarded train, had talk with D. B. Kalelkar, reached Sodepur at 9.30 p.m. Gave interview to U. P. I.
March 4	:	Had talk with H. S. Suhrawardy. Addressed prayer meeting. Left Sodepur at 7.30 p.m. Boarded train to Patna.
March 5	:	Reached Patna in morning. Had discussion with Rajendra Prasad and Bihar Ministers. Addressed prayer meeting.
March 6	:	Had talks with Rajendra Prasad, Arvind Bose, Jayaprakash Narayan, Shrikrishna Sinha and Anugraha Narayan Sinha.
	:	Met Muslim League leaders and Hindus from Chhapra. Spoke at prayer meeting. Had talk with John Wardle Houlton, Relief Commissioner.
March 7	:	Had talk with Syed Mahmud. Met nationalist Muslims' deputation, members of Muslim Students' Federation, khadi workers and Khaksars. Addressed prayer meeting.
March 8	:	Met Muslims from Bhavalpur, Colonel Mahboob Ahmed of I.N.A., a Shia deputation, Sachchidananda Sinha and Anugraha Narayan Sinha. Gave interview to Mohammad Yunus. Spoke at prayer meeting. Abdul Ghaffar Khan arrived.
March 9	:	Gandhiji in interview to U. P. I. said that there was "no present intention of fasting". Had discussion with Binodanand Jha. Addressed Provincial Congress Committee members. His written speech was read out at prayer meeting.
March 10	:	Addressed prayer meeting. Had discussion with Ministers.
March 11	:	Had talk with Muslim League members. Addressed prayer meeting. Met Ministers.
March 12	:	Sent cable to Cavalcade. Addressed prayer meeting at Mangal Talao. Visited ruined houses and mosques on way.

March 13	:	Met Sikh deputation, Shah Nawaz Khan, S. M. Majmudar, Mahamayaprasad, Anugraha Narayan Sinha in afternoon.
	:	Visited ruined houses on way to Ebbadullah Chowk. Addressed prayer meeting.
March 14	:	Gave blessings to Syed Mahmud's son on eve of his wedding. Addressed prayer meeting at Khusropur village.
March 15	:	Had discussion with Muslim League Relief Committee members. Met Hugh Dow, Governor of Bihar. In prayer speech referred to his visit to Governor. Had discussion with Swami Anand and Kedar Nath.
March 16	:	Discussion with Swami Anand and Kedar Nath continued. Had talk with Dr. Syed Mahmud, S. N. Maulvi, Azad Hussain and Hakim Tasadduq Hussain. Met Muslim refugees and women. Had discussion with Bihar Ministers. Commenced silence.
March 17	:	Reached Masaurhi at 5.10 p.m. Addressed prayer meeting.
March 18	:	Visited ruined places. Had discussion with refugees. Had talk with N. K. Bose. Left for Bir at 3.45 p.m. Reached Bir at 5.10 p.m. Addressed prayer meeting. Had talk with Shrikrishna Sinha.
March 19	:	Had discussion with Congress workers. Had talk with village representatives. Addressed prayer meeting at Goriakharhi; returned to Bir. Had talk with Anugraha Narayan Sinha.
March 20	:	Left Bir at 6 a. m. Reached Masaurhi at 9.30 a. m. Met Y. M. Dadoo and G. M. Naicker. Visited Harla village. Addressed prayer meeting.
	:	Sent telegram to H. S. Suhrawardy about increasing cases of loot and arson in Noakhali. Had talk with Ministers.
March 21	:	Left for Hansdih. Saw ruined houses on way. Reached Hansdih at 9 a. m. Had talks with Muslim refugees and village representatives. Visited neighbouring villages. Addressed prayer meeting at Ghorhuan.

March 22	:	Visited Kharant village. Reached Pipalwan. Had talk with women refugees. Arrived in Patna at 10. a. m. Addressed prayer meeting.
March 23	:	Had talks with Syed Mahmud and Gladys Owen. Addressed meeting of women workers of Kasturba Memorial Fund. His written speech was read out a prayer meeting.
March 24	:	Met Gladys Owen. Visited Barhavan. Addressed prayer meeting at Rajghat. Returned to Patna. Lord Mountbatten sworn in as Viceroy and Governor-General of India.
March 25	:	Gandhiji addressed prayer meeting.
March 26	:	In letter to Viceroy, accepted his invitation to visit Delhi. Reached Jehanabad at 3.25 a. m. Visited Kako Relief Camp and Saistabad. Addressed prayer meeting.
March 27	:	Visited Amthua, had talk with Muslims. Visited Belti. Halted at Dhosi. Visited Abdullachak, Julfipur, Abdullapur and Okri. In prayer speech, at Okri, appealed to striking policemen to call off strike.
March 28	:	Had talks with Muslim refugees, representatives from surrounding villages and striking policemen. Addressed Congress workers in afternoon. Addressed prayer meeting at Allahganj. Abdul Bari shot dead.
	:	Gandhiji reached Patna at 9.30 p. m. Concluded third part of his tour programme in Bihar.
March 29	:	Attended funeral of Abdul Bari; offered condolence to family. Met Anugraha Narayan Sinha, Krishna Vallabh Sahay and Jayaprakash Narayan. In prayer speech paid tribute to Abdul Bari. Met Ministers.
March 30	:	Met Jayaprakash Narayan and Prabhavati. Left Patna at 9.30 a. m.
March 31	:	Reached Delhi in morning. Met Jawaharlal Nehru, C. Rajagopalachari, Sucheta Kripalani, G. D. Birla, and Vallabhbhai Patel.
	:	Met Viceroy in evening. Visited ailing Sarojini Naidu. Met Amrit Kaur and Shantikumar Morarjee.

April 1 : Met Abul Kalam Azad, Jawaharlal Nehru, C. Rajagopalachari and Rajendra Prasad in morning. Met Viceroy at 9 a. m.

: Met Choithram Gidwani and workers from Sind. Addressed Inter-Asian Relations Conference. Spoke at prayer meeting.

: Attended Congress Working Committee meeting. Had talk with Mirabehn.

April 2 : Gave message to Maharaja or Kapurthala. Had interview with Viceroy in afternoon. Addressed prayer meeting. Spoke at concluding session of Inter-Asian Relations Conference.

April 3 : Met Abul Kalam Azad, Rajendra Prasad and Amrit Kaur. Delegates from Tibet, Japan and Burma called in. Gandhiji had discussion with Y. M. Dadoo and G. M. Naicker. Addressed prayer meeting.

April 4 : Had talk with refugees from Rawalpindi. Had interview with Viceroy in afternoon. Addressed prayer meeting. Had talk with Egyptian delegates.

April 5 : Had talk with Dr. Sjahrir and European visitors. Met delegates from Malaya. Spoke at prayer meeting.

April 6 : Met J. B. Kripalani, Shankarrao Deo, Jawaharlal Nehru, and Abdul Majid. Participated in mass spinning. Addressed prayer meeting. Met Begum Gazanafar Ali and Vietnamese delegates.

April 7 : Sent telegram to H. S. Suhrawardy appealing for prompt action regarding increasing lawlessness in Noakhali. His written speech was read out at prayer meeting. Discussed constructive programme with two communist visitors.

April 8 : Gave interview to Sir M. Derling. Had discussion with C. Rajagopalachari, Abul Kalam Azad, Rajendra Prasad, Jawaharlal Nehru and other Congress leaders. Gave interview to American journalists. Addressed prayer meeting. Had discussion with Cabinet Ministers.

April 9	:	Had talks with people from Kathiawar and Abul Kalam Azad. Addressed prayer meeting.
April 10	:	Had talk with women workers. Addressed prayer meeting. Discussed draft formula with Jawaharlal Nehru, Abdul Ghaffar Khan, J. B. Kripalani, C. Rajagopalachari, Rajendra Prasad and other leaders; failed to "convince them of the correctness" of his plan.
April 11	:	In letter to Viceroy, conveyed his failure with Congress Working Committee members and expressed his intention to leave for Patna next day. Visited ailing Rajendra Prasad.
	:	Had talk with Y. M. Dadoo and G. M. Naicker. At prayer meeting told people about his decision to go to Bihar.
April 12	:	Met Rajendra Prasad and C. Rajagopalachari and Gopalaswami Ayyangar. Had talk with Sikhs. Called on Viceroy, signed "Joint Appeal" denouncing violence and calling upon all communities to refrain from using force. Met Arab delegation, a Chinese visitor, Baldeo Singh, C. H. Bhabha, Sir Datar Singh, V. K. Krishna Menon, French Ambassador and Congress leaders.
	:	At prayer meeting appealed to people to observe fast on April 13, the last day of National Week. Visited ailing Sarojini Naidu. Left Delhi at night.
April 13	:	Wrote to Viceroy on train. Had discussion with Manibhai B. Desai on Rural Reconstruction Trust, Uruli Kanchan. Reached Patna at 7.10 p. m.
April 14	:	Telegraphed to Viceroy that Congress President should also sign Joint Appeal, but left decision to Viceroy. Addressed prayer meeting. Had talk with Muslim League members.
April 15	:	Met Shah Nawaz Khan. Had talk with Syed Jafar Imam and Bihar Ministers. Addressed prayer meeting. Joint Appeal signed by M. A. Jinnah and issued to Press.
April 16	:	Gandhiji addressed prayer meeting. Had discussion with Ministers.

April 17 : Had talk with women and Congress workers. Gave message to Maharaja of Darbhanga. Met zamindars. Had talk with representatives of Jamiat-ul-Ulema. Addressed prayer meeting.

April 18 : Had talk with Syed Mahmud and other nationalists, Muslims, zamindars, peasant and labour leaders. Addressed prayer meeting. Had talk with Muslim students. Met Anil Roy and Lila Roy.

April 19 : Addressed workers of Hindustani Talimi Sangh and A.I.V.I.A. Attended meeting of A.I.S.A. Met two English women. Talking to Ministers explained ideal conduct for Ministers and Governors in independent India. Addressed prayer meeting.

April 20 : Addressed workers of Hindustani Talimi Sangh and A.I.V.I.A. Addressed prayer meeting.

April 21 : Attended meetings of A.I.S.A. and Hindustani Talimi Sangh. His written speech was read out at prayer meeting.

April 22 : Met khadi workers. Addressed Hindustani Talimi Sangh meeting. Had talk with Ministers. Addressed prayer meeting.

April 23 : Had talk with Muslim League members. Addressed meetings of Hindustani Talimi Sangh and A.I.S.A. Had talk with Peace Committee members. Addressed prayer meeting.

April 24 : Had talk with Houlton. Addressed Harijan workers at Sadaquat Ashram. Addressed prayer meeting. Had talk with Bihar Ministers.

April 25 : Had talk with two Englishmen. Addressed prayer meeting.

April 26 : Addressed prayer meeting. Attended Jamiat Islamia Conference.

April 27 : Had talk with Muslim women. Spoke to I.N.A. men. Addressed prayer meeting.

April 28 : Gave advice to students in writing. Announced his decision to leave for Delhi on April 30.

April 29 : Had discussion at Peace Committee meeting.

		Had talk with Bihar Ministers. Addressed prayer meeting.
April 30	:	Left Patna at 8 a. m. for Delhi.
May 1	:	Reached Delhi in morning. Attended Congress Working Committee meeting. Addressed prayer meeting.
May 2	:	Attended Congress Working Committee meeting. Addressed prayer meeting.
May 3	:	Addressed prayer meeting.
May 4	:	Attended Congress Working Committee meeting. Called on Viceroy. Addressed prayer meeting.
May 5	:	Issued statement to Press regarding proposed non-European rally on question of racial disabilities. Gave interview to Reuter's special correspondent. Addressed prayer meeting. Called on M. A. Jinnah in evening. Had discussion with Socialist leaders.
May 7	:	Addressed prayer meeting. Left Delhi.
May 9	:	Reached Calcutta, put up at Sodepur Ashram. Met Sarat Chandra Bose. Addressed prayer meeting.
May 10	:	Gave interview to Abul Hashem. Addressed prayer meeting.
May 11	:	H. S. Suhrawardy called on Gandhiji. Gandhiji addressed prayer meeting.
May 12	:	His speech was read out at prayer meeting. Had talk with H. S. Suhrawardy.
May 13	:	Discussed with Shyamaprasad Mookerjee scheme for united sovereign Bengal. Addressed prayer meeting.
May 14	:	Visited riot-affected areas in Calcutta. Addressed prayer meeting. Left Calcutta.
May 15	:	Reached Patna. Addressed prayer meeting. Manu Gandhi operated upon for appendicitis; Gandhiji was present during the operation.
May 16	:	Visited Manu Gandhi at hospital. Had talks with Abdul Qayum Ansari, Mridula Sarabhai, Anugraha Narayan Sinha and Jayaprakash Narayan. Addressed prayer meeting.

May 17 : Visited Manu Gandhi. Met Syed Mahmud and Jayaprakash Narayan. Visited Dinapur, could not address prayer meeting due to lack of order in the audience.

May 18 : Sent message for South Africa through Y.M. Dadoo and G. M. Naicker. Had talk with Abdul Qayum Ansari and Mridula Sarabhai. His written speech was read out at prayer meeting. Visited Manu Gandhi at Hospital.

May 19 : Met Y. M. Dadoo, G. M. Naicker, Kamaladevi Chattopadhyaya, Satyanarayan Sinha and Maharaja of Cooch Bihar.

: Visited Barh; addressed prayer meeting. Visited Manu Gandhi at hospital.

May 20 : Met deputation of zamindars and Khaksars. Visited Manu Gandhi at hospital. Visited Hilsa; addressed prayer meeting.

May 21 : Met Bihar Ministers. Visited Bikram; addressed prayer meeting.

May 22 : Visited Fatehpur; addressed prayer meeting.

May 23 : Visited Maner; addressed prayer meeting.

May 24 : Met Khaksars. Left Patna for Delhi.

May 25 : Gandhiji returned to New Delhi after visits to Calcutta and Patna.

May 26 : In New Delhi.

May 27 : Had discussion with Jayaprakash Narayan and co-workers. Called on Acting Viceroy Colville. Addressed prayer meeting.

May 28 : Received Chinese Ambassador who was accompanied by Jawaharlal Nehru; at prayer meeting answered questions.

May 29 : Addressed prayer meeting.

May 30 : Addressed prayer meeting.

May 31 : Addressed prayer meeting.

June 1 : Addressed prayer meeting.

June 2 : Met Viceroy along with other Congress and League leaders. Sought removal of the Governor of North-West Frontier Province. Attended

	Congress Working Committee meeting. In speech, which was read out at prayer meeting, expressed hope of a scavenger girl becoming first President of India.
June 3	: In letter, advised relatives to allow use of ancestral home for national purpose; at Congress Working Committee meeting, advised Socialists to serve party ungrudgingly; addressed prayer meeting.
June 4	: Spoke at Congress Working Committee meeting; met Viceroy; informed prayer meeting that Congress had accepted partition as last resort.
June 5	: In letter, deplored race for power; explained meaning of independence to students; at prayer meeting, announced death of D. D. Kosambi.
June 6	: At 4.30 p.m., met Viceroy; addressed prayer meeting.
June 7	: Addressed prayer meeting.
June 8	: In letter, advised Sarat Chandra Bose to give up struggle for United Bengal.
June 9	: Addressed prayer meeting.
June 10	: Addressed prayer meeting.
June 11	: Addressed prayer meeting.
June 12	: Attended meeting of the Congress Working Committee. Addressed prayer meeting.
June 13	: In letter to Lord Mountbatten, suggested that Jinnah be invited to Frontier Province before holding referendum; at prayer meeting, deplored Travancore State decision to stay "independent" of Constituent Assembly.
June 14	: Spoke at A.I.C.C. meeting; addressed prayer meeting.
June 15	: In the afternoon, received Travancore State delegation; at prayer meeting, talked about future of Princes.
June 16	: In the morning, received Purushottamdas Tandon. Addressed prayer meeting.
June 17	: Met Viceroy; also Jinnah; addressed prayer meeting.

June 18 : Accompanied by Abdul Ghaffar Khan, continued discussion with Jinnah; addressed prayer meeting.

June 19 : Addressed prayer meeting.

June 20 : Addressed prayer meeting.

June 21 : At Hardwar. Visited refugee camp.

June 22 : In Delhi. spoke to women working in refugee camps; addressed prayer meeting.

June 23 : Addressed prayer meeting.

June 24 : Addressed prayer meeting.

June 25 : Addressed prayer meeting.

June 26 : Met Viceroy; addressed prayer meeting.

June 27 : In letter, requested Lord Mountbatten to expedite action on Jawaharlal Nehru's visit Kashmir; addressed prayer meeting.

June 28 : At prayer meeting, spoke on rights and duties.

June 29 : At prayer meeting, continued talk on rights and duties.

June 30 : In telegram to Sivashunmugam Pillai, expressed joy on temple-entry in Rameswaram; in speech, which was read out at prayer meeting, said that "temple-entry should be followed up by true internal reform in temples".

July 1 : Accompanied by Jawaharlal Nehru and Vallabhbhai Patel, met Viceroy; noted down his comments on Indian Independence Bill; addressed prayer meeting.

July 2 : Spoke at Delhi Provincial Political Conference presided over by Jayaprakash Narayan; addressed prayer meeting.

July 3 : Addressed Prayer meeting.

July 4 : In letter, expressed disbelief in civil marriages; addressed prayer meeting.

July 5 : Received Lady Mountbatten; advised Abdul Ghaffar Khan that he and his people should boycott referendum.

July 6 : Addressed prayer meeting.

July 7 : In speech which was read out at prayer meeting,

		wanted Congress-League understanding without Viceroy's intervention.
July 8	:	Had discussion with Sushila Nayyar and Aruna Asaf Ali; was interviewed by deputation from Quetta; also by V. K. Krishna Menon; addressed prayer meeting.
July 9	:	Met Viceroy, addressed prayer meeting.
July 10	:	Felicitated Princess Elizabeth and Philip Mountbatten on their engagement; was interviewed by Arthur Moore; also by Winkleman; addressed prayer meeting.
July 11	:	Addressed prayer meeting.
July 12	:	At prayer meeting, explained reason for making Lord Mountbatten Governor-General of India, while Pakistan preferred Jinnah.
July 13	:	Addressed prayer meeting.
July 14	:	Addressed prayer meeting.
July 15	:	Addressed prayer meeting.
July 16	:	In a letter, informed Viceroy he intended to visit Kashmir as private citizen; at prayer meeting, spoke on language issue.
July 17	:	In discussion with visitors, stressed need for cultivating non-violence of the brave.
July 18	:	Felicitated the Mountbattens on silver jubilee of their wedding.
July 19	:	In letter to Viceroy, expressed readiness to postpone Kashmir visit; gave interview to Naga delegation.
July 20	:	In speech at prayer meeting, said that condition in country did not warrant rejoicing on August 15, Independence Day.
August 1	:	Gandhiji reached Srinagar.
August 4	:	Reached Jammu.
August 5	:	Spoke at Gurudwara Punja Saheb; addressed prayer meeting at Wah Refugee Camp.
August 6	:	Reached Lahore; answered questions put by Congress workers; in evening left for Patna en route to Calcutta.

August 8	:	At Patna, addressing prayer meeting said that 15th August should be celebrated by fasting, spinning and prayer.
August 9	:	Reached Calcutta; put up at Sodepur Ashram.
August 10	:	Gave interview to Congress Ministers of Bengal; received Muslim deputation; at prayer meeting announced decision to postpone visit to Noakhali by two days.
August 11	:	In response to H. S. Suhrawardy's request to extend stay in Calcutta, proposed to live with him and work together till every Hindu and Muslim was safe.
August 12	:	At prayer meeting, announced that he and Suhrawardy would live and work together in disturbed areas until peace was restored.
August 13	:	Moved into "Hydari Mansion" in riot-affected area where, on arrival, faced angry demonstration by Hindus.
August 15	:	Observed Independence Day by fasting, spinning, prayer.
August 16	:	Had discussion with Rev. John Kellas.
August 18	:	At prayer meeting, offered Id greetings to Muslims.
August 19	:	Visited industrial area at Kancharapara where police had resorted to firing near a mosque.
August 20	:	In interview to Press, declined to comment on political matters as he wanted to utilize the media for Hindu-Muslim unity.
August 21	:	Spoke at women's meeting.
August 22	:	Answered questions put by Kasturba Trust trainees.
August 24	:	Invited readers' opinion about the desirability of continuing *Harijan* weeklies.
August 30	:	Was described as "one-man boundary force" by Mountbatten in letter.
	:	In interview, told Randolph Churchill that he still considered partition a "sin".
August 31	:	Addressed Muslim merchants at Grand Hotel. Faced violent demonstration but escaped unhurt.

September 1	: Deeply disturbed by eruption of violence, went on fast at 8.15 p. m. to be given up "only if and when sanity returned to Calcutta". In talk with Rajagopalachari, refused to give up fast.
September 2	: Put off scheduled journey to Lahore; in evening, had talks with Sarat Chandra Bose and P. C. Ghosh.
September 3	: Had discussion with Hindu and Muslim representatives.
September 4	: Broke fast after assurances from leaders of all communities to stop riots and maintain communal harmony.
September 5	: In message to Shanti Sena Dal said : "My life is my message."
September 7	: Visited Gobra Leprosy Hospital and spoke to patients and staff; left for Delhi.
September 9	: Reached Delhi; put up at Birla House.
September 11	: Gave interview to Sikh deputation; visited Irwin Hospital.
September 12	: At prayer meeting, referred to disturbances in North-West Frontier Province.
September 16	: Spoke at R. S. S. rally; abandoned prayer due to objection to recitation from Koran.
September 17	: At prayer meeting, exhorted people to curb anger to qualify themselves for independence.
September 18	: Addressed Muslim gathering in Daryaganj mosque; had discussion with Suhrawardy.
September 21	: Addressed prayer meeting although prayer had to be abandoned, as recitation from Koran was objected to.
September 22	: Announced decision to continue publication of *Harijan* weeklies.
September 24	: In discussion with Jam Saheb of Nawanagar, advised rulers of Kathiawar to remain united.
September 25	: In talk with J. B. Kripalani, reiterated opposition to permanent exchange of population.
September 26	: Had discussion with Suhrawardy.
September 29	: At prayer meeting, expressed disapproval of unfounded Press reports.

October 2 : On his 78th birthday when advised by doctors to take penicillin, declared that Ramanama was his sole remedy.

October 6 : In speech read out at prayer meeting emphasized need for self-sufficiency in food.

October 9 : Had discussion with Suhrawardy.

October 11 : Spoke to Gujaratis who presented purse in honour of his birthday.

October 13 : In speech at prayer meeting emphasized need for cleanliness and sanitation in refugee camps.

October 17 : In letter to Julian Huxley, wrote :"rights to be deserved and preserved come from duty well done"; gave interview to Gujarati correspondents of All-India Radio.

October 19 : In afternoon, explained significance of silence to Lady Handes.

October 20 : Addressed prayer meeting.

October 22 : Had talks with Christian pacifists and Muslims.

October 25 : Had talk with communists.

October 26 : Advised Muslims to resolve on Id not to spill blood but to offer it as sacrifice.

October 27 : At prayer meeting called upon the Services to rise above communalism.

October 30 : Advised Sind Congress leaders to settle down in villages, if they had no courage to return to Sind.

October 31 : At prayer meeting, exhorted people to uphold their religion without any fear.

November 1 : At prayer meeting, referred to condition of refugees in Kurukshetra and events in Kashmir. Met Horace Alexander.

Before November 2 : Gave interview to Ronald Stead.

November 2 : At prayer meeting referred to events in Kashmir.

November 3 : At prayer meeting, spoke in favour of lifting food control.

November 4 : Addressed prayer meeting.

November 5 : Gave interview to Chinese delegation. At prayer meeting, referred to Kashmir issue.

November 6	:	Attended Food Committee meeting and discussed removal of food control. At prayer meeting, referred to his proposal of lifting food control.
	:	In interview to Chinese delegation gave message of peace and non-violence.
November 7	:	Had talk with Indonesian visitors. Visited Tihar village.
	:	At prayer meeting, advised refugees in Delhi to become selfsupporting citizens.
November 8	:	Met Lady Mountbatten. At prayer meeting, advised decontrol of cloth. Gave interview to Burmese delegation.
November 9	:	Addressed prayer meeting.
November 10	:	Visited Panipat. At prayer meeting welcomed accession of Junagadh to Indian Union.
November 11	:	Gandhiji was in Delhi. Had talks with Shankarrao Deo, J. B. Kripalani, Rajendra Prasad, Manibehn Patel and Amrit Kaur. Attended Congress Working Committee meeting. In his address at prayer meeting defended Government of India having taken over administration in Junagadh.
November 12	:	Had talks with Muslim students and H. S. Suhrawardy. Broadcasted message for refugees at Kurukshetra Camp from All India Radio in the afternoon. Attended Congress Working Committee meeting. Addressed prayer meeting.
November 13	:	Attended Congress Working Committee meeting. Had talks with Rajendra Prasad, Sucheta Kripalani, H. S. Suhrawardy, Dr. Jivraj Mehta, Profulla Chandra Ghosh, Shankarrao Deo, B. G. Kher, Jawaharlal Nehru, Prabhavati and Anantrai Pattani.
	:	Addressed prayer meeting.
November 14	:	Attended Congress Working Committee meeting. Had talks with Rajendra Prasad, Mridula Sarabhai, Dr. Kitchlew, Sudhir Ghosh and H. S. Suhrawardy. Addressed prayer meeting. Burma Independence Bill passed in House of Commons.

November 15	: Gandhiji attended Congress Working Committee meeting. Had talks with Rajendra Prasad, J. B. Kripalani, C. Rajagopalachari, Sudhir Ghosh, Jawaharlal Nehru, Dada Dharmadhikari and Anantrai Pattani.
	: Addressed A. I. C. C. meeting. Resolutions on "Rights of Minorities', "Repatriation of Refugees" and "States" passed by A.I.C.C. J. B. Kripalani resigned from Congress Presidentship. Gandhiji addressed prayer meeting.
November 16	: Attended Congress Working Committee meeting. Had talks with H. S. Suhrawardy, Vallabhbhai Patel and Jawaharlal Nehru.
	: Resolutions on "Communal Disturbances", "Private Armies", "Controls", "The Congress Constitution" and "Congress Objectives" passed by A. I. C. C.
Novemebr 17	: Gandhiji attended Congress Working Committee meeting. Had talks with Rameshwari Nehru, A. V. Thakkar, Horace Alexander, Jamnadas Dwarkadas and Rammanohar Lohia. His speech was read out at prayer meeting.
	: A. I. C. C. accepted J. B. Kripalani's resignation, elected Rajendra Prasad as President and concluded its. session.
November 18	: Gandhiji had talks with Rajendra Prasad, Jayaprakash Narayan, Jawaharlal Nehru, Dr. Syed Mahmud, Sucheta Kripalani, Gopalaswami Iyengar, Dewan of Rampur, Shah Nawaz Khan, Dada Dharmadhikari, Gopalrao and Achyut Patwardhan.
	: Explained Congress Resolution on "Rights of Minorities" in his prayer address and appealed to people to support and follow it. Constituent Assembly met for the first time as Dominion Parliament. G. V. Mavalankar elected its Speaker.
November 19	: Gandhiji had talks with Rajendra Prasad, Rameshwari Nehru, Amrit Kaur, Dr. Syed Mahmud, Sir Akbar Hydari, Jairamdas Doulatram, Shah Nawaz Khan,

Mahamayaprasad, H. S. Suhrawardy and Lord Ismay. Addressed prayer meeting.

November 20 : Had talks with Rajendra Prasad, Shankarrao Deo, C. Rajagopalachari, Sophiabehn and Sudhir Ghosh. Visited Refugee camp near Okhla along with Sucheta Kripalani in afternoon. Went to Government House to meet C. Rajagopalachari and ailing Sarojini Naidu. Addressed prayer meeting. Indian Resolution calling for a Round Table Conference on treatment of Indians in South Africa failed to pass in United Nations General Assembly.

: Princess Elizabeth married Philip Mountbatten.

November 21 : Gandhiji had talks with Rajendra Prasad, Shankarrao Deo, Rameshwari Nehru, Choithram Gidwani, K. C. Neogi, Jawaharlal Nehru, Egyptian Delegation, Rammanohar Lohia, Dr. Chimanlal and Harekrushna Mehtab. Addressed prayer meeting.

November 22 : Had talks with Rajendra Prasad, Rameshwari Nehru, Mahavir Tyagi, Gopalaswamy Ayyangar, John Matthai, Shah Nawaz Khan, Mridula Sarabhai, Nalini Sen, Indira Gandhi, Pheroz Gandhi, Gopalrao Kale, Rammanohar Lohia, Sucheta Kripalani, Naliniranjan Sarkar and Vallabhbhai Patel. Addressed prayer meeting.

Novermber 23 : Had talks with Rajendra Prasad, Horace Alexander, B. G. Kher, Morarji Desai, Maharani of Vijayanagar, Sophiabehn, Reddiar, A. V. Thakkar, K. Srinivasan, Dr. Gopichand Bhargava, Vallabhbhai Patel, Khandubhai Desai, Girijashankar Bajpai and Jawaharlal Nehru. Addressed prayer meeting. Visited ailing Manibehn Patel.

November 24 : His speech was read out at prayer meeting. Met Rajendra Prasad, C. Rajagopalachari, Horace Alexander, Mridula Sarabhai, Anantrai Pattani, Khwaja Abdul Majid, Rameshwari Nehru, Brijlal Nehru, Raja of Bilaspur and Amrit Kaur.

November 25 : Had talks with Rajendra Prasad, Khwaja Abdul

Majid, Sophiabehn, Aruna Asaf Ali, Subhadra Gupta, Jawaharlal Nehru, Amrit Kaur and Lady Mountbatten. Addressed prayer meeting.

November 26 : Had talks with Rajendra Prasad, C. Rajagopalachari, Abul Kalam Azad, Rameshwari Nehru, Gopinath Bardoloi and Jawaharlal Nehru. Addressed prayer meeting. Vithoba temple at Pandharpur thrown open to Harijans. Lord Mountbatten resumed office of Governor-General. Ceylon Independence Bill passed by House of Commons.

November 27 : Gandhiji called on Lord Mountbatten. Visited ailing Liaquat Ali. Had talks with Rajendra Prasad, J. B. Kripalani, Sheikh Abdullah, Jamnadas Dwarkadas and Balwantrai Mehta. Addressed prayer meeting.

November 28 : Had talks with American visitors, Sheikh Abdullah, Abul Kalam Azad, Dr. Sjahrir, Vallabhbhai Patel and Jawaharlal Nehru. Spoke at Guru Nanak birthday celebration. Addressed prayer meeting.

November 29 : Had talks with Rajendra Prasad, C. Rajagopalachari, Surendra Mohan Ghosh, Muslims from Panipat and Jawaharlal Nehru. Addressed prayer meeting.

November 30 : Had talks with Maulanas, Kasturbhai Lalbhai Shah, S. Radhakrishnan, Vallabhbhai Patel, Dinshaw K. Mehta and Jehangir Patel. Addressed prayer meeting. Agreement signed between India and Hyderabad.

December 1 : Gandhiji had talks with Lt.-Gen. K. M. Cariappa, Rajendra Prasad, Dinshaw K. Mehta, Jehangir C. Patel and Jawaharlal Nehru. His speech was read out at prayer meeting.

December 2 : Visited Panipat, had talks with Muslim refugees, Muslim leaders and Dr. Gopichand Bhargava. Spoke at public meeting. Met Mridula Sarabhai. Addressed prayer meeting.

December 3 : Had talks with Mehra Chand Khanna, Kamaladevi Chattopadhyaya, Bakshi Ghulam

		Mohammed, Lt.-Gen. K. M. Cariappa and Jawaharlal Nehru. Addressed prayer meeting.
December 4	:	Had talks with Amrit Kaur, Jehangir C. Patel, Khurshed Naoroji, Burmese Premier and Syamaprasad Mukherjee. Addressed prayer meeting.
December 5	:	Had talks with Rajendra Prasad, Anugrahanarayan Singh, Mridula Sarabhai, Ghanshyam Singh Gupta, Jawaharlal Nehru, Renuka Ray, Dr. Jivraj Mehta and Annada Chowdhary. Addressed prayer meeting.
December 6	:	Had talks with Horace Alexander, Khurshed Naoroji, Abul Kalam Azad, Vallabhbhai Patel, Saralabehn Sarabhai, G. V. Mavalankar and M. S. Subbulakshmi. Subbulakshmi sang bhajan at prayer meeting. Gandhiji addressed the gathering.
	:	Inter-Dominion Conference held in Lahore to consider ways and means for restoration of abducted women and forced converts.
December 7	:	Gandhiji addressed Kasturba Gandhi National Memorial Trust meeting. Had talks with Sindhi friends, Vallabhbhai Patel, Jawaharlal Nehru, Sucheta Kripalani and Mridula Sarabhai. In his address at prayer meeting stated that restoration of abducted women should be a matter of first priority with Indian and Pakistan Governments.
December 8	:	Had talks with U. N. Dhebar, Bhaktiba, C. P. Ramaswami, Sucheta Kripalani, J. B. Kripalani, Renuka Ray and Jawaharlal Nehru. His speech was read out at prayer meeting. Control on sugar removed.
December 9	:	Gandhiji had talks with Shankarrao Deo, Saralabehn Sarabhai, Khurshed Naoroji and Jawaharlal Nehru. Attended meetings of Kasturba Gandhi National Memorial Trust and All-India Spinners' Association. Had discussion with women workers of K. G. N. M. Trust. Addressed prayer meeting.
December 10	:	Had talks with H. S. Suhrawardy, Jayaprakash

	Narayan and Satis Chandra Das Gupta. Had discussion with members of K. G. N. M. Trust, teachers and students. Addressed Hindustani Talimi Sangh meeting. In address at prayer meeting dwelt on the activities of A. I. S. A.
December 11 :	Had talks with J. C. Kumarappa, Amrit Kaur and Jawaharlal Nehru. Addressed Constructive Works Committee meeting. Met rulers of Sangli, Aundh, Phaltan, Miraj (Senior) and Ramdurg. Demonstration held in Calcutta against Security Bill.
December 12 :	Gandhiji had talks with D. B. Kalelkar, Shankarrao Deo, Ghanshyamdas Birla and Dr. Gopichand Bhargava. Addressed Constructive Works Committee meeting. Spoke at prayer meeting.
December 13 :	Had talks with D. B. Kalelkar, Acharya Jugal Kishore, R. R. Diwakar, Pandit Sundarlal, Satis Chandra Das Gupta, Lakshmidas and Jamnadas Dwarkadas. Addressed prayer meeting.
December 14 :	Had talks with Y. M. Parnerkar, Perinbehn Captain, Khurshed Naoroji, G. Ramachandran, Saundaram, Satis Chandra Das Gupta, Amrit Kaur and Jawaharlal Nehru. Addressed prayer meeting. Had discussion with constructive workers.
December 15 :	Had talks with Pyarelal, Maulanas, Anantrai Pattani, J. C. Kumarappa and Amrit Kaur. His speech was read out at prayer meeting.
December 16 :	Had talks with Pyarelal, Satis Chandra Das Gupta, Arun Chandra Guha, Princess of Belgium, Amrit Kaur, Vallabhbhai Patel and visitors from Jammu. Addressed prayer meeting.
December 17 :	Sent message to U.P. students. Had talks with Shankarrao Deo, Sushila Pai, Sir Datar Singh, Dr. Acharya, Maharaja of Bhavnagar, Maulanas and Jawaharlal Nehru. Addressed prayer meeting.
December 18 :	Had talks with Rajendra Prasad, Shankarrao Deo, H. S. Suhrawardy, French Ambassador,

Rammanohar Lohia, Dr. Gopichand Bhargava, Swaran Singh and Jawaharlal Nehru. Addressed prayer meeting.

December 19 : Addressed Meos at Jesarah, a village in Gurgaon tehsil. Had discussion with Rajendra Prasad, Vallabhbhai Patel and Jawaharlal Nehru in the morning and again in the evening. Had talks with Pyarelal, Dr. Chandubhai, Dinkarbhai Desai, K. M. Munshi and Maharaja of Kapurthala. Addressed prayer meeting.

December 20 : Had talks with Rana Petis, Sri Prakasa and Jawaharlal Nehru. Met people from Bahawalpur, Mirpur and Jammu. Addressed prayer meeting.

December 21 : Had talks with H. S. Suhrawardy, Brijlal Nehru, Rameshwari Nehru, Sheikh Abdullah, Begum Abdullah, Dr. Kitchlew, Bakshi Ghulam Mohammed, Nawab of Chhatari, Prince of Kutch, Maharaja of Bhavnagar and Anantrai Pattani. Addressed prayer meeting. Met Vijayalakshmi Pandit and Jawaharlal Nehru. United Deccan State formed.

December 22 : Gandhiji had talks with Pandit Sundarlal, H. S. Suhrawardy, Lakshmidas Asar, Raosaheb Patwardhan, Rammanohar Lohia and Jawaharlal Nehru. His speech was read out at prayer meeting. Rajendra Prasad took over as President of Congress.

December 23 : Gandhiji had talks with J. B. Kripalani, Sucheta Kripalani, Lakshmidas Asar, H. S. Suhrawardy, Nawab of Khamwat, Jawaharlal Nehru, Lady Mountbatten, Vallabhbhai Patel and K. M. Munshi. Met local Muslims, people from Bahawalpur and Rawalpindi. Addressed prayer meeting. Had discussion with Vallabhbhai Patel and Jawaharlal Nehru.

December 24 : Met J. B. Kripalani and Maulanas. Addressed prayer meeting. Had discussion with Vallabhbhai Patel and Jawaharlal Nehru in the evening.

December 25 : Had talks with Sevakram, Dinshaw K. Mehta, Jehangir G. Patel, Rameshwari Nehru, Vallabhbhai Patel, Jawaharlal Nehru and women delegates from Indonesia. Met local Maulanas. In address at prayer meeting referred to Kashmir dispute and spoke against inviting a third party for arbitration.

December 26 : Had talks with Sevakram, Dinshaw K. Mehta, Shamaldas Gandhi, U. N. Dhebar, Balwantrai Mehta, Sardar Nihalsingh, Choithram Gidwani and Kikibehn. Addressed prayer meeting. Had discussion with Vallabhbhai Patel and Jawaharlal Nehru.

December 27 : Called on Lord Mountbatten at 10.30 a. m. Had talks with Jehangir C. Patel, Vallabhbhai Patel, Jawaharlal Nehru, deputation from Ajmer led by Haribhau Upadhyaya and Martanda Upadhyaya. Addressed prayer meeting at Sambhal, a village.

December 28 : Had talks with Jehangir C. Patel, Shamaldas Gandhi, U. N. Dhebar, Maharaja of Patiala, Jawaharlal Nehru and Sheikh Abdullah. Addressed meeting of cloth merchants. In address at prayer meeting advocated decontrol of cloth.

December 29 : Had talks with U. N. Dhebar, Shamaldas Gandhi, Balwantrai Mehta, Anantrai Pattani and Jawaharlal Nehru. In address at prayer meeting paid tribute to Hakim Ajmal Khan.

December 30 : Had talks with Rameshwari Nehru, Vallabhbhai Patel, Sheikh Abdullah, Diwan of Kutch and Abul Kalam Azad. In address at prayer meeting appealed to Nawab of Bahawalpur to arrange for evacuation of Hindus and Sikhs. Had discussion with Jawaharlal Nehru and J.B. Kripalani.

December 31 : Had talks with Subhadra Gupta, Anantrai Pattani, Amrit Kaur and Congress volunteers. Addressed prayer meeting. Government of India decided to refer Kashmir issue to United Nations Security Council.

Chapter Eight

Attaining Martyrdom

1948

January 1	:	Gandhiji had talks with Amrit Kaur, Anantrai Pattani, Gyani Kartarsingh and Sardar Dilip Singh. In his address at prayer meeting appealed to Government to enforce prohibition. Government of India took over administration of 25 Orissa States.
January 2	:	Kashmir issue referred to United Nations Security Council. Gandhiji had talks with Dev Prakash Nayyar, Chandrani and Jawaharlal Nehru. Addressed prayer meeting.
January 3	:	Had talks with Rajendra Prasad, Jawaharlal Nehru, Amrit Kaur and Maulanas. Addressed prayer meeting at Wavell Canteen refugee camp. Provisional Government of Junagadh dissolved.
January 4	:	Gandhiji had talks with Rajendra Prasad, Pandit Sundarlal, Zakir Husain, Jawaharlal Nehru, and Muslim leaders. In his address at prayer meeting justified Government of India having taken Kashmir issue to United Nations Security Council. Free Republic of Burma proclaimed.
January 5	:	Gandhiji had talks with Munnalal G. Shah, Subhadra Gupta, Jawaharlal Nehru and Maulanas. In his written speech for prayer meeting commented on decontrol of food.

January 6 : Met Khurshed Naoroji, Krishnan Nair, Raja and Rani of Mandi, Rameshwari Nehru and Brijlal Nehru. Had talk with Jawaharlal Nehru. In address at prayer meeting advised dock workers in Bombay against going on strike. U. N. Security Council adjourned hearing on Kashmir issue. Sikh refugees in a Gurudwara in Karachi attacked by Muslim mob.

January 7 : Gandhiji had talks with Gopalaswamy Ayyangar, M.S. Aney, Abdul Ghani, Rameshwari Nehru and Mridula Sarabhai. Met people from Punjab, Sindh and N.W.F.P. In speech at prayer meeting, remonstrated with Pakistan Government about incident in Karachi.

January 8 : Had talks with D. B. Kalelkar, J. B. Kripalani, Sucheta Kripalani, Kikibehn, Rukmini Erulkar, Vallabhbhai Patel, Anantrai Pattani, A. V. Thakkar, Dr. Kitchlew, Sheikh Abdullah and Jawaharlal Nehru. In his speech at prayer meeting advised students not to go on strike.

January 9 : Had talks with Vallabhbhai Patel, Manubhai Pancholi, Balwantrai Mehta, Mohanbhai Motichand Gadhadawala, Sriman Narayan, Jawaharlal Nehru and Rameshwari Nehru. Addressed prayer meeting.

January 10 : Had talks with Anantrai Pattani, N. V. Gadgil, Iranian Ambassador and Jawaharlal Nehru. In prayer speech assured evacuation of refugees from Bahawalpur.

January 11 : Had talks with Shankarrao Deo, Rajendra Prasad, Bhimsen Sachchar, Sorabji Rustom, Pragjibhai and Anantrai Pattani. Addressed prayer meeting.

January 12 : Vallabhbhai Patel in statement to Press, replied to allegations made by Finance Minister of Pakistan and justified Government of India's stand that settlement of the financial issues could not be isolated from vital issues like Kashmir. Gandhiji met Jamnadas and Vallabhbhai Patel. In written speech at prayer meeting, announced decision to go on fast to establish communal unity. Called on Lord Mountbatten. Had talks with Jawaharlal Nehru, Jamnadas and Devdas Gandhi. M. S. Aney sworn in Governor of Bihar.

January 13 : Gandhiji began fast at 11 a.m. with prayers. Had talk with Vallabhbhai Patel. Met Amrit Kaur, Abul Kalam Azad, Jairamdas Doulatram, H. S. Suhrawardy, Purushottamdas Trikumji and Anantrai Pattani. In address at prayer meeting said he would end his fast when peace returned to Delhi. Train carrying non-Muslim refugees from Bannu attacked at Gujrat railway station by tribesmen; hundreds were killed and wounded and women abducted.

January 14 : Gandhiji continued fast. Had discussion with Jawaharlal Nehru, Vallabhbhai Patel, John Matthai and Shanmukham Chetty. Met deputation from N. W. F. P., Amrit Kaur, Maharaja of Patiala, Gurbachansingh, Sucheta Kripalani, Mehar Chand Khanna, Bakshi Ghulam Mohammed and H. S. Suhrawardy. Was examined by Drs. Jivraj Mehta, Bidhan Chandra Roy and Sushila Nayyar and advised rest. Addressed prayer meeting. Health bulletin announced that "each day's fast increased both immediate and future danger" to Gandhiji's life.

January 15 : Gandhiji met Jawaharlal Nehru, Pandit Sundarlal, Goswami Ganesh Datt, V. T. Krishnamachari, Kasturbhai Lalbhai Shah, Shankarrao Deo, Acharya Jugal Kishore, B. G Kher, Maharaja of Devas, Rajendra Prasad, Shah Nawaz Khan, Jairamdas Doulatram, Shanmukham Chetty and K. C. Neogi. On third day of fast, became considerably weak and had to be carried in an armchair. Spoke briefly on microphone, lying in bed; his dictated speech dealing with questions put by journalists, was read out. Government of India announced implementation of financial agreement with Pakistan regarding balance of payment as gesture of goodwill. Debate on Kashmir issue began in United Nations Security Council.

January 16 : Rajendra Prasad, Jawaharlal Nehru, Abul Kalam Azad, Jayaprakash Narayan, Prabhavati, Shankarrao Deo, Rammanohar Lohia, Sucheta Kripalani, Shah Nawaz Khan and Sikh deputation called on Gandhiji. Health bulletin said that Gandhiji's kidneys were not functioning properly. Gandhiji, lying in bed, spoke a few words on microphone; his dictated speech was read out at prayer meeting. Jawaharlal Nehru, Jairamdas Doulatram, Amrit Kaur and Jayaprakash Narayan addressed public meetings appealing to people to maintain peace and save Gandhiji's life.

January 17 : Gandhiji's condition deteriorated on fifth day of fast. Health bulletin said it was most undesirable to let fast continue and appealed to people to create conditions for ending fast without delay. Abul Kalam Azad, Sir Padmasingh, Gopinath Bardoloi, Jawaharlal Nehru, Satyanarayan Sinha, Lord and Lady Mountbatten, Rammanohar Lohia and Nawab Sadaquat Ali Khan called. Gandhiji had talk with Rajendra Prasad and G. D. Birla. Lying in bed, addressed a few words on microphone; his dictated speech was read out at a mammoth prayer gathering. Abul Kalam Azad, at a public meeting, announced seven conditions on which Gandhiji was prepared to end fast. Representatives of different communities and organizations assembled at Rajendra Prasad's residence in evening.

January 18 : Sixth day of fast. Gandhiji complained of stomach ache, was extremely restless. Over a hundred representatives of various groups and organizations in Delhi came to Gandhiji, signed a declaration of assurance on seven conditions. Rajendra Prasad signed declaration as Congress President. On receipt of assurance prayers were held and Gandhiji broke fast at 12.15 p.m. Gave message to Sikhs on Guru Govind Singh's birth anniversary. Lying in bed, spoke on microphone

		for twenty minutes; his dictated speech was read out at prayer meeting.
January 19	:	Had talks with Jamshedji, Jehangir C. Patel, Dinshaw K. Mehta, H. S. Suhrawardy and Jawaharlal Nehru. Was carried to prayer ground in a chair, his written speech was read out at prayer meeting. Central Peace Committee formed to implement assurances given to Gandhiji. Government decided to decontrol cloth.
January 20	:	Gandhiji had talks with Jamshedji Mehta, Jawaharlal Nehru and Amrit Kaur. While addressing prayer meeting a bomb exploded a short distance away. Gandhiji continued address after the interruption. Madanlal Pahwa was apprehended. United Nations Security Council agreed to set up a three power commission to mediate between India and Pakistan over Kashmir dispute.
January 21	:	Security measures were tightened in Birla House. Gandhiji turned down suggestion for searching people coming to prayer meeting. Met Sikh deputation. Had talks with Iftikhar-ud-Din and Jawaharlal Nehru. Addressed prayer meeting, had to be carried in a chair.
January 22	:	Had discussion with Jawaharlal Nehru. Addressed prayer meeting.
January 23	:	Had talks with Jawaharlal Nehru and Sucheta Kripalani. In his speech at prayer meeting, paid tribute to Subhas Chandra Bose on his birth anniversary. Kathiawar rulers signed covenant approving creation of Saurashtra Province, a United State.
January 24	:	Gandhiji attended Congress Working Committee meeting. In speech at prayer meeting, stressed need to return all abducted women unconditionally. Had talk with Jawaharlal Nehru.
January 25	:	Attended Congress Working Committee meeting. Addressed prayer meeting.
January 26	:	Had talks with Gopichand Bhargava, Prafulla Chandra Ghosh and Annada Chowdhary.

Attended Congress Working Committee meeting. His written speech was read out at prayer meeting.

January 27 : Visited shrine of Khwaja Kutub-ud-Din Bakhtiar at Mehrauli; addressed gathering there. Had talks with Govind Ballabh Pant, Abul Kalam Azad, Maharaja of Vijayanagar, Justice Ramlal, Mehar Chand Khanna, Jawaharlal Nehru and Rameshwari Nehru. Gave interview to Kingsley Martin and Vincent Sheean. Had discussion with R. R. Diwakar, Acharya Jugal Kishore and members of Congress Constitution Sub-committee. Addressed prayer meeting.

January 28 : Had talks with Rajendra Prasad, members of Central Relief Committee, Nawab Sadiq Ali Khan, Jawaharlal Nehru, Amrit Kaur and Vincent Sheean. Addressed prayer meeting.

January 29 : Had talks with Prabhavati, Jayaprakash Narayan, Padmaja Naidu, Krishna Hutheesinh, Indira Gandhi, Rajen Nehru and Sudhir Ghosh. Gave interview to Margaret Bourke-White and General Secretary of Y.W.C.A. Addressed prayer meeting. Prepared draft constitution of Congress suggesting disbanding of Congress organization and setting up a Lok Sevak Sangh. Had talk with Devdas Gandhi.

January 30 : Revised draft constitution of Congress. Had talks with Pyarelal, Sudhir Ghosh, Maulanas and Sindhi deputation. Had discussion with Vallabhbhai Patel, took his evening meal at 4.30 p. m. while discussion continued. Manibehn Patel interrupted discussion to remind Gandhiji that it was time for prayer. Gandhiji started for prayer meeting supported by Manu Gandhi and Abha Gandhi on either side. As he was approaching the prayer ground, three shots were fired at him at close range. Gandhiji sank to the ground breathing his last at 5.17 p.m.

■■■